The Handbook of International Mergers and Acquisitions

David J. BenDaniel

Professor of Entrepreneurship
Johnson Graduate School of Management
Cornell University

Arthur H. Rosenbloom

Chairman of the Board
MMG Patricof & Company, Inc.

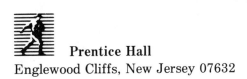
Prentice Hall
Englewood Cliffs, New Jersey 07632

Library of Congress Cataloging-in-Publication Data

BenDaniel, David J.
    The handbook of international mergers and acquisitions / David J.
BenDaniel, Arthur H. Rosenbloom.
        p.   cm.
    ISBN 0-13-472499-2
    1. Consolidation and merger of corporations.   2. Consolidation and
merger of corporations—United States.   I. Rosenbloom, Arthur H.
II. Title.
K1362.B46   1990
346′.06626—dc20
[342.66626]

89-48291
CIP

Editorial/production supervision
  and interior design: *Jean Lapidus*
Cover design: *Lundgren Graphics, Ltd.*
Manufacturing buyer: *Kelly Behr*

© 1990 by Prentice-Hall, Inc.
A Division of Simon & Schuster
Englewood Cliffs, New Jersey 07632

The publisher offers discounts on this book when ordered
in bulk quantities. For more information, write:

Special Sales/College Marketing
Prentice-Hall, Inc.
College Technical and Reference Division
Englewood Cliffs, NJ 07632

Printed in the United States of America

10 9 8 7 6 5 4 3 2 1

ISBN 0-13-472499-2

PRENTICE-HALL INTERNATIONAL (UK) LIMITED, *London*
PRENTICE-HALL OF AUSTRALIA PTY. LIMITED, *Sydney*
PRENTICE-HALL CANADA INC., *Toronto*
PRENTICE-HALL HISPANOAMERICANA, S.A., *Mexico*
PRENTICE-HALL OF INDIA PRIVATE LIMITED, *New Delhi*
PRENTICE-HALL OF JAPAN, INC., *Tokyo*
SIMON & SCHUSTER ASIA PTE. LTD., *Singapore*
EDITORA PRENTICE-HALL DO BRASIL, LTDA., *Rio de Janeiro*

Contents

**Chapter 2 Legal Aspects of Acquiring
U.S. Enterprises   25**

Chapter 4 Accounting Aspects
of International Mergers
and Acquisitions   90

Chapter 6   Tax Considerations in Acquiring Non-U.S. Enterprises   **221**

Chapter 10   Pricing and Negotiations   300

References 353

Index 361

Preface

We have assembled a team of hands-on practitioners to provide their expertise for *The Handbook of International Mergers and Acquisitions.* Those corporate principals, legal and financial advisers, investment and commercial bankers for whom this work is intended, will, we hope, view this *Handbook* as a road map which sets forth in detail the general issues in most international M & A transactions and allows for an insightful solicitation of other expertise on the particular problems associated with a given deal. If we have succeeded in providing such a map, our journey in preparing it will have been worthwhile.

Because of the constantly changing nature of the international M & A environment, we have established a somewhat special updating procedure for this *Handbook*. We are committed to keeping practitioners current by sending future updates to place in the pocket part of this volume.

Important tax, accounting, etc., changes will be noted and sent to the readers for a small charge. Just fill out the enclosed reply card to register.

A driving force behind this *Handbook* is that it has become One World of M & A. The year 1992 and all it holds for international transactions is, at this writing, almost upon us. Russian, Asian, and third world markets beckon invitingly. For a variety of reasons, U.S. companies continue to attract overseas suitors. While the pace of transactions may ebb and flow with world economic conditions, and while currency fluctuations or other considerations may provide an impetus at one juncture for inbound transactions and at another for outbound ones, the likelihood is strong that the years between now and the dawn of the twenty-first century will see an acceleration in the pace of international merger and acquisition transactions.

Merger and acquisition transactions involving U.S. and non-U.S. companies are growing dramatically. With that growth there has been an abandonment of a series of well-established verities known to the deal community. Among them is the fact that it is the U.S. companies who are most often the buyers. The 1988 edition of *Mergerstat Review* reports that the number of non-U.S. companies acquiring U.S. companies ("inbound transactions") has risen from 88 in 1972 to 307 in 1988, an almost fourfold increase. This figure represents 12.6 percent of the total transactions in 1988, up from 11 percent in the previous year. Of the $202.5 billion in M & A consideration paid in such deals since 1975, $120.4 billion or around 59 percent resulted from transactions in the 1986–1988 period. Meanwhile the actual number of U.S. companies acquiring non-U.S. companies ("outbound transactions") fell from 531 in 1972 to 151 in 1988 and of the $47.2 billion spent since 1975, $30.6 billion or 64.8 percent was spent in the 1986–1988 period.

Furthermore, a series of long cherished shibboleths have bitten the dust. Japanese companies are *not* solely interested in buying U.S. securities or real estate. While Sony's CBS Record and Columbia Picture deals loom large, what is even more persuasive is that, in 1990, Japanese companies rank second (to the U.K.) in number of acquisitions of U.S. companies. Not long ago, common wisdom held that European companies would not close hostile transactions nor utilize high leverage. James Goldsmith, WPP, and many others give lie to those presuppositions.

Against this backdrop, the need for a work of this kind has become increasingly clear. There is, to our knowledge, no American text dealing exclusively with international M & A transactions. In attempting to fill the void, we have tried to address the principal functional areas which impact cross-border M & A transaction. Not unsurprisingly, the strategic planning, legal, tax, accounting, negotiating, fund raising, and people/organizational areas covered here are precisely the same ones found in domestic transactions. But international transactions create levels of complexity not found in purely domestic deals and it is the international overlay to such issues which we hope will give this work an original flavor.

We wish to thank John Willig and Jean Lapidus of Prentice Hall for their invaluable aid in getting this Handbook to its readers.

David J. BenDaniel

Arthur H. Rosenbloom

Contributors

WALDO M. ABBOT (Chapter 7) is a Managing Director and head of Chemical Bank's High Technology and Paper Product Groups. He is also responsible for corporate finance activities in the Mid-Atlantic market. Mr. Abbot joined Chemical in 1973 as a trainee in the Treasury Division. In 1974 he accepted a position in the Foreign Exchange Advisory Service where he spent five years including a two year assignment in Europe opening the Brussels office. Mr. Abbot was named Vice President in 1980 while on assignment in the Tokyo office with responsibility for Japanese and foreign multi-national business. In 1981, after his return to New York, Mr. Abbot became the manager of the National High Technology group. In 1986 he assumed additional responsiblity for the Mid-Atlantic region. Mr. Abbot was appointed a Managing Director in 1988. A native of Ann

Arbor, Michigan, Mr. Abbot holds a B.A. from the University of Richmond and an M.B.A from the Wharton Graduate School.

ROBERT M. BATTAGLIN (Chapter 9) is Manager, Human Resources-Business Divisions for Corning Inc. Mr. Battaglin has 15 years of experience in the human resources field, including extensive involvement with Corning's International Operations. Prior to this he held various line positions over a ten year period in Marketing and Sales Management, Manufacturing, Planning and Control. In his current position he manages a team of Human Resources professionals who work exclusively with the various product divisions of Corning, including involvement with their International Operations. Prior to this he was Manager, International Human Resources and Compensation reporting to the senior vice president for Operations in Japan, Latin America and Asia. He had total Human Resources responsibility for the U.S. Headquarters Group and Regional Export offices, plus oversight responsibility for Personnel Policies and Practices, Compensation and Human Resource Planning for Corning's International Subsidiaries and Affiliates. He has played an especially active role in Japan, where Corning has developed a fully integrated operating company starting from a regional sales office base. During this time he also managed Corning's Expatriate Compensation Programs worldwide. Mr. Battaglin is active on the Management Resources and Organization Committee of the National Foreign Trade Council, and is Chairman Elect for 1990-91. Mr. Battaglin holds a B.S. in Engineering from the Illinois Institute of Technology and an M.B.A. from the Graduate School of Business, University of Chicago.

WILLIAM L. BURKE (Chapter 6) is a partner in the New York office of Hughes, Hubbard & Reed. He is a past chairman of the Tax Section of the New York State Bar Association, a past co-chairman of the Tax Section's Committee on Foreign Activities of United States Taxpayers, and a Member of the Committee on Foreign Activities of United States Taxpayers of the Tax Section of the American Bar Association, the International Fiscal Association, and the Tax Committee of the International Bar Association. He has taught courses on international taxation at New York University Law School and is a frequent lecturer on subjects in the international tax area. His undergraduate degree is from Harvard University, and he received his LL.B. degree from the University of Virginia Law School, where he was an editor of the Law Review.

PETER J. CLARK (Chapter 8) is Managing Director of Maplestar Consulting Group, a New York and Montreal management consulting and advisory organization concentrating on strategy and implementation relating to acquisitions, corporate sales and divestivities. Previous to this he was at Coopers and Lybrand, where he founded their acquisition consulting practice. His present practice emphasis spans pre-acquisition, due diligence, and post-acquisition periods. Mr. Clark has personally been involved in more than $2 billion of successful transactions, and is directly involved with the issue post-acquisition integration of differing corporate cultures and strategies. He holds a B.B.A. and an M.B.A from Southern Methodist University.

KEITH D. ENGSTROM (Chapter 9) is retired as Director of Salaried Compensation of Corning Inc. Mr. Engstrom has thirty years experience in the personnel field with Corning, including a three year tour as a loan executive to the Board of Governors of the Federal Reserve system as Director, Division of Personnel. As Director, International Personnel Programs for Corning in the late 1970's, he developed and put in place Corning's basic personnel policies and practices for international operations and designed and established its worldwide expatriate compensation programs. He has experience working with all of Corning's international subsidiaries, affiliated companies and regional sales offices, often putting in place and/or upgrading their personnel programs and organizations. In this and his later role in corporate compensation, he was directly involved with developing the special personnel programs for a series of turn-key/technology sale projects Corning undertook in Eastern Europe, China, and India. He was a Charter Member of and took part in organizing the Management Resources and Organization Committee of the National Foreign Trade Council. Mr. Engstrom holds a B.A. in Economics from Albion College in Michigan.

RUSTIN R. HOWARD is a graduate in international finance from Brigham Young University and has an M.B.A degree from the Johnson Graduate School of Business, Cornell University.

PAUL McCARTHY (Chapters 2 and 3) is a Partner at Baker & McKenzie, Chicago, Illinois. He specializes in U.S. and international acquisitions, and partnership and partnership taxation law. He spent six months on Legal Staff of European Economic Community and he was a professor of law at Boston University Law School 1968–1972 and at Haile Selassie I University Faculty of Law, Addis Ababa, Ethiopia 1966–68. He is a Member of the Chicago and American Bar Associations, including the ABA's Committee on Negotiated Transactions and Committee on Partnerships. He is also a Member of the Board of

Directors of the Chicago Crime Committee and a Governing Member of the Art Institute of Chicago. He holds an M.C.L. from the University of Chicago Law School, a J.D. from the University of Michigan Law School, and an A.B. from Cornell University.

LAURANCE R. NEWMAN (Chapter 1) is Sr. Vice President - Worldwide Service Businesses & Corporate Development for S.C. Johnson & Co. Mr. Newman and his organization are responsible for the corporation's Corporate Development activities including acquisitions, joint ventures, new businesses, and licensing programs worldwide. In addition, Mr. Newman has responsiblity for Johnson's Worldwide Sanitation Service Businesses. Johnson Wax is a private, global company participating in over 45 countries around the world with annual revenues of over $2 billion. Mr. Newman has been involved in over 40 acquisitions and divestitures, as well as a number of licensing and joint venture projects. His prior line business background brings a broad perspective to both the financial and legal aspects of mergers and acquisitions. He holds Bachelor's and M.B.A. degrees from Northwestern.

MICHAEL R. NANUS (Chapter 4) is KPMG Peat Marwick's partner-in-charge of Capital Markets Services in New York. He serves on their Merger and Acquisition Committee. Mr. Nanus has spent a substantial portion of his career assisting acquirers to consummate acquisition transactions. He has worked with leveraged buyout groups in their acquisitions of stand-alone and divisional entities in numerous industries. A CPA, Mr. Nanus is a Member of the American Institute of Certified Public Accountants. Active in the New York State Society of Certified Public Accountants, he has served on its committee on Cooperation with Commercial Accountants, and he has served on its Committee on Cooperation with Commercial Credit Grantors and its Public Relations Committee. In addition, he serves on the editorial board of The Practical Accountant and on the Board of Directors of Management Decision Laboratory at the New York University Graduate School of Business. Mr. Nanus holds a B.S. in Accounting and an M.B.A in Finance, both from New York University.

ARTHUR H. ROSENBLOOM (Chapter 10 and Editor) is Chairman of MMG Patricof & Co., Inc., a New York City based firm specializing in transatlantic mergers and acquisitions. MMG has offices in New York, Palo Alto, London, Paris, Zurich, and Madrid and is part of the MMG Patricof Group, which includes Alan Patricof Associates, Inc., one of the World's largest international venture capital firms. Mr. Rosenbloom's investment banking work has involved him with companies as diverse as First Brands Corporation, VNU, Ringier AG, RJR Nabisco, Act III Communications, Inc., Morgan Crucible, Medical Economics, Hyatt Corp., Rapid-American Corp., Continental Airlines, Inc., and Trans Union Corp. His contributions on investment banking related topics have appeared in *The Harvard Business Review, Forbes, Business Week, Mergers and Acquisitions Magazines, Inc.,* and the *National Law Journal.* A former Adjunct Professor at New York University, Mr. Rosenbloom has lectured before the AICPA, the Financial Executives Institute and forums under the auspices of Inc. Magazine, the Wharton School of the University of Pennsylvania, and the Johnson Graduate School of Mangement of Cornell University. Mr. Rosenbloom holds a Bachelor's degree from Bucknell University, a Master's degree from Columbia University, and a law degree from the Cornell Law School.

DAVID R. TILLINGHAST (Chapter 5) has been former Chairman Committee on Taxation, Association of the Bar of the City of New York, Reporter, American Law Institute Project on International Aspects of U.S. Income Taxation, Consultant to Reporters, American Law Institute revision of the Restatement of the Foreign Relations Law of the United States, Member, Permanent Scientific Committee, International Fiscal Association, Former Vice-Chairman and Secretary, Committee on Taxation, Business Law Section, International Bar Association and Member, Council on Foreign Relations. He is the Author of "Tax Aspects of International Transactions" (Matthew Bender, 1978) (2nd edition, 1984) and numerous articles in professional publications. He holds an A.B. from Brown University (cum laude), and an LL.B from Yale, where he was Note and Comment Editor of the Law Journal.

DANIEL P. TREDWELL (Chapter 7) is a Vice President in Chemical Bank's Private Placement Group, where he has agented several corporate financings. He was also heavily involved in Chemical's restructuring of Kosmos A.S., one of the largest diversified corporations in Norway. He has an M.B.A. from the Wharton School and a B.A. from Miami University.

JAMES B. WINDLE (Chapter 7) is an Associate in Chemical Bank's Corporate Finance Group. He has a B.A. and an M.B.A. from the Darden School at the University of Virginia.

G. CHRISTOPHER WOOD (Chapter 8) is the Organizational Effectiveness Practice Leader within the Resource Management Group of Coopers and Lybrand in New York City. His consulting engagements focus on organizational planning and change, alignment of strategy and structure, and postmerger integration. He has developed a specialization in the area of analyzing the implications of globalization for business strategy, organization structure, and business practices. Mr. Wood is a frequent speaker on improving manufacturing productivity and strategic human resources issues. He has published articles in the Datapro Manufacturing Automation Series and the *Journal of Business Strategy*. He holds a B.A. and an M.A. from the University of Virginia.

DAVID J. BENDANIEL (Editor) is The Don and Margi Berens Professor of Entrepreneurship at the Johnson Graduate School of Management, Cornell University. He has been Senior Vice President for Venture Capital at the American Research and Development/Textron, Group Vice President, Technology Components for Exxon Enterprises/Exxon Corporation, and Manager of the Technical Ventures Operation of the General Electric Company. He has served on the boards of over a dozen new business ventures with international connections. Dr. BenDaniel attended the University of Pennsylvania for a B.A. (with honors) and M.S. in Physics, and the Massachusetts Institute of Technology for a Ph.D. in Engineering. He has also served as a Visiting Fellow and Lecturer at the Harvard Business School.

Chapter 1

Strategic Choices

Laurance R. Newman
Senior Vice President, S.C. Johnson & Co.
Worldwide Services Businesses and Corporate Development

1.0 THE QUEST FOR CORPORATE GROWTH

Internal and external corporate growth has long been a preoccupation of the financial and business communities of the world. If a company is identified as a growth company, it becomes more attractive to the investment community. Growth companies command highprice-earnings ratios, their absolute value on the market is greater, they receive more attention from the analysts, and there is more pizazz in their activities and operations. They promise hope, they promise the future, and they promise much higher share prices than more staid, conventional companies.

1.1 The World Business Community

To achieve corporate growth, companies throughout the world are becoming less and less insular. They view the world as a total business community. Their vision of corporate growth transcends natural borders and encompasses the developed and less developed countries of the world.

In his recent book on the Tri Ad Concept[1], Kenichi Ohmane described the growing realization that the world business and economic community is truly a Tri Ad, managed by the industrial complexes of Japan, North America, and Western Europe. The interaction and combination of these large industrial masses shape the destiny of most corporations. The ability of the corporate management and board to understand the impact and the interaction between these colossuses will, in the long run, determine their company's future. The understanding of global economic impact and how it relates to a business decision made in Chicago, Dusseldorf, or Seoul are requirements for survival in today's rapidly changing economic environment.

Over the past few years, the violent fluctuation in international currencies, the oil crisis, rampant inflation, and the inability of many countries to cope with budget deficits or balance of trade deficits has created considerable business opportunities and economic disasters for companies leveraged in countries plagued with such discontinuities. Those companies with a global vision and a long-term strategy have weathered these economic crises reasonably well. Those that operate at an ad-hoc reactionary basis have seen their volumes and profits fluctuate violently by their numerous reactions to foreign competition and changing economic conditions.

The following chart diagrams the world environment and potential business reaction in a four-factor series of linkages that must work together to provide a company with a proper flexible strategic direction in a changing business environment. (This chart has been modified from the traditional strategic four-factor diagram.)

The strategic management of your business requires the integration and the management of the four key linkages: resources, strategic planning, organization, and strategic control. The formulation of clear mission objectives is the means for conquering the demands put on your organization. If one plans to manage an international enterprise (or one of some multinational dimensions), this understanding is necessary for survival. A number of years ago, one could hardly envision a global marketplace consisting of cars from Japan, steel from Korea, or soft goods from China. The type of strategic diagram previously described allows consideration

[1] *The Coming Shape of Global Competitions*, 1985.

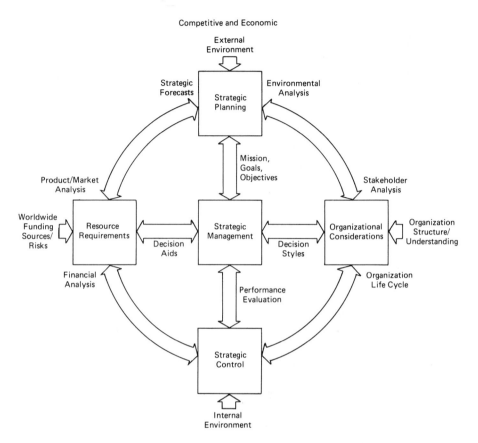

of all those factors in developing current and future product lines and gives recognition to the changing nature of the external environment. It also considers one's organization and how it needs to be adapted to fit the changing links in its strategic management. Proper controls are critical if you plan to manage a far-flung, diverse business organization.

S.C. Johnson Wax, our corporation, like many U.S. multinationals and their non-U.S. counterparts, manages a significant number of critical business units throughout the world. Most of the employees of such companies do not speak the language of the country in which the company is headquartered. A strategic vision and a strategic plan allow them to effectively manage the timing and use of resources to optimize short- and long-term yield.

Organizational strategy flows from a desire to meet a predetermined corporate purpose. To achieve that purpose, top management, and sometimes the controlling shareholders, must have a long-term design. This design will include visions of its markets, its geography, its environment, and its purpose. A corporate strategy requires a comprehensive plan that takes into account the resources a corporation could have available to it and the allocation of them that is necessary to meet that organization's basic mission and priorities.

2.0 CORPORATE STRATEGY

Corporate strategy according to most practitioners is the pattern of decisions in a company that

1. Shapes and reveals its objectives, purposes, or goals,
2. Produces a principal policy and plans for achieving these goals, and
3. Defines the business the company intends to be in and the kind of economic and human organization it intends to be.

As in the case of Maslow's traditional hierarchy of human needs, corporate vision, objectives, and strategies also can be viewed in some hierarchal context. The following chart describes how an organization can order these parameters. Of critical importance in this hierarchy is the feedback element. Only through feedback does one have an opportunity to retest, reevaluate, and readjust goals.

In forming its strategic plan, every company should evaluate its past and current performance. Such a written evaluation enables management to compare its accomplishments against its objectives. Did it accomplish its strategies? Were assumptions about the world environment correct? Is the timing and vision appropriate? Each evaluation is a way of measuring the ability to achieve a company's vision in a timely and orderly fashion. If the report indicates significant shortfalls, one must retest the strategy and vision and ask

1. Did we miss because the environment or economic conditions changed?
2. Did we miss because we misunderstood the market?
3. Did we miss because we are not as adept as our competitors in attacking and managing a competitive marketplace?
4. Did we miss because our vision of the future was at a pace which is faster than the environment itself?

In the consumer products world, many product-technology innovations were far ahead of their time. For example, liquid and low-suds deter-

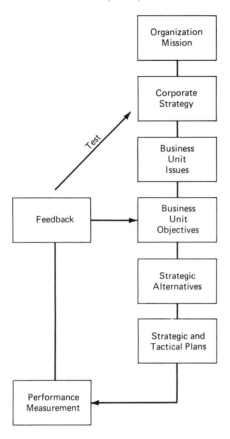

gents have been out for a number of years, but only in the last few years have they made significant impact on the market.

2.1 Global Development Program

There are three key questions that must be addressed.

What business am I in? The classical railroad or transportation business model quoted in so many business cases is critically pertinent as one considers the global corporate growth. If the railroads were in the transportation business, their strategy would have driven development of buses, planes, and maybe cars.

Where are my current markets going? Are they growing? How are they growing, in market potential, distribution, frequency of usage, or what other aspect?

What is our competitive advantage?   Construct a matrix chart by marketplace or products or geography. Ask yourself the questions that relate to

	HIGH	MEDIUM	LOW

1. product differentiation
2. barriers to entry
3. market growth rate
4. future demand curve
5. capital intensity

2.2 Acquisitions Only as a Tactic

In this chapter, it may seem strange to the reader that we have not yet talked about acquisitions. It is intentional. Most of the chapters in this book deal with the transaction and all the business and legal ramifications of its execution. From our perspective, they are all the same issues of an acquisition. The critical issue is *Your Strategy.* This chapter is designed to take you through that strategic process, step by step; so you know why you are making an acquisition and how the acquisition fits your strategy. Many of you who are reading this have been involved in an acquisition. Think for a second. Was it driven by a predetermined strategic plan? Was it opportunistic? Was it both? Was it neither? *Acquisitions should never be a strategic goal of any organization.* They should be the result of a well studied program to identify various alternatives to achieve your corporation's predetermined goal. Many companies espouse a strategy that results in a plan to make an acquisition rather than to properly delineate and define their corporation's objectives. Acquisitions are but one means to achieve identified strategic objectives. Many times in business plans, operating groups use the word acquisition to represent the difference between how far their current business plan will take them and the outer edge of their assigned corporate goal.

Before determining if acquisitions are a viable alternative for achieving a corporate strategy, managers must start with a mission, either at the corporate or business unit level. A mission describes your vision. It describes your world audiences. It talks about where you are going, how you are to get there, and what the world is going to look like when you achieve the result. It relates to identifying the needs of the company's multiple constituencies, its customers, shareholders, employees, and the world in which it transacts business. Given a mission statement, one can turn attention to the kind of objectives that enable the mission to be accomplished.

While it is sad when a company makes acquisitions without a strategy or objectives, it may be sadder when a company pursues second rate entry points to a market because of a declared strategy and the inability to execute properly.

Firms must have a business growth strategy. Firms look for and need to explore growth opportunities on a global basis. A number of strategic analyses have identified the primary four components that contributed to growth-gap analysis between a company's sales potential and its current actual performance.

Product line gap: Closing this gap entails completion of a product line, either in width or depth, or in geography by introducing improved or new products.

Distribution gap: This gap can be reduced by intensifying the coverage and exposure and expanding distribution. This is especially true as we look at global business development.

Usage gap: To increase users, a firm must induce current nonusers to try the product and current users to increase their frequency of usage/purchase.

Competitive gap: This gap can be closed by making inroads into the market position of direct competitors as well as those who market allied products.

When you perform this gap analysis, it is critical to identify your company's gap potentials. In identifying those potentials, you must come to grips with its alternative executions. *This is where acquisitions can play a critical role.* Do you really have the ability, internal resources, or patience to expand your product line in Japan or in Germany or in the U.S.? How can you sell products in Southeast Asia without a sales force? Do you recognize the problem of importing products into Brazil? All of these issues must be examined as you look at the choice between internal and external growth.

The gap analysis should take into account the following checklist. PIMS[2] has suggested this type of analysis when considering organic versus external growth.

[2]This checklist was developed by PIMS. PIMS was organized in early 1972 by the Marketing Science Institute in concert with the Harvard Business School. Using a large database, the PIMS study is predicted on a series of questions concerning what factors influence profitability and by how much, and how return on investment changes in response to changes in strategy and market conditions.

Analysis of Organic vs. External Growth Alternatives

	Domestic			Foreign Target Mkts		
	Low	Med	High	Low	Med	High
1. Market share						
2. Relative market share						
3. Product quality						
4. Market growth						
5. Vertical integration						
6. New-product activity						
7. R&D and Sales						
8. Marketing and sales						
9. Productivity						
10. Capacity utilization						
11. Investment intensity ratio						
12. Inventory level						

3.0 INTERNATIONAL BANKING AND INTERNATIONAL ACQUISITION

In considering and evaluating an international acquisition, foreign currency risks become an issue, but with the globalization of the financial markets, there is increasing ability for a strong company to borrow in local currency to make an acquisition in Japan, the U.K., Germany, the U.S., and Italy; even the USSR and the Eastern Bloc are becoming real possibilities.

Many multinational companies have discovered it easier to raise capital (or debt) in foreign markets and have sought listings on the international exchanges. For example, there are currently around 520 foreign companies listed on the U.K. exchange including 43 of the top 100 U.S. industrial companies, and 9 of the 10 largest U.S. commercial banks.

Banking connections and relationships need to be developed globally, not just in one's corporate locale. By developing and nurturing these relationships, one obtains not only better access to potential merger partners, but also to the financing and financing skills necessary to fund the transaction.

3.1 International Acquisition Perspective

The following international merger and acquisition international perspective section is not intended to be either definitive or comprehensive, but rather is intended to provide the uninitiated with some early perspectives that can guide and direct preliminary evaluation.

What is U.S?   The acquisition process in the U.S. has developed into a finely honed process driven by financial players. Focus is on ROI or ROE. Leveraged buy-outs, restructurings, or consolidation are normal business activities. Money tends to be plentiful, government and union involvement very limited, and exposure risks of international currency and foreign cultures, minimum.

What is Asia?   Asians are not a monolithic group. This is rather obvious, but what are the differences? In their language customs and religion, the Japanese, Chinese, and Koreans are as different as the Irish, Italians, or eastern Europeans. Acquisition activity and the infrastructure to execute it are extremely limited today but will grow as the Asian firms become more attractive acquisition targets.

Japan is changing.   Japan's internal business culture is changing, not by leaps and bounds, but slowly and steadily as Japanese managers begin to see international mergers and acquisitions as a potential viable economic benefit. Most of the major Japanese banks have developed mergers and acquisitions departments. They are designed primarily for foreign (cross- border) transactions, as Japan recognizes the need to have a global presence. The skills and analytical abilities that allow a Japanese company to make a friendly takeover bid in North America or Europe are going to be applied to the Japanese market in time. Mr. Moriya, head of Merrill Lynch Capital Markets in Japan, in a 1987 article in a Japanese mergers & acquisition magazine, indicated that he thought a friendly takeover bid in Japan would come within a year. Historically, Japanese acquisitions were done very privately and very quietly by one company taking over a financially distressed smaller company for the benefit of the employees. The Japanese Ministry of Finance has authorized a study by a university professor to determine the potential effects of mergers and acquisitions on the economy, on employment, and on cultural attitudes. A positive result of that study may result in the government recognizing the potential benefits of acquisitions within Japanese business.

In Japan, 30 percent of the shares may effectively convey control. Culture and experience dictate that you need first to develop a relationship or an alliance with a company before you discuss acquisition, maybe distribute some products for them or work together on a joint venture or a co-venture. Junzo Sawamura, Chief Manager Capital Services Consulting Division, Mitsubishi Bank, has indicated that a U.S. company must be patient enough to spend at least six times as much time to acquire in

Japan as they would in the United States or in Europe. Do most western multinationals have the patience to do this?

M&A Japanese style. Despite considerable writing on the growth and flourishing of the mergers and acquisitions activity in Japan, and despite the optimism, as of yet little has happened. Kenji Suganoya, General Manager, in Yamaichi's Corporate Planning Department, has indicated that, in the Japanese tradition, "to sell a company in Japan is considered shameful in much the same way as [as the failure that caused] an ancient war lord [to] kill himself for surrendering his castle or . . . a captain [to] choose to go down with his ship." In addition, the debt-equity ratio of Japanese companies averages about 80 percent despite considerable recent improvement, compared to only about 50 percent for American companies. Japanese companies, therefore, are more dependent on their banks. The banks become key investors and, in fact, are heavily involved in the decision-making process. Nevertheless, all the Japanese bank merger and acquisition people that I have spoken to truly believe the boom will hit Japan. Attitudes are changing and management is recognizing the desire for restructuring.

If you are going to attempt to acquire in Japan, patience is the key operating word. The probability of your acquiring control immediately is very low, especially as a foreign company.

What is Europe? After the United States, Europe has been the most active participant in cross-border transactions over the last few years. As U.S. companies recognized that a global perspective was critical for their operations to expand and seek new opportunities, Europe became a key target. Europe, as a target, recognized the growth of the middle class and of affluent people throughout the industrial world. The continued evolution of the European economic community allowed U.S. cross-border transactions to participate in a Pan-European perspective. By 1992, the European economic community hopes to complete the opening of the borders between most European countries. The growth of multilanguage labeling and advertising through the sky-channel and other such multicultural devices allows companies to look at acquisitions in Europe on a broader base than country by country.

Even though a cross-border transaction from the U.S. to Europe anticipates a more Pan-European business and marketing environment, it is very important to recognize that the United States of Europe does not exist. Countries and cultures in Europe are still very different. Traditions and cultures will not change but will slowly evolve over time. Technical and legal barriers may be dropped between countries, but emotional, ethnic, and cultural barriers will remain for a considerable period of time.

3.2 Perspectives by Key Countries

West Germany.   Many West German companies evolved postwar and are still run by entrepreneurs or their families. German banks are heavily involved and exercise a great deal of corporate direction and control. Acquisitions are very difficult and very expensive.

Italy.   Italy is probably the most entrepreneurial country in Europe. Companies grow and flourish despite the many changes in the Italian government. Businesses tend to be adventuresome, take risks, and explore new frontiers of fashion and creativity. Separating the entrepreneur from the company is very difficult.

France.   France is evolving from a very insular country into one which is willing to tolerate foreign investment. Recent acquisitions by Henkel and others have set new patterns for the participation of significant foreign investment in the French business climate. The establishment of the right relationship and contacts in France through French intermediaries is absolutely critical to establishing a dialogue with a target company. It is important to understand potential government intervention in issues of redundancy and plant closings. Also, rights and privileges of the workers' council should be anticipated and accounted for.

Spain.   With Spain's recent involvement in the EEC, acquisition activity has increased dramatically. In evaluating acquisitions in Spain, it is important to determine whether the Spanish entity to be acquired will remain competitive once the trade barriers have been dropped. Can you support the cost structure and the market share in a new business environment? Many Spanish companies may be available because the owners recognize a dramatic change in the business culture and climate. Study carefully and more cautiously in Spain.

U.K.   The U.K. is most like the U.S. in terms of the evolution and structure of the acquisition business. U.K. companies have been involved in significant restructurings over the last few years, which have also seen the privatization of major government corporations in automotive, aircraft, and similar industries. The financial infrastructure and the U.K. stock market support acquisition activity within the country. The government is sensitive to and understanding of major restructuring of acquisitions to allow viable economic business operations. The investment banking community is also more highly developed in England than in other European countries. U.K. accounting practices related to goodwill have made U.K. companies very successful bidders in cross-border activities, especially in the U.S. market.

The most important caution to doing a cross-border transaction in Europe is to make sure that your company understands the cultures of the countries in which you are going to do business. Germany is not Italy. Italy is not France. And neither relate directly to Spain or the U.K. in terms of business pace, business culture, and the modes of executing business transactions. For example, do not expect to do European business planning during the month of August. Most of southern Europe is closed during the month of August. You will not change that culture.

Earlier in this chapter we mentioned acquisitions as an alternative strategy to execute a corporate objective. It becomes a viable alternative to the extent that most corporations cannot realize all of their growth by internal means, especially when they operate on a global basis. Most corporations do not have the experience, the infrastructure, or the resources to allow the planting of a flag in a number of countries around the world simultaneously. Hence, acquisitions become a viable avenue for the execution of this strategy. It is critically important that companies recognize the increasing necessity of developing a global view of the world and global business strategies.

A cross-border acquisition can bring the corporation

1. Identified ongoing business with *brand franchises, successful products,* and known *brand names,*
2. *New distribution systems,* especially in regions or parts of the world where it is critical to have a complete infrastructure, including sales force,
3. *Manufacturing facilities,* especially in transporting difficult or costly products where it is critical to have a manufacturing facility near the customer base,
4. *New customers* in terms of geography or products, and
5. *New technology* to enter or serve an identified market.

3.3 Disadvantages of International Acquisitions

Before embarking on foreign acquisition, consider the following common roadblocks.

Culture shock.   Be sure to understand the culture, the people, the country, and the business environment of the potential acquisition. The Japanese and Chinese are very different, as are the Korean and the Taiwanese. The Germans and the French are as different as the Spaniards and the Norwegians. Understand the target business and how it operates. Understand the implications for 1992 in the European community, how they will affect the business of a prospective European seller, and how they will affect the parent company. Understand the cartel laws and how they can affect the ability to manage the acquired business in the postmerger phase.

Management distance.   Des Moines, Iowa is not Paris, France. They are apart, in culture and distance. Management must be comfortable handling an operation very far from its home base.

People problems.   Many countries in the world have an additional player in people management: militant unions, workers councils, countrywide labor problems. Each of these may bring unique sets of people-management issues different from those at home.

Lack of local business knowledge.   The more one knows, the more one knows how little one knows. Do not assume a knowledge of what appears to be a similar business in a foreign country. Having produced Widgets for 50 years in Canberra does not assure the ability to understand Widget production in Capetown or Cape Canaveral. Be sure, before making an acquisition, to truly understand the business in that country.

Poor knowledge of industry and geography.   Many foreign acquisitions fail because the buyer wrongly assumed it knew the seller's country and industry. (This applies to local deals, too.) For example, the outstanding days' receivable in Industry X in Venezuela is 197 days, not 31 days as in the U.S., or, in some countries it may be necessary to make a facilitating payment to get your sanitation permit approved. Many companies do not do sufficient homework concerning the country in which they are making an acquisition.

4.0 ACQUISITION STRATEGY

If we look at the process of selection in a foreign market based upon an acquisition entry strategy (the widget business in France), it must be tempered by considering the basis. Look at some numbers.

If the leader grows with the market, and the market is growing at 20 percent, a company half the size of the leader must grow two and one-half times faster than the leader and the market in order to catch up. A company one-fourth the size of the leader, must grow nearly four times faster than the leader to catch up within five years. *This suggests that companies with low relative market shares in attractive foreign markets are poor acquisition candidates.* The work on market share structure de-

Sales ($M) \ Co.	#1	#2	#3
This Year	100	50	25
5 Years Out	250	250	250
C.G.R.	26%	50%	78%

veloped by the Marketing Science Institute says that, when the market leader is strongly entrenched, it has a low probability of being unseeded without a new technology, service elements, or some device to create significant differentiative, like Federal Express and the FAX machine. The number 2 brand most probably will have half the share of the number 1 brand, and brands 3, 4, and 5 are usually relatively unprofitable. This is especially true in a stagnant business. Acquiring the number 5 brand with no new technology or no unique synergy is probably an effort in frustration.

If an acquisition is a true tactical choice for corporate growth strategy, be willing to walk away from it if the appropriate candidate to meet strategic needs cannot be found. There is nothing sadder than a company which pursues second rate entry points to a market because there was a declared strategy and an inability to execute properly. *Successful acquirers, especially overseas, find it necessary to keep a number of dynamic markets in focus simultaneously.* An acquisition of one of the leading companies in any of the dynamic markets would provide a satisfactory execution of a predetermined strategy. Do not let an acquisition pull the company into a strategic direction that was not planned. On the other hand, do not become wedded to a single strategy that has little likelihood of working.

Many acquisitions are partly opportunistic, but opportunistic purchases should and can be made within a framework of agreed to, well thought-out business development strategies. Otherwise, an acquisition is not opportunistic but truly random. Many acquisition opportunities require quick development of the relationship necessary for an ultimate purchase. This is especially true with auctions which are so prevalent in the U.S. and are becoming more popular in Europe. Having an agreed-to, approved plan from management concerning how to approach a strategic market or markets is absolutely critical to the effective and proper execution of an acquisition program.

Why not just export?   Many companies are innocents abroad. Many push exports even when currency has been devalued, and they find it exceptionally difficult. Many global companies have found that using local nationals to manage their foreign businesses gives them a better chance to build a long term business franchise within the culture of the local country.

Many companies do not understand that putting the right product at the right place at the right time in an overseas market is not the same as shipping its local product to the marketplace.

Examine the planning process.   There is no greater comfort in an acquisition program than to be equipped with a reliable business plan. Try to look out at least five years and attempt to project both earnings and cash flow. Remember when choosing an acquisition partner, each firm inherits the other's cash flow problems.

It is helpful to have a sophisticated planning process in place. Those who do not are at a decided disadvantage and run the risk of entering a partnership long on memories but short on prospects. The decision-making process in business relates to the future, not the past.

Those unused to a planning process often ask, "How can one project five years out with any certainty?" Reliability in planning is derived empirically. A first attempt will be ragged at best; one learns from each planning cycle. There is no time like the present to begin.

Below is a table for measuring the reliability of the company's planning process. The last number in each vertical column up to column 6 is the actual result. All the others are planning numbers.

E. P. S. Plans and Actuals, a Hypothetical Example

Plan ($) Year	1	2	3	4	5	6	7	8	9	10
1	.50	.55	.60	.68	.79					
2	.45	.48	.53	.60	.70	.76				
3		.52	.57	.65	.71	.78	.85			
4			.55	.62	.70	.76	.83	.96		
5				.61	.69	.76	.85	.95	1.05	
6					.70	.79	.86	.99	1.10	1.21
7						.78	.86	.99	1.10	1.21

Year	1	2	3	4	5	6	7	8	9	10
High Est.	.50	.55	.60	.68	.79	.79	.86	.99	1.10	1.21
Actual	.45	.52	.55	.61	.70	.78				
Low Est.	.45	.48	.53	.60	.69	.76	.83	.95	1.05	1.21

The first year's plan was excessive across the board, probably the result of not taking into account all the things that can and do go wrong. Once burned, the second year was more conservative than it needed to be. Each subsequent year showed a better performance.

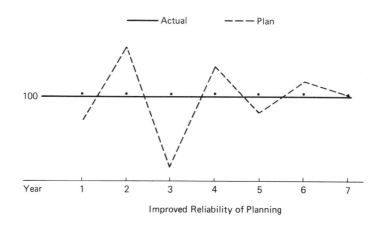

Improved Reliability of Planning

Does this pattern instill confidence about the future of the company in the example? Would it not be desirable to share the plan with a prospective merger partner to determine whether the plan could have the same demonstrated level of reliability. Obviously, it will not do to limit this kind of tracking to the whole corporation for a multi-enterprise or multi-country business. Each unit should be tracked the same way. Another clue to reliability in planning is that plans should be generated from the bottom of the organization, not dictated from the top. The top has the role of setting goals, not writing plans. The best way to make a planning system fall apart is to turn it into a one-way communication.

Before embarking on an overseas acquisition program examine strengths and weaknesses of the acquirer.

As an example, one strength might be the ability to make rapid decisions in a fast changing, competitive environment. A weakness might be the lack of capital to support the next needed surge of growth. Ultimately, the strength and weakness analysis helps in seeking a partner who complements the parent company or where the parent's strengths can help the target.

Also consider your firm's business style and its decision-making tempo. In Peter Drucker's parlance it is called "temperamental fit."

Practically all pharmaceutical companies entered the cosmetic business in the 1960s and were disillusioned by these moves in the 70s. Why? One reason is that a good pharmaceutical product takes years to develop.

A cosmetics product must often be developed in a matter of months. Much of a pharmaceutical company's market planning can be done at a different pace and be reviewed only once or twice a year. You cannot afford to do that in a cosmetics company. Some decisions of great strategic importance have to be made quickly, otherwise, the competition will get to the marketplace first.

The first question a buyer should ask about a seller is, "How is the style of this business different from our own?" This is especially important in cross-border transactions. The style of Japanese business is dramatically different than a U.S. business.

In a recent joint venture transaction in Japan, the potential partners talked about the terms and conditions of the agreement for one and one-half years. While the issues under discussion were critical, most of the time in the process was spent getting the participants to trust each other as business partners. No contract will ensure a strong business partnership if a spirit of trust has not been established.

Be aware of differences in management style and practices. In Japan, the inside Board of Directors tends to meet weekly or monthly and operate the company day to day, while in most western countries, the board meets only quarterly to approve plans and policy.

One of the clear style distinctions one finds is one between a financially-oriented company and an operationally-oriented company. The financially-oriented management style features a hands-off attitude toward day-to-day operations. The operationally-oriented company is characterized by a top management group deeply involved in the operations. Most conglomerates are financially-oriented. Financially-oriented companies are usually aggressive deal makers, tend to favor debt as consideration to drive up the return on equity, and are attracted to deal structures that minimize taxes.

There are certain kinds of companies that usually make suitable partners for financially-oriented companies and others which do not. For example, financially-oriented companies and smaller high tech companies rarely mix well. The financially-oriented company often looks for stability and debt coverage. If problems arise with the subsidiary, it wants easy access to people who can offer a quick fix. High tech companies typically do not fit that pattern. Financially-oriented companies are often good international acquirers because they are comfortable in managing from a distance by the numbers.

Operationally-oriented companies subordinate the making of deals to concerns about how to manage the new subsidiary. They tend to look for growth stability. In an acquisition, they are often meddlesome. It is this meddlesome nature which suggests that an operationally-oriented company should not stray too far from its basic business. If a company is very operationally-oriented and *needs* to participate in the day-to-day decision making, it is likely to be quite frustrated with an overseas acquisition.

Assuming that your strategic development program has identified international as a means to a given corporate strategy, it is important to answer a series of questions.

Who is responsible? Developing and executing a successful acquisition is an entrepreneurial line function, no matter how the individual charged with the program is shown on the corporate organization chart. An individual must be identified and charged with responsibility for the program. He or she will require a wide diversity of international business skills, including analytical ability and negotiating skills, as well as the interpersonal skills to orchestrate a large variety of multicultural technical specialists to aid in the evaluation and execution of an acquisition program. Many companies find it difficult to identify a single individual who possesses enough broadly based skills to be able to take total leadership for an acquisition program. Hence, many operate with a small cadre of business specialists who execute the program together.

For example, S.C. Johnson Wax centralizes responsibility for the identification, evaluation, and execution of all of our acquisitions worldwide within its corporate group in Racine, in concert with local and regional operating managers. We access local operating management and other technical groups to support the process, but focus the formal activity with one group of people who have developed a reasonably high skill in acquisitions.

Where to buy? Identify as part of the strategy a target country or region. This is very critical to orchestrating the appropriate search techniques to identify potential candidates.

What to acquire? The identification of what you are trying to acquire, either in terms of product or company, is contingent on the answer to the previous question of where one wants to acquire. Consideration of volume levels, market position, technical competence, manufacturing characteristics, distribution and warehousing skills, and employee relations are all critical in determining to acquire.

We have the plans and we know our strengths and weaknesses. Now it is time to talk about screening candidates for acquisitions. Some companies determine acquisition candidates on purely financial bases, such as size of revenues and profits, profit margins, rates of return on assets and equity, and the like. Others prefer to give prime consideration to operational elements directed to the business characteristics of the seller. We advocate a screening approach which takes both such concerns into consideration. Here is an example which allows evaluation of several companies on various weighted criteria.

		Companies*					
Criteria	Weight	A	B	C	D	E	F
Expands corporation into its designated field	5	7	6	5	9	2	6
Offers diversification into a new attractive market	3	5					
High technology business and protectable product assets	4	3					
Business not subject to cycles	3	9					
Good sales growth prospects	5	3					
Good historical profitability	4	5					
Makes significant contribution to earnings	4	6					
Market leader with its major products	5	3					
High levels of R&D commitment	4	7					
Controllable size	3	2					
Managerial reputation	4	7					
Good investor reactions	3	0					
	Weighted Total	226					

*Rate on 0–10 scale

Our preference is to spend a long time studying what you want, pare down the list to a manageable number, say half a dozen, and then go to work wooing them. It is amazing how creative, approaches can be, if proper research is done.

This method will not result in instant gratification. Patience is cautioned: Good deals take time to develop.

Why acquire?   It would seem that this question is somewhat redundant if you have worked through an appropriate strategic plan. The process of reasking it provides a double-check on your strategic direction. This question must make business sense. For example: Why should I, a U.K. company, acquire a potato-chip company in the U.S.? Answer: To provide a distribution system for store-delivered snacks that are a technical strength of the company. Why should I, a U.S. company, acquire a pasta company in Northern Italy without a factory? Answer: To provide additional volume opportunities for an under-used manufacturing facility in Milan. Ask the question and answer it as an important double- check to your strategic thrust.

How to go about it.   This question provides some structure and substance to an acquisition search. The answer should define the species and amounts of payment.

1. Is there a financial limit? Is it $3 million or $300 million?
2. What structure is acceptable?
    a. 100% ownership.
    b. Controlling ownership. A U.S. company may want 51% or more for control (public vs. private).
    c. A joint venture with a participating partner.
    d. A local joint venture with a nonparticipating partner.
    e. A collaboration agreement (alliance).
3. Will the deal be friendly or hostile? An unfriendly bid is increasingly seen in Europe, perceived as almost totally irresponsible in Japan, but fairly commonplace in the U.S.

Providing definition and structure to this question and understanding government regulations which may control or restrict the acquisition is very important. Finalize a list of key candidates and develop a marketing program to contact and open negotiations with potential candidates. Understanding your corporation's patience and tolerance is important to the development of the target list and the closing of a transaction. Time differences, cultural barriers, and other elements of international acquisitions take time. Be aware if your corporation will tolerate a one-to-four-year process time.

In larger companies, sponsorship of an acquisition can be a tricky affair. More deals are thwarted from lack of sponsorship than in any other way. Sponsoring managers often are unaware of the time it takes and the frustrations one encounters in an acquisition; it is easy to lose interest. Thus, the operating group responsible for sponsoring a particular overseas target must be excited about the potential of the acquisition and of its ability to address the buyer's strategic needs. In an international acquisition, the sponsor is often the local acquiring company, particularly if the overseas target is to be integrated into the sponsoring company's operation. Sometimes the sponsor is the regional or corporate group, if the acquisition represents a new thrust into the country or business and will be managed independently from other operations.

The workload of an active buyer can be another problem. Activity comes in waves and is hard to organize.

We are advocates of frequent and open communication about pending deals within our corporation. It suits our culture but may not be suitable for everyone. Most management does not like surprises and like to know about and participate in the various acquisition projects under development.

4.1 Finders and Intermediaries

Companies are solicited daily with suggestions from managers, bankers, and business brokers. To maximize deal flow, it is important to be prepared to respond promptly to such suggestions with reasons to support the decision to go forward or not to proceed. One cannot execute this well unless the strategy development and screening process has been solidly carried out.

Step one is to have an approved corporate policy on compensation of intermediaries which is promptly placed in the hands of the intermediaries involved. Keep a log of all suggestions coming in.

Instruct all company managers to refer these unsolicited proposals to you. Tell your managers that they will be responsible for the second fee should a doubling occur. Always inquire pointedly about the relationship between the intermediary and the prospect and make a careful judgment about whether you are getting the right story. It pays to ask the unknown intermediary for references, deals he or she has completed, and satisfied clients.

Intermediaries can play a key role in international transactions. From a philosophical viewpoint, we use them to provide critical interface. For example, in Japan, asking a company if it is for sale is a terrible affront and indicates that you think it is a failure or in financial trouble. However, a board member of the company in whom you have interest could be gently asked over cocktails whether the company has ever considered the possibility of a collaboration with another company. If the answer is yes, the dialogue can begin. The right contact is very important in an international transaction. Be patient. Many times the negotiation of a simple letter of intent or term sheet may take many months. Whether to use an intermediary may depend on the facts related to a particular transaction. Consider the following:

Other U.S. company.   An investment banker may or may not be used by the buyer. Purchase of the target may be due to its restructuring. Sale may be by auction by the target's investment banker.

Other multinational.   An investment banker or other intermediary will probably be very helpful. A local investment banker may be helpful in understanding the company.

Local share, public, or semipublic. Because of the existence of public shares (even though the purchase may involve private and/ or public shares) an intermediary and investment banker may both be very important. They could be the same person, but it is possible that the person who can facilitate the introduction to the company will be the investment banker you want to handle a tender offer.

Private company. Local intermediaries are very important and, in many countries in Asia, South America, and Southern Europe, absolutely critical in arranging for and nurturing the negotiation. Their purpose is not to participate in the negotiations but to support and facilitate the process. Deal structure may be critical because of tax considerations and government regulations.

In any transaction, legal, financial, and appraisal advisors should be involved as quickly as possible; they usually are worth their cost and are far less effective when they get into a deal late in the process.

4.2 Recommendation Document

Once a letter of understanding, a nonbinding letter of intent, or a heads of agreement is negotiated, it is important to develop a single, concise, well-written acquisition recommendation document. This document should be approved by the appropriate executive committee and in most companies, depending on the size of the transaction, by the Board of Directors. The document should contain the following areas of discussion.

1. Recommendation.
2. Strategic objectives that led to the transaction.
3. The company to be acquired and its characteristics.
4. The strategic fit of the company to the strategic plan objectives.
5. Discussion of price and value, including return on investment, return on assets, profit margin, earnings per share effect, and the like.
6. Discussion of business, government, or cultural characteristics of the country or company that are different from those found in the home-based company.
7. Discussion of planned changes in governmental structure that may affect the cost or competitive situation of the business: the completion of the EEC in 1992, the decapitalization effect of South American reevaluation, Hong Kong becoming part of mainland China in 1997.
8. Spend some time discussing an integration plan as part of any acquisition. It is easy to make acquisitions, but much tougher to operate them. Without a strong vision of the operation of the acquired

company, it will be very difficult to effect your acquisition strategy. Before agreeing to acquire, a decision or plan should be in place regarding

a. Who is to run the company,
b. How it is to be run,
c. Cost implications of having your employees in an overseas acquired company,
d. How, if at all, to integrate the company into the buyer company's operation,
e. What functions or people are likely to be redundant to the company,
f. How to handle potential problems with workers' councils, unions, governments in the transition of the company, and
g. How to handle currency fluctuation exposure (this is especially critical in a first international acquisition), dividend payment and government restrictions, increased capitalization, government approval, and the like.

Government permissions.   What permissions are required? Like Hart-Scott-Rodino in the United States, many countries require government permission for a transaction to be made, especially if that transaction requires foreign currency being brought into the country. (Sometimes a foreign government can require a local company to bid against a multinational purchase.) This process of government approval can be time consuming and difficult. Many countries, especially third world countries, have erected legal and procedural barriers to protect local industry. In addition to restricting the level and type of foreign ownership, many countries have erected significant procedural approval processes.

5.0 SUMMARY

International acquisitions are very complex and challenging, but if properly executed and properly integrated, they can add significant volume and profit to a predetermined strategic plan for the company. Keys to success include the following:

1. Orchestrate the strategy carefully,
2. Develop a strong proactive plan to identify, contact, and convince acquisition candidates of the benefit of a transaction with your company,
3. Close only at a purchase price that provides sufficient return on assets or return on investments to execute a long term strategic vision,

4. Perform a thorough due diligence,
5. Negotiate an acquisition contract that offers the best possibible protection, and
6. Execute a well thought out post-merger integration plan.

Following each of these steps offers the best opportunity for a successful
international acquisition that will serve the strategic needs of the acquiring company for many years.

Chapter 2

Legal Aspects of Acquiring U.S. Enterprises

Paul McCarthy
Partner, Baker & McKenzie

The structure of an acquisition of a U.S. business depends in part upon the nature of the legal entity which owns the business (probably a corporation), the business and financial condition of the target as disclosed during the buyer's due diligence investigation, and the business objectives of the buyer. An acquisition by a foreigner will encounter relatively few regulatory requirements, although the United States has recently enacted a new review procedure for acquisitions and takeovers by foreign interests that may affect national security. An acquisition may take the form of a share purchase, asset purchase, merger, or a combination of these, depending upon the interests of the buyer and seller. Acquisition agreements in the United States are usually rather extensive, functioning as a means of structuring and accomplishing the acquisition, producing substantial disclosure concerning the target business, and allocating the risk of the business between buyer and seller.

1.0 REGULATORY FRAMEWORK

1.1 Governmental Approvals

Foreign acquisitions of U.S. businesses are assisted by a general absence of government regulation of foreign investment and the absence of a general system of exchange controls in the United States.

General.   There is no general system of licensing or regulating foreign investment or foreign acquisitions in the United States. However, the Exon-Florio amendment to the 1988 Omnibus Trade Bill authorizes the President to review certain acquisitions, mergers, and takeovers of U.S. companies or businesses by foreign entities. The President is empowered to suspend or prohibit any such acquisition, or order divestment of the acquired company if the acquisition has been completed, if the President finds credible evidence that the foreign person might take any action that threatens to impair the U.S. national security. The President has delegated the authority to investigate to the Committee on Foreign Investment in the United States ("CFIUS"), an interagency group.

The definition of national security has been left vague, just listing three "factors to consider" in making a determination:

- The domestic production needed for projected national defense requirements.
- The capability and capacity of domestic industries to meet national defense requirements, including the availability of human resources, products, technology, materials, and other supplies and services.
- The control of domestic industries and commercial activity by foreign citizens as it affects the capability and capacity of the U.S. to meet the requirements of national security.

The third factor could be interpreted to include even non-defense industries.

The Exon-Florio amendment applies to any transaction that could result in foreign "control" of a U.S. person or entity. This includes the power to make significant decisions, even where only a minority interest is acquired.

The Exon-Florio provisions impose strict time limits for the investigation and review procedure. Review will begin upon receipt by CFIUS of either "voluntary" notice from the parties involved or notice from an appropriate agency of the U.S. government. CFIUS has 30 days to decide whether the transaction should be investigated. If an investigation is warranted, CFIUS has 45 days in which to conduct the investigation, during which it may request additional documents and personal appearances by the parties, and make its decision. The President then has 15 days in which to review and approve the decision. Transactions will be allowed to proceed without interference unless action is taken by the government within these time periods. However, unnotified transactions will continue to be subject to review at any time. Therefore, in case of doubt, it will often make sense to notify the transaction to CFIUS before proceeding with an acquisition.

Foreign-owned enterprises have equal access to federal and state investment incentives and benefits, except as discussed below.

Exchange controls.   The United States exercises few controls over foreign exchange transactions by U.S. citizens or foreigners. No approval of the Treasury Department or other finance authorities is required to make an investment. A foreign-owned enterprise is free to invest capital and to remit profits and repatriate capital abroad without any license or restriction. Interest and royalties paid to a foreign parent are also free of restriction. The U.S. government does monitor foreign exchange transactions of substantial size but only for informational purposes.

Reports.   Foreign-owned enterprises are required to make periodic, direct investment reports to the United States Department of Commerce by the International Investment Survey Act of 1976, if ten percent or more of a substantial enterprise is foreign-owned. Foreign investment in real estate requires additional reports, particularly to U.S. tax authorities, under the Foreign Investment in Real Property Tax Act. The acquisition of 200 acres or more of agricultural land must be reported to the U.S. Department of Agriculture. Real estate acquisitions may also give rise to other reporting obligations. A foreign buyer of industrial property in a rural area should be careful to ascertain whether any portion of the property purchased can be considered agricultural property. No specific report is necessary for acquisition of nonagricultural land.

1.2 Restricted Industries

Foreign ownership of certain restricted industries is limited or regulated by the federal or state government. These include the defense, banking, insurance, domestic air or water transportation, fishing, and radio and television broadcasting industries.

Defense and other government contractors.   Foreign-owned U.S. firms are free to bid on contracts with the federal and state governments. Buy-American requirements tend to look at where the item is produced rather than to the ownership of the producer. However, an enterprise that is foreign controlled or influenced is unlikely to receive a security clearance and so will not be able to contract with the Department of Defense. (An exception is sometimes available for Canadians and U.K. citizens.) A foreign equity interest of more than five percent creates a presumption of foreign control, although the degree of actual control will be the decisive factor. Even loans or licenses from foreign persons may constitute foreign control in some circumstances. Thus, a foreign acquisition could severely damage an enterprise which depends upon defense business. Sometimes, however, such disqualification can be avoided. Foreign owned stock for the whole company or, more likely, the stock of the subsidiary which actually engages in defense business may be placed in a voting trust controlled by U.S. citizens. Other methods of decontrol may also be available.

Banking.   Banking in the United States is regulated on both the state and federal levels. A foreign bank may establish either a federal or state branch to engage in banking directly as long as it is subject to examination by federal or state banking authorities and regularly publishes financial information. A foreign bank may also acquire an existing U.S. bank. If the bank is state chartered, it will be necessary to obtain the consent of state banking authorities. Most state laws do not restrict foreign ownership of state banks, and state regulatory authorities are increasingly willing to approve foreign takeovers. The acquisition of a national bank must be approved by the Federal Reserve Board, but this approval is generally available. A foreign acquirer must comply with the Bank Holding Company Act of 1956, which restricts multistate banking and participation in both domestic banking and domestic commercial activities. All directors of a national bank must be U.S. citizens. A foreign bank's world-wide structure and long- range plans should be examined in detail before it attempts to acquire a U.S. bank.

Investment banking.   Investment banking is strictly regulated in the United States, but the acquisition of an investment banking firm does not require advance government approval, nor are foreign nationals restricted in owning such firms. Many foreigners engage in investment banking activities in the U.S. directly or through U.S. subsidiaries. A foreign-owned firm may be registered as a broker-dealer with the Securities and Exchange Commission and be a member of U.S. stock exchanges and the National Association of Securities Dealers. Commercial bank involvement in investment banking is limited.

Insurance.   Insurance is largely regulated at the state level. The acquisition of an insurance company normally requires state government approval. No state imposes a citizenship or residency requirement on ownership of an insurance company, although some do impose citizenship requirements on directors. Approval of an acquisition is subject to substantial financial disclosure by the acquirer. Even with such disclosure, insurance company acquisitions are sometimes rejected by state insurance commissioners.

Public utilities.   Because they are so closely regulated by the states, the acquisition of a public utility would almost certainly require state government approval.

Communications and power.   Foreign individuals and firms may not obtain a license to engage in radio or television broadcasting from the Federal Communications Commission (FCC), although they may be permitted to operate a radio privately. An FCC license may only be granted to a U.S. corporation if all of its officers and directors are U.S. nationals and not more than 20 percent of the stock is owned or controlled by foreigners. The acquisition of more than 20 percent of a corporation engaged in the telegraph business is similarly restricted. There are no comparable restrictions on the foreign acquisition of a telephone company. Some states do prohibit an out-of-state corporation from engaging in a local telephone business, but such restrictions almost never extend to the citizenship or residency of the shareholders. There is no federal or state restriction on foreign participation in or ownership of other communications businesses, such as newspaper publishing.

Foreign ownership or control of nuclear power facilities is prohibited, but foreigners may control corporations engaged in other power generating businesses, such as hydroelectric facilities.

Transportation.   Foreigners are restricted from participation in domestic maritime and air transportation and may be limited from engaging in railroad transportation under state law.

Maritime shipping between two U.S. ports is limited to U.S. built and registered vessels owned by U.S. citizens. No foreign corporation may participate in this business. A U.S. corporation will qualify as long as its chief executive officer and a majority of a quorum of its board of directors are U.S. citizens and at least 75 percent of its equity is owned and controlled by U.S. citizens. A U.S. registered vessel may only be sold or mortgaged to a foreign person with U.S. government consent. Foreigners are free to engage in international maritime transport with the United States.

Domestic air transport may only be carried out by domestically registered aircraft. Only U.S. citizens, partnerships in which all partners are U.S. citizens, and U.S. corporations in which the chief executive officer and two-thirds of the directors are U.S. citizens and 75% of the stock is held or controlled by U.S. citizens may register an aircraft. Surprisingly, this limitation extends not only to commercial aircraft but to private aircraft as well. The acquisition of more than ten percent of a domestic air carrier's shares is subject to the approval of the Civil Aeronautics Board. The Civil Aeronautics Board may authorize foreign registered aircraft to transport goods and persons internationally if the carrier is technically qualified and the transport is in the public interest, which usually means that the country of the aircraft's registration affords reciprocal privileges to U.S. registered aircraft or that there is a treaty in effect between the United States and the country of registration.

Federal law does not limit foreign ownership of railroads, but many state laws prohibit any out-of-state railroad company from operating within the state. Some states also restrict the nationality or residence of directors of railroad corporations and, in one case, foreign shareholding as well.

Other maritime activities.   Only U.S. registered vessels may engage in domestic towing, salvage operations, or dredging operations. Only U.S. persons or corporations that meet the same requirements as for vessels that participate in domestic maritime transport, may register such vessels. The same management and ownership requirements apply to vessels fishing within U.S. territorial waters. Foreign vessels may fish within the two-hundred-mile or continental-shelf limit of exclusive U.S. fishing rights, subject to control by the Department of Commerce.

Real estate.   There is no federal law that limits foreign ownership of real estate, but several states have such prohibitions. For example, Iowa limits the right of foreigners to own agricultural property. Most such laws are rather archaic and are unlikely to be enforced. They also can be avoided through proper structuring of ownership, like holding it through a U.S. corporation.

Natural resources.   There is no general limitation on foreign exploitation of natural resources in the United States. However, substantial amounts of exploitable land are owned by the Federal Government. Federal lands may be leased for removal of oil, gas, coal, and other minerals only by U.S. citizens, partnerships, or corporations. However, there is no limitation on foreign shareholding or control of such U.S. corporations. Similar rules apply to federal leases of timberland and of the outer continental shelf. Restrictions and reporting obligations also may apply with state-owned property. Some states restrict foreign real estate investment to certain size tracts.

1.3   Other Regulations and Legal Considerations

There are a number of other legal matters that a foreign buyer must consider in connection with an acquisition, including antitrust notification requirements and federal and state securities regulations.

Antitrust regulation.   U.S. antitrust law prohibits any acquisition or merger that would have the tendency to lessen competition or create a monopoly. However, it has been our recent experience that this restriction has only rarely been used to block acquisitions, particularly if the buyer is foreign and has no or only limited existing operations in the United States.

If a U.S. acquisition meets certain minimum size levels (in general, a value of $15,000,000 or more) and the parties are of a certain size (with sales or assets of $100,000,000 or more in the case of one party and of $10,000,000 or more in the case of the other party), a premerger notification must be filed with the Department of Justice and the Federal Trade Commission. Detailed financial and descriptive information concerning the "ultimate parent" of the acquiring and target corporations, their product lines, and the transaction itself must be included. The "ultimate parent" will be the corporation that is highest in the chain of ownership if the actual buyer is a subsidiary. If the ultimate parent corporation is privately owned (as would be the case with many family-owned enterprises), the ultimate parent may be the family itself. Although this may sound burdensome and unnecessarily intrusive, buyers can comply with the law while disclosing only a reasonable amount of business information.

The parties must wait for thirty days to complete the acquisition, although early termination may be requested. It is not permissable to proceed with the acquisition prior to expiration of the waiting period, even if the transaction is made expressly subject to divestment, in case the government later objects. Managerial and financial control of the target must remain with the seller until expiration of the waiting period. However, the effective date of the acquisition may be made retroactive to a date prior to such expiration, thereby giving the buyer the financial benefit of the target company operations during the waiting period.

The Department of Justice or Federal Trade Commission may request additional information at any time during the waiting period, in which case the waiting period will be suspended until the information is provided. Parties should take care that all information provided is accurate and complete, especially if the timing of the acquisition is important.

Hart-Scott-Rodino filings are confidential. U.S. government authorities will not even confirm or deny if a filing has been made. Therefore, filing a notification should not jeopardize an acquisition or create unwanted publicity in the United States or in the buyer's home country.

Securities laws.   The purchase and sale of securities, including the shares of a corporation, are strictly regulated by both federal and state governments.

Issuance of Shares.   A foreign corporation may issue shares or other securities in the U.S. to finance an acquisition. This would typically be the case with an acquisition in which the buyer exchanges its shares for the shares of the target corporation or for its assets. Shares or other securities must be issued pursuant to a registration statement filed with the Securities and Exchange Commission, unless an exemption from registration is available. The most commonly used exemption in acquisitions is the *private offering* exemption, that is, an offering to a limited number of knowledgeable investors. In any case, the buyer is also required to make full disclosure concerning its business affairs and financial condition (or make such information available) to the seller even in a private transaction. Strict antifraud provisions apply to any issuance or sale of shares or securities.

Tender Offers.   A notice must be filed with the Securities and Exchange Commission once five percent or more of any class of a publicly held target's securities are acquired. This must include a statement of the purchaser's intentions. A tender offer is regulated by federal securities law, including the antifraud rules.

Certain states have adopted legislation designed to make hostile tender offers more difficult. Corporations have adopted restrictions in their articles of incorporation and have taken other defensive measures for the same purpose.

Mergers.   It is often simpler to merge with a public corporation than to tender for its shares, although, as described below, a merger is more time consuming. A merger is a joining together of two or more corporations by operation of law. A foreign buyer will not merge directly with the target but will typically establish a U.S. subsidiary to act as the merger partner. A merger with a public company will require the approval of the target's shareholders and so will be subject to securities law regulations. Public shareholder approval must be obtained through a proxy statement which must contain certain prescribed information, including certain financial information on the proposed merger partner and often on its foreign parent.

2.0 STRUCTURING AN ACQUISITION

There are many factors that must be taken into account in structuring the acquisition of a U.S. corporation. Many of these apply in purely domestic transactions, although they tend to be more complicated in an international acquisition.

2.1 Shares or Cash

The use of cash to acquire shares or assets or to effect a merger offers no legal difficulties. This is the form normally used by a foreign buyer.

There may be tax advantages (especially to the sellers) to using shares or other securities to acquire the shares or assets of a target enterprise. The use of shares for this purpose is subject to securities law regulation. As noted above, shares or other securities may only be issued pursuant to a registration statement unless an exemption from registration is available. In addition, the target's shareholders will only be interested in taking shares if there is a significant public market for the shares offered. This is a severe limitation on the possibility of foreign buyers using shares unless they have shares or other securities traded on a U.S. stock exchange, or the seller is willing to accept securities traded on a foreign exchange.

2.2 Acquisition Vehicle

A foreign buyer may acquire shares or assets directly. More often, a foreign buyer will establish a U.S. acquisition vehicle in the form of a partnership or corporation to acquire assets and, often, shares.

Partnership. A U.S. partnership may be a general partnership with unlimited liability for all partners or a limited partnership with limited liability for the limited partners. Corporations may be partners in either type of partnership. A partnership will often be used if the acquired business is to be conducted as a joint venture, since such a structure may offer tax advantages for both U.S. and foreign participants. A partnership may also be used if the target business primarily involves real estate or natural resources. An investment in partnership form may also have advantages for investors from certain countries, such as West Germany.

Corporation. A corporation is the more common form of acquisition vehicle used by foreign buyers. There is but a single form of share company in the United States, the corporation. A corporation may be organized in any state. (There is no national business corporation law.) Delaware corporate law is particularly flexible and, since it has few mandatory provisions, many U.S. corporations are organized under that law. A U.S. corporation may be organized very quickly, since organization does not require prior approval of any governmental authority or involve prolonged review or processing of documents. There is no limitation on foreigners acting as shareholders in a U.S. corporation except for certain regulated industries discussed above. The organization of a U.S. corporation is discussed below.

Holding company. A new corporation may be used to acquire shares, thereby establishing a holding company structure. A U.S. holding company may also be used if assets are to be acquired or if the acquisition is to be effected through a merger. Such a structure is permissable and comparatively simple in the United States, since a U.S. corporation may have a single shareholder and the U.S. members of the corporate group may file a consolidated income tax return. A holding company structure is likely to give the foreign buyer greater flexibility in tax and business planning in the future, especially if it plans to make other U.S. acquisitions.

2.3 Share Acquisitions

This is the simplest form of acquisition, especially if there are only a few shareholders and all are willing to sell. As in any other sale of securities, the sellers will be subject to the antifraud provisions of U.S. securities laws, although it is customary to include a full disclosure provision in an asset acquisition agreement.

Advantages. All assets remain in the target corporation and so few transfer documents are required. Thus, the acquisition may be completed fairly quickly, even if a public tender offer is required, as discussed below. Transfer taxes may also be limited or avoided, although such taxes are relatively low in most states (Florida is an exception for real estate) and so this is less of an advantage in the United States than in most other countries. The target corporation will retain all of its assets, including its licenses, permits, and franchises. In an asset transaction, these can be difficult to transfer because of the need to obtain consents from the issuing government agencies. Important contracts and leases may also be unaffected by the transfer. These matters must be investigated, however, to be certain that the mere change of control of the target will not bring about termination of permits or contracts.

Disadvantages.   The target corporation will usually retain its tax attributes, both favorable and unfavorable, assuming that the business is continued. A disadvantage of the share acquisition is that a higher purchase price paid for the business may not be reflected in the tax basis of the target corporation's assets after the acquisition, unless the seller consents to certain elections. Since these elections are usually quite disadvantageous to the seller, they are only rarely made. The target corporation will retain all of its tax and other liabilities, whether disclosed or undisclosed, although, in a U.S. transaction, the seller will typically indemnify the buyer against any undisclosed liability of the target, as discussed at 3.2, below.

2.4 Asset Acquisitions

Advantages.   The buyer's tax basis in the acquired assets may be increased to reflect the actual purchase price. Also, not all the assets of the target corporation need be purchased. Thus, if one is interested in only one line of business or one division of a corporation, an asset purchase is the most straightforward way to accomplish the transaction, although in certain cases it may also be possible for the target corporation to rid itself of the unwanted business or assets prior to a share acquisition.

Another benefit of an asset acquisition is that not all liabilities need be acquired. However, certain liabilities may pass to the acquirer in any case. For example, certain state property taxes will constitute a lien on the assets acquired. Environmental liabilities may become the responsibility of any subsequent owner of real estate. Substantial pension liabilities may pass to the purchaser under some circumstances. A few states will impose responsibility on the acquiring corporation for product liability claims even for products sold prior to the acquisition. This is true in only a minority of states, however. In the United States, the seller will usually indemnify the buyer against any such liabilities in the acquisition agreement, which may be sufficient protection if the seller is financially sound.

Assets may also remain subject to attachment by creditors of the seller for a period of time after the transaction is closed unless certain bulk sales procedures, including notices to all creditors of the seller, are followed. These procedures are quite inconvenient and are often ignored where the seller is a substantial corporation, in which case the buyer will rely on the seller's indemnification against any claims of creditors. If the selling corporation is insolvent, great care must be taken to avoid any charge of fraudulent conveyance because of inadequate consideration.

Disadvantages.   An asset acquisition is more complex than a share acquisition because all assets must be transferred. Consents to the transfer of certain valuable assets, such as licenses, permits, or contracts, may not be obtainable or may be obtainable only at a significant price. However, we have not encountered any particular difficulty in obtaining consents from public or private parties merely because the ultimate buyer is foreign. Favorable tax attributes of the target corporation will normally be lost.

2.5 Mergers

As noted above, in a merger, two corporations are joined by operation of law. Normally, one corporation disappears and the other continues as the successor to both lines of business. A merger requires the consent of the board of directors and shareholders and a public filing with the state to be effective. Any consideration may be used in a merger. Thus, the shares in the target corporation may be converted to cash, to shares in the acquiring corporation, or to shares in any other corporation.

The principal advantage of a merger is that the transfer of assets and the exchange of target corporation shares are automatic. Shareholders of the target corporation have no option to retain their shares. No separate transfer documents are required. Transfer taxes normally do not apply in a merger.

Valuable permits, contracts, and the like may also be easier to transfer in a merger than in an asset sale, but these do not remain in the same corporate entity unless the merger is accomplished by merging the buyer's subsidiary into the target corporation. Such a reverse merger is possible in the United States, leaving the target as the surviving corporation. In such a reverse merger, it is still possible to eliminate the target's shareholders by automatically converting their shares to cash or to shares in the buyer or any other corporation.

A merger with a publicly held corporation may be time consuming because of the need to hold a meeting of the shareholders and to comply with U.S. proxy rules. If the publicly held target is attractive to other potential bidders, the delay in effecting a merger may allow these other bidders to compete for the target, increasing the price of the shares and, possibly, frustrating the acquisition. Our foreign clients are often reluctant to battle, or even compete, with other bidders. In such cases, we often start with a friendly tender offer for sufficient shares to approve a merger. This may be completed quickly. If the tender is successful, timing will no longer be important, and any remaining shareholders can be eliminated through a merger of the acquisition vehicle with the target.

2.6 Financing an Acquisition

It is increasingly common to finance an acquisition with the assets or future profits of the target corporation. This is called a leveraged buy-out. The assets of the target enterprise may be pledged to a bank or other financial institution, or the buyer may issue high interest, subordinated debt instruments, normally referred to as *junk bonds*. Such bonds consti-·tute securities and must be registered with the Securities and Exchange Commission unless an exemption from registration is available. We find that foreign buyers only rarely use local U.S. debt financing (leveraged or otherwise) for an acquisition, although this may be due primarily to recent high interest rates in the U.S.

Foreign buyers are more likely to use shareholder loans to finance an acquisition, especially if they have borrowed in their own countries, which is another form of leveraged buy out, since it is the target that will effectively repay the borrowing. Since dividends are not deductible by the paying U.S. corporation, it is generally advantageous to treat payments to foreign shareholders as interest. However, such shareholder loans must bear a U.S. market interest rate, must be treated as loans, and must not constitute too great a portion of the company's financing in comparison to its share capital. Interest payments (and dividends) to foreigners may be subject to U.S. withholding tax.

3.0 DOCUMENTATION

A foreign buyer will find that a U.S. acquisition will go through several stages, each characterized by a form of documentation.

3.1 Letter of Intent

This sets out the principal points upon which the parties have agreed. It is useful in identifying important issues between the parties. Its disadvantage is that it may delay the preparation and signing of a definitive contract.

Except for certain matters, such as confidentiality, standstill, and the like, a letter of intent is typically made not legally binding between the parties. However, in the United States, the parties are considered to be morally bound, and an American party will be most reluctant to make important changes in the terms set out in the letter of intent. A letter of intent may also create legal liabilities if one of the parties fails to negotiate the definitive agreement in good faith. Thus, it is important that all matters of importance to the foreign buyer, especially the material terms and the structure of the transaction, be considered and reviewed with counsel before a letter of intent is signed. If the seller is a public company, the signing of a letter of intent may also require public disclosure of the transaction.

3.2 Acquisition Agreement

With or without a letter of intent, the parties and their attorneys must prepare and negotiate a definitive acquisition agreement. It should set out all of the rights and obligations of the parties, both before and after the closing. A foreign buyer should expect a complete explanation of all aspects of the agreement, since that is the key element in the transaction. A foreign buyer should never fear to appear unsophisticated and should take nothing for granted. We find that many foreign buyers make unwarranted assumptions based on business and legal practices in their own countries. We always try to explain all elements of the acquisition agreement and related agreements in terms that take into account the buyer's own experience. We also try to draft documents that make them easier for the client to understand, avoiding unnecessary "lawyer's" terminology. Nonetheless, questions from clients are always appropriate and welcome.

Acquisition agreements in the United States tend to be fairly long. The principal features of a U.S. acquisition agreement are described below.

Subject of acquisition.   The property to be acquired by the buyer, whether assets, shares, or a combination of both, should be specified. Any assets or businesses to be excluded must also be identified. If a merger is contemplated, this will be described.

Price.   The price paid for a U.S. enterprise may be fixed, subject to adjustment or contingent. The cash price in a share acquisition or merger will usually be fixed, although the seller may guarantee that the net worth of the target corporation will be a certain minimum. If it does not reach this minimum, the price may be adjusted. Net worth would in such a case be determined by a postclosing audit. Such audits, often by an independent accounting firm, are quite customary in the United States and would only rarely be resisted by a U.S. seller. An audit affords the foreign buyer substantial protection, but an audit can only supplement the buyer's own preclosing due diligence investigation, discussed below.

In an asset transaction, the seller's cash is normally excluded. The price paid for property, plant and equipment and non-balance sheet intangibles, such as intellectual property, will be fixed, but the price for current assets, particularly inventory and receivables, will depend upon the level of such assets as of the closing. These and any other items subject to adjustment will be determined by an audit conducted immediately after the closing.

If a target's earnings history is short or subject to question, the parties may make part of the purchase price contingent on future earnings performance. Such a payout arrangement is fraught with difficulty, since the buyer will wish to operate the purchased business freely, but the seller will have a continuing interest in it and so wish to impose significant limitations on the buyer.

Allocation of price.   It is advantageous to allocate the purchase price to specific assets, at least in an asset transaction. The parties will normally agree to use these allocations for all tax purposes. The parties are not completely free to make any allocation they wish. Any allocation is subject to challenge by the tax authorities, who have an interest in allocating as much of the purchase price as possible to nondepreciable items such as goodwill.

Payment.   An acquisition agreement normally calls for payment by wire transfer at the closing, although bank (cashier's) checks are sometimes used. The mechanics of payment are discussed under "Closing," below.

A portion of the price may be paid on a deferred basis through the issuance of a promissory note. This will permit the purchase to be more easily financed out of the assets and future profits of the acquired business. It may also provide a means for satisfying any claims that the buyer may have after the closing. Therefore, a foreign buyer should always consider this possibility, even though it may not be customary in the buyer's own country.

Assumption of liabilities.   In a sense, all liabilities are assumed in a share transaction or merger, since after the closing the buyer will own the debtor corporation or a successor in interest to the debtor corporation. Normally, only the target corporation's assets are exposed to such liabilities, although this would be of little solace to the buyer. As noted above, this risk is mitigated somewhat by the seller's indemnity against any undisclosed liabilities that one customarily finds in U.S. acquisition agreements.

In an asset acquisition, the liabilities to be assumed and excluded should be covered in considerable detail. The buyer will have to assume the obligations under all contracts assigned. The buyer should also consider assuming trade payables, since it is the buyer who will have the greatest interest in seeing that suppliers of goods and services are satisfied. The amount of the liabilities assumed should be considered a part of the overall purchase price. Any liabilities not specifically assumed by the buyer will be retained by the seller.

Representations and warranties. These are usually quite extensive and cover the areas of greatest concern to the buyer. These areas are discussed under Section 4, below. Acquisitions in the United States are made on the basis of full disclosure of all aspects of the purchased business. Representations and warranties are designed to provide disclosure of information about the target enterprise. They are not principally intended to form the basis of claims after the closing, although they may in fact do so.

Covenants. Any matters to be carried out between the signing of the contract and the closing will be set forth as specific covenants of one party or the other. The most significant such covenant is that which requires the seller to conduct the business in the ordinary course. It will typically prohibit the seller from engaging in any major transactions without the advance approval of the buyer.

Conditions. The preconditions to closing the transaction will also be set forth in the acquisition agreement. Typical such conditions are the continued accuracy of the seller's representations and warranties, the performance of seller's covenants, the rendering of legal opinions, the execution of ancillary agreements, and the absence of any material adverse change in the business.

Closing. The transfer documents to be executed and delivered at the closing, as well as the method of payment of the purchase price, should be specified. The mechanics of closing a U.S. acquisition are described below.

Indemnification. If a public company is acquired, it is impractical in most cases to obtain any continuing indemnity from the public shareholders after the closing, and the target's management and controlling shareholders, if any, will generally refuse to accept the responsibility alone. In this situation, the representations and warranties will expire at the closing and there will be no ongoing indemnity obligation. The burden is then on the buyer to verify all facts about the target prior to the closing. The buyer will be aided in this by the fact that the target has been subject to the public disclosure obligations of U.S. securities laws.

If the target is privately owned, the acquistion agreement will require the seller to indemnify the buyer for any misrepresentations, breaches of warranties, or breaches of covenant. The buyer will be subject to a similar obligation in favor of the seller. The indemnification provisions will also allocate responsibility for the conduct of the business both before and after the closing. In this sense, these provisions represent an allocation of risk between the two parties. An indemnification provision will also specify the period following the closing during which one party will be responsible to the other party. The parties have a natural desire to have their indemnification obligations end. Such "survival" periods are typically specified between one and three years, although, as noted below, environmental indemnifications are often unlimited in time. Indemnification provisions may also specify that claims may only be made after all claims reach a certain minimum level. Once this level is reached, the agreement may permit a party to assert all claims or only those in excess of the minimum. Less frequently, an agreement may provide a maximum claim that may be asserted, typically all or a set portion of the purchase price of the business.

3.3 Other Agreements

The acquisition agreement may provide for a variety of ancillary agreements to be executed at the closing. These may include a noncompetition agreement, employment agreements with one or more of the sellers or key employees of the target, and ongoing leases and licenses. These are discussed under "Closing," below.

4.0 PRINCIPAL LEGAL CONCERNS OF THE BUYER

The representations and warranties in the acquisition agreement focus upon the matters of greatest concern to the buyer. As noted above, representations and warranties are designed to elicit information about the target company. Thus, they play a vital role in the buyer's investigation of the target company. The disclosures made in the acquisition agreement will be based in part on the due diligence investigation performed by counsel for the seller and will be further verified by the investigation of buyer and buyer's counsel. This investigation may be more far-reaching than would be encountered in the foreign buyer's own country. The expense involved should be weighed against the added protection afforded the buyer.

4.1 Corporate Authority and Organization

The seller will represent that the selling entity is properly organized and that the persons acting on its behalf are duly authorized to do so.

However, in the United States, the buyer and its counsel will also independently verify this thorough examination of the target's books and records, as well as public filings. A share acquisition agreement will also contain a representation that the target corporation is properly organized. However, the buyer will also rely upon the opinion of legal counsel to the seller concerning the seller's organization and authorization. Typically, buyer's counsel will only independently verify the validity of the original organization of the target corporation in a share acquisition. In other cases, the buyer will rely on the seller's representations and the opinion of seller's counsel.

4.2 Financial Statements

The acquisition agreement will indicate that the financial statements that have been presented to the buyer (which may or may not be attached to the agreement) have been prepared in accordance with generally accepted accounting principles on a consistent basis. Financial representations will be included even if all financial statements have been audited by a reputable accounting firm. Usually, they will also contain specific representations as to certain assets, such as inventory and accounts receivable. These will be audited after the closing as well.

4.3 Compliance with Law

Environmental compliance.   In the United States, the buyer will inherit legal responsibility for any environmental problems existing on any real property purchased, whether the transaction is in the form of an asset acquisition, share acquisition, or merger. Environmental liabilities represent one of the most significant traps for the unwary buyer, domestic or foreign. Therefore, the buyer will want full disclosure of any such problems. These will include any failure by the business to comply with environmental laws or any environmental permits for day-to-day operations. Of equal concern are any hazardous waste materials that may be stored or buried on any real property. The removal of such waste can be incredibly expensive. In certain industries, it may be appropriate to have an environmental audit of the premises, including soil borings and air and water tests, to ascertain the presence and extent of any such problems. The buyer will also want to confirm that any waste materials that have been carried off the premises have been handled and disposed of in accordance with applicable legal requirements. A purchaser may become liable for the improper off-site disposal of waste material by a predecessor or even by an unrelated third party, such as a waste disposal service retained by a previous owner of the business. Environmental permits or licenses will have to be transferred in the case of an asset acquisition, or new permits will have to be obtained. It will also be necessary to consult with environmental authorities to be certain that the permits will be respected upon the change of ownership in a share acquisition. In certain states, such as New Jersey and Connecticut, the advance approval of state authorities may be required in order to complete the acquisition. Because environmental liabilities are so extensive in scope, the seller's environmental indemnities are usually unlimited in amount and time.

Other licenses and permits.   Every business will operate with a variety of governmental licenses and permits, including general business licenses, building permits and certificates of occupancy relating to structures, boiler permits and other permits to operate certain forms of machinery and equipment, and vehicle licenses and registrations. In addition, specific governmental licenses and franchises may be necessary for certain kinds of businesses. It may be possible to transfer these licenses and permits to the buyer in an asset acquisition. More often, however, new licenses and permits must be obtained. Arrangements for the transfer or obtaining of such licenses must be made so that they are in place at the closing if the business is to continue without interruption. Even vehicle licenses may present problems, since their transfer may take some time.

Government licenses and permits, are generally not assignable even though they may be very material to the business. They may also terminate in the event of a material change in control of a target corporation. The latter is more often imposed by practice on the local level than by statute. In such cases, the buyer will want to be certain that it can obtain its own licenses and permits prior to the closing. The agreement will generally call for disclosure of the licenses and permits used by the business.

Compliance with other laws.   The buyer will wish to confirm that the business operates in compliance with zoning laws and other local laws regulating the use of real estate. Zoning law compliance is not always covered by title insurance. The buyer will also be concerned about compliance with federal occupational safety and health laws. It is unlikely that the seller will be able to give absolute assurance of such compliance, but the buyer will want to know that the seller is at least not aware of, and has not received notice of, any violations. The buyer may also want some assurance that the seller is not aware that it has violated any laws relating to equal employment opportunities or hiring or other laws affecting employment and employment practices.

The foregoing compliance matters may also be the subject of specific provisions in the indemnification section of the agreement. Even if it is not possible for the seller to give absolute assurance of compliance in certain areas, the seller can expressly retain responsibility for noncompliance. This allocation of risk and responsibility is one of the major negotiating points in any U.S. acquisition.

4.4 Employees

Employment protection. Unlike many foreign jurisdictions, there are no statutes in the United States requiring that employees be retained or given specific severance pay upon termination of employment in an acquisition, although federal and some state laws require advance notice if an entire plant is to be closed. Employees have no right to review or approve an acquisition of their employer. Employees do not automatically become the employees of the acquiring corporation in an asset purchase, although they will do so in a share acquisition or a merger. However, a foreign buyer should not assume that it has an entirely free hand in dealing with employees. Most American employers have adopted employment policies which are legally binding on the employer. These will often provide for some form of termination compensation unless the employees are offered employment with substantially the same salary and, perhaps, benefits by the acquiring corporation. For this and other reasons, the seller will often insist that the buyer agree to employ its existing work force and may also want to specify the terms and conditions of that employment. As with other economic issues, these matters will be settled between the buyer and seller through negotiation, although there may also be a strong psychological element on the part of the seller. Related matters, such as accrued vacation pay, will also have to be dealt with, since the employees will expect to retain these accrued benefits after the closing. A foreign buyer will want to be particularly sensitive to employee expectations.

Labor agreements. In a stock purchase or merger, the buyer will be bound by any collective bargaining agreement to which the target corporation is a party. A purchaser will only be bound in an asset acquisition if it expressly assumes the collective bargaining agreement. A buyer will usually want to take advantage of the anxiety of the work force to renegotiate the terms of employment. Consequently, it will generally resist assuming any collective bargaining agreements. The buyer will, however, be required to recognize any existing labor union and bargain with it in good faith. Many foreign buyers will find American labor unions easier to deal with than their foreign counterparts.

Termination notice. The federal government and some state governments, as well as many labor contracts, require advance notice when industrial plants are closed. Depending upon the degree of continuity in an acquisition, such statutes or contract provisions may apply. Federal law also requires that a terminated employee be allowed to continue any employer-sponsored health program for a period of up to eighteen months but at the cost of the employee. Certain states, such as Massachusetts, may impose this economic cost on the employer.

Pensions and other benefits.   If the seller or target corporation has maintained any employee benefit programs, including pension plans, responsibility for continued adequate funding of these obligations may pass to the buyer, even in an asset acquisition. Such plans are subject to extensive federal regulation. A buyer of a business may also incur significant obligations created prior to the acquisition, including making up any underfunding of the pension plan. The seller in an asset acquisition would generally want the buyer to continue its existing pension plans, since termination of a plan can be quite expensive and time consuming. Termination is only possible if the buyer is willing to have a plan that is more or less comparable, although not necessarily identical, to the seller's existing plan. In any acquisition, the seller's or target corporation's pension plan should be examined in detail by experts (lawyers and actuaries) hired by the buyer, in order to avoid having the buyer incur substantial unexpected liabilities.

4.5   Material Assets

Physical facilities.   The buyer will want to obtain clear title to any plants or other real estate owned by the seller or target corporation since these would generally be material to the operation of the business. Title to real estate is transferred by a deed, which is publicly recorded. (Title certificates are also used in certain locations.) There is no notary of the kind found in many civil law countries. In most U.S. states, title to real property is investigated and assured by specialized title insurance companies. The title company will insure clear title, subject to certain specified exceptions, such as identified mortgages and easements. Title insurance should be obtained even if a target corporation is being acquired and no real property is actually being transferred. Usually, the buyer should also obtain a survey of the property, which indicates the location of all buildings and easements, such as utility lines, and other matters affecting the physical layout of the property, and which also discloses any difficulty with access to the property. As noted above, the buyer may also wish to obtain an environmental audit. The buyer will want to insure that the property is being used legally and in compliance with all building codes and zoning ordinances; these will be covered by title insurance only if specifically requested and paid for. In an asset acquisition, the transfer of real estate will entail state and local transfer taxes, but with certain exceptions, these tend to be far lower than in most other countries.

Intellectual property.   In many businesses, intellectual property will constitute a substantial basis of economic success. The buyer will want to conduct a thorough investigation of title to all intellectual property, including trademarks and patents, and will want to insure that title to such property can be effectively transferred to it in the case of an asset acquisition. A foreign buyer may be particularly interested in the extent of foreign protection of the acquired intellectual property. The buyer will also want to be assured that all necessary consents to the assignment of any intellectual property licenses have been obtained. This may be necessary even in the case of certain stock acquisitions, if the license is terminable upon a material change in control of the target enterprise.

A major issue which we encounter with foreign buyers in some acquisitions is the unwillingness of the seller to assure the buyer that its patents are valid. Such a warranty goes far beyond a mere representation of good title. A significant number of challenged patents are ruled invalid in the United States, and so a warranty of validity will generally be resisted by U.S. sellers.

Agreements and licenses.   Agreements and licenses may be quite material to the success of a business and yet may be jeopardized by an acquisition. (For example, following the recent foreign acquisition of Firestone, General Motors announced that it would no longer purchase tires from Firestone as original equipment on its automobiles.) An acquisition agreement will require disclosure of any contract above a certain size or extending beyond a certain duration, both to advise the buyer of the commitments to which the business is subject and to advise the buyer of the consents which must be obtained to assume such agreements or leases. The other party to such contracts or leases may be reluctant to consent to assignment without compensation if, for example, the rent is below market.

4.6 Liabilities

Product liability.   A principal concern of any foreign buyer of a U.S. business is strict liability for personal injuries resulting from products sold. As in most other countries, the manufacturer or seller of a product in the United States is liable for any damages that may be sustained as a result of the manufacturer's or seller's negligence. However, under the American doctrine of strict liability, one who sells a product is liable for any physical harm caused to the ultimate user or consumer or to its property, if the product at the time of sale is in a defective condition (such that it is unreasonably dangerous to the user). The seller is engaged in the business of selling the product, and the product may be expected to and does reach the user or consumer without substantial change. Combined with the propensity of American juries to award substantial damages, the doctrine of strict liability makes product claims a material cost of doing business in the United States. Any buyer will want to obtain some assurance from the seller that such exposure will not be unreasonable in amount. The buyer will also want to investigate the historical experience of the seller in order to ascertain whether the business itself involves undue risks.

In a stock purchase or a merger (or in an asset acquisition in a few states), the buyer will also be concerned about assuming responsibility for products sold prior to the closing. Although the seller may represent that it knows of no such liabilities, there is no way that the seller can give complete assurance in this regard. Therefore, the parties will want to allocate responsibility as part of the indemnification provisions. We often provide that the seller will remain responsible for any products sold (or shipped) prior to the closing and that the buyer will be responsible for products sold (or shipped) after the closing. Indemnification for product liability will often either be unlimited in time or limited to the applicable statute of limitations. This statute of limitations may be quite long since it generally will only begin to run at the time the person is injured, which may be long after the product is sold or shipped.

Tax liabilities.   In an asset acquisition, the buyer will almost never become directly liable for taxes based upon the operation of the business prior to the closing. Certain ad valorem taxes may constitute a lien on the assets purchased, however. In the case of a share acquisition or merger, any tax liabilities (and other tax detriments) will come with the target corporation. In this case, it is normal for the seller to accept complete responsibility for any tax liabilities attributable to the operation of the business prior to the closing and to indemnify the buyer against any such liabilities. Such indemnification would generally run for the period of limitations.

Other liabilities.   In the United States, the seller will generally represent that there are no undisclosed liabilities of the business, whether contingent or otherwise. If the target corporation should have any such undisclosed liabilities, they will usually be the responsibility of the seller pursuant to an indemnification obligation. In an asset acquisition, the buyer will expressly not assume any liabilities other than those specifically identified in the agreement.

4.7 No Material Change

The seller will generally represent that there has been no material adverse change in the operations or financial conditions of the target business since the date of the most recent financial statements or some other cut off date. In addition, lack of any material adverse change will often be a condition of closing. A typical provision in an acquisition agreement will limit the seller's right to conduct the business other than in accordance with past practice and will prohibit the seller from making any material change in the business, making any major purchases or investments, incurring any significant obligations or liabilities, or changing compensation or other employee benefits without the consent of the buyer.

5.0   OTHER LEGAL MATTERS

There are a number of other legal matters that may be of concern in an acquisition.

5.1 Distributors and Agents

It is customary in an acquisition agreement to require disclosure of all distribution and sales representative agreements and arrangements. These are material to the operation of some businesses. Unlike many other countries, in the United States the buyer will be relatively free to terminate distributors and sales representatives without, in most states, being liable for any mandatory termination compensation payments. Few states have statutes requiring such compensation. However, there is a general trend in the United States against arbitrary or abusive terminations. Thus, a buyer should be careful to document that any such terminations are pursuant to a reorganization of the acquired business's distribution arrangements. The buyer should also be sure that such terminations are not motivated by matters constituting violations of the antitrust laws. For example, it would be illegal to terminate a price-cutting distributor in an attempt to control pricing.

5.2 Immigration

A foreign acquirer will often contemplate sending executives and skilled technical experts to assist with the conduct of the business after the closing. These individuals may easily visit the United States on temporary business visas (a B-1 visa) for short periods of time. In the case of a transferring executive, appropriate visas are available, but obtaining them may be somewhat time consuming. Any important personnel transfers should be planned with the help of experts well in advance of the closing.

5.3 Importation of Parts and Components

All matters pertaining to the importation of merchandise into the United States fall within the exclusive jurisdiction of the federal government. Most products imported into the United States are subject to the payment of import duties, generally payable on an ad valorem basis and determined by their specific classification. The customs authorities have the right to challenge any claimed valuation, particularly where the transaction is between a foreign parent and a U.S. subsidiary. If a foreign buyer plans to use an acquired corporation, for example, to assemble parts and components imported from abroad, it will want to ascertain at an early point that it will be able to import such parts and components freely (which is almost certainly the case) and obtain some guidance as to the import duty cost of such importation.

There are a number of special forms of customs entry, such as foreign trade zones, that may be of particular interest to a foreign buyer. Products of foreign origin may be shipped to a foreign trade zone located in the United States without making a formal customs entry or paying any U.S. customs duties. Such foreign products may be stored, sold for export, or assembled while located within the zone and then reexported, all without incurring any U.S. customs duty.

A foreign buyer may encounter certain restrictions on imports into the United States, particularly antidumping and countervailing duties. These are imposed when products are imported at what the customs service considers to be an unjustifiably low price. In certain cases, quotas may be imposed on certain limited kinds of products. If the acquired business will be dependent on imported materials or components, the foreign buyer should review its plans and anticipated pricing with customs counsel prior to proceeding with an acquisition.

6.0 ORGANIZING THE ACQUISITION VEHICLE

Whatever the form of the acquisition, it is likely that the buyer will want to organize a U.S. corporation to act as the acquisition vehicle. The corporation will be organized prior to the closing and probably prior to signing the acquisition agreement. Alternatively, the acquisition agreement may be signed by the buyer and assigned to the acquisition vehicle prior to the closing. Organizing a U.S. corporation will involve a number of steps.

6.1 Initial Decisions

The principal matters that need to be determined by a foreign buyer in order to organize a U.S. corporation and prepare it to operate are the name of the corporation, the state of incorporation, its principal place of business, its initial capital, the identity of the shareholders, the number, name, and addresses of directors and officers, and if the corporation will operate after the closing, the fiscal year and any banking relationship. A corporation may choose any name as long as it is not confusingly similar to that of another corporation. The state of incorporation will usually be the same as the principal place of business, although as noted above, Delaware is a popular choice for state of incorporation, especially if the acquisition vehicle is not a wholly-owned subsidiary.

6.2 Public Filings

A U.S. corporation is formed by filing a Certificate or Articles of Incorporation (the terminology depends on the state of incorporation—both terms are substantially equivalent) containing information required by state corporate law. Typically, this is only the name of the corporation, its principal place of business in the state, and its authorized and issued capital shares (discussed in Section 6.5, below). The Articles may also include the names of the initial directors and other matters of concern to the shareholders. The Articles or Certificate will be signed by one or more incorporators, who need not be shareholders.

6.3 Organizational Meetings

Unless the directors are appointed in the Certificate or Articles, the incorporator or shareholders will hold an initial meeting to elect the directors. The directors will then hold an initial meeting to elect the officers, accept subscriptions for shares and authorize their issuance, approve a seal, select a fiscal year and, normally, authorize the opening of a corporate bank account. At the initial or a subsequent meeting, the directors will also approve the acquisition of the target and the execution of the acquisition agreement and related documents.

6.4 Capital and Financing

U.S. corporations may issue common and preferred shares. Common shares fully participate in the economic life of the corporation. Preferred stock may carry any sort of preference for dividends or distribution of assets upon dissolution. Shares may be voting or nonvoting.

Shares may be issued for cash, personal or real property, or services already performed. No public appraisal or court approval is required to value contributed property.

To provide flexibility, it is normal to authorize more shares than will initially be issued. No fixed percentage of the authorized shares must be subscribed or paid for.

6.5 Corporate Structure and Management

A corporation consists of three principal organs, the shareholders, the board of directors, and the officers.

Shareholders.   As noted earlier, a U.S. corporation may have a single shareholder. Shareholders elect directors and approve extraordinary acts and transactions, such as a merger, the sale of substantially all assets, or the dissolution of the corporation. They may also approve amendments to the articles of incorporation or bylaws. Shareholders normally do not declare or approve dividends or approve the balance sheet.

Shareholder meetings (including the initial meeting) may be held by proxy. In lieu of a formal meeting, a consent resolution signed by all (in some states, a majority) of the shareholders may be used to take any action required of the shareholders.

Board of directors.   An American corporation is managed by its board of directors, although they may delegate substantial authority to officers. Directors declare dividends and recommend such actions as a merger or dissolution to the shareholders. The corporation may have a single director, although a larger number is more common. Directors need not be shareholders, and so qualifying shares are never needed. Directors generally need not be citizens or residents of the United States or a particular state. An exception exists for those regulated industries noted above.

Unlike in many foreign jurisdictions, U.S. directors act as a body and do not represent the corporation individually. There is no managing director of an American corporation. Directors may not meet through proxies but may meet through a conference telephone call and may act through written consent resolutions signed by all of the directors. Corporations may not act as directors.

New close corporation statutes permit the shareholders to manage the corporation and dispense with the board of directors, but these are not often used by foreign investors.

Officers.   The officers consist of a president, one or more vice-presidents, a secretary, and a treasurer. The officers are elected by the board of directors and may be removed at any time. The president is normally the chief executive officer of the corporation. A vice-president will act in the absence of the president. The secretary is responsible for maintaining all corporate books and records. The secretary may be called upon to confirm the authority of the president or other officer to act for the corporation. The treasurer supervises the financial affairs of the corporation.

7.0 CLOSING

The closing of a U.S. acquisition will be organized primarily by legal counsel for the buyer and seller. A closing will typically involve the following matters.

7.1 Transfer Documents

The transfer documents to be executed and delivered at the closing will depend upon the nature of the transaction. In a stock purchase, the seller will deliver certificates representing all of the shares in the target corporation accompanied by an executed stock power of attorney authorizing the transfer of the shares on the stock books of the target. In a merger, the parties will execute a formal plan of merger (in most states) for filing with the secretaries of state of the jurisdictions in which the respective corporations are organized. This document may be considerably shorter than the definitive merger agreement. It will often have to be notarized. These formalities will be accomplished immediately prior to the closing and the plan of merger may actually be sent ahead to the appropriate state capital(s) so that it is ready for filing on the day of the closing.

An asset acquisition is more complicated. Real estate will be transferred by deeds for each parcel. Deeds will typically have to be notarized and recorded in the locality in which the real estate is located. Recording will be completed on the day of the closing or shortly thereafter. The title insurance company will execute and deliver a binder insuring title to the real estate. Personal property will be transferred by bill of sale, which requires no formalities. Agreements and other intangibles will be transferred by a form of assignment, which may be combined with the bill of sale. Separate assignment documents may be required for patents and certain other assets, some of which are subject to formal requirements.

7.2 Payment

In an international acquisition, payment is more often effected by wire transfer than cashier's check. The disadvantage of a cashier's check is that it will have to be deposited for collection, and so funds may not be actually available to the seller on the day of closing. This can cause the loss of a substantial amount of interest. Wire transfers make funds immediately available once the transfer is acknowledged by the seller's bank, but delays do sometimes occur. It has been our experience that international wire transfers are more likely to be delayed on a Monday or Friday because of the large volume of other transfers and transactions on those days. Therefore, it is preferable to hold a closing in the middle of the week whenever possible. If the closing must be held at the beginning or end of the week or timing is crucial, payment may be made by a federal funds cashier's check, which is somewhat inconvenient for the buyer to obtain but which provides immediately available funds to the seller.

7.3 Other Agreements

A number of ancillary agreements may be executed at the closing. These are likely to include the following.

Noncompetition agreements. There are both business and tax reasons why the buyer would want the seller to agree not to compete with the purchased business for some period of time after the closing. Such agreements are generally enforceable provided that they are reasonable and designed to preserve to the buyer the benefit of the acquisition.

Employment agreements. It is not unusual for the seller of a privately held business, and possibly members of his family, to have been employed by the corporation prior to the acquisition. A significant consideration in agreeing to sell the business may be some assurance of continuity of employment. In larger transactions, the buyer will want to assume that certain key individuals will be available to operate the target business after the closing. This is most often true of top executives and important technical personnel. In these cases, either the buyer or seller may require that employment agreements be executed with such key persons at or prior to the closing.

Leases and licenses. It may not be possible to transfer all of the tangible and intangible property necessary to operate the business to the buyer. For example, the seller may continue to use key software or technology in its retained businesses. In such cases, tangible property may have to be leased and intangible property licensed to the business.

Service agreements.   If the buyer is purchasing a portion of an integrated business, the buyer may not receive a fully stand-alone operation. In this case, the seller may have to provide postclosing services to the buyer on a short-term or, occasionally, long-term basis. Computer access is a common example of such a postclosing service provided by the seller.

7.4 Other Documents

A number of other documents may also be delivered at the closing. These would include legal opinions from counsel for both parties. It is also normal to deliver a certified copy of the Certificate or Articles of Incorporation of the target company as well as a certificate issued by the appropriate secretary of state indicating that the target company is in "good standing" in its state of incorporation. It is also customary for the management of the target (and for the buyer) to deliver a certificate affirming that all representations and warranties in the acquisition agreement are true and correct as of the day of closing. The officers and directors of the target company in a stock acquisition will deliver written resignations.

8.0 U.S. ACQUISITION LEGAL CHECKLIST

The following checklist represents the various matters addressed by attorneys in the course of an acquisition. The approach to a given acquisition will vary with circumstances, but the matters covered are set out in more or less chronological order.

The point at which a foreign buyer should consult a U.S. attorney will also vary. If there is any significant question about the legal permissibility of the acquisition, an attorney should be consulted at the very outset. In other cases, an attorney will become involved after the buyer has conducted an initial investigation into the business and financial aspects of the target and has determined that the acquisition is desirable from the business point of view. A foreign buyer should always bear in mind that such a purchase is a significant transaction in an unfamiliar environment, an environment in which acquisitions are quite complicated and where the pitfalls are many. Except for an agreement to keep information received during the buyer's initial investigation confidential, a U.S. attorney should be consulted before any document is signed, including the letter of intent, and prior to deciding on the form and structure of the transaction.

Legal Checklist U.S. Acquisitions

I. Initial due diligence
   A. Preliminary investigation of business
      1. Financial statements
      2. Business operations
   B. Confidentiality agreement
      1. Access to information about target
      2. Confidential treatment of target information
II. Regulatory considerations
   A. Foreign investment approvals
      1. CFIUS investigation: National security
         a. Notice requirements
         b. Investigations and time limits
      2. Government restrictions on foreign ownership
         a. Defense: Federal
         b. Banking and other financial institutions: State and Federal
         c. Insurance: State
         d. Air and maritime transport: Federal
         e. Ownership of ships and aircraft: Federal
         f. Communications and power: Federal
         g. Railroads: State
         h. Towing, salvage, and dredging: Federal
         i. Fishing: Federal
         j. Natural resources: Federal
         k. Agriculture: State
         l. Other real estate: State
   B. Other limitations and notices
      1. Hart-Scott-Rodino premerger notice
      2. Takeover and public tender legislation
         a. Federal: Williams Act
         b. State
      3. Other securities law considerations
         a. Proxy rules: Merger
         b. SEC registration or exemption if shares or other securities
            used as consideration
   C. Bulk transfers
      1. Notice to creditors
      2. Other formalities
III. Structuring the transaction
   A. Purchase price
      1. Shares or other securities
      2. Cash or notes

B. Choose acquisition vehicle
   1. Foreign parent
   2. New or existing local subsidiary
      a. Formalities to establish new corporation
      b. Time requirements for new corporation
C. Choose form of acquisition
   1. Share acquisition
      a. Simplicity or complexity
      b. Continuity of business
      c. Contracts, permits, and tax attributes
      d. No transfer taxes
      e. Liabilities
   2. Asset acquisition
      a. Simplicity or complexity
      b. Transfer taxes
      c. No continuity of contracts, permits, or tax attributes
      d. Liabilities
   3. Merger (often not available)
      a. Simplicity or complexity
      b. Some continuity of business, contracts, or permits
      c. Possibly avoid transfer taxes
      d. Liabilities
IV. Principal documentation
A. Letter of intent
   1. Outline of transaction
   2. No-shop
   3. Access to information
   4. Confidentiality
B. Acquisition agreement
   1. Description of transaction
      a. Transfer of assets, shares, or merger
      b. Price and payment terms
      c. Price allocations (asset transfer)
      d. Price adjustment
   2. Liabilities assumed (asset transfer)
   3. Representation and warranties (see Legal due diligence, V, below)
   4. Covenants
      a. Conduct of business
      b. No-shop
      c. Confidentiality
      d. Standstill
      e. Consents to assignent and nonassignable contracts
      f. Future employment of key personnel

5. Conditions to closing
    a. Representations true and covenants performed
    b. No adverse change in business
    c. Related agreements executed
    d. Legal opinions
    e. No litigation affecting transaction
    f. Government approvals (Hart-Scott-Rodino, etc.)
    g. Other consents and approvals (material contracts, leases and licenses, loan agreements, etc.)
    h. Transfer or issuance of material permits.
6. Closing (See VI below)
7. Indemnification
    a. Coverage
    b. Threshold or deductible amount
    c. Survival of obligations (time limits)
8. Dispute resolution and governing law
    a. Arbitration
    b. Choice of forum
C. Other agreements
    1. Noncompetition agreement
        a. Parties covered
        b. Scope (time, field, and geography)
        c. Legality and enforceability
        d. Tax incidents
    2. Employment agreements
        a. Key employees
        b. Selling shareholders
        c. Tax incidents
    3. Leases and licenses
        a. Nontransferable property
        b. Commingled property
    4. Services agreement
        a. Transition to permit target to achieve standalone capability
        b. Essential commingled services
    5. Parent or other guaranties
    6. Ongoing supply or distribution agreements
    7. Escrow agreement
V. Legal due diligence
(These are normally also covered by the representations and warranties.)
A. Corporate matters
    1. Organizational documents (particles of incorporation and by-laws)

2. Corporate records (minutes of shareholders and director meetings, stock transfer records)
3. Annual and other reports (include proxy statements and 10-K's and 10-Q's if a public company)
4. Lists of shareholders, officers, directors, auditors
5. Capitalization
   a. Number of shares
   b. Identity and status of shareholders
6. Identification of and information concerning subsidiaries
B. Corporate authorization
   1. Shareholder and director approval requirements
   2. Resolutions
   3. Shareholder and voting agreements
C. Financial matters
   1. Financial statements
      a. Five years audited financial statements (if available) including balance sheets, income statements, consolidated and consolidating statements, and other financial information
      b. Most recent unaudited financial statements
      c. Projections, if any
   2. Identify bank accounts
   3. Financings
      a. Loan and credit agreements and other lending documents
      b. Financing leases, sale and leaseback transactions, installment purchases
      c. Recorded and unrecorded security interests, UCC searches
      d. Compliance reports to lenders
   4. Reports to and from, and correspondence with, auditors
   5. Tax matters
      a. Copies of federal income tax returns for 5 years
      b. Audit reports
      c. I.R.S. notices
      d. Settlement documents
D. Government reports and filings
   1. Material permits and licenses
   2. Reports to and from government agencies
   3. Correspondence with government agencies
   4. Government applications
   5. Other evidence of noncompliance with law, regulations, etc.
E. Material agreements
   1. Joint venture or partnership agreements
   2. Long-term agreements

      3. Significant personal property leases

      4. Material insurance policies

      5. Agreements or arrangements with officers, directors, or other affiliates

      6. Customer lists

      7. Noncompetition agreements

      8. Guaranties

      9. Product warranties

     10. Other material contracts

F. Intellectual property

      1. Patents

      2. Trademarks

      3. Computer programs

      4. Copyrights

      5. Know-how

      6. Licenses

      7. Infringement claims

G. Real estate

      1. Title insurance binders

      2. Surveys

      3. Deeds or equivalent

      4. Mortgages

      5. Leases

H. Employee matters

      1. Employment contracts

      2. Employee benefit documents (pension plans and trust documents, insurance policies, etc.)

      3. Labor contracts

      4. Employee lists

      5. Employee records (payroll, turnover, etc.)

I. Environmental matters

      1. Government reports (see D above)

      2. Environmental audits and surveys (internal and external)

      3. Environmental permits and authorizations (reports and records)

      4. On site survey and testing

J. Litigation and liabilities

      1. Copies of all judgments, decrees, or orders applicable to target

      2. Description of all current and threatened litigation. including names of attorneys to contact

      3. Description of government investigations in last 5 years (see also D above)

  4. List and description of product liability claims in last 5 years

  5. Copies of significant court filings in any pending litigation

  6. Name of responsible insurance company, if any

VI. Organize acquisition vehicle

 A. Formalities

  1. Reserve corporate name in relevant states

  2. File certificate or articles of incorporation

  3. Draft by-laws

  4. Draft minutes for organizational meetings

 B. Capital

  1. Prepare and execute share certificates

  2. Enter share issuance in stock record books

 C. Management

  1. Hold organizational meetings of shareholders and directors

  2. Adopt by-laws

  3. Elect directors

  4. Elect officers

  5. Authorize acquisition and execution of acquisition documents

 D. Other organizational matters

  1. Obtain taxpayers identification number

  2. Prepare minute books

  3. Qualify corporation in necessary states

VII. Closing

 A. Transfer documents

  1. Deeds

  2. Bill of sale

  3. Assignment of agreements

  4. Assignments of other intangible assets

 B. Payment

  1. Wire transfers or cashier's checks

  2. Promissory note

 C. Corporate formalities

  1. Shareholder and director approval

  2. Election of new directors and officers

 D. Other matters

  1. Related agreements

   a. Noncompetition agreement

   b. Employment agreement

   c. Leases and licenses

   d. Services agreements

  2. Legal opinions

3. Update certificate, representations true and correct as of closing
4. Certified articles of incorporation and good standing certificates
5. Resignations

Chapter 3

Legal Aspects of Acquiring Non-U.S. Enterprises

Paul McCarthy
Partner, Baker & McKenzie

The acquisition of a business outside the United States will involve most of the complexities inherent in acquiring a U.S. enterprise, along with a few surprises. In the international context, additional obstacles and considerations will arise, some because of rules imposed by many non-U.S. jurisdictions and others that are inherent in any international acquisition. These additional obstacles may take the form of

Investment approvals,

Exchange control approvals or consents,

Tax clearances,

Clearances under local or international competition laws,

Unusual problems arising in the due diligence investigation of a foreign target,

The necessity of agreeing on an allocation of the purchase price among assets located in various jurisdictions, and

Burdensome mechanics required to comply with local law or practice relating to the documentation necessary to effect the acquisition for local purposes.

All of these factors will be further complicated if the acquisition is multi-national in scope.

As in a domestic context, an acquisition may take the form of a share purchase, asset purchase, or merger, although the latter is considerably less common abroad. Although acquisition agreements tend to be shorter outside the United States, they are becoming more like U.S. agreements in many jurisdictions. It is likely that a U.S. acquirer will continue to look to the acquisition agreement as a means of obtaining substantial information about the target company and allocating business risks between buyer and seller.

1.0 REGULATORY FRAMEWORK

The acquisition of a non-U.S. company will generally be subject to numerous government approvals and notices, including

Foreign investment approvals,

Exchange control approvals,

Antitrust or antimonopoly clearances or consents, and

Tax clearances, filings, or payments.

These may vary depending upon the nature, size, and structure of the business conducted and the manner in which it is acquired, as well as on the size of the enterprise. The assets and business of the acquiring entity may often be relevant as well.

1.1 General Requirements

In some cases, an approval, clearance, or consent may have to be obtained in advance of the acquisition. In other cases, it is only necessary to notify the appropriate governmental authority. A failure to obtain a required governmental approval may make the acquisition void or voidable. In other cases, the failure may not affect the validity of the acquisition, but may deny the buyer the right to remit earnings or repatriate capital, or cause it to lose tax or other benefits or incentives.

As in the United States, there are certain industries which are considered to be particularly sensitive. These include such industries as banking, communications, computers, public utilities, shipping, and transportation. Outside of these sensitive industries, government approvals may be fairly routine. However, even routine approvals may be quite time consuming, requiring anything from two weeks to six months. In controversial situations, approvals may take longer and may even be unobtainable.

Government approvals are of such importance that they should be considered in detail during the course of negotiations and prior to the execution of a definitive acquisition agreement. It is desirable for the parties to agree in advance which party will be primarily responsible for obtaining relevant approvals, although both parties should cooperate in this endeavor.

In a multinational acquisition, the parties should also consider whether it will be appropriate to delay all closings until all government approvals are obtained or whether it will be possible to proceed with the acquisition of entities in some countries while leaving other acquisitions for a delayed closing after all approvals have been received. The entire transaction will have to be made subject to obtaining any approvals to acquire an entity that is vital to the entire transaction. Where a particular entity is not vital to the enterprise as a whole, a delayed closing is appropriate. It may also be possible to provide for a reduction in the purchase price in the event that a required approval is never obtained. In any case, the acquisition agreement should make the closing in a given country subject to obtaining all necessary government approvals in that country. It would often be a violation of foreign law to sign an unconditional acquisition agreement.

The need for government approvals may also affect the structure of the acquisition. For example, under current French law, the acquisition of shares in a French company will generally require the approval of the French Treasury Department, but the acquisition of shares in a non-French holding company which owns shares in a French company will only require postclosing notification to the French authorities.

1.2 Approvals and Notifications

Foreign investment approvals.   A number of countries impose approval requirements on foreign purchasers simply because they are nonresidents of the country in which the target enterprise is located. In France, for example, all non-EEC direct investments require the prior authorization of the Treasury Department of the French Ministry of Economy and Finance. The acquisition of 20 percent or more of the equity of a French company is considered to be a direct investment.

In a simple, small acquisition, the approval process would ordinarily take several weeks. In a large, complex transaction, the process may take several months. Foreign investment, including the acquisition of a foreign-owned company, is also subject to government approval in Japan.

Many countries restrict foreign ownership of commercial ventures regardless of the industry involved. For example, India limits foreign equity participation in industrial companies to 40 percent. Similar restrictions appear throughout Latin America, the Middle East, and Asia. In other countries, such as Korea, the degree of foreign ownership permitted depends on the sector of the economy involved and may also depend, as a practical matter, on whether there is an already established local or foreign owned business operating. In yet other countries, such as Indonesia, the percentage of foreign ownership may determine the kinds of activity (such as local distribution) in which the enterprise may engage.

Exchange control approvals.   In some countries, foreign direct investment is also subject to foreign exchange control approvals. Without such approvals, it may not be possible later to repatriate profits or capital, interest or royalties. In such cases, the transfer of funds in connection with an acquisition of a business will often require exchange control approval.

For example, in Italy, the sale of the stock of an Italian company by an Italian company or resident must be effected through an Italian bank. The parties will have to obtain a valuation of the stock from a committee of the stock exchange. The bank will complete the transaction only if the price agreed upon is approximately the same as, but not less than, the appraised value. Otherwise, a special authorization of the foreign exchange authorities is required. Italy also requires posttransaction exchange control notice.

Foreign exchange control approvals are required in a number of other countries, including Sweden and Japan. However, many West European countries impose no such exchange control requirements. The United Kingdom, for example, abolished all such restrictions in 1979. Prior government foreign investment approval would also be required in most countries outside Western Europe and Japan, including India and most countries in South America.

The ease of obtaining foreign exchange approvals may depend upon whether the seller is already in full compliance with local exchange control laws. Therefore, the buyer should always request a representation to that effect from the seller. If the seller is not in full compliance and does not hold all appropriate approvals, it may be time consuming (or impossible) to obtain approval for the acquisition.

Restricted industries.   As noted above, any acquisition that will result in the transfer of an enterprise from local to foreign control may come under intense governmental scrutiny if a particularly sensitive industry is involved. This has been particularly true in France where, with respect to such areas as electronics, data processing, and defense, approval may not be available at all or may be made conditional upon continued substantial French participation.

Reports.   In certain countries, no prior approval is needed for an acquisition but the government must be notified after the fact. Among these would be Venezuela and Italy, as well as France in the case of an indirect acquisition.

1.3 Other Regulations and Legal Considerations

There are a number of other legal matters that must be considered in connection with an acquisition outside the United States, including competition law notification and labor law compliance.

Competition law.   In the European Economic Community, the need or advisability for approval depends upon whether the acquiring company and the company that is being acquired hold, at the Community level, a significant share of the relevant product or service market. This requires an analysis of the market share of the target company and that of competitors. Generally, if the market share of the parties prior to the acquisition is less than 20 percent the EEC, there would not normally be any problem. Under the present draft of the EEC Regulation on mergers, premerger filings are required if certain thresholds are exceeded.

The prior approval of the German Cartel Office is also required if the target has some substantial connection to Germany and the world-wide sales of seller and buyer are sufficiently large, even if market shares in Germany are minimal. However, the decision to actually grant approval depends upon the parties' market shares in Germany. This approval can take up to four months to obtain. However, we have generally been able to obtain quicker approval in noncontroversial situations.

The circumstances of an acquisition may also make it advisable to obtain competition law approval in France or the United Kingdom. It can usually be obtained in one to two months.

A Hart-Scott-Rodino filing may be required in the United States if the target company holds operating assets in the United States or has aggregate sales to the United States of more than $25,000,000 in its most recent fiscal year.

Employment and labor law.   Employees receive far greater legal protection in many foreign countries than in the United States. This will make it appropriate to include quite explicit covenants, representations, and warranties on these points. We have generally found European sellers of businesses to consider employment matters to be quite significant and so to devote a substantial amount of attention to these concerns during negotiations. These matters are discussed below.

As in the United States, the employees of most foreign targets will learn of the acquisition only after the deal is struck. However, employees are given a role in conducting the business in certain European countries, and this role may be important in the case of an acquisition. For example, if a target company in the Netherlands has more than thirty-five employees, it will be required to have a works council. Under the Netherlands Works Councils Act, the works council must be consulted whenever there is a transfer of control of a Netherlands enterprise or a merger of a Netherlands enterprise with another company. This consultation is supposed to take place prior to management's final decision on the matter, although this is observed more in the breach. The works council is not given a veto over the acquisition, but if management's final decision is contrary to the works council opinion, an appeal may be taken to court. In our experience, however, acquisitions are almost never blocked. Buyers generally find it in their interest to become involved in the dealings with the works council to insure good labor relations after the acquisition is completed.

Similarly, it may be appropriate or even required for the workers committee to be consulted before a French company is acquired, at least if the employees or their conditions of employment will be affected by the acquisition. The same comment applies generally to a number of other countries, both inside and outside Western Europe.

2.0 STRUCTURING THE ACQUISITION

2.1 Shares or Cash

Cash is the normal consideration used in an acquisition of a foreign target. Shares and other securities are used only rarely. Shares of the U.S. parent may be used without filing a registration statement with the Securities and Exchange Commission as long as certain steps are taken to insure that the shares or other securities are not redistributed to the United States. However, the foreign buyer may want to obtain securities for which there is an established market, and it may be that the only market available for such trading is a U.S. stock exchange. In this case, the shares should be registered. However, the seller may not need registration in the United States if the buyer's shares are traded on other stock markets, such as London or Tokyo.

2.2 Acquisition Vehicle

The vehicle used to acquire the foreign target will depend upon the buyer's overall tax planning and the structure of the target company. If the target company is operating in a variety of jurisdictions through local subsidiaries, it may be possible to acquire each subsidiary or to acquire the shares of the company that is the parent of those subsidiaries. For instance, as noted above, an indirect acquisition of a French company avoids the need for French government approval. Much also depends upon the structure of the buyer's own foreign operations. The organization of a foreign acquisition vehicle is discussed in Section 4, below.

2.3 Share Acquisitions

As in the United States, this is the simplest form of acquisition.

Advantages.   All assets remain the target corporation, and so few transfer documents are required. Transfer taxes may also be limited or avoided. This is particularly important in many foreign countries because such taxes may be very substantial, ranging as high as 14 percent on asset transfers in France. The target corporation will retain all of its assets, including licenses, permits, and franchises, which might otherwise be difficult to transfer. The same would probably be true with contracts and leases.

Disadvantages.   The target corporation will retain all of its tax attributes. The target will also retain all of its liabilities. Disclosure of such liabilities may be more difficult in a foreign context, as discussed below.

2.4 Asset Acquisition

Advantages.   Not all of the assets of the target need be purchased. Thus, if a single line of business is being sold, the transaction will have to be structured as an asset acquisition. Also, not all of the target's liabilities need be acquired. However, in many foreign countries, the sale of substantially all of the assets which constitute business (what would be referred to in the United States as a bulk transfer) will carry with it more than would be the case in the United States. For example, in many European countries, the sale of a business means that the employees of the business automatically become employees of the buyer.

Disadvantages.   As in the United States, an asset acquisition is more complex than a share acquisition because separate transfer documents must be drafted for the various assets. Certain assets, such as licenses and contracts, may require third party consents in order to be transferred. As noted above, transfer taxes are quite substantial in many foreign countries.

2.5 Mergers

Mergers are not available in all countries. Even where available, they may differ substantially in theory and practice from the United States. For example, in Canada, a merger is considered to be the joining of two separate businesses, which continue together after the merger. One company is not considered to be the survivor while the other disappears. However, this theoretical difference appears to have little significance in practice.

Where a merger is available, its principal advantage is the same as that of the United States. That is, the transfer of assets from the target to the buyer is automatic, although certain filings may have to be made to record the transfer. This may greatly facilitate the transfer of valuable permits and contracts. However, there is probably no country in which the merger may be structured with the flexibility available in the United States, particularly with the use of various forms of consideration and reverse mergers.

3.0 DOCUMENTATION

3.1 Letter of Intent

This sets out the principal points upon which the parties have agreed. It is useful in identifying important issues between the parties. Its disadvantage lies in that it may delay preparing and signing a definitive contract. A letter of intent is not legally binding between the parties. Parties outside the United States feel free to propose departures from the letter of intent to a greater extent than would an American party. Nonetheless, all matters of importance to the parties, especially the structure of the transaction, should be considered and reviewed with counsel and other consultants before a letter of intent is signed. Disclosure of the signing of a letter of intent is not normally required outside the United States.

3.2 Acquisition Agreement

Acquisitions in many foreign countries involving only nationals of those countries are often done without the formalities followed in the

United States. In particular, acquisition agreements will be much shorter, often without any representations and warranties. However, if a U.S. or other sophisticated buyer is involved, the acquisition agreement will be similar to that used in the United States but with more detailed treatment of those areas, such as employees, which constitute more substantial risks outside the United States.

In the case of a multinational acquisition, it will often be advisable to use more than one agreement, a master agreement which will govern the transaction as a whole and local agreements which will govern only the transaction in each country. This approach permits the local agreements to be shorter than they might otherwise be, thereby simplifying translation and similar problems in the event that the agreement has to be registered with local authorities. It may also avoid having each local taxing authority try to reallocate the purchase price to increase the local income or transfer taxes. The principal features of a non-U.S. master agreement and local agreements are described below.

Price and payment.   As in the United States, the price may be fixed or be subject to adjustment. The purchase price as well as the amount allocated to each transaction will be set out in the master agreement and the amount allocated to the local transaction be repeated in each local agreement.

In an asset transaction, the price paid for fixed assets will be set, while the price for current assets will be determined by the level of those assets at the closing. This will normally be established through a postclosing audit. A pay out arrangement for determining the price is quite rare abroad.

The allocation of the price among the various entities acquired may be quite significant. The agreement should provide that the parties will follow these allocations for tax purposes in every jurisdiction. This provision only appears in the master agreement. It is also advisable to allocate the price among the various assets purchased in an asset transaction in each local agreement.

Payment will normally be made by wire transfer. If local asset agreements are used, payment may have to be made simultaneously in a number of jurisdictions. This will require substantial coordination, with inevitable delays.

Assumption of liabilities.   All liabilities are included in a share transaction or merger, although the seller may indemnify the buyer against certain liabilities, particularly those that are undisclosed or contingent at the time of the closing. In an asset transaction, the buyer will have to assume responsibility for all agreements and leases assigned. The buyer should also normally assume responsibility for trade payables, since it is the buyer who has the greatest interest in seeing that suppliers of goods and services are fully paid. As noted above, certain other liabilities, such as for employees, will transfer to the buyer automatically by operation of law.

Representations and warranties.   These will cover the main areas of concern to a buyer. They are discussed in greater detail in Section 5, below. The notion of full disclosure is less known outside the United States, although sophisticated sellers will not be surprised by the extent of the representations. On the other hand, if a family-owned company is being acquired in Europe, the sellers may flatly refuse to provide the extensive representations common in the United States. In that case, the buyer will have to choose with care the particular matters that it wishes covered and independently investigate any other important matters. A multinational acquisition normally includes the representations and warranties only in the master agreement.

Covenants.   As in the United States, these will cover those matters that ought to take place between the signing and the closing. In particular, the seller will be required to conduct the purchased business in the ordinary course and will be prohibited from engaging in any major transaction without the consent of the buyer. In a multinational transaction, most pre- and post-closing covenants will appear only in the master agreement. However, it is often useful to include covenants that describe local matters in local agreements as well in order to provide an explanation of what takes place. For example, the local agreements might describe the transfer of local employees, the treatment of benefits, and the like.

Conditions.   Typical conditions are the obtaining of any required government and other approvals, the execution of ancillary agreements, and sometimes, the absence of any material adverse change in the business. Among sophisticated parties, legal opinions are increasingly common. However, in acquiring a family-owned business, the buyer should not be surprised to find the seller reluctant to provide such opinions. For instance, a French entrepreneur will not be accustomed to relying on attorneys to anywhere near the same extent as in the United States. The same is true in Japan. Attorneys are used as counselors more frequently in England and Germany. In a multinational acquisition, there is no need to include the conditions in the local asset agreement. A comprehensive provision in the master agreement will suffice.

Closing. The master agreement will describe the mechanics of closing, as will the local agreements. The typical legal mechanics of foreign closings are described in Section 5, below.

Indemnification. In an acquisition between sophisticated parties, an indemnification provision of the kind used in the United States may be included. In a multinational acquisition, this would generally be included only in the master agreement, since it will likely be the ultimate parent that the buyer will wish to have given the indemnities. As in the United States, the indemnification provisions are designed to allocate the risks of the business between the buyer and seller. In the case of the acquisition of a family business, an indemnification provision may be very difficult to obtain, since it is totally unfamiliar to the sellers.

4.0 PRINCIPAL LEGAL CONCERNS OF THE BUYER: DUE DILIGENCE

As in the United States, any representations and warranties in the acquisition agreement will be designed to cause the seller to disclose material information of greatest concern to the buyer. However, in certain cases, these representations and warranties will be less extensive than in the United States. Moreover, even if an unsophisticated seller is willing to make certain representations, it may not fully appreciate all the ramifications of those representations. Therefore, the buyer should independently verify as much as possible about the target through its own efforts as well as with the assistance of attorneys and other consultants with a local presence. (In this as in many other areas, general experience and familiarity with international transactions will not suffice.) The buyer should be aware that the sources of such information may differ substantially from those available in the United States. Not only will the information itself differ, but that which is most relevant may be quite different from that which would be relevant in a U.S. context. It is always a mistake to simply use U.S. concepts in representations, warranties, or legal opinions, without taking account of local differences.

The existence of a commercial registry in most civil law countries means that substantial information about a target may be publicly available. The commercial registry information on a share company will, in many jurisdictions, include not only the name of the company, its principal place of business and its capital (including issued but not fully paid-in capital) but also the directors of the company, their authorization to represent the company, and any restrictions on that authority. In England and many other countries, annual financial statements will be on file at the companies register.

The principal concerns of an American buyer of foreign entities are likely to be the following.

4.1 Corporate Organization and Authority

The buyer will want to confirm that the target company is properly organized. This is particularly important in a stock acquisition. However, the means of ascertaining this may differ substantially from the means used in the United States. For example, in France one can confirm that the company is enrolled with the commercial register and obtain an extract from the commercial register indicating the company's capital and who has the authority to act for the company. It may be possible to obtain an official copy of the memorandum of association in many, though not all, countries. In some countries, this may be certified by the commercial register or, as in Belgium, by a notary.

There is no concept of "good standing" in most countries outside the United States. Good standing in the United States generally means that all franchise taxes have been paid and all filings have been made. In many countries, there are no ongoing franchise fees or taxes, and no periodic filings are required. This is the case, for example, in Germany. Therefore, including a representation or seeking a legal opinion that a company is in good standing is meaningless and should be avoided. If the buyer insists on some equivalent of good standing, it is possible for the seller to state that there exists no condition or circumstance which would permit the dissolution of the company without further administrative action or notice on the part of shareholders, creditors, or the local court.

4.2 Employees

As noted above, employment law is considerably more developed in many western countries than in the United States. The best known case is Japan where employees may enjoy a right to lifetime employment, if only by custom. However, in many countries, much of this is regulated by law, independent of any particular arrangements with the employer. Therefore, it is not sufficient to rely on representations and warranties in the acquisition agreement, although appropriate covenants should be included to provide for the parties' respective responsibilities vis a vis employees. Rather, the buyer should seek competent advice from counsel about the implications both of the transaction and of acquiring the employees of the target.

Employment protection.   Often, the employees will automatically transfer with the business. Then it is not necessary for the buyer to offer employment or take any other steps in this regard. With these employees, the buyer will inherit all attendant liabilities, especially in the event they are ever terminated. In some countries, the buyer must offer employment on terms no less favorable than those offered by the seller. Otherwise, the employees will be considered to have been terminated and may be entitled to substantial termination compensation from the seller. Once these responsibilities have been identified and quantified, it is possible to assess whether one should seek to have the seller assume some of them. For example, in Italy an employee has a right to indemnity upon termination of employment, even by voluntary retirement, which is dependant upon length of service. Standard U.S. pension representations might not pick up this liability. In some countries, it is possible in an asset acquisition to treat the employee as having been terminated and give him the right to receive this indemnity immediately. It is also possible to treat employment as continuous with the buyer. In the latter case, it may be appropriate to have the seller pay the buyer an amount equal to the accumulated indemnity as of the closing. This would also be possible in a share acquisition.

Employee benefits.   The handling of employee benefit matters may be simpler in certain countries than in the United States. In some West European countries, such as France, pensions are largely statutory and are paid out of government operated funds. There actually is no pension fund to transfer and no pension liability to assume. All such liabilities are held by the government and are funded by taxes similar to social security in the United States, although the benefits tend to be far more extensive. In Germany and a number of other countries, private insurance is used to fund pensions. It will be necessary to obtain the cooperation of the insurance company to be certain that there is no gap in coverage.

In the United Kingdom, there are pension schemes quite similar to the defined benefit and other pension plans found in the United States. These are closely governed by the Finance Act of 1970. Adequate and extensive provisions may be required in order to ensure that the buyer acquires the assets necessary to discharge the responsibilities it is assuming. However, such assets may only be transferred to a new pension plan with the consent of each employee.

Labor agreements.   Labor unions may be significant factors in any business in many countries outside the United States. Even in an asset transaction, the buyer may be required to assume all obligations under a collective bargaining agreement. In some countries, the collective bargaining agreement is negotiated between the union and a group of employers. In that case, the buyer will have little or no opportunity to renegotiate the agreement at the time of the acquisition.

4.3 Compliance with Law

Environmental matters.   Environmental regulation in most countries has not reached the level it has in the United States. Asian countries have been notorious in ignoring environmental concerns. Even in Europe, many governments have not yet sought to regulate the disposal of waste and the clean-up of hazardous sites to any great degree. However, the awareness of problems in the environmental area has been on the rise everywhere, and one can expect greater regulation in the future. It is, therefore, prudent to investigate any target for potential environmental difficulties. It may actually be easier to get a seller to assume continued responsibility for environmental matters arising out of the conduct of the business prior to the closing, since that exposure appears to be slight today. On the other hand, such a proposal will be viewed as rather unusual and may arouse suspicion and even hostility.

Licenses and permits.   As in the United States, businesses will be required to operate under a variety of governmental permits and licenses. If anything, such regulation is more extensive and more strict than in the United States. If shares are acquired, the target will typically come with such permits and licenses intact, provided that the all governmental authorizations have been obtained. This assumes that the particular business is not restricted with respect to foreign ownership or change in ownership.

In the case of an asset transfer, as in the United States, such permits and licenses may not be assignable, and new permits and licenses must be arranged for at or prior to the closing. Obtaining new permits may be extremely time consuming.

If there is a change in the management of the target, the new managers may be required to have permits to operate. For example, in France, if the manager of a French share company or limited liability company is not a citizen of an EEC country, a commercial card must be obtained. This will take some months, and so adequate preparation should be made to avoid delays. In other countries, residence and work permits must be obtained for new expatriate managers.

4.4 Liabilities

Product liability.   It is generally true that product liability claims outside the United States are far smaller than inside the United States. This is in part due to cultural norms. In the United States money is considered an appropriate compensation for any injury. In many other countries, however, there is a far lesser likelihood of someone bringing a lawsuit in response to an injury, even where someone appears to be at fault. In Japan, bringing a lawsuit is socially discouraged. Also, the

American doctrine of strict liability has not yet been adopted in most other countries. Even where a lawsuit is prosecuted successfully, the size of the award is unlikely to even approach those in the United States. Nonetheless, one can expect a gradual increase in the likelihood of product liability claims in various countries, particularly in Western Europe in light of the recent EEC Directive on product liability law.

Tax liabilities.   If stock is acquired, the target corporation will carry with it all of its tax attributes, positive and negative. Tax avoidance, and even fraud, is common in many countries. We were involved with the acquisition of one substantial Italian company that maintained three separate (and inconsistent) sets of books. The U.S. buyer wished to correct such practices after the closing, since the target would have to be integrated into the U.S. company's accounting system. Also, the subsidiary of a U.S. company will always be more visible to local tax authorities. However, this entailed substantial tax costs for prior years for the target company, costs which the seller was most reluctant to accept. In fact, the seller did not wish to see such matters disclosed to the tax authorities at all. It is less likely that the buyer in an asset acquisition will assume any tax liabilities, and the buyer will be free to set up its own accounting system. However, certain assets may be encumbered with tax liens, the existence of which may be very difficult to ascertain. This liability may have to be covered through indemnities.

Other liabilities.   The notion of full disclosure is viewed as a bit unusual outside the United States. Therefore, a request for a representation that there are no undisclosed liabilities in the business, contingent or otherwise, may make a seller somewhat uncomfortable. However, such a representation is, if anything, more important in this context. No one wishes to purchase a business on a caveat emptor basis. An appropriate indemnification provision should also be included, especially if the seller is reluctant to make a representation on this broad basis.

4.5 Financial Statements

Accounting practices vary greatly from country to country, and the presentation of financial information may seem quite unfamiliar. Nonetheless, there are generally accepted accounting principles in most western countries and in Japan. Therefore, the seller should be required to confirm that the financial statements that it has presented to the buyer are so prepared.

With privately held companies, however, this will in fact not often be the case. In such instances, there would be little alternative to the buyer other than to prepare closing financial statements under the supervision of an accounting firm. Although the statements may be audited, they are inherently less reliable than audited statements prepared by accountants familiar with the company and with the full cooperation of management.

The seller of a privately owned firm will often resist any substantial reliance on outside experts. This will vary from country to country. In Germany, for example, businesspeople often rely on lawyers, tax advisers, and accountants. Therefore, there is a greater likelihood that audited financial statements will be available with respect to the target's past operations and that preparation of an audited closing financial statement will be acceptable to the seller. By contrast, French businesses people rarely rely on outside experts, and then primarily for such extraordinary matters as litigation. In one recent instance, the seller of a French company refused to agree to an audit of the company books as a partial determinant of the purchase price and even refused to deal with the buyer's attorneys and accountants. Although this reluctance was undoubtedly due in part to a desire to avoid disclosing inadequacies in the target's inventories and other accounting matters (concerns often present with a U.S. seller of a family company), the psychological aspects of the matter were quite significant. Therefore, care would be taken at the letter of intent stage to spell out in detail exactly what will be done with respect to such matters. The buyer should not rely on the inclusion of even a well-known accounting term like "certified" in describing closing financial statements. It is also useful to have the seller's financial statements translated into a U.S. presentation by an accountant knowledgeable about both accounting systems.

4.6 Material Assets

Physical facilities.   The buyer will want to be certain that it has title to any plants or other real estate owned by the seller or target corporation. Title insurance is virtually unknown outside the United States, although it is occasionally used in Canada. In most common law jurisdictions, the buyer will rely upon an opinion of counsel based upon an examination of the records at the registry of deeds or the equivalent. In civil law countries, real estate will often be transferred by notarial deed. In this case, the notary plays a function far beyond that of a notary public in the United States. The notary functions as a government-appointed attorney, acting in effect for both parties, to insure that proper title has been conveyed. The notary will also deal with all other formalities of transfer. It is up to the notary to insure that there are no material encumbrances on the property.

Transfer taxes tend to be far more significant outside the United States. As noted elsewhere, these may range as high as 14 percent in

France. As one might expect, the stated consideration for the transfer may come under some scrutiny.

Intellectual property.   Intellectual property may be a very important part of the target business. Intellectual property systems vary substantially from country to country. In many countries, registration of a trademark, for example, is of vital importance in protecting one's rights. Without registration, all rights to enforce a trademark against third parties may be lost. At the same time, actual local use of the trademark may not be a prerequisite to registration. This is the case, for example, in Japan. Therefore, it is important to the buyer to ascertain that all of the intellectual property necessary to operate the business is not only transferred to the buyer but is also properly registered.

In England and other commonwealth countries, a registered user agreement must be executed and entered into by any party which uses a trademark of which it is not the owner. If not handled properly, the trademark could be lost.

The buyer will want to look into all of these matters to insure that the intellectual property that it believes it is getting will in fact be transferred in a form that will be fully enforceable against third parties.

In most countries, unless specifically restricted, an agreement is assignable. A principal exception would be where the agreement is by its very nature personal to the other party, as for example, in the case of an employment agreement with respect to the employee. However, these rarely arise in acquisition situations. In an asset transaction, all agreements will have to be scrutinized to determine whether there is any limitation on their assignability. In our experience, an agreement or license abroad rarely provides for termination solely because of a material change in ownership of one of the parties. However, such a restriction is possible as a matter of contract or regulatory law, and all material documents must be scrutinized to ascertain this.

5.0 ORGANIZING ACQUISITION VEHICLE

One encounters a variety of business forms outside the United States. In France, the commercial code provides for no less than eight forms of business entity, of which seven have separate legal personalities. The rules governing such entities will be crucial if, as is often the case, the buyer must organize a local company to hold acquired shares or assets. An acquisition vehicle will generally be in corporate form, either a corporation in common law countries (principally England, Canada, Australia, India, Pakistan, Hong Kong, Singapore and other former British colonies) or, in many civil law countries (which include Western Europe, South America, Japan and Korea), a share company or a limited liability company. These are discussed below.

5.1 Corporations: General

English and other Commonwealth country corporations are similar to those in the United States, although they do tend to be more structured than in the United States. In many civil law countries, a limited liability company tends to be used for smaller enterprises. A share company will be used for larger enterprises, particularly those whose shares are held by the public. The rules applicable to limited liability companies tend to be fairly flexible, and these are particularly useful for wholly-owned subsidiaries. By contrast, share companies are subject to numerous formalities and restrictions. However, their shares may be freely traded.

The discussion below describes a generic share company and a limited liability company. The specific rules applicable to these companies in particular jurisdictions vary substantially and should be reviewed in detail with competent local counsel.

5.2 Share Companies

Share companies are similar to U.S. corporations, but more formal.

Formation.   A share company will be formed when its organic document is enrolled with the commercial register in the location of its principal place of business. Unlike the United States, where Delaware corporations are common, there is currently no "Delaware" in Europe. A share company whose principal place of business is in Germany would not be organized in France, for example.

It may take a considerable period of time to organize a share company in many foreign jurisdictions. Bureaucratic delays will result in anywhere from several weeks to several months between the filing of the appropriate documents and the organization of the company. This delay factor should be borne in mind if a buyer contemplates organizing an offshore company to facilitate an acquisition. Attorneys in some countries keep "shelf" companies available for their clients, but acquiring such companies inevitably involves some risks if the company had operated previously at all or had been originally organized for another shareholder.

Capital.   The capital of a share company is represented by shares, which are typically freely transferable, subject only to any applicable securities laws. Shares may be issued for cash or property. However, it would generally be necessary to obtain a public appraisal or court approval to establish the value of any property contributed. This adds a considerable complication to the acquisition of assets and their contributions to a newly organized local subsidiary.

In a number of jurisdictions, shares are represented by certificates, which may be registered or bearer in form. Shares have a specified par value; no-par shares are generally unknown.

Corporate structure.   A share company consists of two principal organs, the shareholders and the directors. Most civil law countries require that there be more than one shareholder, usually three to seven. There is generally no limitation on foreigners acting as shareholders although foreign investment in some countries may require some form of government approval. Shareholder meetings may be held by proxy. However, consent resolutions of the kind used in the United States are generally unknown.

The directors in many share companies function like both officers and directors in a U.S. corporation. Thus, the directors both manage the share company and represent it in its dealings with others. In some countries, such as Germany, there are two boards of directors, one performing a supervisory function and the other managing the day-to-day affairs. In France, the board of directors may supervise the management of the company while the chief executive officer (the *président-directeur général*) actually conducts the company's affairs.

Many countries require that a majority or some other fixed number of directors be citizens of the country. In France, a new *président-directeur général* who is not a citizen of an EEC country must obtain a commercial card before acting in this capacity. This can be a time-consuming matter. Directors may delegate their authority to others and so may act through proxies. They do not generally act through written consent resolutions.

5.3 Limited Liability Companies

A limited liability company corresponds to the SARL in France, the GmbH in Germany, and the Yuren Kaisha in Japan. There is no equivalent to the limited liability company in England. A limited liability company, for many purposes, is more flexible than a share company.

Formation.   A limited liability company will typically be organized through the enrollment of a deed or agreement among the participants with the local commercial register.

Capital. The capital of a limited liability company will normally be characterized as interests or quotas rather than shares, since a share denotes something which may be freely traded. Quotas may not be freely traded.

A limited liability company will typically be required to have more than one quotaholder, although the number of required quotaholders may be less than that for a share company.

Quotas may be issued for cash or personal or real property. However, as with a share company, contributions in kind must go through some form of public appraisal or court approval to value the contributed property.

Corporate structure. A limited liability company will have two principal organs, the quotaholders and the managers.

In most west European countries and Japan, there is no limitation on corporations or foreigners acting as quotaholders in a limited liability company except in certain restricted industries. However, foreign investment in this or any other form may be subject to prior government approval.

Like the directors of a share company, the managers of a limited liability company act both as directors and officers of the company in that they are authorized to represent the company individually. Their authority may be limited by an appropriate notation in the commercial registry, and this will be binding upon third parties who deal with the company. However, it is customary for managers to exercise fairly wide powers in managing the business.

6.0 CLOSING

6.1 Mechanics of Closing

The legal mechanics of closing an acquisition abroad may be quite complicated, involving a number of formalities, documents and filings. In a multinational acquisition, it will be necessary to provide a means to have simultaneous closings in a number of different countries since certain acts will have to be carried out within the country in question. Often this can be done through the use of informal escrows whereby the local closing takes place one or two days in advance of the master closing. All of the documents will then be left with a local attorney to be delivered to the parties when he is notified that the master closing has taken place.

Even a closing of the sale of stock in a single country may involve complications that are unfamiliar to a U.S. buyer. For example, in purchasing a French share company, whether alone or as part of a larger transaction, it will be necessary to transfer the shares in a transfer document signed with certain specific language, that is, *"bon pour transfer de_____ actions de capital."* Without these words, the transfer may be ineffective. In other countries, such as Austria, the transfer document must be by means of a notarial deed, that is, a formal document executed in front of a notary.

A transfer document will have to be signed by an authorized representative of the transferor, often in the country in question. It is normal to use a formal power of attorney, legalized before a consulate whenever possible.

In many jurisdictions, such as France or the Netherlands, shares are not represented by certificates that may be endorsed or delivered. Share ownership is evidenced only by an entry in the share registry book of the company. Therefore, the transfer will have to be recorded in the share registry by a representative of the transferor or transferee in order for the transfer of ownership to be effective. Alternatively, the transfer may have to be notified to the company within a certain number of days of the transfer. Director or shareholder approval may be required, especially if there is a shareholder agreement in effect.

The transfer of shares can be made even more complicated by the fact that the number of shareholders will be large. In a French share company, for example, there must be at least seven shareholders, often requiring nominee shareholders. Also, a director of a share company must become a shareholder within three months of appointment as a director, further increasing the potential number of nominee shareholders. Such nominee shareholdings may be transferred at the closing. This is now true even with respect to the directors under a recent amendment to French company law.

The seller's representatives as directors will usually be required to resign, effective at the closing, but subject to the election of new directors. Since new directors may have to be elected by the shareholders, it will be necessary to have a shareholders meeting at the time of the closing. Notice requirements should be observed. Since a notice period may be fairly long, this requires advance planning.

As noted above, many countries require that directors must be shareholders (or become shareholders within a certain period of their appointment). These qualifying shares of directors should be made subject to executed transfer documents held by the company so that their shares may easily be transferred if they cease to be directors. The appointment and resignation of directors at the closing may also have to be published or filed with the local commercial register.

6.2 Other Agreements

A number of ancillary agreements may be executed at the closing.

Non-competition agreements.   As in the United States, there are sound business reasons why the buyer will want the seller to agree not to compete with the acquired business after the closing. The enforceability of such agreements will depend upon local law, although most countries will enforce them if they are reasonable in duration and geographical scope. Any tax benefits derived from the use of such a covenant will depend on local law.

Employment agreements.   It is likely that the buyer will want some assurance that key employees will remain with the business. This may be accomplished in part through a statement in the agreement that the seller is not aware of any plans of key employees to leave and an agreement not to employ them for some period after the closing. The buyer may also want the assurance that is available through having key employees enter into a formal employment agreement. Written employment agreements are generally more common outside the United States. Therefore, this should be relatively easy to accomplish.

Leases and licenses.   If the seller is going to retain some tangible or intangible property of significance to the business, it will be necessary to have the acquired company be empowered to use it under a license or lease. Appropriate forms of agreement are known in most countries, but if they call for payment outside the country in which the leased facility is located or the licensed trademark or technology is used, exchange control or other government approval may be required. Local formal requirements should also be respected, such as a registered user agreement for trademarks in the United Kingdom and many Commonwealth countries.

7.0 NON-U.S. AND MULTINATIONAL ACQUISITION CHECKLIST

The checklist attached indicates the principal matters addressed by attorneys in the course of an acquisition in more or less chronological order. The point at which attorneys should become involved will also vary. However, anyone contemplating an acquisition in a foreign country or countries is likely to encounter rules and practices that are not only different but also unlikely to be even anticipated. Therefore, an attorney experienced in multinational transactions should be consulted at the very outset.

Legal Checklist: Multinational and Other Non-U.S. Acquisitions

  I. Initial due diligence (nonlegal, done by purchaser)
     A. Preliminary investigation of business
        1. Financial statements
        2. Business operations
     B. Confidentiality agreement
 II. Regulatory Considerations
     A. Foreign investment approvals
        1. Government restrictions on foreign ownership
        2. Government approvals and notices
           a. Advance notices and waiting periods
           b. Postclosing notices
     B. Exchange control approvals
     C. Antitrust limitations and approvals
        1. Mandatory
           a. Germany: Cartel Office approval
           b. Other countries
        2. Advisory
           a. EEC: Premerger notice to Commission
           b. France
           c. United Kingdom
           d. Other countries
     D. Consultation with employees
        1. Netherlands: Works Council
        2. France
        3. Other countries
III. Structuring the transaction
     A. Purchase price
        1. Shares or other securities
        2. Cash or notes
     B. Choose acquisition vehicle
        1. Foreign parent
        2. New or existing local subsidiary
           a. Formalities to establish new corporation
           b. Time requirements for new corporation
     C. Choose form of acquisition
        1. Share acquisition
           a. Simplicity or complexity

          b. Continuity of business
          c. Contracts, permits, and tax attributes
          d. No transfer taxes
          e. Liabilities
      2. Asset acquisition
          a. Simplicity or complexity
          b. Transfer taxes
          c. No continuity of contracts, permits, or tax attributes
          d. Liabilities
      3. Merger (often not available)
          a. Simplicity or complexity
          b. Some continuity of business, contracts, and permits
          c. Possibly avoid transfer taxes
          d. Liabilities
IV. Principal documentation
   A. Letter of intent
      1. Outlines of transaction
      2. No-shop
      3. Access to information
      4. Confidentiality
   B. Purchase agreement: Single country transaction
      1. Description of transaction
          a. Transfer of assets, shares, or merger
          b. Price and payment terms
          c. Price allocations (asset transfer)
          d. Price adjustment
      2. Liabilities assumed (asset transfer)
      3. Representation and warranties (see Legal due diligence, V, below)
      4. Preclosing covenants
          a. Conduct of business
          b. No-shop
          c. Confidentiality
          d. Other
      5. Other covenants
          a. Transfer of employees
          b. Obtain consents and approvals
      6. Conditions to closing
          a. Government approvals
          b. Transfer and issuance of material permits
          c. Other consents and approvals (material contracts, leases and licenses, loan agreements, etc.)
          d. No adverse change in business

       e. Legal opinions (not always available outside the U.S.)
       f. Representations true and covenants performed
       g. No litigation affecting transaction
       h. Related agreements executed
    7. Closing (See VII, below)
    8. Indemnification (less common outside U.S.)
       a. Coverage
       b. Threshold and deductible amount
       c. Survival of obligations (time limits)
    9. Dispute resolution and governing law
       a. Arbitration
       b. Choice of forum
C. Master and local agreements (multinational acquisitions)
    1. Master agreement
       a. Description of overall transaction
       b. Overall price
       c. Allocation of price
       d. Representations and warranties
       e. Preclosing covenants
       f. Other covenants
       g. Conditions to closing
       h. Coordination of local closings
       i. Indemnification
       j. Dispute resolution and governing law
    2. Local agreements
       a. Description of local transaction
       b. Local price
       c. Payment mechanism
       d. Covenants, if any, applicable only to local transfer
       e. Local closing mechanics
D. Other agreements
    1. Noncompetition agreement
       a. Parties covered
       b. Scope (time, field, and geography)
       c. Legality and enforceability
       d. Tax incidents
    2. Employment agreements
       a. Key employees
       b. Selling shareholders
       c. Tax incidents
    3. Leases and licenses
       a. Nontransferable property
       b. Commingled property

    4. Services Agreement
      a. Transition to permit target to achieve stand-alone capability
      b. Essential commingled services
    5. Parent or other guaranties
    6. Ongoing supply or distribution agreements
    7. Escrow agreement

V. Legal due diligence
(These are normally also covered by the representations and warranties.)
  A. Corporate matters
    1. Organizational documents (statutes, etc.)
    2. Corporate records (minutes of past meetings, etc.)
    3. Annual and other reports
    4. Lists of shareholders, officers, directors, auditors
    5. Capitalization
      a. Number of shares
      b. Identity and status of shareholders
      c. Any noncash consideration paid for shares
    6. Identification of and information concerning subsidiaries
  B. Corporate authorization
    1. Shareholder and director approval requirements
    2. Resolutions
    3. Powers of attorney
    4. Shareholder and voting agreements
  C. Financial matters
    1. Financial statements
      a. Five years audited financial statements (if available), including balance sheets, income statements, consolidated and consolidating statements, and other statements
      b. Most recent unaudited financial statements
      c. Projections
    2. Identify bank accounts
    3. Financings
      a. Loan and credit agreements and other lending documents
      b. Financing leases, sale and leaseback transactions, installment purchases
      c. Recorded and unrecorded security interests and title retention arrangements
      d. Compliance reports to lenders
    4. Reports to and from, and correspondence with, auditors
    5. Tax matters
      a. Copies of income tax returns for 5 years

    b. Copies of other significant tax returns

    c. Audit reports

    d. Settlement documents

D. Government reports and filings

    1. Material permits and licenses

    2. Reports to and from government agencies

    3. Correspondence with government agencies

    4. Government applications

E. Material agreements

    1. Joint venture or partnership agreements

    2. Long-term agreements

    3. Significant personal property leases

    4. Material insurance policies

    5. Agreements or arrangements with officers, directors or other affiliates

    6. Customer lists

    7. Noncompetition agreements

    8. Guaranties

    9. Product warranties

    10. Other material contracts

F. Intellectual property

    1. Patents

    2. Trademarks

    3. Computer programs

    4. Copyrights

    5. Know-how

    6. Licenses

G. Real estate

    1. Evidence of title

    2. Deeds or equivalent

    3. Mortgages and hypothecations

    4. Leases

H. Employee matters

    1. Termination rights and indemnities

    2. Individual and general agreements

    3. Labor unions and agreements

    4. Employee benefits

I. Environmental matters

    1. Regulatory reports

    2. Internal reports

    3. On-site survey and testing

J. Litigation

    1. Copies of all judgments, decrees, or orders applicable to target

     2. Description of all current and threatened litigation, including names of attorneys to contact

     3. Copies of significant court filings

     4. Name of responsible insurance company, if any

VI. Organize acquisition vehicle

     1. Formalities

     2. Capital

     3. Management

VII. Closing

    A. Transfer documents

     1. Execution (power of attorney, etc.)

     2. Formalities (notarial deed, etc.)

     3. Mandatory language on transfer documents

    B. Governmental formalities

     1. Notices

     2. Filings

       a. Foreign investment

       b. Exchange control

       c. Tax

    C. Corporate formalities

     1. Notice to or filings with corporation

     2. Shareholder and director approval

     3. Nominee shareholders

     4. Election of new directors and officers

    D. Other documents

     1. Related agreements

     2. Legal opinions

     3. Certification of representations as true and correct as of closing

Chapter **4**

Accounting Aspects of International Mergers and Acquisitions

Michael R. Nanus
Partner, KPMG Peat Marwick

In a mergers and acquisitions (M & A) environment, accounting is a vehicle to communicate the economics of a target business to the purchaser and the potential financing sources for a proposed transaction.

The association of accounting with mergers and acquisitions is a most natural and important concept. The successful consummation of an acquisition transaction is based, in part, on the ability of a seller to communicate information about a target to a purchaser and the purchaser's ability to interpret, synthesize, evaluate, and react to such information. Accounting is a principal vehicle for communicating this information and for moving the negotiating parties closer to each other and to the closing of their deal. The final measure, however, of the ultimate postclosing success of the transaction is also dependent on accounting, the internal accounting controls necessary to monitor and manage the acquired operations, and the generally accepted accounting principles (GAAP) which supports the issuance of financial statements for different purposes and to different users throughout the world. Accounting, therefore, is like many other things in life: It is often hard to live with, but most definitely impossible to live without.

The first part of this chapter, "Understanding Financial Information," presents a comparative analysis of similarities and differences in the GAAP followed in various countries around the world. Next is a discussion of "Evaluating the Target," where the process of due diligence is described and examples of information that should be obtained from the target company and critically reviewed are provided. Finally, "Postacquisition Considerations" summarizes control objectives and procedures to be implemented for managing the business, as well as external financial reporting and audit requirements in a number of different countries.

1.0 UNDERSTANDING FINANCIAL INFORMATION

Once we acknowledge that accounting is a communications vehicle, or a language, it is relatively easy to identify an immediate problem in pursuing acquisitions on an international basis—the lack of one common language to link countries around the world to one another. This dilemma is real whether we are talking about a spoken language or a written one. Like a tourist who is not fluent in the language, a purchaser not well versed in the local GAAP which underlies financial information of a target company is at an extreme disadvantage.

Prospective purchasers must make informed investment decisions based upon available data and must have the ability to compare specific acquisition opportunities with other similar ones. Hence, they require financial information, even transnational information, to be understandable and comparable. The differences in GAAP between countries can have a significant effect on proposed merger and acquisition transactions. Some of the variations are so significant that prospective buyers in a particular country will not consider certain types of acquisitions in another. For example, in countries where goodwill is required to be amortized against income over a period of years, companies can be discouraged from making acquisitions where a premium might have to be paid for strategic market position, undervalued or hidden assets, or exceptional earnings performance.

Alternatively, a company which does not consolidate its foreign subsidiaries may be free to make its decisions on the basis of the investments' economics alone. One of the criteria, therefore, in identifying an international acquisition candidate is to determine whether local accounting policies treat such a transaction in a favorable way.

Below is a brief overview of some of the major and most frequently encountered areas of difference between U.S. GAAP, which is this author's frame of reference, and the accounting principles followed elsewhere around the world.[1] In Table 4.1, such differences are graphically presented on a country-by-country basis for the U.S., Brazil, Australia, Canada, France, Federal Republic of Germany, Japan, and the United Kingdom.[2]

1.1 Accounting for Long-Term Investments in Share Capital of Other Entities

In the U.S., the method of accounting for investments in other companies is generally based on the percentage of voting securities of the investee owned by the investor. Control is usually determined on the basis of the percentage of voting securities owned. In rare circumstances, other factors may override the ownership test, for example, the investment is temporary in nature or the investee cannot repatriate earnings because of foreign laws. The three methods generally employed in the U.S. are consolidation, equity method, and cost method.

Consolidation.   When the investor controls more than 50 percent of the voting securities of another company, the investee company is known as a subsidiary and is generally considered to be a part of a parent. Line-by-line consolidation of the subsidiary's financial statements with the financial statements of the parent is considered to be the most informative disclosure and is usually necessary for fair presentation under U.S. GAAP. The U.S. Securities and Exchange Commission (SEC), however, generally does not permit consolidation if the investor is a registrant and owns 50 percent or less of the voting securities of another company except in unusual circumstances. Significant intercompany transactions between the parent and its subsidiaries are eliminated in the consolidated financial statements. The practice of consolidation is seldom followed outside the U.S., U.K., and Canada, except in the case of companies that are publicly owned and except among European Economic Community (EEC) member countries where consolidated financial statements will be required in 1990.

---

[1]Peat Marwick Main & Co., *Public Sale of Securities in the United States: A Guide for Foreign Issuers*, 1987

[2]Orsini, Larry L., McAllister, John P., and Parikh, Rajeev, *World Accounting*, Matthew Bender & Co. Inc., 1986.

TABLE 4.1 Summary of GAAP Country by Country

	U.S.	Brazil	Australia	Canada	France	Germany	Japan	U.K.
Accounting for Long-Term Investments in Share Capital of Other Entities	*Consolidation.* For greater than 50% control of voting securities of another company. Significant inter-company transactions are eliminated in consolidated financial statements.	Same as U.S.	Same as U.S.	Same as U.S.	Same as U.S.	Same as U.S.	Same as U.S.	Same as U.S.
	Equity Method. For 20% to 50% control. Investment stated at net asset value. Equity in investee's earnings or loss included in investor's income statement.	Equity method must be used if book value of controlled company is 10% or more of net worth of investor; equity pickup related to changes in investee's equity, not its income.	Equity method not acceptable for statutory purposes and, if used, the company must present supplementary equity financial statements.	Same as U.S.	Not used.	Not used.	Not allowed.	Same as U.S.
	Cost Method. For less than 20% control. Investment is stated at cost. Dividends paid by investee company are included in earnings by investor.	Rarely used.	Cost method used normally where investment is 50% or less.	Same as U.S.	At year-end, investments are written down to their underlying net worth, if below cost.	Cost method used for less than 50% control.	Cost method used for less than 50% control but if market price is at least 50% less than cost and decline does not appear to be temporary, market price is used.	Same as U.S.

(continued)

TABLE 4.1 (continued)

	U.S.	Brazil	Australia	Canada	France	Germany	Japan	U.K.
Translation of Foreign Currency Financial Statements and Accounting for Foreign Currency Transaction	*FASB #52 Translation Adjustments.* Certain foreign assets and liabilities translated into U.S. dollars at current exchange rate; gains and losses reported as separate component of stockholders' equity. *Transaction Gains and Losses.* Weighted average exchange rate used to translate revenues and expenses; gains and losses recognized in income in accounting period they occur.	Many companies use FASB #52 but more commonly used is current-rate translation approach.	No accounting standards; however, FASB #8 usually used and there is movement toward FASB #52. Transaction gains and losses, some as U.S. Long-term losses are amortized.	Similar considerations as FASB #52.	No officially prescribed method exists. Prevailing practice is to apply rate of exchange at transaction date and treat difference from settlement date exchange rate as an exchange gain or loss.	No accounting standards and no general practice exists, since foreign subsidiaries are excluded from consolidation. Realized gains and losses recognized in income when they occur. For short-term receivables and payables, unrealized gains deferred, unrealized losses are not.	Similar to FASB #52 approach.	Same as U.S.
Investment in Debt Securities	Debt securities are stated at amortized cost. Value may not be written up to appraisal or market values but values may be disclosed in notes to fi-	Same as U.S., except that straight-line amortization is also acceptable.	Stated at cost, but amortization not required; write-down to market required if value perma-	Same as U.S., except that straight-line amortization is also acceptable.	Stated at cost, but amortization not required; write-down to market required if value permanently impaired.	Stated at cost, but amortization not required; write-down to market required if value perma-	Same as U.S., except that amortization method is straight-line.	Same as U.S.

(continued)

	nancial statements. If security is permanently impaired, it should be written down to net realizable value. Discounts and premiums amortized over life of investment, using the interest method.					nently impaired.	nently impaired.
Inventories	Reported in financial statements at lower of cost or market at balance sheet date. Methods: Specific identification FIFO LIFO Average cost For manufactured inventories, inventory costs include allocation of overhead.	FIFO may be used. LIFO not allowed. Moving average method most common because it results in lower inventory than FIFO, and, therefore, lower taxes.	Same methods as U.S. except LIFO not allowed.	Same methods as U.S. except LIFO not acceptable for tax; standard cost method also used.	Same methods as U.S. except LIFO not permitted.	Same methods as U.S. For manufactured inventory costs may include production overhead.	Same methods as U.S. Other methods include base-stock, retail and purchase price methods.	Same methods as U.S. Overhead is allocated to costs of inventory.
Reserve for Unspecified Future Losses	Contingency reserves or general reserves not allowed. Required are valuation reserves for anticipated losses, established via charges to current earnings (shown as a deduction from related asset account on balance sheet).	No specific rules exist but basically follows U.S.	Same as U.S. although rarely are they created since there is no tax benefit.	Same as U.S.	Same as U.S.	Same as U.S.	Same as U.S.	Same as U.S.

TABLE 4.1 (continued)

	U.S.	Brazil	Australia	Canada	France	Germany	Japan	U.K.
Accounting for Capital Leases	Leases that are in substance either purchases, sales, or financing transactions are accounted for as such. Leased property is recorded as an asset in lessee's accounting records and liability for future lease payments is also established if lease transfers substantially all rights and risks of asset to leasee.	Generally accepted practice treats operating and capital leases as rentals but pronouncement is planned similar to U.S.	Same as U.S. although current practice is not to capitalize.	Same as U.S.	All leases recorded as operating leases but disclosures of leases are required.	Same as U.S.	Commercial Code and Security and Exchange Law are silent on leases but common practice is same as U.S.	Same as U.S.
Deferred Income Taxes	Required income taxes are provided against current period income as reflected in financial statements even though all or some of such income will not be reported for tax purposes in current period and taxes will not be payable currently (deferral method).	Most companies still record and recognize income tax strictly as computed for tax purposes.	Liability method used; otherwise same as U.S.	Same as U.S.	Accounting for deferred income taxes not practiced. Accounting for taxes recognizes taxes currently payable only.	Same as Brazil and France.	Same as Brazil, France and Germany. Deferral method is forbidden.	Liability method used (otherwise same as U.S.)
Fixed Assets and Depreciation	Furniture, equipment, and leasehold improvements are recorded at historical cost and depreciated	Same as U.S. (machinery, furniture and fixtures must be monetarily corrected at least annually.	Same as U.S.	Same as U.S.	Same as U.S.	Same as U.S.	Same as U.S.	Same as U.S. although fixed assets may be revalued.

	on a systematic basis over remaining useful life of asset (or terms of lease for leasehold improvements).						
Research and Development Costs	Generally expensed in period incurred.	Same as U.S.	Same as U.S.	Usually same as U.S., but may also be included as an intangible asset and amortized over 5 years or less.	Same as U.S.	Usually same as U.S., but R&D costs for new products or techniques may be capitalized and amortized within 5 years.	Same as U.S.
Capitalization of Interest Expense	Capitalized as part of historical cost.	*Not* allowed, but in preoperation period, interest expense is deferred until normal operations are achieved. Interest expense must be disclosed in financial statements.	No recognized standards but only interest costs on construction projects in period before fixed asset is put into use are capitalized.	Most interest is expensed although interest expense related to finance cost of internal manufacturing or construction may be capitalized.	Interest is generally expensed, but capitalization permitted for long-term construction projects.	Appears to be same as U.S. in common practice.	No standards, but normal practice is same as U.S.
Accounting Changes	Change in accounting principle or method is reported in income statement in period the change occurs. The effect of accounting changes on prior periods is presented as a cumulative amount, net of tax, below income from continuing operations.		Same as U.S.	Same as U.S.			Same in U.S., U.K., Australia, and Canada. Varies in other countries but in general all should follow U.S.

(continued)

TABLE 4.1 (continued)

	U.S.	Brazil	Australia	Canada	France	Germany	Japan	U.K.
Debt Issue Expense	Debt issue costs are recorded as a deferred charge and amortized to income over life of debt issue.	Same as U.S. Amortized 5–10 years.	Same as U.S. except amortization must be completed in 5 years or less.	Optional, but common practice is same as U.S.	Same as U.S.	Bond issue costs are expensed.	Same as U.S. Amortized over 3 years.	
Business Combinations	Purchase method with acquisition recorded as cost; acquired assets and liabilities recorded at fair values.	Usually used.	Used only.	Both methods used along with reverse takeover method where company issues enough voting shares as consideration so that control of combined company passes to shareholders of acquired company.	Purchase method used only.	Used only.	Very few corporate acquisitions have occurred but purchase method will be used since goodwill is tax deductible.	Same as U.S.
	Pooling of interests method.	Rarely used.	Not acceptable.		Not used.	Not allowed.		Same as U.S.
Goodwill	Goodwill is recognized only on acquisition of an enterprise accounted for by purchase method. Good-	Same as U.S. usually, although amortization is optional.	Same as U.S. but amortization must be completed in 20 years. In	Same as U.S.	Same as U.S. except amortized over 5 years or over its useful life.	Same as U.S. except amortization must be completed in 5 years.	Same as Germany.	Same as U.S.

...will is capitalized and amortized over a period not to exceed 40 years.

certain circumstances, goodwill may be revalued.

Inflation Accounting	SFAS 89 applies only to public U.S. companies. Foreign issuers must comply if currencies cumulative inflationary effect is 100% over the most recent 3 year period. SFAS 89 encourages but does not require income adjusted for impact of changing prices for specific goods and services used by company, and purchasing power gain (loss) on net monetary items for public companies with assets of $1 billion or more or inventories and P.P. and E. of $125 million or more.	Corporation law requires financial statements be monetarily corrected (constant currency rather than constant cost information).	No requirements. Statement of accounting practice in current cost accounting not widely used.	Required for public companies with total assets of $350 million or more, and total inventory and P.P. and E. of $50 million or more.	No standard yet but will be one in near future. Tangible and intangible fixed assets may have been revalued according to legal revaluation or management decision.	Accounting for inflation not required. It is recommended but it has not been followed.	No legal requirements address accounting for inflation.	Current Cost Accounting.

Equity method. When the investor controls 20 percent to 50 percent of the investee's voting securities or has a subsidiary that is not consolidated, the investment is generally stated at the underlying net asset value, with the equity in the investee's earnings or loss included in the investor's income statement for the current period (equity accounting). Any dividends received are treated as an adjustment to the basis of the investment. This method of accounting for 50 percent-or-less owned companies and subsidiaries not consolidated is followed by the U.K. and Canada, but is not recognized as an acceptable method of accounting in many other countries.

Cost method. When the investor controls less than 20 percent of the voting securities of another company, the investment is generally stated at cost. Dividends declared or paid by investee companies that are carried at cost are included in the investor's earnings for the current year. The timing of recognition of dividend income differs in certain foreign countries where dividend income is recognized in each year, regardless of whether the dividends have been formally declared or paid.

1.2 Translation of Foreign Currency Financial Statements and Accounting for Foreign Currency Transactions

The accounting policies of recognition and accounting for foreign exchange gains and losses vary significantly from country to country. The current practice in the U.S. under Statement of Financial Accounting Standards (SFAS) No. 52, issued by the Financial Accounting Standards Board (FASB), distinguishes between translation adjustments and transaction gains and losses. Translation adjustments arise when a foreign entity's financial statements are translated into U.S. dollars at the current exchange rate. Translation adjustments are not included in determining net income for the period. They are accumulated as a separate component of equity until disposal or substantial liquidation of the related foreign entity takes place.

Transaction gains and losses arise when exchange rate changes affect transactions of the enterprise. Transaction gains and losses are generally recognized in income in the accounting period that they arise. However, if the transaction represents a hedge of a foreign currency commitment or a net investment in a foreign investee, the unrealized gain or loss is accounted for in the same manner as a translation adjustment.

The accounting policies of many countries allow for either deferral of unrealized exchange gains or losses or capitalization of such gains and losses as part of the related asset. Some countries apply historical or current rates of exchange, depending on the nature of the account or transaction, and recognize all gains and losses in the current period. Other countries require that only realized gains and losses be recognized in the accounts; still others require the recognition of unrealized losses (but not unrealized gains) in addition to realized gains and losses.

1.3 Investment in Debt Securities

U.S. accounting principles require that debt securities held for investment purposes be stated at amortized cost. Such investments may not be written up to appraisal or market values, although these values must be disclosed in the notes to the financial statements. If the security is determined to be permanently impaired, it should be written down to net realizable value. There is no provision for any subsequent write-up should appreciation occur.

In the U.S., amortization is calculated using the interest method, while the straight line method is used in certain other countries, notably Brazil and Japan.

1.4 Deferred Income Taxes

Generally accepted accounting principles in the United States require that income taxes be provided against current period income as reflected in the financial statements, even though all or some of such income will not be reported for tax purposes in the current period and taxes will not be payable currently. This means that, even though certain amounts of current period accounting income are not currently taxable, income tax expense must be provided in the financial statements against both income on which taxes are currently payable and income on which the tax liability is deferred regardless of the length of that deferral.

In Brazil, France, Germany, and Japan, the concept of deferred taxes is not recognized and, instead, such countries record only the amount of tax that is currently payable or record income taxes solely on a cash basis.

1.5 Fixed Assets and Depreciation

In the U.S., fixed assets such as furniture, equipment, and leasehold improvements are recorded at historical cost and depreciated on a systematic basis over the remaining useful life of the asset (or terms of the lease in the case of leasehold improvements). In Brazil it is accepted practice to write up longer-term assets to higher values that reflect inflation indexes provided by the government. The U.K. permits assets to be written up to appraised value. Depreciation in such cases is based on the new value of the assets.

1.6 Research and Development Costs

In the U.S., R&D costs are generally expensed in the period incurred. France and Japan permit deferral of R&D costs, including costs of personnel, materials, equipment, facilities, and intangibles directly related to R&D activities, to future periods that may benefit from R&D activities.

1.7 Inflation Accounting

A subject of much debate throughout the world has been the question of how to account for the impact of inflation. In the U.S., SFAS No. 89 encourages, but does not require, that the following information be disclosed by public companies that have assets in excess of $1 billion or inventories and property, plant, and equipment in excess of $125 million:

Income adjusted for the impact of changing prices for specific goods and services used by the company (current cost) and
Purchasing power gain or loss on net monetary items.

If included, the inflation-adjusted data disclosed by public companies must be presented as supplementary information to the basic financial statements. The basic financial statements continue to be prepared on the basis of historical cost.

SFAS No. 89 is applicable only to U.S. public companies and has not been extended to foreign issuers by the SEC. However, the SEC does require foreign private issuers with financial statements denominated in a currency of a country that has experienced a cumulative inflationary effect of 100 percent over the most recent three-year period to present supplementary information about the impact of changing prices. The supplementary information should quantify the effects of changing price on the company's financial condition and results of operations. In Canada, inflation accounting is required for public companies having a specified minimum amount of assets.

Requirements for disclosure of the impact of inflation differ widely in other countries. Australia, Germany, and Japan have no requirement for disclosure of inflation-adjusted financial information. Brazil allows for the write-up of certain assets (usually long-term assets) on the basis of certain inflation indexes provided by the government and other sources. Depreciation taken reflects the adjusted asset values and accordingly may result in the reporting of current or replacement costs in the income statement. There also are countries that either require or permit disclosure of inflation-adjusted financial statements prepared on different bases than constant-dollar or current cost (as specified by SFAS No. 89).

1.8 Capitalization of Interest Expense

U.S. accounting principles require the capitalization of interest costs as part of the historical cost of certain "qualifying" assets if the asset requires a period of time to get it in the condition and to the location of its intended use and if interest costs are incurred during that period. In general, capitalization of interest costs applies to major assets constructed for a company's own use or assets intended of sale or lease that are constructed or produced as discrete projects, like ships, aircraft, real estate developments.

In France, the interest costs incurred during construction or production of such assets are considered to be period costs. Therefore, the interest costs are charged to income rather than capitalized as part of the cost of the assets, although interest related to the financing of costs of certain internal construction may be capitalized.

1.9 Accounting Changes

In the U.S., a change in an accounting principle or its method of application, in most cases, is reported in the statement of income in the period the change occurs. The effect of the accounting change on periods prior to the change is presented as a cumulative amount, net of tax, below income from continuing operations. Australia, Canada, and the U.K. follow the same practice as the U.S.

1.10 Debt Issue Expense

U.S. accounting principles require the deferral and amortization of debt issue costs. The SEC also requires that some portion of lump-sum fees paid to investment bankers in takeover or leveraged buy out transactions be included in debt issuance costs. Therefore, the debt issue costs are recorded as a deferred charge and amortized to income over the life of the debt issue. In Brazil, Australia, and Japan, the amortization periods are limited irrespective of debt maturity dates. Alternatively, in Germany, the full amount of debt issue costs is charged against earnings in the year incurred.

U.S. GAAP also specifies the accounting treatment for any discount or premium that arises on the sale of long-term debt securities. Debt discount or premium must be reported as a direct deduction from or addition to the liability and be amortized as interest expense or interest income over the life of the debt. The method of amortization must produce a constant rate of interest on the amount of debt outstanding in any period (Interest Method).

1.11 Accounting for Business Combinations (Mergers and Acquisitions)

A business combination occurs when one entity acquires part or all of another entity for cash, shares, or other consideration. The principal authoritative literature applicable to accounting for business combinations in the U.S. is represented by Opinions 16 and 17 of the former Accounting Principles Board (APB). APB Opinion 16 became effective for combinations initiated after October 31, 1970, and APB Opinion 17, for intangible assets acquired after October 31, 1970. While the successor to the APB, the Financial Accounting Standards Board (FASB) has issued several statements and interpretations clarifying the prescribed accounting treatments in specific situations, the basic theory underlying business combination accounting in the U.S. has withstood the test of time, particularly the "merger mania" of the 1980s, and has remained relatively constant.

APB Opinion 16 acknowledges that for accounting purposes, there are two distinct types of business combinations: (1) a pooling of interests and (2) a purchase. The Opinion identifies twelve criteria, grouped into three broad categories, to test whether a particular combination should be accounted for as a pooling of interests. If the combination meets all twelve criteria, pooling of interests accounting is required, not optional. Conversely, if the combination fails to meet one or more of the criteria, purchase accounting is imposed. Certain countries, including Australia, France, and Germany do not recognize the pooling of interests method as an acceptable accounting method. In the U.K. and Canada, both the purchase method and pooling-of-interests method may be used; however, the conditions for determining which method is appropriate may differ. Consequently, some business combinations accounted for as poolings in the U.S. may be reflected as purchases in other countries, and vice versa. Differences may also exist in the determination of the amount of goodwill, as noted later. Significant differences in the carrying values of assets and liabilities and in the results of operations of the combined companies can result from applying purchase accounting rather than pooling of interests accounting. During the past ten years, there has been a significantly greater number of purchases compared to poolings.

1.12 Purchase Contrasted with Pooling in the U.S.

Contrasting the theories of purchase and pooling accounting can begin with the following definitions of "purchase" and "pool," which appear in *Webster's New Collegiate Dictionary.* "Purchase," as a noun, is defined as something obtained especially for a price in money or its equivalent. "Pool," as a noun, is defined as an aggregation of the interests or property of different persons made to further a joint undertaking by subjecting them to the same control and a common liability.

APB Opinion 16 defines a purchase as the acquisition of one enterprise by another, or anything that does not qualify as a pooling. A pooling, on the other hand, is defined in accounting terms as the presentation as a single interest of two or more common shareholder interests that were previously independent, including the combined risks, opportunities, and rights of ownership. In this context pooling is synonymous with merger.

What do the differences in these definitions mean in an economic sense? A purchase combination implies that one entity is acquired by another, thus creating a change in control of the acquiree and the loss of its ability to control its own destiny. In a purchase transaction, a majority, if not substantially all, of the stockholders of the acquiree exchange their stockholder interests in the net assets of their company or business in exchange for cash, equity, debt of the acquirer or its affiliates, or a combination thereof. Depending on the fair market values of the individual assets and liabilities, the net discounted value of expected future cash flows, the acquiree's competitive position in its marketplace, or domestic or international market conditions in general, the historical carrying or "book" value of the acquiree's net assets may or may not bear any resemblance to the purchase price offered by the acquirer. Accordingly, in a transaction accounted for as a purchase, a new cost basis of accounting must be applied to the assets and liabilities acquired, regardless of previous accounting by the acquiree, to be consistent with the theory that the accounting value of an acquired asset is its cost of acquisition.

Whereas a purchase implies a change in control of one of the combining entities, a pooling gives rise to a continued sharing of control by the stockholders of each of the combining entities in a proportion determined by the relative market values of their respective ownership interests prior to the combination. A pooling, therefore, is the addition of two or more groups of net assets, or stockholder's equity, in an assets-and-liabilities sense and in terms of the actual common stock ownership in the combined enterprise. APB Opinion 16 summarizes the sharing concept of a pooling by stating that the pooling method:

shows that stockholder groups neither withdraw or invest assets but in effect exchange voting common stock in a ratio that determines their respective interests in the combined enterprise. . . . Certain attributes of combining enterprises indicate that independent ownership interests are combined in their entirety to continue previously separate operations.

A final significant distinction between a purchase and a pooling is that in real terms, a purchase is consummated through the exchange by the acquirer of a significant proportion of cash and debt to the seller relative to the total purchase price. A pooling, on the other hand, is effected principally through the exchange of voting common stock by each of the combining entities, with only minor amounts of cash or debt permitted to be included as part of the aggregate consideration exchanged.

1.13 Application of Purchase Accounting

Standard historical cost principles.   Under purchase accounting, the cost of an acquired entity becomes the new basis for recording the investment in the net assets of the acquiree in the financial records of the acquirer. This concept is reasonably consistent around the world where purchase accounting is applied. If the purchase price consists of consideration other than cash, the cost of such consideration is determined by its fair market value or the fair market value of the net assets received from the acquiree, whichever is more readily determinable. In most transactions accounted for by the purchase method, a major component of the total purchase price is cash, although the acquiree may accept the acquirer's notes and/or stock as part of the aggregate consideration.

Cost of an acquired entity.   There are three general categories of costs that ultimately determine the total acquisition cost to be accounted for under the purchase method:

1. The up-front purchase price to be paid to the seller by the closing date of the transaction,
2. Contingent consideration to be paid in the future based on the occurrence of events identified in the acquisition agreement, and
3. Transaction costs of consummating the acquisition that will be paid to parties other than the seller.

The up-front price can be either a fixed amount stated in the acquisition agreement or a price based on a formula applied to certain financial data at or prior to the closing date. In either case, any consideration that must be exchanged between buyer and seller after the closing date is characterized as contingent consideration.

Contingent consideration usually results from one of the following events occurring after the closing date:

An audit of the acquiree's financial statements as of the closing date and/or for the period ending thereon, which determines that adjustments to the up-front price are required pursuant to a contractual formula applied to such financial statements,

The achievement of contractually specified earnings levels (an earn-out formula), or

The nonachievement of contractually specified market values for securities issued to the seller as part of the up-front price.

Contingent payments are not recorded as a component of the cost of an acquired entity until resolution of the uncertainty giving rise to the contingency is reasonably assured.

Transaction costs have become much more visible to the public as a result of the megadeals (like the RJR Nabisco, Beatrice and Revlon leveraged buyouts) of the 1980s. Such costs, frequently as high as five percent or more of the purchase price, encompass a wide variety of services necessary to consummate the acquisition, and include

Commissions to finders or other intermediaries,

Fees to investment bankers, attorneys, accountants, actuaries, engineers, or other outside consultants, and

Commitment or origination fees and other costs relating to financing the acquisition.

Allocating costs to net assets.   The valuation of the assets and liabilities of an acquired business by the acquirer is the essence and often the most difficult consequence of accounting for a business combination under the purchase method. The previous carrying values of the acquiree's assets and liabilities give way to what could be an entirely new series of values, based on the total acquisition cost (including transaction costs) allocated to individual assets and liabilities based on their relative fair market values. The former stockholders' equity of the acquired company is eliminated.

All of the assets acquired and liabilities assumed are reviewed to determine their fair market values at the acquisition date. The most typical valuation concepts are summarized below.

- *Cash and Account Receivables.* Most frequently valued at their carrying values prior to acquisition, assuming that such assets can be converted into other liquid assets at the option of the holder within a reasonably short period. Receivables should be valued after considering allowances for returns, discounts, unearned interest, and bad debts.

- *Marketable Securities.* Net realizable value.
- *Inventories.* For finished goods, net realizable value less a normally expected gross profit, and for raw materials, current replacement cost. In almost all situations, any LIFO reserve maintained by the acquiree prior to the acquisition is eliminated.
- *Property, Plant, and Equipment.* Fair market value as determined by independent appraisals for land, buildings and improvements, and machinery and equipment.
- *Accounts Payable and Accrued Expenses.* Carrying values prior to acquisition, assuming cash payments to be made within a reasonably short period.
- *Notes Payable and Long-Term Debt.* The net present value of cash payments to be made using a current interest rate applicable to the type of debt being assumed.
- *Pension Plan Obligations.* The excess or deficiency of assumed projected benefit obligations (as defined by FASB Statement of Financial Accounting Standards 87 to be the actuarial present value of pension benefits attributed to the pension benefit formula to service prior to an "as of" date) relative to plan assets transferred to the acquirer gives rise to a liability or an asset to be recorded. The data necessary for valuing the net liability or asset should be reviewed by a consulting actuary.
- *All Other Liabilities.* The net present value of cash payments to be made in the future, using an appropriate discount rate.

Total acquisition cost and aggregate fair value of new assets.
Once all of the acquired company's tangible assets and liabilities have been individually fair valued, the net fair value is compared to the total acquisition cost. In many situations, a difference between the two represents an excess of acquisition cost over the net fair value of assets acquired, resulting in a residual value for one or more intangible assets. After consideration is given to identifying the value of specific intangibles such as patents, trademarks, "bargain" leases, and the like, the remaining excess of acquisition cost over net fair value of assets is classified as goodwill. In accordance with APB Opinion 17, goodwill is amortized against the future earnings of the combined entity over a period not to exceed forty years. There are several situations that indicate that goodwill should be charged off over a substantially shorter period, based on the nature and expected useful lives of the principal assets acquired or based on industry practice.

In some countries, goodwill is recognized only on the acquisition of an enterprise and represents the excess of the purchase price paid over the *book value* of the net assets acquired, not an *adjusted value*, as in the U.S. While some countries have provisions for capitalization and amortization of goodwill similar to those in the U.S., Australia, Germany, and Japan require immediate write-off against current earnings over substantially shorter periods of time relative to the U.S. Brazil permits goodwill to be carried indefinitely as an intangible asset without amortization.

When the difference between the total acquisition cost and the fair value of the net assets acquired results in an excess of fair value over cost, a careful evaluation of the reasons for the apparent "bargain purchase" must be made. Under APB Opinion 16, noncurrent assets (other than marketable securities classified as noncurrent) should be written down to the extent of the excess of fair value over cost, and any remaining excess should be classified as negative goodwill and credited to the future earnings of the combined entity over a period not to exceed forty years. In evaluating the circumstances underlying an apparent bargain purchase, it is sometimes determined that the net realizable value of inventories is less than originally estimated or that there are liabilities not previously recorded by the acquiree.

Accounting for contingencies.   Contingent consideration is one of the components used in arriving at the total acquisition cost to be accounted for when such contingency contribution is either paid or becomes payable to the seller and when cash or other assets of the acquirer (other than its own shares of stock) is the medium of payment; it is then most frequently classified as additional goodwill. Often, however, there are contingencies with respect to the acquiree that are not capable of being resolved prior to the consummation of the acquisition. Litigation and governmental investigations into environmental concerns are two examples of preacquisition contingencies. SFAS 38 requires that such items be considered in the fair valuing of the assets and liabilities of the acquiree as follows.

1. After evaluating the contingency, it is determined whether the creation or impairment of an asset or the incurring of a liability is probable, and whether the result can be quantified.

2. If a resulting asset or liability from 1, above, is determined within one year after the closing date (referred to as the allocation period), an adjustment is made to the allocation of the total acquisition cost based on the fair value of the asset or liability arising from resolution of the contingency.

3. If, after the allocation period, an asset is created or impaired or a liability is incurred as a result of the resolution of a preacquisiton

contingency, it is accounted for in the period of resolution through a credit or charge to earnings.

Purchase accounting and income taxes. SFAS 96 provides new guidance in dealing with the financial statement implications of income taxes for business combinations accounted for as purchases.[3] APB Opinion 16 requires that amounts assigned to the assets and liabilities assumed in a purchase business combination be recorded at fair value. Frequently, such values differ from the tax bases of the assets acquired and liabilities assumed (for example, because the combination is a tax-free exchange). In such circumstances, SFAS 96 requires that differences between the tax bases and the fair values of the assets acquired and liabilities assumed be recognized by recording deferred tax assets and liabilities in the same manner as for other temporary differences. Present practice under APB Opinion 11 requires the tax effects of basis differences to be considered in assigning values to assets acquired and liabilities assumed (the net-of-tax approach).

The following example illustrates the effect of SFAS 96 on individual financial statement amounts in a purchase combination.

Assume Company A acquires another enterprise in January 1989 for $280,000 in a nontaxable transaction that is accounted for as a purchase. The assets acquired have a fair value of $300,000, but no tax basis. The tax rate is 40 percent. The purchase price is allocated as follows.

	SFAS 96	APB Opinion 11
Identifiable assets	$ 300,000	$ 180,000
Deferred tax liability	(120,000)	—
Goodwill	100,000	100,000
	$ 280,000	$ 280,000

Assume also that prior to recording depreciation on the assets acquired and the amortization of goodwill, consolidated pretax income for 1989 is $100,000. The assets acquired are being depreciated using the straight-line method over ten years; goodwill is being amortized over twenty years. Further assume that there are no other temporary differences and that income taxes currently payable are $40,000 ($100,000 × 40 percent). The following illustrates the effects on the 1989 income statement of applying SFAS 96.

[3]Peat Marwick Main & Co., *Accounting for Income Taxes: A Summary of FASB Statement 96*, 1988.

	SFAS 96	APB Opinion 11
Pretax income before depreciation and amortization	$ 100,000	$ 100,000
Depreciation	30,000*	18,000
Amortization of goodwill	5,000*	5,000*
Pretax income	65,000	77,000
Income taxes:		
Currently payable	40,000	40,000
Deferred (benefit)	(12,000)	—
Net income	$ 37,000	$ 37,000
Effective tax rate	43.1%	51.9%

*No U.S. tax deduction.

Under SFAS 96, the effective date of which has been deferred until fiscal years beginning on or after December 15, 1991, the accounting for previously reported purchase business combinations depends on whether the enterprise elects to restate its previously issued financial statements.

SFAS 96 also changes the accounting for net operating loss (NOL) and tax credit carryforwards acquired in a purchase business combination. If the benefit of an NOL or a tax credit carryforward is not recognized at the date of acquisition (which generally will be the case), its subsequent recognition first reduces goodwill and then noncurrent intangible assets. Any remaining benefit is recorded as a reduction of income tax expense.

Under APB Opinion 11, the benefit was recognized first as a reduction of goodwill, then as a reduction of other noncurrent assets acquired, with any remaining benefit being credited to negative goodwill.

1.14 Requirements for Pooling of Interests Accounting

The pooling of interests method of accounting, which is rarely used outside the U.S. (Canada and the U.K. excepted), treats a business combination as the uniting of the ownership interests of two or more companies by an exchange of equity securities. No acquisition is recognized because the combination is accomplished without disbursing resources of the constituents. Ownership interests continue and the former bases of accounting are retained.

For the concept of this union to be transformed into pooling of interests accounting, twelve conditions must be met. These conditions are described next.

ATTRIBUTES OF COMBINING COMPANIES

1. Each of the combining entities has not been a division or subsidiary of another business entity for at least two years prior to the initiation date of the proposed combination.

2. Each of the combining entities is independent of the other combining entities to the extent that no combining entity owns more than ten percent of the voting common stock of any other combining entity prior to the initiation date of the proposed combination.

For purposes of applying the above two tests, the initiation date of a proposed business combination is the date on which the significant terms of the combination are formally communicated to the stockholders of any of the combining entities, or the date on which the stockholders of any combining entity are notified in writing of an exchange offer, whichever is earlier.

The principles reinforced through the implementation of these tests are that for a combination to qualify as a pooling, the parties to the transaction are (1) autonomous entities from a control standpoint and in their authority to consummate a proposed combination without intervention by a higher corporate or "ultimate owner" layers and (2) free from prior economic interest in one another that would make the negotiations between them leading to the combination non-arm's-length.

MANNER OF COMBINING INTERESTS

3. The combination is completed via a single transaction or through a plan incorporating a number of transactions to be accomplished within one year after the initiation date.

4. The combination is effected through the exchange of common stock for substantially all of the combining entities' common stock ("substantially all" means 90 percent or more of total outstanding voting common stock).

5. The equity interest in the common stock of the combining entities is not altered in anticipation of the proposed combination for at least two years prior to the initiation date and for the period between the initiation date and the closing date. For purposes of applying this test, normal dividends distributed to stockholders within two years of the initiation date do not represent a change in the equity interest of the combining entities' common stock.

6. None of the combining entities reacquires its voting common stock for purposes related to the proposed combination. Treasury stock *systematically* acquired in connection with existing compensation plans such as stock options is permitted.

7. The ratio of the interest of an individual common stockholder to those of other common stockholders in a combining enterprise remains the same as a result of the exchange of stock to effect the combination, or each common stockholder who exchanges stock receives a voting common stock interest exactly in proportion to its voting common stock interest before the combination is effected.

8. The voting rights represented by the shares of common stock owned by all of the combined stockholders are exercisable and not restricted.

9. The combination is resolved at the time the plan of merger is consummated, which means that there are substantially no contingent shares of stock to be issued after the closing date.

The most common implementational problems resulting in the inability to account for a business combination as a pooling of interests are:

Securities other than voting common stock are used in the exchange.

Nonrecurring or unusual distributions to stockholders have been made within the past two years.

More than ten percent of the shares exchanges were acquired in the treasury over the past two years.

The plan of combination provides for contingent consideration.

Stockholders in the combined entity have a restriction in certain of their voting rights.

ABSENCE OF PLANNED TRANSACTIONS

10. There is no agreement for the combined entity to retire or to reacquire any of the shares of stock used to effect the combination.

11. No other financial arrangements are made for the benefit of former stockholders of a combining entity.

12. There are no plans to dispose of a significant portion of the assets of the combining entities for at least two years after the consummation of the combination, except for resolving duplicate or excess capacity.

The last three tests are consistent with the theory that for a transaction to qualify as a pooling, it must be consummated quickly and without a hidden agenda, side deals, or contingent arrangements that could effect stockholder interests. Similarly, if certain assets essential to the operations of one of the combining companies are owned outside of such com-

pany, pooling of interests accounting is prohibited, since ownership interests in the combining company would not be combined in their entirety.

1.15 Application of Pooling of Interests Accounting

Unlike purchase accounting, there are no valuation issues inherent
in reflecting a business combination as a pooling; rather, an arithmetical
combining of financial statements accounts is achieved on a virtually line-
by-line basis. The basic procedures to be followed for pooling of interests
accounting can be summarized, as follows:

- Assets and liabilities are combined at the previous carrying values
  reported by the combining entities; no goodwill results.
- Stockholders' equity of the separate entities is combined.
- Results of operations are reported as if the combination had been
  consummated at the beginning of the current accounting period;
  prior period financial statements should be retroactively adjusted
  to reflect the combination as if it had taken place at the beginning of
  the earliest accounting period presented for comparative purposes.
- All transaction costs of business combination accounted for as a
  pooling are expensed as incurred.

1.16 Financial Statement Implications Compared

To illustrate the impact on the financial statements of the combined
entity of applying either purchase or pooling of interests accounting in a
specific transaction, assume the following facts.

Company A and Company B agree to combine under an agreement whereby
A issues to B shares of its common stock, having a market value of $45 per
share or $4.5 million in the aggregate, in exchange for all of B's issued and
outstanding common stock.

The individual balance sheets for A and B as of December 31, 1988,
are presented below.

	Company A	Company B	
	Book or Carrying Value	Book or Carrying Value	Fair Value
Current assets[a]	$5,000,000	$1,000,000	$1,100,000
Fixed assets[b]	3,000,000	3,000,000	4,000,000
Other assets[c]	800,000	500,000	600,000
	$8,800,000	$4,500,000	

	Company A	Company B	
	Book or Carrying Value	Book or Carrying Value	Fair Value
Current liabilities	1,500,000	500,000	500,000
Long-term debt[d]	2,500,000	1,000,000	950,000
Common stock			
($10 par value)	3,000,000	1,000,000	
Paid-in capital	200,000	500,000	
Retained earnings	1,600,000	1,500,000	
	$8,800,000	$4,500,000	

a. The entire difference between B's book value and fair value of current assets is attributable to inventory. Both companies use FIFO inventory procedures.

b. The remaining life of B's fixed assets is twenty years.

c. The remaining life of B's other assets is ten years.

d. The long-term debt of B will mature in ten years.

The separate income statements for A and B for 1989, the first year of combined operation, are presented below.

	Company A	Company B
Sales	$4,000,000	$2,000,000
Cost of Sales	2,000,000	1,000,000
Gross profit	2,000,000	1,000,000
Expenses	800,000	400,000
Net income	$1,200,000	$ 600,000

The balance sheet of the combined entity under both pooling and purchase accounting is as follows.

	Pooling of Interests[a]	Purchase
Current assets	$ 6,000,000	$ 6,100,000[b]
Fixed assets	6,000,000	7,000,000[b]
Other assets	1,300,000	1,400,000[b]
Goodwill	—	250,000[d]
	$13,300,000	14,750,000
Current liabilities	$ 2,000,000	$ 2,000,000
Long-term debt	3,500,000	3,450,000[b]
Common stock ($10 par)	4,000,000	4,000,000[c]
Paid-in capital	700,000	3,700,000[c]
Retained earnings	3,100,000	1,600,000[c]
	$13,300,000	$14,750,000

a. The pooling column represents the sum of the individual assets, liabilities, and stockholders' equity of A and B as presented in their separate balance sheets.

b. The difference in value arises from the use of fair value to record these assets and liabilities under purchase accounting ($100,000 additional inventory, $1,000,000 additional fixed assets, $100,000 other assets, and $50,000 less long-term debt) rather than book or carrying value under pooling of interests accounting.

c. All of the stockholders' equity accounts of B are eliminated as a result of purchase accounting. Retained earnings of A are unchanged. Common stock and paid-in capital of A are reconciled as follows:

	Prior to Combination	Issuance of Common Stock*	After Combination
Common stock	$3,000,000	$1,000,000	$4,000,000
Paid-in capital	200,000	3,500,000	3,700,000
	$3,200,000	$4,500,000	$7,700,000

*100,000 shares at $10 par value and $45 market value.

d. Goodwill is calculated as the difference between the purchase price (no transactions costs assumed) and the net fair value of the assets and liabilities transferred, or as follows.

Purchase price	$4,500,000
Less:	
Inventory	(1,100,000)
Fixed assets	(4,000,000)
Other assets	(600,000)
Plus:	
Current liabilities	500,000
Long-term debt	950,000
Goodwill	$ 250,000

The 1989 income statement for the combined entity under pooling and purchase accounting appears below.

	Pooling of Interests[a]	Purchase
Sales	$6,000,000	$6,100,000
Cost of sales[b]	3,000,000	3,100,000
Gross profit	3,000,000	2,900,000
Expenses[c]	1,200,000	1,271,250
Net Income	$1,800,000	1,628,750

a. The pooling column represents the sum of the individual revenues and expenses of A and B as presented in their separate income statements.

b. Reconciliation of cost of sales is accomplished as follows:

Reported on B's income statement	$1,000,000
Reported on A's income statement	2,000,000
Reported under pooling of interests income statement	3,000,000
Write-off of increase in inventory (all attributed to 1989 as goods recorded on a FIFO basis are sold)	100,000
Reported under purchase income statement	$3,100,000

c. Expenses are reconciled from pooling to purchase as follows.

Reported on B's income statement	$ 400,000
Reported on A's income statement	800,000
Reported under pooling of interests income statement	1,200,000
Depreciation of increase in plant assets (1,000,00 ÷ 20)	50,000
Depreciation of increase in other assets (100,000 ÷ 10)	10,000
Amortization of discount on long-term debt (50,000 ÷ 10)	5,000
Amortization of goodwill (250,000 ÷ 40)	6,250
Reported under purchase income statement	$1,271,250

In pointing out the inherent problems in understanding financial information, we have covered only the broad, basic areas in which U.S. accounting principles, practices, and methods are most commonly found to differ from those of other countries. Innumerable further differences in theory and in implementation not dealt with herein arise at the level of specific application of these principles. In addition, there may be other broad areas that are less frequently encountered in which significant differences occur. Differences in disclosure requirements also exist between the U.S. and other countries, such as in the areas of business segment reporting, pension data, and oil and gas reserve information.

In evaluating a potential merger or acquisition candidate, its financial statements should be revised to the extent that its basic accounting policies conform to those used by the purchaser. Such a process may not be easy, since records may be inadequate and/or the need to revise several years' historical accounts could prove to be a time-consuming job. This exercise should be completed as early as possible within the overall acquisition process.

When acquiring a foreign-based listed or public company, it may also be necessary to conform the accounts of the acquirer with those generally accepted in the country of the target. This would typically be the case if common stock was being issued by the acquirer in exchange for shares in the target. As we will see later, in the United States, for example, a foreign buyer must be prepared to revise its own accounting policies to produce financial statements in conformity with U.S. GAAP, or to provide disclosure reconciling the non-American accounts to those which would be generally accepted in the U.S.

1.17 The SEC and Foreign Securities Issuers[4]

A consideration of the philosophy of the SEC in a situation where a non-U.S. company is acquiring a U.S. company using U.S. public funds must begin with the role the Commission plays in the United States. The SEC was created to establish a more efficient capital market by providing adequate protection for investors, hence increasing their confidence in U.S. capital markets. It is the policy of the SEC to fulfill its role primarily through regulations that require full, fair, and adequate disclosure of information to investors on securities issued and traded in the public market.

Non-U.S. issuers are generally treated in the same manner as domestic issuers. They are confronted with no special barriers if they wish to enter U.S. capital markets. This is consistent with the free enterprise philosophy of the United States, which has traditionally held that free market forces should determine the direction of capital flows throughout the world so that economic efficiency is maximized. This philosophy permits U.S. investors the freedom to invest their money wherever they desire. Accordingly, the SEC permits foreign companies to enter U.S. capital markets freely if they are willing to comply with its regulations and requirements to provide full, fair, and adequate disclosure.

Foreign issuers may find the disclosures required by the SEC burdensome, both because the SEC requirements are generally more extensive than disclosure requirements in other countries and because of differences in accounting principles between the U.S. and other countries. To alleviate this burden, the legislation that created the SEC was amended in 1964 to permit the Commission to grant certain special exemptions to the issuers of foreign securities provided these exemptions do not diminish protection of U.S. investors.

As a result, some of the reporting requirements of foreign issuers are less stringent than those for domestic issuers. The Commission has occasionally relaxed specific rules when asked to do so by foreign registrants on the grounds that hardship would result from compliance.

The problem of how to enable foreign issuers to overcome the substantial problems of adapting their practices to U.S. requirements without increasing the risk to investors has traditionally been approached by the SEC from different directions for accounting and for auditing questions. On accounting matters, the Commission is flexible. U.S. GAAP is not imposed on foreign companies. Instead, foreign issuers may file financial statements based on foreign accounting principles as long as a reconciliation of their financial statements to U.S. generally accepted accounting principles is included when there are material differences between the

[4]Peat, Marwick, Main & Co., *Public Sale of Securities in the United States: A Guide for Foreign Issuers*, 1987.

foreign principles and U.S. GAAP. The reconciliation is generally presented in the footnotes to the foreign issuer's financial statements.

In summary, foreign issuers are welcomed in the U.S. capital markets on essentially the same basis as domestic issuers. This means that foreign issuers must comply with the time-comsuming and often costly regulatory requirements of the SEC.

2.0 EVALUATING THE TARGET

After a target's financial information has been translated by the purchaser from an accounting point of view, the next step to consider in the acquisition process is the qualitative evaluation of the target, or due diligence. A due diligence, or businessman's review,[5] is a challenging and interactive exercise in which the acquisition team conducts an investigative analysis of the operating and/or financial areas of the target's business. The review is international to the extent of the geographical dispersion of the target operations, assets and markets, and can be an integral part of the planning for post-closing multi-national corporate and tax structures of the combined company. Its overall objective is to assist the purchaser in assessing the risks, rewards, and opportunities of a potential merger or acquisition. The review procedures vary and must be adapted to meet the needs of almost each acquisition. In addition to in-house personnel designated by the purchaser, the acquisition team frequently includes accountants, lawyers and other outside specialists.

2.1 Scope

The scope of a businessman's review may be narrow or broad. The most typical narrow-scope review is initial fact-finding. Initial fact-finding may, for instance, be limited to obtaining information about the target company's operations (by discussions with target company management and its independent accountants, if any, and a review of their working papers). This level of due diligence may be useful when an acquirer is in the early discussion stages of a potential merger or acquisition and needs general information about the company being considered.

On the other hand, a broad-scope businessman's review, whether performed in stages or with all procedures authorized at the outset, may include expanded fact-finding or procedures designed to provide conclusions or recommendations. The following procedures are typical of expanded fact-finding.

---

[5]Peat, Marwick, Mitchell & Co., *Businessman's Review Practice Guide*, 1981, and as updated.

- Make inquiries or seek other corroborating evidence supporting target management's comments about its company's operations, interim financial information, employment contracts, sales backlog, and so on.
- Perform fact-finding procedures with respect to the target's
  —ownership and management,
  —products, markets, and major competitors,
  —status of litigation, if any,
  —sales methods, product distribution, salesmen's compensation, pricing policies, and terms,
  —product development efforts,
  —relative position in the industry (comparative data on sales, backlog, earnings, dividends and certain key ratios, usually covering the past several years),
  —principal suppliers and terms.
  —age, capacity, and use of property, plant, and equipment, capital commitments and future capital requirements, subsidiaries and the amount and method of handling intercompany transactions,
  —long-range plans and budgets, relationships with stockholders, creditors, customers, and the community, and
  —personnel administration, interdepartmental coordination, organization, labor market, employee contracts, strike record, and the like.

The following examples illustrate businessman's review procedures designed to provide conclusions or recommendations.

- Evaluate the target's marketing, planning, administrative, or other functions.
- Apply specific procedures to identified elements, accounts, or items of the target's financial statements.
- Assess the adequacy of data processing operations in meeting the needs of the target.
- Apply specific procedures to all or a part of the company's system of internal accounting controls.
- Read projected income statements, cash flow projections, or other prospective information.
- Perform an in-depth review of the target's employee benefit plans.
- Perform an in-depth review of the target's tax posture.
- Perform an in-depth review of the tax aspects of a proposed acquisition or merger.
- Perform a value analysis review of the company.

- Provide assistance or advice on the strategy for negotiating an acquisition or merger.

2.2 Procedures

Fact-finding is the means used most often to obtain requested information about a target. It includes the following procedures:

- Systematic inquiry—asking the right questions,
- Observation and critical analysis—evaluating responses to inquires in light of other data gathered, knowledge of the industry, and a general understanding of business risks and how they interrelate, and
- Follow-up—making additional inquiries and seeking corroborating evidence when necessary.

Because of the flexible nature of a businessman's review, the fact-finding process cannot be standardized. The manner in which such efforts progress depends on the needs of the purchaser. The extent of corroborating evidence sought, if any, depends on judgment, the circumstances, and whether such evidence is required as a part of the predetermined scope of the review. The approach followed should never be mechanical; the acquisition team should always be able to react to additional information uncovered.

In performing fact-finding procedures, obtaining information on a target company through inquiring and observation can be difficult. Even the most experienced review team should be alert to certain pitfalls inherent in the process. For various reasons the target company's management may view the due diligence process as somewhat adversarial, despite previously positive negotiations, causing them to be uncooperative or inclined to color the facts to present the company in its best possible light.

In addition, the process of inquiry requires experience at asking the right questions along with an intuitive grasp of how deeply one can probe without disrupting the progress being made toward an acquisition, merger, or other agreement. Some of the more frequent pitfalls encountered are given below.

2.3 Frequent Pitfalls In Evaluating a Target

Omitting key questions or question areas.   Perhaps the most important qualitative characteristic possessed by the due diligence team is business acumen. Such acumen is developed over time through involvement in other fact-finding missions. Without experience, it is difficult to ask the right questions; over time, however, the members of the team should have acquired a natural understanding of how potential business risks interrelate. For example, take the case of a manufacturer who sells machinery through independent dealerships. Inquiries about these dealerships should focus on the terms of dealership agreements, floor-planning arrangements, and customer financing on which the company is directly or contingently liable, as well as on the size and financial stability of the dealers themselves, along with the possibility that the company may be forced to acquire one or more dealerships in order to sustain its marketing efforts.

Failure to utilize appropriate industry or technical expertise. Inquiries often cover areas requiring a specialized understanding of scientific terms, productive processes, unusual industry conditions, and so on. The team should prepare for these areas by involving the appropriate experts or specialists prior to initial fact-finding if possible. For example, a manufacturer of precision aircraft parts may use numerous metal-forming events to create each product. The effectiveness with which these events are integrated may be measurable only by an industrial chemist.

Vague or unclear responses. Inquiries may be hindered by the inability or unwillingness of management to respond in a well-defined fashion. Company managers also may be concerned that a specific answer would be in conflict with previously obtained information. To some extent, persistence in follow-up inquiry can overcome this problem. Nonetheless, inquirers are often not able to draw out the information needed to describe a business area adequately.

Incomplete information. Management may seek to increase the perceived attractiveness of the company by providing partial responses to various inquiries. For example, it may be disclosed that overall employee turnover has declined 20 percent in the past year without mentioning that a key level of skilled employee has actually experienced increased turnover. An alert inquirer can often pursue question areas to minimize such hidden information.

Incorrect information. Unless the team is charged with the verification of certain information received, it may be impossible to determine whether one is receiving accurate responses. The inquirer should at all times be observing events which may be in conflict with the answers or information being received. When possible, the inquirer also should ask several managers to provide their perspectives on a given area of inquiry.

Responses in inappropriate form. Very often, in an attempt to save time, management will react to a request for information by providing documents or answers which do not directly satisfy the request. For example, assume a request is made for a summary of independent dealerships which sell a company's product, along with the key terms of each dealership agreement. Management may supply voluminous legal documentation which must be scrutinized at length in order to uncover the information desired. This presents the team with the choice of devoting extra time to this task or redirecting management to respond more precisely.

Lack of cooperation. The willingness of a company's shareholders to permit business inquiries to be made by outsiders does not guarantee the understanding and cooperation of management. During the inquiry process, managers must satisfy normal responsibilities simultaneously with unusual requests for information. In the case of a prospective acquisition of the company, managers may feel their positions are endangered through cooperation. The result can be an unwillingness to participate satisfactorily in the due diligence review.

Demand for further commitment prior to proceeding. Inquirers may find that management is not expecting the depth of review it is subject to. The prospective seller may decide to cut off the inquiry process and require that, in order for additional time to be devoted to describing the company, a formal agreement be reached (if one has not already been reached). In effect, this is a negotiating ploy which must be dealt with by the purchaser.

Limitations on access to people or operating locations. Management may decide that, rather than cut off inquiries or refuse to answer all questions, it will limit the team to one or several persons at a single location, possibly away from the heart of operations. If the review is intended to be an in-depth fact-finding mission, such limitations can undercut the purchaser's objectives. Access to the right persons in an organization and direct observation of operations and productive facilities are almost always crucial to a satisfactory description of the business.

Delays in response. The problems mentioned above can surface in the form of slow responses to requests for information. For example, interim financial statements available within a few days or a week of the period covered may be withheld for several weeks. Such delays can create severe difficulties in meeting contractual deadlines relating to an acquisition, merger, or other agreement.

To summarize: The inquiry process cannot be standarized. The flow of questioning must be adapted to the information received. Sources of information and the willingness with which it is provided are unlikely to match the purchaser's needs. Specialists should be used when needed.

Below are a few brief examples of mistakes that can be made when performing fact-finding procedures. This list is not comprehensive but illustrative in nature.

Considering the cash flow potential of different business segments without understanding the tax treaties between various countries which could impact the ability to repatriate earnings,

Evaluating operational efficiency without considering severance statutes in different countries,

Obtaining a summary of pension assets and vested benefits without information as to the underlying assumed rates of return on plan assets,

Analyzing overall employee turnover without regard to specific employee classifications,

Describing an independent dealer network without examining the past history of dealer additions and/or cancellations,

Failing to consider the impact of socio-economic or political changes on future operating potential (e.g., 1992),

Observing general cleanliness, safety features, and work flow without noticing the attitude of employees,

Inquiring as to the reputation of past accountants without obtaining an explanation for why they were dropped,

Discussing methods of buying and selling commodities or financial instruments without inquiring about whether appropriate protective financial steps (like hedging) are taken,

Failing to follow up on pending items,

Failing to inform the purchaser of delays in obtaining information which the seller may wish to stress during negotiations,

Obtaining internal projections without understanding the basis for their preparation,

Listing the selling shareholders without investigating their relationship to one another and/or their motivations in considering a sale,

Analyzing past tax returns without asking if they have been subject to a tax audit,

Comparing relative product contributions to revenues on a dollar basis without considering relative unit sales, and

Failing to establish a clear, initial understanding as to the specific objectives for the overall due diligence process and for the businessman's review in particular.

2.4 What to Look For

The end product of the due diligence process is a level of comfort for the purchaser with respect to the quality of the operation being acquired.

In evaluating a prospective target, it is often difficult to separate the financial and nonfinancial areas of investigation, since there are numerous overlaps. For example, the evaluation of the target's management and staff personnel is a nonfinancial consideration, but the amount of their compensation and fringe benefits, as well as the adequacy of amounts provided therefore in the target's financial statements is clearly a financial concern. Since accounting tends to have a quantitative emphasis, we shall concentrate on the financial aspects of evaluating the target, specifically on the assets, liabilities and operations reported in its financial statements.

The checklist at the end of this chapter outlines the types of information about the target that the acquisition team normally needs to obtain. What the purchaser is looking for in accumulating and studying such data can be highlighted below for major financial statement captions.

CASH

Periodic cash flow (and working capital) requirements. This is a real concern in financing the proposed acquisition.

Opportunities for improved cash management.

Restrictions on the use of cash based upon existing agreements with lenders.

RECEIVABLES

Existence and business validity of amounts owed.

Aggressiveness of target in approving customers' credit and in expediting collections.

Exposure to bad debts and adequacy of financial statement provisions.

Predictability of returns, allowances, and other customer credits.

Value as part of an ongoing borrowing base of collateral.

Profile of overall customer base to the extent derivable from a detailed aging of individual customer accounts.

Relationship of receivables to sales.

INVENTORIES

Existence and ultimate saleability.

Reasonableness of inventory cost accumulation and overhead allocation systems.

Strategic business purpose for overall inventory levels, including raw material, work-in-process, and finished goods components.

Effectiveness of inventory management program.

Net realizeable values within defined operating cycle.

Financial statement exposure for quality control and environmental problems.

Relationships of inventories to accounts payable.

Value as part of an ongoing borrowing base of collateral.

PROPERTY, PLANT, AND EQUIPMENT

Existence and usage relative to capacity.

Adequacy of insurance coverage.

Net realizable value of assets not held for production.

Capital expenditure and repair and maintenance requirements.

Appropriateness of previous depreciation policies.

Value as part of an ongoing borrowing base if collateral.

Extent to which productive assets are leased, rather than owned.

INTANGIBLE ASSETS

Current business value as compared to historical cost of acquisition.

Appropriateness of amortization period.

Relationship of intangible assets to total assets.

DEBT

Historical availability of credit, annually and seasonally.

Borrowing profile of the target, to the extent determinable from the terms and conditions of credit agreements, including interest rates, degree of collateralization significance of affirmative and negative covenants, and maturities.

Ability to assume existing debt.

Amount of credit available relative to the borrowing base of assets, historical and ongoing.

ACCOUNTS PAYABLE

Profile of suppliers to the extent determinable from a detailed schedule of amounts owed to vendors.

Relationship of accounts payable to inventories.

Accumulation and financial statement recording of all known liabilities.

Exposure for open purchase commitments, if any.

Opportunities to improve cash flow through accounts payable management.

COMMITMENTS AND CONTINGENCIES

Accounting policy for accrual of contingencies
Employee benefit obligations, both before and after retirement.
Exposure to litigation and unasserted claims.
Availability of and amounts outstanding under letters of credit.
Guaranty of indebtedness or performance of others.
Extent of uninsured risks.
Exposure to product liability or warranty.
Appropriateness of expense cutoff, as accrued in the balance sheet.

SALES

Appropriateness of revenue recognition policies.
Trends in sales units compared to prices.
Relationship of sales to working capital requirements.
Proximity of actual sales to budgeted amounts.
Correlation between historical sales and amounts projected in the future.
Exposure to loss of significant customers.
Exposure to settlements related to sales under government contracts.
Relationship of sales persons' compensation to sales.
Cost-effectiveness of advertising and promotion programs and the timing of reflecting expenditures for such in the financial statements.

COST OF SALES

Relationship of production cost changes to sales prices.
Impact of inventory shrinkage in assessing overall level of production control.
Proximity of actual gross profits to budgeted amounts.
Correlation between historical costs and amounts projected in the future.
Cost exposure relative to changes in sources of supply.
Explanations for one-time charges to cost of sales.

GENERAL AND ADMINISTRATIVE EXPENSES

Explanations for one-time, on nonrecurring charges
Effect of transactions with related parties on financial position and results of operations, including goods and services provided to the target without charge (such as computer processing, treasury functions, personnel administration, and the like).

Opportunities to reduce costs on a going forward basis, including operating synergies.

TAXES

Exposure to additional income and taxes for previous years.

Extent to which tax returns are filed in jurisdictions where target is deemed to be operating.

Effectiveness of previous tax planning on a domestic and international level.

Tax attributes of the target that have the potential to carry over to the purchaser.

Nature and extent of differences between income and expenses reported in the financial statements and tax returns.

Nature of nondeductible expenses.

Extent to which the current tax posture of the target helps or hinders the tax structure contemplated for the proposed acquisition, on a global basis.

3.0 POSTACQUISITION CONSIDERATIONS

To this point the accounting aspects of mergers and acquisitions have been associated with events and processes that have occurred prior to the actual consummation of the transaction: First, there is a need to understand the accounting bases for financial information about the target that has been provided to the purchaser. Once the purchaser relates the accounting principles and methods underlying such information to his own country's GAAP, the due diligence process accelerates in a substantive way and the assets, liabilities and operations of the target are evaluated qualitatively by the acquisition team.

If the purchaser and seller are ultimately able to agree on all of the terms and conditions for a specific deal, a written agreement is executed and a closing date is scheduled. The closing date for an acquisition has a twofold significance: First, it signifies the official transfer of ownership of the target from the seller to the purchaser; second, it confirms the responsibilities of the purchaser to integrate the newly-acquired entity into its own operating and/or reporting systems. Some acquired companies will be operated as fully self-sufficient, standalone businesses, while others will be completely merged or otherwise operationally combined with the purchaser's existing business and lose all or a part of their previous identity.

Since a substantial number of international acquisitions result in acquired companies operating as individual free-standing entities (particularly true in the case of acquisitions of U.S. companies by non-U.S. acquirers), a great deal of effort will be required in order to ensure that the acquirer can monitor the financial position and results of operations of its new business from a distance, even though representatives from the parent will often be permanently on site. In order to react quickly to sudden changes in sales volumes, production costs, local and/or global economic conditions, and the like, the new acquisition will need to be well controlled and organized in a manner conducive to reliable financial reporting, both internal and external reporting. Thus, the next section of our discussion focuses on the concept of *internal* control within the new company, and in the final section we discuss *external* financial reporting responsibilities and audit requirements which the new company may face in a number of different countries around the world.

3.1 Understanding Internal Controls

Internal control refers to all of the various methods and measures adopted within an entity to safeguard its assets, check the accuracy and reliability of its accounting and other data, promote operational efficiency, and encourage adherence to prescribed managerial policies.[6] In discussing internal control, one needs to distinguish between administrative controls and accounting controls.

Administrative controls include, but are not limited to, the plan of organization and the procedures and records that are concerned with the decision processes leading to management's authorization of transactions. Such authorization is a management function directly associated with the responsibility for achieving the objectives of the organization and is the starting point for establishing accounting control of transactions.

Accounting controls comprise the plan of organization and the procedures and records that are concerned with the safeguarding of assets and the reliability of financial records and consequently are designed to provide reasonable assurance that

1. Transactions are executed in accordance with management's general or specific authorization.
2. Transactions are recorded (1) to permit preparation of financial statements in conformity with the recognized and accepted accounting principles of the country in which the operation is located and (2) to maintain accountability for assets.

[6]Peat, Marwick, Mitchell & Co., *Action Plan for Reviewing Internal Accounting Controls,* 1978, and as revised.

3. Access to assets is permitted only in accordance with management's authorization.

4. The recorded accountability for assets is compared with the existing assets at reasonable intervals and appropriate action is taken with respect to any differences.

The two types of controls are not necessarily mutually exclusive; certain procedures and records may serve as both accounting controls and administrative controls. For example, maintaining personnel records provides wage and salary information necessary for accounting controls, but it also can provide performance evaluation information to be used in obtaining greater productivity from personnel assignments, and so be an administrative control. Notwithstanding the overlap that may exist between accounting and administrative controls, the accounting and finance officers of the acquirer will be concentrating on the accounting controls necessary to measure the performance of the acquired assets and operations and report the results of such measuring process to top management.

Objectives of internal accounting control. The objectives of internal accounting control can be classified into three categories (authorization, accounting, and safeguarding) which will be referred to as the broad objectives of internal accounting controls.

Every system of internal accounting control must satisfy these broad objectives, but the manner in which this is accomplished will vary from company to company based on the types of assets involved and the complexity of the company's operations.

In an effective system of internal accounting controls, appropriate segregation of duties plays an important role. In most cases, the duties related to the three broad objectives of internal accounting controls—authorization, accounting, and safeguarding—should be segregated by having them performed by different individuals.

Authorization. The core of the internal accounting control system rests on the premise that all transactions proceed from a plan of authorization. Thus, certain transactions will be specifically authorized and others will be authorized by an established policy or operating procedure. For example, specific authorization may be needed to acquire a building costing $10,000,000, but periodic supply purchases may be made in accordance with previously established limitations. In no event, however, should any transaction occur without some form of authorization.

Accounting. This broad objective means a company's accounts and records should reflect transactions as executed. Transactions should be properly described, entered in appropriate accounts, and recorded in the accounting period to which they relate, in the actual amounts involved. If these procedures are followed, it should be possible to prepare reliable financial statements from the records and accounts, and to maintain accountability for assets.

Safeguarding.   To achieve the objective of safeguarding assets, limiting access to authorized persons is necessary. Depending on the nature of the assets involved, a variety of devices for limiting access may be used. For example, access to certain assets, such as valuable securities maintained in safe deposit boxes, might require the presence of two or more senior company officials, whereas access to cash, inventory, and other assets may require other means of cross-verification. The problem of safeguarding assets requires sensitive handling because sufficient access must be allowed so that business operations are not stifled, and yet access must be restricted to authorized persons.

As a further step in the process of accounting for and safeguarding assets, it is necessary at various intervals to compare the assets actually on hand to the amounts recorded. The frequency with which these comparisons are made will vary with the nature of the assets. In a company with a high dollar amount of inventory consisting of many different items, some loss will result through physical deterioration, errors in record keeping, etc. In this case, an adequate system of internal accounting controls would include a periodic comparison of the records to inventory on hand, so that appropriate adjustments for loss and corrections may be made.

3.2 Administration of the Accounting Function

Delineated controls over transaction processing may not function properly because of human error. Consequently, consideration should be given to the supplemental controls that can minimize this potential for error. These controls usually include:

- Budgeting procedures providing for realistic comparison of budgeted to actual results and for timely investigation of significant variations,
- Internal financial reports covering areas of control responsibility (responsibility reporting) that are promptly issued after the close of the reporting period,
- Procedures for comparing nonfinancial reports prepared by operating departments with data included in financial reports (comparison of sales forecasts to physical inventory listings to check for potentially obsolete inventory),

- Staffing appropriate in numbers of personnel needed to process the accounting data effectively, the skills required in the processing function, and the integrity of the personnel, and
- Accounting policies and procedures defined in current manuals which include charts of accounts, account content descriptions, record retention policies, and the like.

3.3 Protection of Physical Assets

Use of company assets is a necessary part of day-to-day operations of a business but, to safeguard assets, use should be limited to authorized personnel. Protection of physical assets may be accomplished through various procedures, including

- Restricting access to offices, plants, and other company premises to authorized personnel by use of guards, fences, locked areas, and so on,
- Protecting assets subject to deterioration from the elements,
- Storing important records in facilities that are either locked or under continuous surveillance,
- Storing negotiable documents in protective containers, such as fireproof safes or vaults, to which no person has sole access,
- Maintaining written disaster plans and off-premises storage of backup files for all critical records,
- Investigating the integrity of personnel hired to fill sensitive positions, and
- Periodically reviewing the adequacy of insurance coverage.

3.4 Internal Audit Function

Many companies have internal audit function as an additional element of control. Activities frequently carried out by internal auditors may consist of

- Reviewing and appraising the soundness of accounting and administrative controls,
- Ascertaining the extent of compliance with established policies, plans, and procedures,
- Ascertaining that company assets are accounted for and safeguarded from losses,

- Ascertaining the reliability of accounting and other data developed within the organization, and
- Recommending improvements in controls.

Like other general controls, internal auditing does not directly affect the validity of data produced as a result of the various transactions. This function can, however, contribute significantly to the control consciousness of the business.

3.5 Transaction Cycle Approach to Controls

When transactions are both frequent and of a similar type, accounting systems and procedures are adopted to process each phase in the transaction cycle on a regular basis. Internal accounting controls within a transaction cycle may be exercised in several different departments and encompass several activities.

The transaction cycle approach to consideration of controls may be outlined as follows:

- Identify the operation's transaction cycles.
- Identify specific objectives within the transaction cycles to achieve the broad control objectives for any transaction—authorization, accounting, and safeguarding.
- Identify the control procedures designed to achieve the specific objectives.

Identifying transaction cycles.   The type and number of transaction cycles vary from entity to entity, but major cycles generally relate to frequent and similar transactions. The major transaction cycles typical of a manufacturing company are as follows.

- *Revenue Cycle:* Transactions that occur in the basic revenue generating process. Typical activities include:
  —order entry,
  —shipping,
  —billing,
  —credit and collection,
  —maintenance of receivable records, and
  —cash receipts.
- *Expenditure Cycle:* Transactions that occur in the acquisition of goods and services in exchange for payment. Typical activities include:

—requisitioning and purchasing,
—receiving,
—accounts payable,
—cash disbursements, and
—payroll.
* *Production Cycle:* Transactions that occur in the production of goods for resale. Typical activities include:
—inventory recordkeeping,
—material usage, and
—inventory costing.

This list is not intended to be all inclusive, nor is it illustrative of nonmanufacturing entities. For example, significant transaction cycles for financial institutions might include loan origination, obtaining deposits, and processing payments.

3.6 Specific Cycle Control Objectives and Procedures to Achieve Them

For the three transaction cycles named above, specific cycle control objectives have been identified and classified under the previously mentioned broad objectives of internal accounting controls, authorization, accounting, and safeguarding, in Tables 4.2, 4.3, and 4.4 that follow. Examples of procedures to achieve the specific cycle objectives are also presented in the three tables. Performing all listed procedures might not be necessary; one or more of the example procedures might be followed, or alternatives not listed may be used. For each procedure the departments or functions likely to be involved are also identified. It should be noted that these tables can also be employed during the due diligence process to evaluate the overall control-consciousness, as well as specific controls, of the proposed target.

3.7 Computer Controls

The reporting process encompasses obtaining input from transaction records as the basis for making accounting entries to a general ledger, and preparing financial reports. Many operations' transactions are frequently processed and recorded with the aid of computer facilities. Therefore, when reviewing controls within transaction cycles, controls over computer facilities and operations also must be considered.

If controls in the computer area are unsound, the entire system of internal accounting controls is subject to risk despite the quality of controls in all other aspects of company operations. Since the computer or data processing center (EDP) acts as a kind of service bureau to other

TABLE 4.2 Revenue Cycle

Control Objectives	Procedures to Achieve Control Objectives	Department or Function						
		Order Entry	Shipping	Billing	Credit & Collection	Maintenance of Receivable Records	Cash Receipts
Authorization							
1. Products and services should be provided only on the basis of appropriate authorization.	Clear criteria and policies for customer acceptance.	X			X		
	Maintenance of an approved customer master file.	X		X			
	Procedures for adding to, deleting from, or changing information in the master file.	X		X			
	Approved shipping order required for products to leave premises.	X	X				
2. Credit terms for products and services should be granted on the basis of appropriate authorization.	Written credit policies.	X			X		
	Credit limits established for individual customers.	X			X		
	Documentation of specific approval of credit granted in excess of established limits.	X			X		
	Assignment of responsibility for approval of credit granted to new customers.	X			X		
3. Prices for products and services should be properly authorized including allowances, discounts, and freight.	Maintenance of master files of approved selling prices, standard allowances and discount terms, shipping terms, etc.	X		X			

(continued)

TABLE 4.2 (continued)

Control Objectives	Procedures to Achieve Control Objectives	Order Entry	Shipping	Billing	Credit & Collection	Maintenance of Receivable Records	Cash Receipts
							Department or Function
Authorization (cont.)							
	Periodic independent reviews of sales records to ascertain conformity with established policies.			X			
	Established procedures for adding to, deleting from, or changing information included in the master files.	X		X			
4. Entries and adjustments within the revenue cycle should be properly authorized.	Assignment of criteria and/or responsibility for approvals of sales returns,			X	X		
	credit memos over stated amount, and			X	X		
	write-offs of receivables over a stated amount.				X		
	Approved receiving report required for acceptance of product returned.			X	X		
	Approval of entries and adjustments.			X	X	X	X
Accounting							
5. All products and services delivered, and only those delivered, should be recorded.	Use and control of prenumbered bills of lading and shipping order forms.		X	X			

Control procedure			
Maintenance of shipping logs listing shipping order forms in numerical order to facilitate accounting for prenumbered documents.	X	X	
Matching of prenumbered sales invoices to shipping documents.		X	
Procedures to control back orders and partial shipments.	X	X	
Rechecking of quantities of orders filled by a second individual.	X		
Matching of prenumbered sales invoices to shipping documents.		X	
Independent check of sales invoices as to pricing, mathematical computations, allowances, etc.		X	
Independent and prompt investigation of customer queries and complaints.	X	X	X
Policies for investigation of credit balances.		X	X
Use of a chart of accounts and accounting procedures manual containing adequate details and clear instructions.		X	X
Use of standard journal entries.		X	X
Sales cutoff procedures.		X	X

6. Individual invoices should be prepared accurately and on a timely basis.

7. All sales and related activities and transactions (e.g., cost of sales, selling expenses, receivables) should be properly recorded, classified, and summarized.

(continued)

TABLE 4.2 (continued)

Control Objectives		Department or Function					
Procedures to Achieve Control Objectives		Order Entry	Shipping	Billing	Credit & Collection	Maintenance of Receivable Records	Cash Receipts
Accounting (cont.)							
Use of prenumbered sales invoices.				X		X	
Periodic reconciliation of subsidiary accounts with general ledger accounts.				X		X	
Independent and prompt investigation of customer queries and complaints.				X	X	X	
Statements mailed to customers periodically with subsequent investigation of any differences reported.						X	
Maintenance of an aged trial balance of accounts and notes receivable.						X	
Use and control of prenumbered forms.				X		X	
Maintenance of sales register or journal.				X			
Procedures to record sales-related transactions (e.g., cost of sales).				X			
Independent check of journal entries for supporting documentation,				X		X	

Control objective	A	B	C	D
mathematical computations, and account distribution.				
Period-to-period comparisons of recurring journal entries.	X			
Procedures to ensure that related receivables and payables are recorded within the same accounting period where shipments are made or services rendered directly to customers by vendors.	X			
8. Cash receipts should be accurately and promptly recorded, classified, and summarized.				
Posting of cash receipts promptly to the accounts receivable subsidiary records.			X	
Comparison of initial recording of cash upon receipt to bank deposit slips and accounting entries.			X	X
Statements mailed to customers periodically with subsequent investigation of any reported differences.			X	
Maintenance of cash receipts register or journal.				X

Safeguarding

Control objective	A	B	C	D
9. Effective collection procedures should be established.				
Assignment of responsibility to oversee established collection policies and procedures.		X		
Timely investigation of past due accounts.		X		
Control and follow-up on accounts written off.		X	X	

(continued)

139

TABLE 4.2 (continued)

Control Objectives	Procedures to Achieve Control Objectives	Department or Function					
		Order Entry	Shipping	Billing	Credit & Collection	Maintenance of Receivable Records	Cash Receipts
Safeguarding (cont.)							
10. Cash receipts should be adequately protected from theft or misappropriation.	Independent control of cash items upon receipt (e.g., lock box, pre-listing of cash receipts with subsequent comparison to bank deposit slip).						X
	Checks stamped with restrictive endorsement upon receipt.						X
	Independent surprise counts of cash funds on hand.						X
11. Records, operating systems, processing areas, and physical assets should be protected from misuse or destruction.	Keeping important records in storage facilities that are locked or under continuous surveillance.			X	X	X	
	Restricting access to offices, plants, etc., to authorized personnel by use of guards, locked facilities, etc.		X	X		X	X
	Assignment of responsibility for custody of notes.				X	X	
	Protection of important records against physical hazards (e.g., fireproof cabinets).			X	X	X	

TABLE 4.3 Disbursement-Expenditure Cycle

Control Objectives	Procedures to Achieve Control Objectives	Department or Function					
		Purchasing	Receiving	Accounts Payable	Disbursements	Payroll	Other
Authorization							
1. The purchasing of products and services should be initiated only on the basis of appropriate authorization.	Purchase orders initiated on the basis of purchase requisitions or other appropriate documentation approved by authorized personnel (e.g., heads of departments requesting purchases).	X					
	Policies established for approving issuance of purchase orders covering such matters as personnel authorized to approve types, quantities, prices, and terms of products and services to be purchased; competitive bidding procedures; maintenance of multiple buying sources; long-term contractual supply commitments; and capital expenditures; and	X					

(continued)

TABLE 4.3 (continued)

Control Objectives	Procedures to Achieve Control Objectives	Department or Function					
		Purchasing	Receiving	Accounts Payable	Disbursements	Payroll	Other
Authorization (cont.)							
	nonroutine transactions (e.g., related party transactions, employee purchases).						X
	Policies established for authorization to acquire products and services not covered by purchase orders.						
2. Products and services should be obtained from properly authorized vendors.	Clear criteria for vendor acceptance.	X					
	Maintenance of approved vendor master file.	X					
	Procedures for adding to, deleting from, or changing information in the master file.	X					
	Approvals needed when competitive bids are required but not requested or when other than the lowest bidder is used.	X					

time cards or other documentation of time worked, and overtime, shift changes, department changes, etc.		X
Approval of payrolls by persons outside the payroll department.		X
4. Compensation rates and payroll deductions should be properly authorized.		
Written authorization (outside the payroll department) required for individual wage or salary rates and changes.	X	
Signed payroll withholding forms required for payroll deductions.	X	X
5. Disbursements should be made by appropriate personnel only for authorized expenditures.		
Check signers designated by the board of directors.		
Checks prepared only on the basis of appropriate documentation.	X	
Review of supporting data by persons who sign checks.		
6. Entries and adjustments within the disbursement-expenditure cycle should be properly authorized.		
Approval of journal entries and adjustments.	X	X
Approval required for adjustments made to amounts due vendors.	X	
Approval required for garnishments, termination payments, corrections to gross or net pay, special payments, etc.		X

(continued)

143

TABLE 4.3 (continued)

Control Objectives	Procedures to Achieve Control Objectives	Purchasing	Receiving	Accounts Payable	Disbursements	Payroll	Other
Accounting							
7. The receipt and acceptance of requested goods and services.	Requirement to inspect, count, and weigh products received.		X				
	Preparation of written receiving reports.		X				
	Appropriate record of receipts (e.g., prenumbered receiving reports, receiving log that sequentially lists such receipts).		X				
	Omission of quantities from copies of purchase orders furnished to receiving department.		X				
8. Amounts due to vendors and others for products and services received should be accurately determined and promptly recorded and classified.	Use of and control over prenumbered receiving reports to ascertain that receipt of goods and services is recognized within the appropriate accounting period.			X			
	Maintenance of a record of open purchase orders and commitments.	X					
	Vendor invoices received directly from the mail opener by personnel			X			

sons who process them for payment.

Control over vendor invoices established immediately upon receipt. — X

Duplicate copies of invoices clearly marked immediately upon receipt to prevent duplicate payment. — X

Reconciliation of monthly statements from vendors to unpaid vendor invoices or accounts payable subsidary ledgers. — X

Procedures established for processing vendor invoices, such as — X

comparison of terms, prices, and quantities to purchase orders,

comparison of items and quantities to receiving reports,

mathematical check of footings, extensions, and discounts,

check of account distribution,

check vendor invoices not covered by purchase orders for appropriate documentation and approval, and

evidence of final approval indicating that the above procedures were performed.

(continued)

TABLE 4.3 (continued)

Control Objectives	Procedures to Achieve Control Objectives	Department or Function					
		Purchasing	Receiving	Accounts Payable	Disbursements	Payroll	Other
Accounting (cont.)	Investigation of unmatched purchase orders, receiving reports, and vendor invoices.			X			
	Freight bills compared to vendor invoices and receiving reports.			X			
	Maintenance of an accounts payable subsidiary ledger that is periodically reconciled with general ledger.			X			
	Return purchases controlled to ensure that the vendor will be charged.			X			
	Procedures to ensure that related receivables and payables are recorded within the accounting period when shipments are made or services rendered directly to customers by vendors.			X			
	Procedures for adjustment resulting from settlement of disputed items.			X			

Procedures for partial payments of vendor invoices to avoid duplicate payment upon completion of order. — X

Stop payment orders issued on checks outstanding for a stated period of time with follow-up as necessary. — X

Procedures for purchases made for employees. — X

9. Cash disbursements should be recorded based upon a recognized liability.

Checks prenumbered and accounted for. — X

Review of supporting data by persons who sign checks. — X

Persons who sign checks or control use of facsimile signature independent of — X

the purchasing department or other department requesting the specific expenditure; and

persons approving vendor invoices for payment.

Comparison of payments to detail accounts payable listing, voucher register, payroll register, or other records. — X X

Maximum check amount for payroll checks. — X

(continued)

TABLE 4.3 (continued)

Control Objectives	Procedures to Achieve Control Objectives	Purchasing	Receiving	Accounts Payable	Disbursements	Payroll	Other
					Department or Function		
Accounting (cont.)							
	Special procedures (e.g., manual signatures) for certain types of unusual checks (e.g., large amounts, special payroll checks, adjustment checks).				X	X	
	Procedures for voiding, explaining, and disposing of voided checks.				X	X	
10. Labor used should be accurately determined and promptly recorded in the proper accounting period.	Time cards or other attendance records used as a basis for preparation of wage payrolls.					X	
	Attendance hours reconciled to actual labor hours paid.					X	
	When employees are paid on the basis of output, payments based on labor tickets or other output records reconciled with production records.					X	
	Compensation rates periodically compared to rate authorizations (e.g., union contracts).					X	
	Persons who perform the following functions independent of each other:					X	

approving hours worked,

preparing payroll,

operating the facsimile signature machine,

signing payroll checks, and controlling facsimile signature plate.

Check of calculation of payroll deductions (e.g., by agreeing in total with predetermined control totals or by sufficient checking of individual amounts).

Payroll deductions recorded in separate control accounts; payments of payroll deductions agreed to such amounts.

Cutoff procedures established to ensure that payrolls are accrued in the proper period.

Deposits to imprest bank account compared to net payroll.

Use of a chart of accounts and accounting procedures manual containing adequate details and clear instructions.

Procedures for disbursement-expenditure cycle entries and adjustments established, such as

11. Purchases of goods and services, cash disbursements, and payroll should be properly recorded, classified, and summarized.

(continued)

149

TABLE 4.3 (continued)

Control Objectives	Procedures to Achieve Control Objectives	Department or Function					
		Purchasing	Receiving	Accounts Payable	Disbursements	Payroll	Other
Accounting (cont.)							
	use of standard journal entries; use of prenumbered forms; review and approval of account coding and distribution; periodic reconciliation of subsidiary accounts to general ledger accounts; and use of imprest payroll bank accounts.						
	Procedures established for developing, summarizing, and reporting tax information.				X	X	X
	Maintenance of a voucher register or purchase journal.				X		
	Maintenance of a payroll register or journal.						X
	Maintenance of a cash disbursements register or journal.					X	
Safeguarding							
12. Records and unused documents (e.g., checks, vouchers, check requests)	Keeping important records stored in areas that are locked or under continuous surveillance.	X	X	X	X	X	

should be protected
from theft, misuse,
destruction, or misap-
propriation

Control						
should be protected from theft, misuse, destruction, or misappropriation						X
Restricting access to offices, records, and critical forms to authorized personnel by use of guards, locked facilities, etc.		X	X	X	X	
Supply of unused checks stored in a safe place and under the custody of persons who do not sign checks manually, control the use of facsimile signature plates, or operate the facsimile signature machine.	X	X				X
Invoices and supporting documentation cancelled upon payment by the person who manually signs the checks or controls the use of the facsimile signature plate, or by persons who did not prepare checks or approve vouchers for payment.			X	X		
Spoiled checks mutilated to prevent reuse and kept in a file for subsequent inspection.		X	X			
Checks mailed without allowing them to return to persons who prepared checks or approved vouchers for payment.			X			
Facsimile signature plates locked in a safe place when not in use.		X	X			X

(continued)

151

TABLE 4.3 (continued)

Control Objectives / Procedures to Achieve Control Objectives	Department or Function					
	Purchasing	Receiving	Accounts Payable	Disbursements	Payroll	Other
Safeguarding (cont.)						
If the custodian of the facsimile signature plate is not the machine operator, determination by the custodian that only authorized checks have been signed.				X	X	
Prohibition of signing of checks in advance of their being completely filled out.				X	X	
Rotation of persons distributing payroll checks.					X	
Procedures established to control unclaimed wages.					X	

TABLE 4.4 Production Cycle

Control Objectives	Procedures to Achieve Control Objectives	General Accounting	Cost Accounting	Production Control	Warehousing
			Department or Function		
Authorization					
1. Products should be produced only upon proper authorization.	Production schedules or job orders approved by designated personnel.			X	
2. Movement or transfer of materials and goods for production should occur only upon proper authorization.	Use of material requisitions to obtain materials from storerooms.				X
	Use of movement or transfer forms for movement of goods from one department to another or to finished goods.			X	
	Approval of transfers of inventory to other locations.			X	X
3. Entries and adjustments within the production cycle should be properly authorized.	Approval of journal entries and adjustments.	X	X		
	Approval of adjustments to perpetual records, accounting records, budgets, standard costs, bills of materials, etc.	X	X		
Accounting					
4. The inventory cost system should accurately determine and properly summarize, classify and report production and other inventory costs and economic activity (e.g., transfers and adjustments).	General ledger control of inventory cost systems.	X	X		
	Established policies for classification of production costs (e.g., direct and indirect labor, overhead).	X	X		
	Perpetual inventory system with quantities and values.		X		

(continued)

TABLE 4.4 (continued)

Control Objectives / Procedures to Achieve Control Objectives	General Accounting	Department or Function		
		Cost Accounting	Production Control	Warehousing
Accounting (cont.)				
Use of bills of material.		X		
Review and investigation of variances from standard costs.		X		
Established procedure to accumulate inventoriable costs, such as		X		
production reports or material requisitions used as a basis for raw materials put into production,				
production reports used to accumulate direct labor hours,				
direct labor hours reconciled to payroll records of actual hours paid, and				
overhead applied to inventory at predetermined rates.				
Inventory valuation policy in accordance with generally accepted accounting principles and covering such matters as basis for determining and valuing obsolete, slow-moving, damaged, or over-stocked products,	X	X		

determination and treatment of estimated shrinkage,				
determination and use of market values, and				
treatment of variances.				
Periodic review of inventory costs.			X	X
Transfer to finished products based on production reports.	X	X	X	X
5. Periodic verification and determination of inventory quantities should be undertaken.				
Complete periodic physical inventory (or cycle counts).	X		X	X
Adjustment of detailed inventory records to physical inventory count.			X	X
6. Entries and adjustments to the production cycle should be accurately determined and properly summarized, classified, and reported.				
Use of a chart of accounts and accounting procedures manual containing adequate details and clear instructions.			X	X
Use of standard journal entries.			X	
Use of prenumbered standard adjustment forms.			X	X
Review and approval of account coding and distributions.			X	X
Cutoff procedures for production and transfers to finished goods.		X	X	X
Summarized entries to record production and transfer to finished goods.		X	X	X

(continued)

TABLE 4.4 (continued)

Control Objectives	Procedures to Achieve Control Objectives	Department or Function			
		General Accounting	Cost Accounting	Production Control	Warehousing
Safeguarding					
7. Inventory should be protected from unauthorized use or removal and against physical deterioration.	Goods adequately safeguarded against loss by theft by being kept in locked buildings, rooms, or enclosures.				X
	Separate areas maintained for receiving, storekeeping, and shipping functions.				X
	Responsibility for protection and control of the various classes of inventory specifically assigned.			X	X
	Movement of inventory subject to verification by the area assuming responsibility for it.			X	X
	Control over consignments in and/or out.		X		X
	Control over inventory at outside locations (e.g., vendors, public warehouses).		X		X
8. Records should be protected from theft, misuse, destruction, etc.	Keeping important records in storage facilities that are locked or under continuous surveillance.	X	X	X	X
	Restricting access to office, plants, etc. to authorized personnel by use of guards, locked facilities, etc.	X	X	X	X
	Protection of important records against physical hazards (e.g., fireproof cabinets).	X	X	X	X

departments, a company should be concerned with controls within EDP itself as well as those over the movement of data into and out of EDP. Three aspects of the data-processing procedure deserve special attention.

1. *Organization and Operation of EDP.* Personnel involved in running EDP should not have access to any books of original entries or perform any other incompatible functions outside of EDP. Within EDP itself, the functions of the system design and programming should be separated from those related to operating and processing of data. If this separation of duties is maintained, the possibility of manipulating data for one's personal benefit will be reduced considerably.
2. *Hardware and Software.* Equipment and programs should be analyzed for appropriate controls and should be safeguarded against use by unauthorized persons or for unauthorized purposes.
3. *Input and Output.* Data should be furnished to EDP only on the basis of appropriate authorization. The department forwarding the data to EDP should develop a procedure to determine that data are complete when delivered to and received from EDP.

These control areas are but a few of the many that deserve consideration when computers are in use. Table 4.5 contains controls that should be imposed upon computer facilities so that this significant aspect of company operations can be considered in the overall integration plan.

4.0 FINANCIAL REPORTING AND AUDIT REQUIREMENTS

As stated previously, the reporting process of a company involves obtaining input from transaction records as the basis for making accounting entries to a general ledger and ultimately preparing financial reports. In multinational organizations, preparation of internal and external financial reports or statements typically requires consolidation and other procedures, such as translation of financial statements into the reporting currency of the parent company.

While internal management reporting requirements are determined on a company-by-company basis, external financial reporting, accounting principles used to generate financial statements contained in reports to "outsiders," and requirements for audits of such financial statements by external auditors are all prescribed on a country-by-country basis.

The financial reporting obligations of the acquirer and acquiree, on a postacquisition basis, can indeed be burdensome. Compliance with statutory and/or financing requirements, however, mandates the issuance of financial statements. Accordingly, both the parent and the acquired com-

TABLE 4.5 Computer Controls

Control Objectives	Procedures to Achieve Control Objectives	Department or Function					
		User Activity	Data Control	Data Processing Management	Computer Operations	Computer Library	Systems Development & Programming
Organization and Operation							
1. The (EDP) department should be organized to provide adequate segregation of duties and functions.	Separation of the following functions within the EDP department: application programming, including design, initial development, and maintenance, systems programming including initial generation of the operating system and its maintenance, operations covering all program processing, control and reconciliation of processing input and output to authorized personnel, and control of master and data files.		X	X	X	X	X

Control Procedure						
2. There should be segregation of functions between the EDP department and other departments.						
Provide physical as well as functional segregation and rotate personnel within a function.		X	X		X	X	X
Segregation of processing performed by the EDP department from the following noncompatible functions:	X	X					
initiation and authorization of transactions,							
initial recording of transactions,							
custody of assets other than computer equipment,							
changes to master files, and							
error correction unless the errors originated in the EDP department.							
3. Competent and thorough surveillance and review should be performed by EDP management.							
EDP management routinely reviews processing time, master and data file usage, and scheduling reports and logs.				X			

(continued)

TABLE 4.5 (continued)

Control Objectives	Procedures to Achieve Control Objectives			Department or Function				
		User Activity	Data Control	Data Processing Management	Computer Operations	Computer Library	Systems Development & Programming
Organization and Operation (cont.)							
4. Administrative and operational procedures should be instituted to establish an effective and control-conscious EDP department.	Procedures such as published organization charts, comprehensive written job descriptions, published policy and procedure manuals, continuing education programs, employee performance reviews, rotation of duties of personnel, formal procedures for forms control and record retention, formal activity logging and review procedures, physical security,		X	X	X	X	X

off-premises backup for important master files, documentation, and programs, insurance coverage, and disaster planning, including backup facilities and testing procedures.			
5. The EDP department should maintain objectivity and independence from source and user departments. Report to a high-level individual who has sufficient authority to ensure that the department will receive adequate support and effective management.		X	
Systems Development and Maintenance			
6. Systems design, programming techniques, and operating procedures should be standardized to promote operational efficiency and processing accuracy. Procedures generally found in systems and procedures manuals, operator manuals, and user manuals.	X	X	X
		X	
			X

(continued)

TABLE 4.5 (continued)

Control Objectives	Procedures to Achieve Control Objectives	User Activity	Data Control	Data Processing Management	Computer Operations	Computer Library	Systems Development & Programming
				Department or Function			
Systems Development and Maintenance							
7. New systems should produce greater benefits than other alternatives.	An operational plan established for new systems development that includes the following: initiation of development based on an overall priority plan, involvement of several departments including EDP, users, systems, and forms control in the design and development process, review and approval at each significant phase of the developmental process, documentation based on standards, adequate testing based on standards, and	X		X			X

controlled implementation and conversion of data.

8. Changes to programs after implementation should be controlled.

Changes to programs after their implementation reviewed, approved, documented, and tested with the same stringent procedures and methods used for the initial development of the system. | X

Hardware

9. Computer equipment should be maintained in good working order.

Control features inherent in the computer hardware, operating system, and other supporting software used to provide control over processing and operations and to report hardware malfunctions. | X

Follow equipment manufacturer's suggested scheduled preventative maintenance and hardware testing routines to ensure that hardware is performing accurately. | X | X

Provide necessary environmental controls in the computer room to protect equipment against | X | X

(continued)

TABLE 4.5 (continued)

Control Objectives	Procedures to Achieve Control Objectives	Department or Function					
		User Activity	Data Control	Data Processing Management	Computer Operations	Computer Library	Systems Development & Programming
Hardware (cont.)							
	excessive humidity, temperature, and other atmospheric conditions. The computer room should be protected against fire.						
	Formal procedures utilized for reporting hardware malfunctions.			X	X		
Access							
10. Only authorized personnel should have access to computer hardware, programs, program documentation, and data files.	Access to computer hardware limited to authorized individuals by			X	X		X
	control of traffic through the computer room by the use of special locks, limited access ways, and security, and						
	control of application programmers' and systems analysts' access to computer hardware.						

(continued)

Where remote terminals are used on a computer system, access to those terminals should be:

 physically restricted through the use of partitions, locked doors, and other physical means, and

 logically restricted through the use of passwords, terminal access keys, usage, and access logs, and monitored activity listings from each terminal. When passwords are used to control access, passwords should be assigned to specific individuals or groups and changed on a regular basis.

Access to program documentation limited to those persons who require it in the performance of their duties by separation of system design and programming functions from computer operations and

X   X   X   X

165

TABLE 4.5 (continued)

			Department or Function			
Control Objectives	Procedures to Achieve Control Objectives	User Activity	Data Control	Data Processing Management	Computer Operations	Computer Library	Systems Development & Programming
Access (cont.)	keeping program documentation in a secure place.						
	Access to production (current application) programs and master files limited to those individuals authorized to process or maintain particular systems.			X	X	X	
	A librarian function utilized to control the issuance and storage of all computer files.					X	
Data and Procedural							
11. There should be prompt and accurate processing of accounting imformation.	A control and balancing function performed by a separate group within the EDP department or by the appropriate user departments.	X	X				
	Written procedures prepared for computer operators.			X			X

Written procedures available for preparation of input for processing.				X
Off-premises backup provided for important files, data files, and programs as well as all necessary documentation for programs and operations.				X
Schedules for processing and output prepared and utilized by appropriate personnel.		X		X
Internal auditors:		X		
review new system development for adequate controls, auditability, and implementation,				
determine compliance with policies and procedures, and				
review existing systems on an ongoing basis.				X
12. There should be a review to ascertain adherence to established policies and procedures.		X		
Input				
13. There should be assurance that input is complete.		X	X	
Establish control totals in the user department prior to submitting data to EDP. Control totals may include record counts, hash totals, dollar totals, etc.				

(continued)

TABLE 4.5 (continued)

Control Objectives	Procedures to Achieve Control Objectives	Department or Function					
		User Activity	Data Control	Data Processing Management	Computer Operations	Computer Library	Systems Development & Programming
Input (cont.)							
	Verify that input data is received on a timely basis from user departments and physically controlled in the EDP department. Control may be achieved by using batch controls, document control numbers, efficient production scheduling, etc.	X	X				
	Review input forms for completeness prior to updating master files. This can be done manually in the user department prior to submitting documents to EDP and can also be economically performed by using programmed controls.	X					X

14. There should be assurance that errors or other rejected data are properly reentered into the system.	Proper control over processing rejected transactions, including: positive identification of rejected records, review and approval of the correction, and prompt reentry of the correction into the system where it will be subjected to the same input controls as the original data.	X	X
15. There should be assurance that only authorized transactions are accepted for processing by EDP.	Authorization can take many forms including: written approval on source documents, general authorization to process all of a department's transactions, and use of identification numbers, security codes, passwords, etc. for remote terminal users.	X	X

(continued)

TABLE 4.5 (continued)

Control Objectives	Procedures to Achieve Control Objectives	User Activity	Data Control	Data Processing Management	Computer Operations	Computer Library	Systems Development & Programming
Input (cont.)							
16. There should be assurance that input media are designed to reduce and control errors.	Use of concise and easily coded forms.	X					X
	Use of preprinted and pre-coded forms where appropriate.						X
	Instructions for completing forms should be clearly documented.	X					X
17. There should be assurance that all codes used to record data are substantiated.	Application programs to test the validity of input codes where feasible.	X					X
18. There should be assurance that movement of data between physical locations or during processing are controlled.	Application programs to verify control totals.		X				
	Prenumbered and controlled batching techniques established by user departments and/or control groups whenever appropriate.	X	X				
	Data transmitted by computers or terminals with transmission verification techniques.	X					X

Processing

	Description				
19. Data should be complete, accurate, and reasonable.	The computer's ability to perform logical testing utilized to perform editing routines on important data fields of an input record.		X		X
20. Data accuracy should be maintained throughout processing.	The use of the computer's ability to perform logical testing to ensure that data accuracy is maintained throughout processing by using programmed procedures included in each job step during the processing cycle.		X		X
21. Proper data files should be used for input.	Application programs to check internal header and trailer labels for data stored on magnetic media or control cards for data stored on punched cards.		X		X
	External labels checked by the machine operator to ensure that the correct files are being processed.	X	X		

(continued)

TABLE 4.5 (continued)

Control Objectives	Procedures to Achieve Control Objectives	Department or Function					
		User Activity	Data Control	Data Processing Management	Computer Operations	Computer Library	Systems Development & Programming
Output							
22. Output data should be complete and reasonable.	Input control totals reconciled to output control totals. This reconciliation may be performed with programmed reconciliation reports, or by manually reconciling totals on output reports with input control totals.	X	X				
	Input data compared item by item to output data to the extent considered reasonable or feasible by the user or control group. Detail review procedures would usually be employed for updating important master files or for error corrections.	X	X				
23. Output reports should be distributed to authorized personnel only.	The person receiving output reports clearly identified to EDP personnel responsible for distributing reports.	X	X				

24. Machine-sensible output should be properly identified and controlled.	Report recipients verify that all reports are promptly received.	X	X		X	X
	All magnetic media data files with appropriate internal leader and trailer labels as well as external labels and card files identified by control cards.				X	X
Documentation						
25. There should be assurance that adequate documentation exists for each application that describes the system and the procedures for performing the data processing function for that application.	An acceptable level of documentation for a computerized system, including flowcharts, operator's instructions, user manuals, etc.		X			X
File						
26. There should be assurance that enough backup exists to permit the file to be recreated if data is destroyed during processing.	Retention period of source documents adequate to permit reproducing transaction files.	X	X			
	Tape or disk files subjected to adequate on-premises and off-premises backup support.		X		X	

(continued)

TABLE 4.5 (continued)

Control Objectives	Procedures to Achieve Control Objectives	Department or Function					
		User Activity	Data Control	Data Processing Management	Computer Operations	Computer Library	Systems Development & Programming
File (cont.)							
27. There should be assurance that files are physically protected against damage by fire or other accidental damage or misuse.	Magnetic files stored in a temperature and humidity controlled, fireproof environment.			X			
	All important master files reproduced periodically and the duplicate copy stored off-premise. If this technique is not employed, some alternate form of master file protection (e.g., fireproof vault is used).			X		X	
	Files under the control of a librarian who controls distribution of the files, monitors expiration dates, etc.					X	

pany must coordinate the preparation of financial statements on a global basis.

In the pages that follow the financial reporting requirements, authoritative sources for acceptable accounting principles, and objectives for independent audits are summarized for the following[7]:

United States
Canada
Mexico
Brazil
France
Federal Republic of Germany
United Kingdom
Hong Kong
Japan

Note that the summaries included here were compiled within the twenty-four-month period prior to the publication date for this book. The reader should inquire therefore, regarding more recent legislation or regulations that would impact the discussion that follows.

4.1 United States

Public companies

Statutory Reports.   Companies whose securities are listed on a national securities exchange, those with securities traded over the counter and with total assets of over $3 million and 500 or more holders of one class of equity securities, or companies with over 300 holders of a class of securities registered under the Securities Act of 1933 must file annual and quarterly reports with the Securities and Exchange Commission (SEC). The form and content of the financial statements as well as any required schedules are prescribed in Regulation S-X. The annual report on Form 10-K must contain a comparative balance sheet as of the ends of the most recent and preceding fiscal years. Comparative income statements and statements of changes in financial position (statement of cash flows replaces changes in financial position for fiscal years ending after July 15, 1988) must be included for the most recent and two preceding fiscal years. Notes to the financial statements are required as of the end of the two or three most recent fiscal years, depending on the nature of

---

[7]Peat, Marwick, Mitchell & Co., Worldwide Financial Reporting and Audit Requirements: A Peat Marwick Inventory, 1986, as updated.

the note. Annual financial statements must be audited; quarterly financial statements need not be audited. All financial statements and schedules must be in English. Consolidated or combined financial statements are required, although there are limited circumstances under which certain subsidiaries might not be consolidated.

Tax Returns.   Returns must be filed annually with the Internal Revenue Service (IRS). Tax returns must be prepared in compliance with the rules and regulations encompassed by the Internal Revenue Code. Auditor involvement is not required, and returns are strictly confidential.

Foreign companies.   Foreign companies are generally treated in the same manner as domestic companies. They are confronted with no specific barriers if they wish to enter U.S. capital markets. Because some foreign companies may find SEC requirements more extensive than disclosure requirements in their own countries and because of differences in accounting principles, the SEC can grant certain special exemptions to foreign companies provided these exemptions do not diminish the protection of U.S. investors.

Statutory Reports.   Foreign companies are automatically subject to the registration and reporting provisions of the Securities Exchange Act of 1934 if they have total assets in excess of $3 million and a class of equity securities held by 500 or more persons, of whom 300 or more reside in the United States. Foreign companies automatically become subject to the 1934 Act by taking any of the following actions: (1) listing a class of securities on a U.S. national securities exchange, (2) registering an offering of securities pursuant to the Securities Act of 1933 when there are more than 300 shareholders on a worldwide basis for a class of securities, and (3) electing to comply with the 1934 Act although the asset and security holder tests are not met.

A foreign company subject to the 1934 Act must file the appropriate forms required under the Act or establish an exemption from the Act's requirements.

In the absence of an available exemption, the foreign company must comply with the 1934 Act by filing the appropriate forms to meet both the registration and the continual reporting requirements of the Act. The form used by most foreign companies to meet their initial registration and annual reporting requirements is Form 20-F. Form 20-F requires disclosure of certain items of financial and nonfinancial information about the registrant, including specified financial statements, footnotes, accountants' report, and financial schedules. Foreign companies are required by the 1934 Act to file interim reports during the year on Form 6-K, disclosing information about the registrant that has been disclosed publicly in its home country. Foreign companies considered equivalent to U.S. domestic companies (because of ownership of 50 percent or more of their shares by U.S. residents, the extent of their U.S. operations, or the composition of their board of directors) are required to file the same reports within the same period of time applicable to U.S. registrants. Financial statements filed as part of Form 20-F may be based on the accounting principles followed in the registrant's country of domicile. However, if there are material differences between the foreign principles and generally accepted U.S. accounting principles, a reconciliation to U.S. accounting principles and SEC Regulation S-X must also be filed. Fiscal-year financial statements required in either a registration statement or an annual report filed with the SEC must be audited by an independent public accountant.

The audit examination of a foreign company, however, must satisfy the same requirements as the audit of a domestic company; that is, the SEC must be satisfied that generally accepted U.S. auditing standards were applied in the accountants' audit of the financial statements for all periods presented.

Audits and accounting

Independence.   Certified public accountants must be independent of the corporation. This is required by the SEC, the American Institute of Certified Public Accountants (AICPA), and the various state boards of accountancy.

Auditors' Reports.   These generally state whether the financial statements "present fairly" the financial position, results of operations, and cash flows in conformity with generally accepted accounting principles applied on a consistent basis.

Authoritative sources.   Generally accepted auditing standards are prescribed by the AICPA. Generally accepted accounting principles are prescribed by the Financial Accounting Standards Board.

4.2 Canada

Public companies

Statutory Reports.   Companies may be registered federally or in one of ten provinces. Securities acts in the provinces have differing definitions of public or reporting companies. Generally, they include companies that offer their securities to the public. The legislation also specifies reporting disclosure and audit requirements. The requirements for a company incorporated in Ontario are presented here and are similar to the requirements of other provinces. Public companies are required to file annual and interim reports with the Provincial Securities Commission. The Securities Act requires that comparative financial statements be prepared, and that they include a balance sheet, an income statement, a statement of surplus, a funds statement, and notes. Financial statements must be prepared in accordance with generally accepted accounting principles as set forth in the Handbook of the Canadian Institute of Chartered Accountants (CICA). The auditor generally reports only on the current year. The annual financial statements must be audited, but the interim statements need not be audited. Reports are usually in English. However, financial statements that are filed or distributed in Quebec generally must be in French, and Quebec shareholders can request such statements in French. Each public company must file separately. Consolidated statements are generally required.

Tax Returns. Returns are filed annually with Revenue Canada, which also collects the corporate income tax imposed by all of the provinces except Ontario, Quebec, and Alberta, which require the filing of a provincial corporate tax return. Provincial capital tax returns are required in British Columbia, Saskatchewan, Manitoba, Ontario, and Quebec. Returns must be completed in the form prescribed by the Income Tax Act, and must be accompanied by financial statements for one year and the auditors' report, if any.

Private companies

Statutory Reports. These reports are required of private incorporated companies, whether registered federally or provincially. However, the specific requirements differ substantially between these jurisdictions. The presentation here covers the Federal requirements only.

Statutory Reports must be filed by companies registered under the Canada Business Corporation Act (CBCA). The CBCA generally requires that comparative financial statements be prepared, although the auditor only reports on the current year. The Act requires that the statements include a balance sheet, an income statement, a statement of retained earnings, a funds statement, and notes. Financial statements must be prepared in accordance with the *CICA Handbook*. Consolidated financial statements are generally required. No specific chart of accounts is mandated, but there are specific record-keeping requirements. Filings may be in English or French. In addition, if a company provides interim financial statements or related documents to shareholders, a public authority, or a stock exchange, these materials must also be filed with the Director of Corporate and Consumer Affairs.

Audits and accounting

Independence.   In order to issue an audit report, chartered accountants must be independent of the corporation. The CBCA generally disqualifies any person from being an auditor who is not independent of the corporation being audited, its affiliates, and the directors or officers of the corporation and affiliates.

Auditors' Reports.   The reports generally state whether the financial statements "present fairly" the corporation's financial position, results of operations, and changes in financial position in accordance with generally accepted accounting principles applied on a consistent basis.

Authoritative Sources.   The *CICA Handbook* is the authoritative source for accounting principles and auditing standards.

4.3 Mexico

Listed public companies

Statutory reports.   These must be filed with the National Investment Commission. The reports, which must be in Spanish, include balance sheets, income statements, funds statements, statements of shareholders' equity, and notes to the financial statements, all usually covering two years. The reports must be audited by an independent public accountant and by an appointed statutory auditor (*comisario*). The *comisario* is usually the company's independent public accountant, but it may be a third party. The *comisario's* responsibilities include attendance at all meetings of the board of directors and certain legal powers and responsibilities. The reports are published in the *Official Gazette.* In addition to the annual report, companies must file unaudited quarterly information, which includes balance sheets, income statements, and other financial data, with the National Investment Commission.

Tax Returns.   Returns must be filed annually with the Ministry of the Treasury and Public Credit. A current-year balance sheet, an income statement, and certain other specified forms must be included in the return. The returns must be in Spanish, need not be published, and are not available to the public. Returns may be filed on a consolidated basis. Auditor involvement is not required, except when returns are on a consolidated basis.

Private domestic incorporated companies

Statutory reports.   Requirements are the same as for listed public companies, except that reports need not be published, are not available to the public, and an audit by an independent public accountant is not required.

Audits and accounting

Independence.   This is required of all independent public accountants and is regulated by the Code of Professional Ethics issued by the Mexican Institute of Public Accountants. The statutory auditor may be shareholder in the company, but not an employee.

Auditing Standards and Accounting Principles.   These principles were developed and established by the Mexican Institute of Public Accountants.

Auditor's report.   In their reports, independent public accountants must attest that the financial statements "present fairly" the financial position and results of operations of the company.

4.4 Brazil

"Open capital" public corporations (public-listed)

Statutory reports.   These reports must be filed with the Securities Commission and the Commercial Registry (CVM). The report must contain comparative financial statements (current and prior-year amounts), which include balance sheets, income statements, funds statements, statements of accumulated profits or losses or statements of changes in shareholders' equity, and notes to the financial statements. An audit of the financial statements, regulated by the CVM, is required. The statements must be in Portuguese and in a format prescribed by the CVM. It is possible to file on a group basis, and consolidated or combined statements are required when the "open capital" company has investments in controlled companies that exceed 30 percent of shareholders' equity or when the company is designated to be, effectively, a group. Proper books must be maintained, and there is a long list of legal requirements, including a specified format for filing with the CVM.

Tax Returns.   Returns are filed annually with the tax authority, which is the Ministry of Finance. They include financial statements for one year that provide a condensed balance sheet, an income statement, and a taxable income calculation (there is no auditor involvement).

Other corporations

Statutory reports.   Requirements are the same as for "open capital" corporations, although no audit is required.

Audits and accounting

Independence.   Independence is required by the federal accounting commission (CFC) established by law to pronounce on accounting matters, and by CVM regulations.

Auditors' Reports.   These must indicate whether, in the opinion of the auditor, the financial statements "present fairly" the financial position of the company and the results of its operations in conformity with generally accepted accounting principles applied on a consistent basis.

Principal Authoritative Sources for Accounting Principles and Disclosure Requirements.   The CVM, which is, in effect, the Brazilian SEC, and Law No. 6.404, which prescribes the form and content of financial statements for corporations and empowers the CVM to regulate publicly listed corporations. Accounting practices in Brazil are essentially those prescribed by corporation law supplemented by income law. Both the CFC and the Brazilian Institute of Accountants issue pronouncements on accounting matters.

4.5 France

All commercial business entities

Statutory Reports.   These reports must be prepared for shareholders. The reports comprise historical financial statements for two years, including a balance sheet, an income statement, and a funds statement, together with notes to the financial statements, prepared in accordance with the requirements of the mandatory chart of accounts (Plan Comptable General), in conformity with the EEC Fourth Directive. A directors' report to shareholders, or equivalent thereof, is also required. The reports must be in French, records must be retained for ten years, and specific charts of accounts are mandated for specific industries. The statutory reports, based on historical financial information, are required to be audited and reported on by the statutory auditor (*commissaire aux comptes)* for all S.A.s and S.C.A.s. For other entities, audits are required depending on certain differing criteria with respect to balance sheet totals, net sales, and number of employees. In addition to the above information for shareholders, and in order to meet public filing requirements, entities that meet certain criteria are required to prepare information principally for distribution by management to the Workers' Committee, relating to current indebtedness and prospective financial information in the form of forecast income and funds statements. This requirement was introduced over a three-year period from 1986 for all except small entities, depending on differing criteria relating to the turnover, or number of employees. The statutory auditor is required to review this information and report thereon as considered necessary. Similarly, entities with over 300 employees must also establish a "social report" on employee matters for submission to the Workers' Committee and employment authorities. This also requires review by the statutory auditor.

Tax Returns.   Returns are filed annually with the local inspector of taxes. An audit is not required. The returns must be prepared on special preprinted tax declaration forms, which include a statutory balance sheet and income statement together with supporting analyses and certain information contained in footnotes referred to in the statutory reporting section. Permission can be requested from the tax authorities to file on a group basis, but this is granted for only a very limited number of cases. Consolidated or combined statements are not required.

Publicly quoted companies and groups

Statutory Reports.   Requirements, in addition to the requirements described for commercial business entities, are summarized as follows. Those companies, including their subsidiaries, where the balance sheet total exceeds F10 million must publish in the *Official Gazette* a balance sheet, an income statement, and a list of their shareholdings in other companies. A five-year summary of comparative financial information is required. Consolidated financial statements are currently recommended by the stock exchange. For financial periods beginning January 1, 1986, in accordance with the EEC Seventh Directive, audited consolidated financial statements for quoted and public companies are mandatory. For other companies, audited consolidated financial statements will be mandatory for financial years beginning January 1, 1990. In addition, quoted companies must publish unaudited interim financial information in the Official Gazette, representing quarterly sales for the period, with cumulative figures for the year (and comparative figures) and an interim six-month's report. The statutory auditor is required to review and report on the half-yearly information.

Audits and accounting

Independence.   This is required and is defined both by law and by the ethics code of the profession.

Responsibilities of Auditors.   These are prescribed by statute and are wide-ranging. In addition to determining whether the financial statements and financial information provided to the shareholders are fairly stated, the auditors must report to the board on irregularities discovered, make recommendations on accounting principles, and report to legal authorities on any misdemeanors discovered.

Auditors' Reports. These must present two standard types of audit opinions: (1) the general report on the financial statements and financial information provided by the board of directors and (2) the special report on related-party transactions. In the general report, the auditors attest to the presentation of a "true and fair view."

Authoritative Sources for Accounting Principles. Sources include the law entitled *Plan Comptable General Revise* and pronouncements from the *Conseil National de la Comptabilite*, the *Ordre des Experts Comptables*, *Compagnie Nationale des Commissaires aux Comptes*, and the *Commission des Operations de Bourse*, as well as other material provided by various groups of accountants.

4.6 Federal Republic of Germany

Public limited companies

Statutory Reports. One-year audited financial statements containing a balance sheet and an income statement in mandated format, together with the annual management report, must be filed annually with the Trade Register of the registered office of the company after approval by the shareholders at the annual general meeting. The auditor is required to submit to the Board of Management a long-form report on the results of the examination which is not available to the public. Within the report the auditor must state whether or not the accounting records are in compliance with the law and the company's statutes and may also present an analysis of the financial statements and of financial position and results of operations. If there are domestic subsidiaries, consolidated financial statements also must be filed, together with a report from management thereon. These must, subject to certain exemptions, include domestic and foreign subsidiaries. The consolidated financial statements are audited and reported as above. If the company is a member of a group, it may have to prepare a report on relations with related enterprises for submission, after audit, to a supervisory board. This report is not published or filed. The company must publish the financial statements, including the auditors' report, in the federal gazette. There are no specific record-keeping requirements.

Tax Returns. Returns are filed annually and are due May 31. Income has to be declared on a calendar-year basis. In cases where a company's fiscal year is not the calendar year, the company must report the income of the fiscal year ended in the calendar year for which a return is filed. The returns include a balance sheet and an income statement. An audit is not required for tax purposes. The return must be in German, and it is not possible to file on a group basis.

Private limited companies

Statutory Reports. Audited financial statements are required annually of these entities if they meet two of the following three size criteria
for three consecutive balance sheet dates set out in the Disclosure Law:
total assets exceed DM125 million, turnover exceeds DM250 million, and
the number of employees exceeds 5,000. Reporting, auditing, filing, and
publication requirements are generally the same as for public limited
companies. If the company and its domestic subsidiaries together meet
the size criteria set out above for three consecutive years, or if a subsidiary is in an AG form, consolidated financial statements and a report from
management thereon must be prepared. Foreign subsidiaries must be
consolidated beginning in 1990. Exemption from the consolidation requirement is available if the company is a subsidiary and an upstream
company (which may be foreign), prepares and files audited consolidated
financial statements with a report from management thereon, and publishes the financial statements in the federal gazette. The exempting consolidated financial statements and report from management should be in
compliance with the Disclosure Law.

Audits and accounting

Independence. Requirements for auditors are set out in the bylaws
of the WP Chamber and in the Stock Corporation Act of 1976.

Auditors' Reports. The auditors must state in their reports
whether the accounting records, financial statements, and management
report comply with the law and company statutes. The financial statements and management report must present as accurate a view as possible of the financial position and results of operations within the framework of the law and company statutes.

Authoritative Sources for Accounting Principles. The AG Law
(public companies), the GmbH Law (private companies), the Disclosure
Law, the Credit Institute Law, and the Insurance Law, as well as research
studies by committees of the WP Institute.

4.7 United Kingdom

Public and private companies

Statutory Reports. Reports of all companies (limited and unlimited) must be sent to all shareholders and debenture holders and must be
presented before the shareholders at a general meeting, usually the annual general meeting. An audit, by a qualified auditor, of the financial
statements contained in the reports is required for all companies, except

for dormant companies that pass a resolution not be audited. Limited companies must also file the statutory reports with the Registrar of Companies; these reports are available for inspection by the public. Companies that are statutorily defined as small or medium (in terms of specified balance sheet totals, sales, and number of employees) may take advantage of provisions (modified accounts) that allow less-detailed reports to be filed, but the full report must be prepared for shareholders. The reports must include annual financial statements with comparative figures comprised of a balance sheet, an income statement, a funds statement (which is required by accounting standards unless the annual sales are below £25,000), an audit report, and notes. Also required is a directors' report to shareholders, which is reviewed by the auditors to ensure that it is consistent with the statements. Normally, consolidated statements are required by law to deal with a holding company and its subsidiaries, except where the holding company is itself a wholly owned subsidiary of another company incorporated in Great Britain. Accounting standards require that consolidated statements include the results of associated companies accounted for by the equity method of accounting. The reports must be in English. It is not possible to file on a group basis, and each subsidiary company must file its own financial statements. The preparation of an additional balance sheet and an income statement based on current cost principles is not mandatory. Specific record-keeping requirements are prescribed by law. The stock exchange requires listed companies to publish biannual interim results, which need not be audited, by sending them to shareholders and debenture holders, or by paid advertisements in two national newspapers. This interim statement and the annual statutory report must be filed with the stock exchange.

Tax returns. Supported by a copy of the audited financial statements, tax returns are filed annually for corporation tax purposes with the Inland Revenue for a company's accounting period. No auditor involvement is required by law.

Unincorporated branches of overseas companies

Statutory Reports. These must be filed annually with the Registrar of Companies. The report must cover the whole of the overseas company's operations rather than just those relating to the branch. The content of the report is the same as for companies incorporated in Great Britain, but the branches do not yet have to comply with the new disclosure requirements introduced by the Companies Act 1981. It has generally been the practice of the Registrar to accept financial statements prepared in accordance with overseas standards comparable to those of Great Britain. No audit is required. If the reports are in a language other than English, a certified translation into English must also be submitted on filing with the Registrar of Companies.

Tax Returns.   Requirements are the same for public and private companies, except that the accounts to support the return are the accounts of the branch only.

Audits and accounting

Independence.   Independence is required by law and by the U.K. accountancy bodies.

Auditors' Reports.   These are required by law to state whether the financial statements present a "true and fair view" and have been prepared in accordance with the Companies Act 1985.

Authoritative Sources for Accounting Principles.   The *Companies Act 1985, Statements of Standard Accounting Practice* issued by the professional accountancy bodies, the continuing obligations for companies admitted to the stock exchange, and international accounting standards insofar as they are adopted by the accountancy bodies.

4.8 Hong Kong

Companies incorporated under the companies ordinance

Statutory Reports.   These are required annually for companies incorporated in Hong Kong under the Companies Ordinance, that is, public companies (listed and nonlisted) and private companies (domestic companies and incorporated subsidiaries of foreign companies). Public companies also file their reports with the Registrar of Companies. The reports contain audited financial statements for the current year, with corresponding amounts for the preceding year, including a balance sheet, an income statement, a funds statement, and notes. The funds statement is not required for companies with annual sales of less than HK$1 million, private companies that are exempt from certain disclosure requirements, banks, insurance companies, shipping companies, and charitable and nonprofit entities. A directors' report is also included, but it usually is not audited. Other disclosure requirements are specified by the Companies Ordinance. If the report of a public company is not in English, a translation in English that is certified to be correct must be filed. If a company has subsidiaries, audited group financial statements (usually in consolidated form) are required unless the holding company is as of year-end a wholly owned subsidiary of another corporate body. Whenever a subsidiary is excluded from group statements on the grounds that the result would be harmful or on grounds of dissimilar businesses, approval must be obtained from the Financial Secretary. Record-keeping requirements call for proper books of accounts to be kept at the registered office of the company or at such other place as the directors think appropriate. These books must be preserved for seven years. If the books are kept outside Hong Kong, financial statements must be sent to Hong Kong at intervals not exceeding six months, disclosing the financial position of the business.

Tax Returns.   Returns are filed annually with the Inland Revenue Department, which issues standard forms to taxpayers for completion and return to the department. For companies incorporated in Hong Kong, audited financial statements must be submitted with the profits tax returns. Auditors may act as tax representatives for clients. The returns must include financial statements that cover the basis period relevant to the year of assessment, including a balance sheet, an income statement, and notes. A funds statement is not required, but one is usually included if it has been prepared. For the profits tax returns, a prescribed form must be completed that presents certain general information on the company and its transactions with nonresidents. A computation of assessable profit must be prepared. It is not possible to file on a group basis because taxes are assessed on each entity and there is no group relief.

Audits and accounting

Independence.   This is required by the Companies Ordinance and by the HKSA, as well as by the Securities Ordinance in the case of audits of security dealers.

Responsibilities of Auditors.   Responsibilities include reporting to shareholders on whether the audited financial statements have been prepared in accordance with the Companies Ordinance and whether they present a "true and fair view."

Authoritative Sources for Accounting Disclosure Requirements. Sources include the Companies Ordinance and, for accounting principles, the HKSA, which is incorporated by the Professional Accountants Ordinance and authorized to regulate the accountancy profession as the only statutory licensing body of accountants in Hong Kong.

4.9 Japan

Public limited companies

Statutory Reports.   These must be filed semiannually with the Ministry of Finance (MOF), under requirements of the Securities and Exchange Law, and with the securities exchanges. All companies listed on the Japanese stock exchanges and nonlisted companies that file registration statements with the MOF must appoint both a statutory auditor and an independent auditor. The independent auditor examines the financial statements and information of an accounting nature, while the statutory auditor examines all other areas. (See Audits and Accounting, below, for the respective responsibilities of statutory and independent auditors.) A full scope audit is required for the annual financial statements, and an interim examination is performed in connection with the semiannual statements. In the interim report the auditor indicates whether the semiannual statements provide "useful information relative to the interim period constituting part of a fiscal year." These requirements apply to all listed companies and to unlisted companies that issue new shares to the public or whose shareholders have sold their shares to the public (50 or more persons) in amounts aggregating 100 million yen or more during the past two years. The requirements apply only to the parent company financial statements, which are considered the primary financial statements. However, audited consolidated financial statements, in the form of an attachment to the annual report, must also be filed annually with the MOF and with the securities exchanges. If the aggregate sales, assets, or net earnings of a subsidiary do not exceed ten percent of the sales, assets, or net earnings reported in the consolidated financial statements, the subsidiary may be excluded from consolidation. The reports must present financial statements as prescribed by the MOF: a balance sheet for two fiscal year-ends and an income statement for two fiscal periods. Statements of profit appropriations for two fiscal periods are also required, and a two-year comparative statement of manufacturing costs is attached to the income statement. Notes to the financial statements cover two fiscal periods. Fourteen special schedules are required for one fiscal period only. A business report that accompanies the financial statements must contain such specified information as a description of the company's main business and locations, capital investments, relationships with a parent company or subsidiaries, a discussion of results of operations and the status of assets (covering at least the last three years), outstanding problems, the major shareholders and any investments the company has in these shareholders, and events subsequent to the balance sheet date. The independent auditor's opinion covers information of an accounting nature that appears in the business report. It is presumed that the statements will be in Japanese, although there is no requirement that foreign languages not be used.

Tax Returns.   Returns are filed in accordance with the requirements of the Japanese tax laws, semiannually and annually. Financial statements should be attached to the tax returns, which are filed with local tax authorities.

Limited companies

Statutory Reports.   These must be prepared at least once a year, in accordance with the Japanese Commercial Code. The audited financial statements are to be maintained at the head office of the company for five years for inspection by shareholders and creditors, and at branch offices for three years. An audit of the financial statements by an independent auditor is required of all limited companies with capital stock of more than 500 million yen or total liabilities of 20 billion yen or more. Limited companies with no more than fifty shareholders and a minimum capital of 100,000 yen must prepare statutory reports annually, with no specific due dates. Financial statements and a statutory auditor's report are to be maintained at the head office of the company for inspection by shareholders and creditors. A company may voluntarily appoint a number of statutory auditors, in accordance with its articles of incorporation. For companies with capital of over 500 million yen, the statutory auditors must examine areas in addition to financial statements. A notice, including financial statements and the statutory auditor's report (as well as that of the independent auditor, if applicable), is to be sent to shareholders two weeks before the annual meeting. The reports include financial statements as prescribed by the Japanese Commercial Code, consisting of a balance sheet for one fiscal year-end and an income statement for one fiscal period. A proposal of profit appropriation should also be included, and certain information, including significant accounting policies, must be disclosed in footnotes. Eleven special schedules are required, as well as any other schedules considered necessary under the circumstances. See Public Limited Companies for the required business report. The language question is also covered under Public Limited Companies; some foreign affiliated companies do present the statements in their own language.

Audits and accounting

Independence.   Requirements for CPAs are specified in detail under the Japanese CPA law and related regulations. In general, neither auditor nor spouse can have any interest, financial or otherwise, in a company the auditor is to audit.

Responsibilities of Auditors.   These are specified for statutory auditors and independent auditors, and differ depending upon whether a company being audited reports under MOF requirements or under the requirements of the Japanese Commercial Code (JCC) for limited companies.

Auditors' Reports.   These must state whether, in the auditors' opinion, the financial statements "present fairly" the company's financial position and the results of its operations.

Authoritative Sources for Accounting and Auditing Standards.
Sources include the MOF (for reporting under the Securities and Exchange Law), the Corporate Accounting Deliberation Board (an advisory body to the MOF), the Ministry of Justice (for reporting under the Japanese Commercial Code), and the Japanese Institute of Certified Public Accountants. In addition, financial statement and schedule forms are issued by the government ministries responsible for certain industries, including construction, shipbuilding, securities, railroads, automotive transportation, banking, maritime operations, insurance, electric power, and gas.

Special Comment.   It is common for firms engaged in international operations to adjust their financial statements to U.S. GAAP, particularly if they are affiliated with U.S. companies, but also if they are Japanese companies that have international reporting requirements because of overseas financing. In addition, it is not unusual for companies with European affiliations to follow U.S. GAAP reporting. In such cases, a company must issue another report in accordance with the JCC, if the company meets the statutory size requirements or if local shareholders request such a report.

5.0 CHECKLIST FOR INFORMATION FROM TARGET COMPANY

I. General Information and Background
   A. Exact corporate name.
   B. Address.
   C. Date and state of incorporation.
   D. States in which qualified to do business.
   E. Location of minute books, bylaws, and certificate of incorporation.
   F. History of business activities, including predecessor organizations.
   G. Description of products and industry.
   H. Corporate organization—subsidiaries, divisions and branches.
      1. Names and locations.
      2. Description of operations.
   I. Fiscal year.
   J. Capitalization—authorized and issued capital stock.
      1. Rights of each class of stock and other securities.
      2. Stockholders' agreements and terms thereof.

3. Names of principal stockholders and holdings, including options.
K. Long-term debt-amount and major covenants.
L. Bank depositories and average bank balances.
M. Credit references, rating, and borrowing ability.
N. Location of company records.
O. Accountants—name and address.
P. Attorneys—name and address.
Q. Insurance agent or broker—name and address.

II. Personnel
A. Directors and their affiliations.
B. Officers and key employee positions, duties, age, health, salary, service, experience, personal plans for the future, retention outlook, and stockholdings.
C. Organization chart and description of policy manuals.
D. Employee contracts—terms, expiration dates.
E. Number of employees in production, sales, administration, etc.
F. Union contracts—terms, expiration dates, and number of members.
G. Strike record, labor morale, and handling of labor relations.
H. Labor market, turnover experience, and recruiting results.
I. Method of determining salaries.
J. Pension, profit sharing, insurance, stock bonus plans, deferred compensation, and severance plans.
K. Comparison with industry as to number of employees, hours per week, wage rates, training programs, benefits, etc.
L. Backup for key management positions.
M. List with brief details of former directors, officers, and senior management who have left during period under review.

III. Operations
A. Description, including significant changes in past few years.
  1. Production capacity and percent of utilization.
  2. Production methods (scheduling, purchasing, and inventory controls).
  3. Significant production costs.
  4. Acquisitions or discontinued operations.
B. Principal suppliers, terms, and prospects for future.
C. Distribution methods and terms (also, brokers or agents and compensation arrangements).
D. Critical lead times for materials, make, or buy practices.
E. Subsidiaries or divisions, their operations and intercompany transactions.
F. Government contracts and subcontracts.

G. Seasonal factors; reliance on other industries.

H. Public and stockholder relations.

IV. Sales

    A. Description of market; amount of export sales.

    B. Number of orders, customers, and names of principal customers.

    C. Sales by product for past five years and for past twelve months.

       1. Penetration of market by product.

       2. Possibilities of increase through existing lines and by diversification.

    D. Sales comparison with industry for past five years and for past twelve months.

    E. Sales backlog, accounts receivable activity, and customer continuity.

    F. Sales correspondence, returns, and allowances.

    G. Sales policies and method of compensation of sales personnel.

    H. Pricing policies and fluctuations in past five years.

    I. Principal competitors and effect of competition.

    J. Relative size in industry and status.

    K. Competitive advantages and disadvantages.

    L. Anything significant in product lines produced in past few years.

    M. Credit terms; any special arrangements.

    N. Missing product lines.

    O. Advertising program, cost past five years, and other sales promotion programs.

    P. Research and development program, cost, history, scope, potential, results and work by outsiders.

    Q. Anticipated technological achievements by company and/or industry.

V. Earnings and Dividends

    A. Earnings results compared with budget for past five years and for last twelve months; gross profit margins; and reasons for variations, nonrecurring income, and expenses.

    B. Earnings comparison with industry for past five years.

    C. Dividend and earnings record for past five years in total and per share.

    D. Level and changes in fixed and variable costs.

    E. Effect of government wage or price controls.

    F. Analysis of selling and general and administrative expenses.

    G. Anticipated economies and cost changes.

VI. Production Facilities
  A. Land.
    1. Acreage and location.
    2. Cost.
    3. Assessed value and real estate taxes.
    4. Fair market value.
  B. Buildings.
    1. Description, location, layout, and floor space.
    2. Age and condition.
    3. Capability to expand or add on.
    4. Depreciation, reserve, method, rate, and policies.
    5. Assessed value—real estate taxes.
    6. Fair market value.
    7. Insurance coverage.
  C. Title to realty.
  D. Machinery and equipment.
    1. Description.
    2. Age, condition, efficiency, and insurance coverage.
    3. Depreciation, reserves, methods, rates, and replacement policies.
    4. Total acquisitions during past five years.
    5. Analysis of most recent additions.
  E. Future plant, machinery and equipment requirements.
  F. Capitalization versus repair policies.
  G. Capital expenditures and repairs for past five years.
  H. Percentage relationship of production costs and comparison with industry.
  I. Efficiency of operations in light of technological change.
  J. Subcontracting done by others.
  K. Capital commitments.
  L. Facility contracts or leases.
  M. Surplus or idle buildings or equipment.
VII. Assets
  A. Cash position, present, and projected—restrictions, compensating balances, etc.
  B. Age and number of accounts receivable (several years normally analyzed).
  C. Provision for bad debts for past five years and current allowance.
  D. Inventories.
    1. Location, including consigned goods.
    2. Finished goods by product.

    3. Work-in-process by product.

    4. Raw materials by product.

    5. Pricing methods.

    6. Accounting procedures and practices.

    7. Provisions for obsolete or slow-moving stock (several years normally analyzed).

  E. Analysis of notes receivable.

  F. Analysis of investments.

  G. Subsidiaries.

    1. Assess impact on parent company's balance sheet.

    2. Determine what information, if any, must be obtained for review.

  H. Analysis of other assets.

   I. Patents held—rights, licenses granted, and values.

  J. Goodwill and other intangibles—basis of evaluations and/or amortization.

VIII. Liabilities

  A. Short-term borrowings and unused lines of credit.

  B. Analysis of accounts payable.

  C. Commitments for new buildings, machinery, and inventories.

  D. Long-term loans outstanding and terms, assets pledged, and payment status.

  E. Debentures outstanding and terms.

  F. Dividends and interest accrued.

  G. Lease commitments.

  H. Insurance coverage, fidelity bonds, and amounts of present claims, if any.

   I. Unfunded pension costs.

  J. Contingent liabilities—warranties, patent infringements, loss contract compensation for services, and contracts subject to termination or renegotiation.

  K. Litigation history and present status, unasserted claims, etc.

IX. Taxation

  A. Federal income tax returns for past five years.

  B. Results of past IRS examinations; latest year examined and open years.

  C. Is a consolidated Federal income tax return filed? Are taxes allocated in accordance with a formal agreement?

  D. List of foreign subsidiaries, foreign tax credits, and analysis of taxes provided on undistributed foreign earnings.

  E. Domestic and foreign intercompany pricing policies, including DISC sales.

  F. States in which company qualifies to do business.

G. State tax returns filed for past five years and type—results of past examination and open years.

H. Taxes paid versus amounts recorded in financial statements for past five years.

I. Accounting policy regarding deferred taxes—details of all significant timing differences.

Chapter **5**

Tax Considerations in Acquiring U.S. Enterprises

David R. Tillinghast
Partner, Hughes, Hubbard & Reed

1.0 STRUCTURING OF TRANSACTION

1.1 Tax-Free Reorganization

From a tax point of view, there are two basic patterns of structuring a merger or acquistion. The first, called a tax-free reorganization, is what we traditionally think of as a merger, that is, the acquistion by one company of all assets or shares of another in a transaction in which the shareholders of the merged company receive shares in the acquiring company. Transactions of this kind are called tax-free because generally neither the merged company nor its shareholders recognize taxable gain or loss as a result, although the shareholders carry over the tax cost, or basis, in their merged company shares to the shares they receive in the exchange, so that they may later recognize the inherent gain. Moveover, the acquiring company succeeds to the tax attributes of the merged company under a type of pooling rule.

1.2 Taxable Purchase

The second general type of transaction is a taxable purchase, that is, an acquisition by one company of shares or assets of another in exchange for some consideration, usually cash or debt obligations but in some cases shares or warrants to buy shares in combination with cash or debt. Such a transaction is called taxable because the selling shareholders, the company selling assets, or possibly both recognize taxable gain or loss on the exchange; the acquiring company also accounts for the transaction as a purchase, taking a new cost basis in the shares or assets acquired.

Over the years, a third kind of transaction, referred to here as a hybrid transaction, has evolved. The reasons for this will be discussed in section 3.3.

1.3 Cash Purchases

During the last decade, the U.S. acquisition market strongly favored cash purchases, many of them structured as leveraged buy-outs, transactions in which an acquiring party or group raised the lion's share of the purchase price for an acquisition through several tiers of borrowings, the most junior class being high-yield junk bonds for which Drexel Burnham, among others, became so famous. This preference was largely a creature of the tax law, which contributed two important incentives to structuring transactions in this way. Of these, the Tax Reform Act of 1986 did away with one and diminished the significance of the other.

Before the Tax Reform Act of 1986, an acquiring company would typically make a cash acquisition of the assets of the target company or, using a special provision found in Section 338 of the Internal Revenue Code, make a cash acquisition of shares which was treated as an acquisition of assets. The target company was deemed to have been liquidated and a new target company created to hold the assets. The object was to step up the basis of the assets acquired (or deemed acquired) without a corresponding tax on the target company. This kind of tax arbitrage arose because the price paid was almost always more than the tax basis (tax book value) of the assets in the hands of the target company. By buying or being deemed to buy the target company's assets, the acquiring company (or, in the case of a foreign acquiring company, a U.S. subsidiary created for this purpose) could step up the basis of the assets to current value and thus increase allowable depreciation and amortization deductions, as well as minimize taxable gain on any future asset dispositions. At the same time, the target company itself recognized only limited amounts of gain, the so-called recapture items. The result was a tax mismatch: a full step-up in the basis of all target company assets to current value at the price of only limited gain recognition by the target company.

2.0 THE 1986 TAX ACT

The 1986 Act, repealing what was known in the United States as the General Utilities rule (named after a landmark case), now requires that in this situation the target company recognize *all* taxable gains inherent in its assets. With relatively infrequent exceptions (referred to in C.1 of the Checklist), this makes a purchase of target company assets disadvantageous; the current tax incurred by the target company is a cost greater than the present value of the increase in the future stream of deductions to the acquiring company, not only because of the timing aspects but also because not every asset purchased will give rise to depreciation or amortization deductions. Most notably, a premium paid in excess of the current fair market value of identifiable assets is treated as the cost of acquiring good will, which cannot be amortized for tax purposes.

The second tax inducement to leveraged buy-out transactions is the deductibility of interest incurred to finance the acquisition in computing U.S. income tax. Often transactions were arranged so that the interest was deductible, in effect, against the otherwise taxable profits of the company acquired. The 1986 legislation did not alter this rule in any fundamental way. By reducing the U.S. income tax rates (from 46 to 34 percent for corporations and from a maximum of 50 percent to an effective maximum of 33 percent for individuals), however, it reduced the U.S. tax benefit of the interest deductions. While this has not done away with the tax subsidy to debt financing of acquisitions, it has affected the price which an acquirer using leverage can offer for a U.S. company. In the case of a foreign acquirer, a greater benefit may be obtainable if the interest is deductible in its home country; this possibility is discussed below.

3.0 FOREIGN PURCHASES OF A U.S. COMPANY

3.1 Avoidance of Tax-Free Transaction

Some of the major tax inducements to structuring the acquisition of a U.S. company as a cash purchase have therefore disappeared or moderated. In practice, however, a foreign company seeking to acquire a U.S.

company will often avoid structuring the acquisition as a tax- free transaction. There are two principal reasons for this.

First, because the tax-free reorganization provisions of the Internal Revenue Code were framed with traditional mergers in mind, they do not lend themselves readily to many kinds of acquisition transactions which are common today. They are not easily adaptable to partial acquisitions of, for example, divisional assets or fractional share interests. Nor do they work very well in tender offers or hostile transactions. Those limitations apply to U.S. and foreign acquirers alike.

Secondly, all of the varied forms of tax-free reorganization contemplate the use of shares as the sole, or at least the principal, consideration to be received by the target company's shareholders, and many foreign acquirers are unwilling to deliver shares. (Some transactions are framed as mergers for corporate law purposes, but unless shares are delivered as the principal consideration, these are considered purchases for tax purposes.) Many companies are themselves closely-held and do not wish to issue a block of shares to outsiders. Others may wish, as a matter of financial planning, to leverage the acquisition (typically, for example, by borrowing the purchase price in U.S. dollars, to be repaid out of target company earnings). Most importantly, however, the issuance of shares in the United States could require the foreign acquirer to comply with Securities and Exchange Commission disclosure requirements; and this some foreign companies are simply unwilling to do. Here, the foreign acquirer may be at a disadvantage against a U.S. competitor which already may be subject to the SEC rules or willing to comply with them.

If a U.S. shareholder of the target company simply sells shares for cash, the shareholder will recognize a taxable gain (or loss) and the cost of this will be factored into the acceptable price. If, on the other hand, the transaction could be structured as a tax-free reorganization, the shareholder would recognize no taxable gain and might accept a lower price. In some cases, a potential foreign acquirer has had to contend with a competing tax-free bid for the target company from a potential U.S. acquirer. Even if another bid is not on the table, the foreign acquirer must compete against the hypothetical value to the target company's shareholders of receiving tax-free treatment.

3.2 Alternatives to Tax-Free Transactions

The tax advisor to a would-be foreign acquirer is often asked how to frame an offer for an American target company which is competitive with the target company's tax-free alternatives. The answer depends, of course, on the particular circumstances, but in principle there are three approaches: (1) pay more; (2) devise an alternative "as good as" a tax-free one; or (3) despite the obstacles, construct a tax-free offer yourself. Of these, the first may be the most effective but obviously involves a direct increase in the acquisition cost; so most foreign acquirers seek another solution.

Some have persuaded target company shareholders that they are at least as well off if they sell their target company shares in an installment sale. Under the Internal Revenue Code, the gain recognized upon a taxable sale of shares can be deferred to the extent that the purchase price is evidenced by promissory notes of the purchaser. In such a case, gain is recognized ratably as the notes are paid off. The shareholders must wait for their cash, of course. In the interim, however, the promissory notes bear interest, normally at market rates, and this represents a return on the pretax value of the shareholder's position.

Foreign acquirers following this approach have emphasized that, although a tax-free transaction sounds as though it escapes tax altogether, it does not; it merely defers tax until the shares of the acquirer received in the exchange are themselves sold. (Since the tax basis of the holder in the new shares is a carryover of the basis in the shares surrendered, the built-in gain does not disappear.) The fact is that many investors do sooner or later sell shares they receive in tax-free exchanges, because eventually they want to reduce the investment to cash or convert it into another holding. To the extent this is true, the effect of a relatively long-term (or medium-term) installment sale recognition may not be very different.

If, moreover, the shareholders of the target company want "upside" participation or if they are more optimistic than the foreign acquirer about the prospects of the target company, a contingent pay format can be adopted. Under this approach, the foreign acquirer agrees to pay a base price in cash or promissory notes and then agrees to pay more if specified benchmarks are reached, for example, earnings or sales targets or the failure of potential claims to be asserted. While the contingent payment feature complicates the computation of the shareholder's taxable gain, proceeds may nevertheless be reported on the installment method, so that tax is imposed on the shareholder only as cash is received.

Unfortunately, the installment sale format is not a viable solution in some cases. Installment reporting of target company shareholders' gain is not allowable if *either* (1) the target company shares are traded in an established securities market or (2) the promissory notes delivered to the shareholders are in registered form or otherwise readily marketable. In some cases, moreover, the foreign acquirer will find the shareholders of the target company insistent on a tax-free exchange. While there are many reasons for this, the most common one is estate planning.

In a typical case, the shareholders of the target company will include one or more older individuals whose basis in their shares is low. This may be true even in the case of a public company if a substantial block is held by management or a family group. Unlike younger shareholders, these older individuals often intend to hold any shares they own until their death, when the tax basis of the shares in the hands of their estates will step up to the fair market value at the date of death. For them, the installment sale is not satisfactory, since it requires recognition of the current gain, even though the cash impact is deferred.

A striking example of this was provided in the case of National Starch. Even though this was a publicly-traded company, a substantial block of its stock was owned or controlled by its chairman and his wife, both of whom were over eighty years of age. After a tax-free merger of National Starch into Merck fell through, the company was sought by Unilever, which was stymied in its attempts to purchase it by the chairman's refusal to go along with a transaction which would result in a taxable gain on the shares which he and his wife owned.

3.3 Hybrid Transactions

In such circumstances, foreign acquirers have been successful (as was Unilever) in structuring hybrid transactions which are tax-free to such shareholders without requiring the issuance of stock of the foreign acquirer. There are several variations of this technique, which are described in the Appendix. They center, however, on the idea of letting the target company shareholders who desire tax-free treatment retain shares of preferred stock in the target company or a comparable U.S. subsidiary of the foreign acquirer, which, under certain conditions, can be redeemed at the option of the holder. In proper circumstances, other shareholders of the target company can be offered cash or installment notes instead.

One way in which this has been done is to have the target company recapitalize. The older shareholders exchange their common stock for preferred stock, while other shareholders retain common stock. This can qualify as a tax-free E reorganization, even though it is immediately followed by a taxable sale of all or any desired portion of the common stock. (See Appendix at B.5.)

A second technique involves the merger of the target company into a newly formed U.S. subsidiary of the foreign acquirer in a transaction qualifying as a forward triangular merger. (See Appendix at B.3.) Again, target company shareholders receive preferred stock of the subsidiary, although the merger may incorporate a cash option allowing up to 49 percent of the target company shareholders to elect to receive cash instead, making the transaction taxable to them but not to others. In Unilever's acquisition of National Starch, an even more ingenious technique, involving a tax-free incorporation transaction followed by a cash merger freeze out, resulted in tax-free treatment to shareholders receiving preferred stock of the U.S. subsidiary, even though more than 50 percent of the National Starch shareholders received cash. (See Appendix at B.6.)

One shadow over preferred stock transactions of the kind described above is created by the so-called thin capitalization or debt-versus-equity problem. Under proper circumstances, the Internal Revenue Service asserts the right to treat what is nominally preferred stock as being in substance debt; if this assertion is upheld, the result is to deny tax-free treatment to target company shareholders. This means that extraordinary protections to the preferred shareholders, such as take-out commitments by the foreign acquirer or highly restrictive convenants limiting the business of the subsidiary issuing the preferred stock, must be carefully weighed. Nevertheless, there are clearly cases where preferred stock will be treated as just that and where the tax-free requirements can be met.

3.4 Tax-Free Reorganization by a Foreign Buyer

If, despite the obstacles, a foreign acquirer wishes to structure a merger or acquisition in the form of a tax-free reorganization, several different forms of transactions may be employed. These are described in the Appendix. Some of the tax-free reorganization definitions require that the *only* consideration to the shareholders of the target company be voting shares of the foreign acquirer. (Whenever the delivery of shares is required, the certificates actually delivered may be American Depositary Receipts, or ADRs, which are treated for tax purposes as the underlying shares themselves.) A more commonly used transaction form, a forward triangular merger in which the target company is merged into a newly created shell U.S. subsidiary of the foreign acquirer under state corporate merger statutes, requires only that shares constitute the majority of the consideration delivered, and these may be nonvoting shares. To the extent that a target company shareholder receives cash or other nonshare consideration, however, the shareholder will recognize taxable income or gain.

3.5 Other Issues

The Internal Revenue Code provisions governing tax-free reorganizations are among the most complex in the U.S. tax law, and a complete discussion of all of the questions which may need to be dealt with cannot be presented here, although all of the principal questions are covered in the Appendix. There are, however, a few issues which deserve mention.

In determining whether a transaction qualifies as a tax-free reorganization, all related transactions which form part of the acquisition plan will be taken into account under the step transaction doctrine. Thus, for example, if target company shareholders by prearrangement immediately sell shares they receive in the transaction, they may be treated as receiving cash; and this in turn may affect the tax-free character of the transaction to other shareholders. While this is largely a concern of the target company shareholders, the foreign acquirer may be required to participate in framing a solution; among other things, resales of shares by target company shareholders may involve substantial SEC problems. When Attwoods PLC, an English company, acquired Eastern Waste Management, the Eastern shareholders bargained out among themselves the number of shares they each would be permitted to dispose of under an SEC registration statement which Attwoods agreed to file. When the target company is publicly held, such agreements are impossible, of course; in those cases management of the target company may be asked to make a representation that it knows of no concerted plan by shareholders to sell off shares received in the transaction, and this is normally sufficient to avoid a tax problem.

The step transaction doctrine also applies to preliminary steps in an acquisition plan. For example, in a famous series of litigations, the courts held that ITT's acquisition of the Hartford Fire Insurance Company pursuant to a share-for-share tender offer failed to qualify as a B reorganization (which requires the delivery of *only* voting stock) because a prior purchase by ITT of some Hartford stock for cash was part of the over-all acquisition plan and thus was a step in the integrated transaction.

As this case illustrates, it may be difficult for an acquiring company to complete a "tax-free" transaction after it has made "toe-hold" purchases of a target company's shares for cash. The greatest leeway is allowed by the forward triangular merger format referred to above, where prior cash purchases of target company shares will not detract from the tax-free nature of the subsequent merger as long as those purchases account for less than half of the total number of target company shares.

A particular annoyance for the foreign acquirer is the fact that a tax-free reorganization can be accomplished only if the surviving company (whether the target company or a U.S. subsidiary) is directly owned by the foreign acquirer itself. The Internal Revenue Code definitions mandate that the shares to be delivered in a tax-free reorganization be shares of the company that ends up with the target company's business and assets or shares of that company's immediate parent. This is inconsistent with the corporate structure which many foreign acquirers already have in place. For example, it is not generally possible to have a U.S. target company acquired by a tax-haven holding-company subsidiary in exchange for foreign parent company shares and still have the acquisition qualify as a tax-free reorganization. What can be done, however, is to have the target company assets dropped down into a second-tier U.S. subsidiary following the acquisition. Alternatively, at some later time when, as American lawyers say, the original acquisition is "old and cold," so that the step transaction doctrine will not apply, the foreign acquirer can drop the shares of the target company or the acquiring U.S. subsidiary down through any number of tiers of intervening subsidiaries until they come to rest in the desired place.

The final point to be noted in respect of tax-free reorganizations is that when shares of a foreign acquirer are received by target company shareholders, certain special requirements imposed by Section 367 of the Internal Revenue Code apply; but in practice this is infrequently a problem. The normal tax-free rules apply unless after the transaction an individual target company shareholder owns 5 percent or more of the shares of the foreign acquirer. A shareholder who exceeds this level of ownership, which is rare, can still procure tax-free treatment by signing an agreement with the Internal Revenue Service to recognize any gain later if the foreign acquirer disposes of the target company or substantial portions of its assets.

Whatever form the merger or acquisition of a U.S. company takes, the foreign acquirer should consider an attempt to pay part of the acquisition cost in a form which will produce on-going tax deductions. We noted before that asset purchases designed to step up the basis of depreciable or amortizable target company assets are no longer generally advantageous. What may still be advantageous, however, is to *create* depreciable or amortizable assets. The opportunities for this depend on the particular circumstances, but one common technique is to pay a portion of the total acquisition price to the target company shareholders (and, in the case of an asset purchase, the target company itself) in exchange for a covenant not to compete, that is, an agreement that for a specified number of years after the transaction, they (or it) will not reenter the business which has been sold. Payments for such a covenant are deductible for tax purposes if made periodically or, if made in a lump sum up front, amortizable over the life of the covenant.

Traditionally, sellers have resisted the allocation of acquisition price in this manner because amounts so received are taxable to them as ordinary income, whereas gain on sale of shares has traditionally been taxed at preferential capital gains rates. At the present time, the United States taxes capital gains and other income at the same rates; but even if some differential in rates is reintroduced in the future, allocation of some amount to a covenant not to compete may still be advantageous. Suppose, for example, that the top U.S. individual income tax rate went to 30 percent, that the rate of tax on capital gains was set at 20 percent, and that the corporate income tax rate went to 35 percent. An acquiring company could "gross up" a payment to a target company shareholder for a noncompetition covenant by 15 percent (a little more than necessary to give him the same after-tax amount) and still net approximately 25 percent in tax benefit compared to a payment for shares, although the benefit would accrue only over a period of years.

If the acquisition is structured to be tax-free to the target company shareholder (whether as a tax-free reorganization or a hybrid transaction), payments of cash may nevertheless be made for covenants not to compete, without affecting the tax-free nature of the underlying transaction, since these payments are not considered payment for the target company's shares. Of course, target company shareholders will more forcefully resist the allocation of consideration to the covenants in this case, because the alternative is a tax-free receipt of additional shares in exchange for their target company shares.

To the extent that a foreign acquirer uses shares to acquire a U.S. company, it obviously does not require funding. When the acquisition will be made for cash, however, the foreign acquirer will often make additional borrowings to fund the purchase. While nontax factors may play the most important role in determining the place and terms of the borrowing, there are important tax considerations to be taken into account.

With some exceptions, interest incurred by a U.S. company is deductible for tax purposes, even when the debt is used to fund a share or asset acquisition. Often if a foreign acquirer forms a U.S. holding company subsidiary to acquire the target company, the U.S. holding company borrows dollars in the U.S. market. This will generally permit the interest to be written off against the on-going profits of the target company or other U.S. operating subsidiaries held by the U.S. holding company through the filing of a consolidated U.S. tax return. In some transactions, the target company itself will also borrow, before or after the acquisition.

Alternatively, as suggested above, the foreign acquirer, or a finance subsidiary located in some other country, can borrow to fund the purchase, contributing or relending the proceeds to the purchasing subsidiary. This might give rise to deductions allowable against a higher rate of tax and, therefore, give a greater tax benefit. This will not always be beneficial, however. In some countries, interest on debt incurred to acquire a U.S. company may not be deductible. Even if it is, if the foreign acquirer intends to service the debt out of the earnings of the target company (or from other U.S. sources), U.S. withholding tax may be incurred on dividends or interest paid to the foreign acquirer or its finance subsidiary to transmit the cash needed for repayment. In this connection, the Internal Revenue Service's accelerating attacks on conduit debt financings must be carefully considered.

One funding mechanism which has been used with advantageous U.S. tax consequences is the issue by a U.S. holding company subsidiary of deep discount debt. Subject to certain generally applicable but seldom effective limitations on interest deductions (noted in the Checklist), original issue discount is accrued as an interest expense over the life of the obligation, thus creating deductions without cash outflows. In principle, equivalent amounts are includable in the taxable income of the lender, but this effect may be of limited importance. Many lenders in the domestic U.S. capital markets are tax-exempt (pension funds and charitable organizations). Moreover, discount earned by non-U.S. lenders not engaged in business in the United States, while taxable in principle, is subject to a withholding tax only to the extent of payments actually made by the borrower. Thus, a zero coupon obligation is subject to no withholding tax until maturity. Even then, no tax will be withheld if the foreign lender has disposed of the obligation to a U.S. person. Note, however, that the foreign lender must be unrelated to the borrower; discount on debt to related foreign parties is deductible only when included in income by the lender. This technique may be barred under legislation introduced in 1989.

4.0 SUMMARY

The foregoing is only the simplest summary of the sometimes daunting complexities which a foreign acquirer may encounter in planning the tax aspects of a U.S. merger or acquisition. Experience shows, however, that tax problems seldom stand in the way of deals which otherwise make sense. If anything, the sophistication of U.S. tax advisers leads them to suggest transactional structures which are rejected by the foreign acquirer not because they are not viable but because they offend the foreign acquirer's sense of what is appropriate under the circumstances. It is the task of the U.S. tax advisor not only to originate ideas which will save U.S. taxes in the merger or acquisition but also to shape these ideas to the policies and objectives of the foreign acquirer. It is essential that the way in which the deal is structured satisfy *all* of the foreign acquirer's legal and business requirements. Taxes should never be the tail that wags the dog.

5.0 CHECKLIST

A. Selection of Basic Tax Pattern
   1. A tax-free transaction: A merger or an acquisition of the target company's assets or shares for shares of the foreign acquirer.
      a. No currently taxable gain or loss to target company or its shareholders.
      b. Shareholders carry over the tax basis in their target company

shares to the shares received, so that inherent gain or loss may be recognized later.

   c. Foreign acquirer (or a U.S. subsidiary) inherits the tax attributes of the target company.

2. A taxable transaction: A purchase of the shares or assets of the target company for cash or cash and debt.

   a. The target company or its shareholders recognize taxable gain or loss.

3. A hybrid transaction, embodying some elements of the taxable and the tax-free.

   a. For example, a transaction may be taxable to some shareholders and tax free to others.

B. Factors in Selection of Tax Pattern

1. Tax free format requires issuance of foreign acquirer's shares (or ADR's representing such shares).

   a. Registration under Securities Act of 1933 may be required.

   b. Even if not, foreign acquirer may become subject to regulation under the Securities Exchange Act of 1934.

   c. In cases where SEC considerations are not determinative, target company shareholders may not accept foreign acquirer's shares.

   d. May also be inconsistent with foreign acquirer's desire to borrow to leverage the acquisition.

2. Tax-free rules do not

   a. Readily permit partial acquisitions (e.g., divisional assets or partial share interests) or

   b. Lend themselves to tender offers or hostile takeovers.

3. Must consider tax objectives of target company's shareholders.

   a. Pointing toward a taxable format.

      i. Desire for cash or equivalent is important in case of a publicly-traded target company, where substantial positions are held by arbitrageurs.

      ii. Desire to recognize taxable loss.

   b. Pointing toward a tax-free or hybrid format.

      i. Desire to defer recognition of taxable gain.

         (A) Typical in a family-owned company, where shares have been owned a long time and the tax basis is low.

         (B) Of critical importance where there are older family members

            (1) If they defer recognition until death, they never pay tax on gain, because of step-up in basis of shares to date-of-death value.

         (C) Desire for upside potential or equity interest following the acquisition.

C. How to structure a deal when the foreign acquirer does not want to deliver its shares but target company's shareholders want to defer tax.
  1. Buy assets of target company
     a. Features
        i. No current taxable gain or loss to shareholders. Eventual gain or sale or liquidation of shares, but postponed.
        ii. Gain or loss recognized by target company.
     b. Disadvantages
        i. Usually disadvantageous for target company to recognize taxable gain, which can be avoided in sale of shares. Exceptions:
           (A) Target company's basis in assets is higher than shareholders' basis in shares, so that there is a loss, no gain or little gain at the corporate level, although substantial gain at shareholder level.
           (B) Target company's taxable gain is offset by net operating loss carryover which will otherwise be unusable (see F below).
  2. Use an installment sale format
     a. Features
        i. Purchase of shares in exchange for promissory notes.
        ii. Shareholders can individually elect to defer taxable gain and recognize it only ratably as notes are paid off.
           (A) Timing of recognition is flexible because a shareholder can trigger gain by disposing of the notes.
           (B) Can be sold as being as good as a tax-free deal, because even if sellers got shares in exchange, at some point they would sell them.
              (1) If interest is paid on notes (see below), shareholders get return on pre-tax principal amount.
           (C) If sellers want upside participation or if foreign acquirer is unsure of the value of the target company, a contingent pay format can be used: The foreign acquirer pays a base price in cash or notes and agrees to pay more if specified benchmarks (earnings, sales, or absence of claims) are met.
           (D) Sellers still can report gain as received, although the contingency complicates the computations.
     b. Disadvantages:
        i. Interest must be paid on the notes, or else it will be imputed. This would produce a tax to shareholder on accrual basis when he has no cash in hand.

       ii. The notes cannot be in registered form or readily market-
          able.

      iii. Does not work in all cases:

        (A) Installment treatment is not available if the shares of
            the target company are traded on an established securi-
            ties market.

        (B) It does not preserve the benefit of the step-up in basis
            at death (see B.3, above). Gain is fixed at the time of
            the sale, although time for recognition is postponed.

3. Structure a hybrid transaction
   a. Features
      i. There are various forms (see Appendix), but one basic idea
        is to allow target company shareholders to exchange target
        company shares for a nonvoting preferred interest, while the
        foreign acquirer or its U.S. subsidiary buys target company
        common stock for cash.

        (A) This is a tax-free transaction to target company share-
            holders that take preferred stock and

        (B) A taxable transaction to those that sell for cash and

        (C) A taxable transaction to the foreign acquirer.

   b. Disadvantages
      i. Depending on form, some SEC involvement unless target
        company is privately held.

      ii. Foreign acquirer invests cash but does not get a step-up in
        basis of target company assets.

D. Consider Allocating Consideration to Tax-Deductible Items
  1. Basic Issue
   a. Purchase price of shares gives rise to no tax benefit until shares
     are sold.

   b. Purchase price of assets of target company *may* give rise to
     increased depreciation or amortization deductions but only to
     the extent that the target company recognizes current gain on
     the sale, and this is generally disadvantageous.

  2. Possible Solutions
   a. Make payments to target company or its shareholders for a cov-
     enant not to compete.

   b. Separately license or acquire patents or trademarks for royalty
     (or other contingent payments).

   c. Build in more compensation for key shareholder-executives.

  3. Effects
   a. In each case, this creates a deductible stream of payments. If a
     lump sum is paid up front for a covenant not to compete, this
     can be amortized over the period covered.

   b. In each case, this creates ordinary income, rather than capital gain, to the recipient. Under current U.S. tax law, there is no difference in rate. Even if a rate differential is reintroduced, the tax difference to the recipient may be less than the tax benefit of the deductions to the Foreign Acquirer
 4. Caveats
   a. Compensation and noncompetition payments must be structured to avoid the so-called golden parachute rules.
   b. The Internal Revenue Service will carefully scrutinize the justification for shifting consideration to these items.
E. Consider Tax Alternatives in Funding the Purchase Price
 1. Basic Issues
   a. If foreign acquirer will borrow to fund the purchase, in what country will it be most advantageous to deduct the resulting interest expense?
   b. Can deductions be generated in two countries for the same interest expense?
   c. Factors to Consider
      i. Interest deductible in U.S. reduces U.S. tax (currently 34%) and this may produce smaller tax benefit than a deduction allowable in the foreign acquirer's home country.
      ii. Home country may not allow deduction for interest incurred in acquiring a U.S. company.
      iii. If debt is to be serviced out of earnings of target company in U.S., withholding taxes on dividends paid by target company must be considered.
   d. Possible Solutions
      i. Foreign acquirer borrows in its home country, contributes the funds to a tax haven subsidiary (preferably in a jurisdiction, such as the Netherlands, having a suitable income tax treaty with the United States), and that subsidiary lends the funds to a U.S. subsidiary making the acquisition. If allowable under the home country's tax law, this can create a double deduction for interest.
         (A) Caveat: U.S. Internal Revenue Service attacks on tax-haven conduits are increasing.
      ii. U.S. subsidiary formed to make the acquisition issues deep discount obligations to unrelated lenders.
         (A) Under U.S. tax rules (subject to limitations discussed below), original issue discount is accrued as an interest expense over the life of the obligation, thus creating deductions without cash outflows.
         (B) If U.S. subsidiary acquires at least 80% of shares of the target company (or its assets), there is no U.S. tax cost

in making the target company's earnings available to
service the debt.

   (C) Discount earned by U.S. lenders is taxable as accrued,
   but many are tax-exempt (e.g., pension funds).

   (D) Discount earned by non-U.S. lenders is in principle subject to U.S. withholding tax, but withholding is made
   only out of interest actually paid.

      (1) A zero coupon obligation gives rise to no withhold-
      ing tax until maturity, and a foreign lender can dis-
      pose of the obligations before that time.

   e. Limitations on Deductions for Interest in U.S.

      i. Acquisition indebtedness is nondeductible but this is a tooth-
      less tiger because

         (A) $5,000,000 of interest is allowed as a deduction each
         year in any event.

         (B) Limitation applies only if debt is subordinated *and*
         either convertible or issued as a unit with shares or war-
         rants to buy shares.

      ii. No accrual of original issue discount allowed on debt issued
      to *related* foreign lender until there is an actual payment
      subject to withholding tax.

      iii. Interest deduction may be lost if the borrowing is made by
      a U.S. subsidiary which is a dual resident company *and* the
      subsidiary has a loss *and* the loss can be used to offset
      group profits in another country (e.g., Australia).

   f. Caveat

      i. If U.S. subsidiary borrows in a currency other than U.S. dol-
      lars, foreign currency gain or loss may result and, unless
      fully hedged, this may produce U.S.-taxable gain or loss.

      ii. Congress is currently considering proposals which would
      further restrict the deductibility of interest on acquisition
      indebtedness.

F. Take Account of Limitations on Use of Net Operating Loss Carry-
overs

   1. The Basic Problem

      a. Generally net operating loss (NOL) of a U.S. company can be
      carried forward to offset taxable income for a period of 15 years.

      b. When a company is acquired, the use of NOLs may be restricted.

   2. The Limitations

      a. The NOL is disallowed altogether if the principal purpose of the
      acquisition is to secure the loss. This limitation will seldom
      apply in a normal business transaction.

      b. The NOL is also disallowed altogether unless the business of
      target company is continued for at least two years.

c. The so-called separate return limitation year (SRLY) and built-in loss limitation prevent use of preacquisition NOLs of target company (or losses built in as of acquisition date) to offset income of other U.S. companies in U.S. group of the foreign acquirer.

d. Under 1986 Tax Reform Act, a stringent metering rule limits the extent to which any remaining NOL can be used. This limitation applies regardless of whether the acquisition is tax-free, taxable, or hybrid.

e. Basic limitation

    i. Each year the amount of the otherwise allowable NOL which can be used is limited to the value of the shares of the target company at the acquisition date, multiplied by the long-term tax-exempt rate (an interest rate published by the Treasury Department and based on rates of interest on long-term U.S. government obligations).

    ii. This is a very complex provision with a large number of special rules.

        (A) Allowable NOL may be adjusted to take account of built-in gains or losses as of the acquisition date.

        (B) Capital contributions to target company to pump up value of its shares may be disregarded.

        (C) Special rules apply in Chapter 11 (insolvent reorganization) cases.

    iii. Under 1987 Act, if a loss company acquires a profitable company (other than in a taxable acquisition of assets), it cannot offset its losses by built-in gains inherent in acquired company's assets.

6.0 APPENDIX

A. The tax-free transaction

    1. General characteristics of this form of transaction

        a. It must meet one of the specific statutory definitions of reorganization (discussed below).

        b. It must be entered into for a valid business purpose and contemplate a continuity of the business enterprise in modified form.

        c. There must be a continuity of interest; shareholders of the target company must continue to hold a substantial equity interest in the foreign acquirer.

          i. IRS view: shares must be at least 50% of total price

    ii. Some reorganization definitions require that *only* stock be used

    iii. For the types of equity interests which can be used and the form in which they may be delivered, see 7, below

    iv. If shareholders of the target company who receive shares in the reorganization itself have a preexisting commitment or plan to sell them, the continuity test may be applied as if they received cash.

2. Under the integration or step-transaction doctrine, if the over-all acquisition plan contemplates more than one step, all of them will be viewed together in determining whether a transaction qualifies.

    a. Suppose, for example, the foreign acquirer wants to make a cash tender offer for shares of the target company, followed by a statutory merger of the target into a U.S. subsidiary in which the target company shareholders get shares of the acquirer. The merger and the tender offer will be viewed together in determining whether there is a tax-free reorganization.

3. Tax consequences of tax-free reorganization

    a. To target company shareholders

        i. No taxable gain or loss is recognized.

        ii. Basis in shares surrendered carries over to shares received.

        iii. If a shareholder receives nonshare consideration in addition to shares, this constitutes "boot" which is taxable either as a dividend (generally, if all shareholders receive it pro rata) or as capital gain to the extent it does not exceed the shareholder's over-all gain.

        iv. Caveat: Shareholders could recognize fully taxable gain in some limited circumstances described in 9, below

    b. To the target company: No taxable gain or loss

    c. To the foreign acquirer

        i. It (or a subsidiary) takes a basis in assets equal to their basis in the hands of the target company (no step-up).

        ii. It inherits the tax attributes of the target company (e.g., accounting methods), although net operating loss carry-forwards will be restricted.

4. The most commonly used forms of tax-free asset acquisitions

    a. Forward Triangular Merger: The target company is merged into a U.S. subsidiary of the foreign acquirer in a statutory merger under state law; shareholders of the target company receive stock of the foreign acquirer in exchange for their stock in the target company.

        i. The stock of the foreign acquirer may be voting or non-voting.

     ii. The U.S. subsidiary must acquire substantially all of the assets of the target company.

  b. The C Reorganization: A U.S. subsidiary of the foreign acquirer acquires substantially all of the assets of the target company *solely* in exchange for voting stock of the foreign acquirer, as well as an assumption of specified liabilities. As part of the plan of reorganization, the target company is liquidated and the stock of the foreign acquirer is distributed to its shareholders.

     i. Caveat: Even one dollar of consideration other than voting stock disqualifies the transaction.

       (A) This bars a toehold purchase for cash.

       (B) But cash can be given in lieu of issuing fractional shares.

5. Considerations in choosing the form of a tax-free asset acquisition

  a. The statutory merger route is usually easier to follow.

     i. Its main disadvantage is that *all* liabilities of the target company, disclosed or undisclosed, are inherited.

       (A) For the possibility of a "hold-back" or escrow of shares to meet undisclosed liabilities, see 8, below

  b. The C reorganization is normally used only when it is essential that the foreign acquirer not assume undisclosed liabilities.

     i. It is mechanically a more difficult transaction than a merger (every asset must be conveyed, while in a merger all assets pass by operation of law).

     ii. The solely voting stock requirement is a disadvantage.

6. The most commonly used forms of tax-free share acquisitions

  a. The Reverse Triangular Merger: The foreign acquirer forms a new shell U.S. subsidiary, and this is merged into the target company in a state law statutory merger. In the merger, the foreign acquirer receives shares of the merged company, while the shareholders of the target company receive shares of the foreign acquirer.

     i. The surviving company must end up with substantially all of the assets of both the target company and the shell subsidiary.

     ii. At least 80 percent of the consideration delivered to the shareholders of the target company must be voting shares of the foreign acquirer.

  b. The B Reorganization: A U.S. subsidiary of the foreign acquirer acquires at least 80% of the shares of the target company *solely* in exchange for voting shares of the foreign acquirer.

     i. It must acquire 80% of voting power of the target company's voting shares, plus 80% of the total number of nonvoting shares.

     ii. Here, as in the C reorganization, only voting shares may be used; one dollar of cash or debt (other than in lieu of fractional shares) totally disqualifies the deal.

   c. A tax-free share-for-share exchange can be framed in the context of a hybrid transaction, described below.

   d. The B reorganization is seldom used because

      i. The "solely for voting stock" requirement is onerous;

     ii. A share-for-share tender, unlike a merger transaction, is not a freeze out transaction.

7. What constitutes stock for purposes of a tax-free transaction

   a. *Any form* of stock may be used. For example,

      i. ADRs are treated as representing the underlying deposited shares.

     ii. Unless voting shares are expressly required, nonvoting may be used.

    iii. Straight or convertible preferred stock may be used, although if preferred is used together with common stock, it may be Section 306 stock, which gives rise to ordinary income, rather than capital gain, when disposed of.

     iv. Warrants and convertible debt are not stock, however.

   b. When delivery of *voting stock* is required:

      i. ADRs representing voting stock are treated as voting stock.

     ii. IRS has approved issuing voting stock into a voting trust and delivering voting trust certificates to target company shareholders.

       (A) But voting trusts normally exist only for a period of years (often, a maximum of ten).

8. Use of contingent consideration in tax-free transactions

   a. Hold back and deferred issuance of contingent shares

      i. In general, IRS will not rule favorably on the tax-free nature of the transaction unless at least 50% of the maximum amount of stock which may be issued is issued at the outset.

     ii. Deferred issuance of shares is treated as an installment transaction subject to imputed interest rules, so that some of the shares later received will give rise to ordinary income inclusion to the target company shareholder even though the underlying transactions remain tax-free.

   b. Issuance of shares in escrow

      i. IRS ruling policy here again requires that at least 50% of the maximum number of shares be issued unconditionally.

     ii. Since the shares are issued as of closing date (and exchanging shareholders are entitled to dividends), no interest is imputed on the shares issued into escrow.

       (A) Exchanging shareholders will recognize gain or loss upon later forfeiture and cancellation of shares if the

shares are recaptured to satisfy a shareholder obligation (e.g, breach of representation) and appreciation in
the shares is applied to satisfy the obligation, but no
gain or loss will be recognized if the forfeiture is only an
adjustment to the purchase price (e.g., failure to attain
specified earnings level).

9. Two particular problems for the foreign acquirer
    a. Section 367 of the Internal Reveune Code and the regulations
       thereunder provide that some transactions normally tax-free to
       the shareholders of the target company may be taxable to some
       or all of them when the shares they receive are shares of a for-
       eign company. This problem arises only in relatively limited cir-
       cumstances, however. The Section 367 rule is inoperative, and
       the general tax-free rules apply to the transactions described
       above if after the transactions either
        i. The individual shareholder owns less than 5% of the voting
           power and value of the shares of the foreign acquirer or
       ii. The individual shareholder owns 5% or more and
           (A) If the shareholders of the target company collectively
               own less than 50% of the voting power and value of the
               shares of the foreign acquirer, the shareholder files with
               the IRS an agreement to recognize gain if, within a five
               year period, the foreign acquirer disposes of the target
               company's shares or substantial portions of its assets or
           (B) If the shareholders of the target company collectively
               own 50% or more, the shareholders file a similar agree-
               ment covering a ten-year period.
    b. In each of the transactions described above, the U.S. subsidiary
       involved must be *directly* owned by the foreign acquirer.
        i. For example, if the foreign acquirer owns shares of foreign
           holding company and the foreign holding company owns
           shares of a U.S. subsidiary, none of the above transactions
           works. It will be necessary to establish a directly owned
           U.S. subsidiary to participate in the transaction.
       ii. But it may be possible to rationalize the structure after the
           transaction.
           (A) For example, assets received by the directly-owned U.S.
               subsidiary can be dropped down into a second-tier U.S.
               subsidiary without affecting the tax-free nature of the
               transaction.
           (B) At a later date, when the original acquisition is "old
               and cold," the shares of the directly-held U.S. subsidi-
               ary can be dropped down into another (new or existing)

U.S. subsidiary, so that the acquisition vehicle ends up as a second-tier (or lower tier) subsidiary.

B. Forms of Hybrid Transactions
  1. The Cash Option Merger
      a. Nature of Transaction: Target company is merged into a U.S. subsidiary of the foreign acquirer in a forward triangular merger, under the terms of which shareholders of the target company receive shares of the foreign acquirer or, to the extent they so elect, cash.
          i. Aggregate cash payable limited to less than 50% of total consideration payable, to assure compliance with the continuity of interest test.
          (A) This requires provision for proration of cash, if honoring all elections would require more than specified maximum.
          ii. Sometimes the foreign acquirer will want to insist on paying cash for minimum percentage of shares (e.g., to prevent excessive dilution or limit added dividend requirement).
      b. Useful where the foreign acquirer is willing to issue some shares and some target company shareholders want shares, while others want cash.
      c. Tax effects
          i. For all parties other than shareholders of target company who receive cash, tax consequences are identical with those of an all-shares forward triangular merger.
          ii. For a shareholder of the target company who receives cash,
          (A) If only cash is received (no shares), this is simply a taxable transaction.
          (B) If shares plus cash are received, the cash is treated as "boot"
  2. Cash Tender Offer followed by forward triangular merger
      a. Nature of Transaction: The foreign acquirer or a U.S. subsidiary makes a cash tender offer for shares of the target company, and this is followed by a forward triangular merger in which the remaining target company shares are exchanged for shares of the foreign acquirer.
      b. Useful where the acquisition is hostile or the foreign acquirer wants to establish a toe-hold position to place potential competitive bidders at a disadvantage.
      c. Tax effects are the same as in the cash option merger: The tender and the merger will be integrated for tax purposes.
  3. The Funded Subsidiary Preferred Stock Merger
      a. Nature of Transaction: Target company is merged into a U.S.

subsidiary of the foreign acquirer in a statutory merger (not a triangular merger) in which shareholders of target company receive nonconvertible preferred stock of the subsidiary.
  i. Preferred stock normally has rights to optional redemption at some future date; subsidiary may have option to call for redemption and there may be a mandatory redemption schedule.
  ii. The foreign acquirer may fund the dividend and redemption obligations of the subsidiary (which of course will own operating assets of the target company or put them in subsidiary whose stock it owns) by contributing cash to its capital, allowing the subsidiary to hold liquid, income-producing assets. Alternatively, these obligations may be funded by the subsidiary itself, in effect accomplishing a "bootstrap" acquisition of the target company.
  iii. Alternatively, acquiring corporation can guarantee dividend and redemption obligations
    (A) Caveat: Care must be taken not to make the preferred stock so secure that the IRS treats it as debt.
  b. Useful where the foreign acquirer wishes to purchase for cash or to accomplish a "bootstrap" acquisition and does not wish to issue its own securities, but shareholders of the target company insist on a tax-free transaction (e.g., to preserve prospect of step-up in basis at death).
    i. Redemption features may be tied to death and need of estate for cash to pay death taxes.
  c. Tax effects
    i. The statutory merger is a tax-free reorganization
    ii. Special considerations for shareholders of the target company
      (A) Preferred is not Section 306 stock, because they acquire no other shares.
      (B) Ultimate redemption can produce capital gain.
4. The Funded Subsidiary Preferred Stock with a Cash Option Merger
  a. Nature of Transaction: Like the transaction discussed in 3, above, but with the cash option feature discussed in 2, above.
  b. Useful where the considerations referred to in 3 are present, but some shareholders of the target company prefer a taxable transaction for cash.
    i. Note, however, that 50% of shares must be acquired for shares to satisfy the continuity of interest requirement.
  c. Tax effects: As described in 2 and 3, above.
5. Recapitalization of Target Company Followed by Cash Purchase of Shares

    a. Nature of Transaction: Pursuant to agreement, target company adopts plan of recapitalization calling for (possibly disproportionate) exchange of a new preferred stock (possibly having redemption features like those described in 2, above) for shares of its common stock; then the foreign acquirer purchases the remaining common shares for cash (or debt) in a taxable (possibly installment sale) transaction.

    b. Useful where considerations referred to in 2, above, apply, but 50% or more of the shareholders of the target company want cash, so that the continuity of interest test cannot be met.

        i. Difficult to assure acquiring company that it will acquire 100% of common stock.

    c. Tax effects

        i. The recapitalization exchange of preferred for common stock is a tax-free transaction; the continuity of interest requirement is not applicable, so that the exchange itself is tax-free, even though shares are thereafter sold as part of same plan.

            (A) If undervalued, shareholders taking preferred stock may be deemed to have made a gift or paid compensation to shareholders who sell for cash.

        ii. Preferred stock is Section 306 stock to a shareholder who retains preferred and common stock, but not to shareholder who exchanges all common for preferred stock.

        iii. Shareholders who sell common stock recognize taxable gain.

        iv. To the foreign acquirer, the transaction is a taxable purchase of common shares.

6. Exchange Offer by U.S. Subsidiary Followed by Freeze Out Cash Merger

    a. Nature of Transaction

        i. The foreign acquirer forms U.S. subsidiary, agreeing to contribute cash in return for all common shares.

        ii. Simultaneously, U.S. subsidiary offers to exchange shares of its preferred stock for shares of the target company.

        iii. Upon completion of i and ii, U.S. subsidiary forms second-tier subsidiary, which is merged into the target company in a cash merger, eliminating remaining minority shareholders of the target company.

    b. Useful in that this achieves the effect of 4, above, without requiring 50% of target company's shares to be acquired for stock; improves on 5, because nonexchanging shareholders can be forced out in the merger.

    c. Tax effects

        i. Steps i and ii under **6.a** constitute a tax-free incorporation transaction.

    (A) Dispositions of stock received in the incorporation transaction can disqualify it; but this rule looks only to those participating in the incorporation.

    (B) Effect is that participating shareholders exchange shares of the target company for preferred stock of U.S. subsidiary without recognition of taxable gain.

  ii. Shareholders frozen out in succeeding cash merger will recognize taxable gain or loss.

 iii. No gain or loss recognized by any of the participating corporations.

Chapter **6**

Tax Considerations in Acquiring Non-U.S. Enterprises

William L. Burke
Partner, Hughes, Hubbard & Reed

If the domestic tax scene is thought of as a two dimensional surface, the transnational tax scene has the appearance of a three dimensional holograph. All of the usual tax considerations relevant to a purely domestic acquisition continue to apply, frequently with a special twist. To this must be added the interplay of the United States internal rules with a wholly separate tax system and possibly an overlaying treaty.

In the case of an acquisition of a foreign enterprise by a United States corporation, the international aspects give rise to two dominating concerns not present in the purely internal United States transaction. The first is the often critical importance of choosing the right structure from the start. The other is that the United States ultimately taxes its corporations on their worldwide income, which engenders a complex set of income deferral and foreign tax credit rules.

1.0 INITIAL STRUCTURAL DECISIONS

1.1 Problems of Subsequent Changes

More (and most costly) mistakes may be made in the tax planning for the structure of the ownership and funding of a foreign venture by a United States company than in any other single area of the tax planning for an out-bound transaction. The United States tax system is extraordinary in the freedom it offers to restructure business activities within the United States once it is in corporate form. The United States imposes additional limitations, however, to insure and frequently to accelerate taxation of deferred income or unrealized gain when ownership of a business passes out of or into direct taxation in the United States tax system. And foreign systems frequently are much more restrictive in the changes they permit to be tax free under their income and transfer tax laws.

Without covering all the possible tax consequences, the point can be illustrated by supposing that the acquisition involves a business in a foreign country and considering the following three situations: (1) the acquired business is first operated as a branch of a United States subsidiary and it is later desired to transfer the business to a foreign subsidiary, (2) the business is acquired in a foreign subsidiary and it is later desired to transfer the business to a branch of a United States subsidiary, and (3) the business is acquired through a foreign subsidiary owned directly by the United States parent and the United States parent later wishes to transfer the stock of the foreign subsidiary to a foreign regional holding company.

The transfer of a branch from a United States corporation to a foreign subsidiary can raise a number of United States tax problems. One potential problem area is inventory. While inventory generally can be contributed to the capital of a domestic subsidiary without United States tax, the transfer of such items to a foreign subsidiary generally will be treated by the United States as a taxable sale. As a result, if the LIFO inventory method is being used in the business, the tax deferred benefit built up in any LIFO reserve is likely to be lost. Moreover, the foreign country may not treat the transfer as taxable. In that event, any built-in appreciation in the inventory will be taxed later in the foreign system. If the later foreign tax cannot be used as a credit because of the United States foreign tax credit limitations, there effectively will be double taxation of the appreciation in the inventory.

Another potential problem area is accumulated tax losses. Suppose the branch, while commercially successful, has operated at a tax loss for United States or foreign tax purposes (for example, because of the combination of the interest charges and rapid depreciation allowances). Structuring the operation as a branch of a United States subsidiary can allow the losses to be used currently in a consolidated return to offset income of other United States operations. When the branch is transferred to the foreign subsidiary, however, the net loss for United States tax purposes will be recaptured as taxable income in the United States. The foreign country also may disallow use of the branch's losses by the new foreign subsidiary. As a result, the effective use of the tax loss may be forfeited or at least significantly deferred.

Yet another potential problem area is intangibles. If certain intangibles such as patents or trademarks are transferred, the United States will restructure the transaction to treat the transfer of those intangibles as licensed for an arm's-length royalty (at values redetermined periodically). An adverse consequence is that the deemed revenues will also be treated as U.S. sourced income so that the resulting United States tax liability cannot be satisfied by use of foreign tax credits. As a consequence, the only practical course may be actually to license such intangibles to the foreign subsidiary for an arm's-length royalty. This will permit the revenue to be treated as foreign source in the United States for tax credit purposes, but it also raises the problems of potential pricing disputes with foreign tax officials, withholding taxes on the royalties, and possible creation of unuseable tax losses in the foreign subsidiary.

The restructuring of a wholly-owned foreign subsidiary into a branch of a domestic subsidiary similarly can pose problems.[1] On the United States side, the transaction would be treated as a tax-free reincorporation, provided the United States parent agrees to include in its taxable income as a dividend any previously undistributed earnings and profits (as computed for United States income tax purposes) that arose while the foreign subsidiary was owned by the United States parent. Passing differences between earnings and profits and taxable income, the deemed dividend terminates the deferral of United States taxation on any earnings of the foreign subsidiary.[2] If the United States parent does not agree to such a dividend, the IRS at its option may treat the transaction as a taxable sale of stock by the United States parent.

The foreign tax consequences may be even more severe. The liquidation of the foreign subsidiary may be treated as a taxable sale of its assets. and the usual transfer taxes for a sale of the business may apply, including transfer tax on the transfer of any goodwill associated with the

---

[1] The occasions on which it is desired to change an existing foreign subsidiary into a United States subsidiary with a foreign branch may be relatively infrequent, but not unheard of. Among the tax reasons for such a restructuring would be to make more effective use of economic losses if the acquisition were not a success and the business were losing money or expected to be sold at a loss. In some cases, it could also prove helpful under the recently promulgated interest expense allocation rules for foreign tax credit computations.

[2] United States tax earnings and profits can vary from United States taxable income in a number of ways, but actual economic profit generally tends to be reflected more fully and earlier in earnings and profits than in taxable income. As a result, the income recognition required on the restructuring may go beyond mere termination of deferral to accelerate taxable income beyond what would have arisen if the business had been placed in the United States subsidiary from the start.

business. Not all of those taxes may be useable or even available as a foreign tax credit against United States tax liabilities.

Restructuring to transfer the stock of the foreign subsidiary to a regional holding company organized in another country is probably the most frequent form of subsequent restructuring that is raised for consideration. A regional holding company can appear desirable after operations are acquired or started in several countries in the same region using separately incorporated subsidiaries for each country. At one time in the past, this kind of restructuring could not have been done on a tax-free basis from the United States side, and United States companies had to settle for group management without a regional corporate holding company to facilitate financing and other purposes. Current United States rules now permit the creation of such a regional holding company, but only if the United States parent agrees to subsequently treat the transfer of stock to the foreign holding company as a taxable transfer in the event that, within a period of ten years, the regional holding company disposes of the stock other than by distribution on a liquidation.

The moral is thus clear: unlike a purely domestic transaction, the initial choice of structure may not be freely changed later.

1.2 Tax Residence

Few United States acquirers are willing to conduct the foreign business operation as a part of the same legal entity as the United States operations. With the exception of banks and some service operations, nontax considerations generally move the business decision in the direction of a separate entity. That decision raises the issue of the tax residence of the separate entity.

Tax residence rules vary among countries. For corporations, the United States bases residence solely on place of incorporation (or deemed incorporation in the case of a corporation availing itself of the special Delaware domestication rules). Other countries use place of management and control or an even more vague "center of the enterprise" concept. And some use an expansive definition that includes corporations organized within the country plus corporations organized elsewhere with the requisite activity (management and control, center of enterprise, and so forth) in the country. Rules for residence of partnerships can be even more vague.

A change in tax residence will not necessarily affect the extent to which the business itself is taxed, at least when the operation is within one country. But it can involve a number of important consequences. One is the extent to which payments by the entity of such items as interest, royalties, dividends, and rental payments for personal property will be subjected to withholding taxes, and by which country. Both availability of tax treaty benefits and the applicable internal tax law rules of a country may be affected. A second consequence, discussed further below, is the timing of income and tax credit inclusions in the United States tax system. A third is that if the transaction involves the acquisition of an existing entity, the change in the entity's tax residence may be treated as a taxable sale of assets and liquidation of the entity under the foreign tax law, precipitating immediate tax liabilities.

To illustrate the effect, assume a foreign corporation in foreign country X, a country that bases residence on management and control and treats a change of residence as a taxable liquidation. Assume the stock of this corporation is acquired by a U.S. corporation with a European headquarters in London to which it immediately transfers supervisory management and control. Assume further that the corporation has unrealized appreciation in its assets of 100 monetary units, has regular earnings of 100, and pays a dividend to its new United States parent. The result would be that income tax would be due to the original foreign country on a deemed sale of the corporation's assets (including goodwill) as a result of the change of residence. The original country would still tax the income from the business done in it (which would be all the income). Dividends to the United States shareholder would give rise to United Kingdom advance corporation tax and a United Kingdom withholding tax of 5 percent of the dividend. Moreover, the United Kingdom advance corporation tax would not be refunded or used because the United Kingdom corporate tax liability would be satisfied with tax credits from the tax paid to the original country on the branch income of the now United Kingdom-resident subsidiary. As a result, if all the corporate income tax rates (and advance corporation tax rates) were 36 percent, instead of a cash receipt of 54.4 and a potential foreign tax credit of 9.6 in excess of its United States tax liability if the subsidiary had remained a tax resident of the original country, the United States parent would have a cash receipt of approximately 21.8 and a potential foreign tax credit of 42.2 in excess of its United States tax liability. Even if the foreign country did not tax the transfer of residence or the foreign country continued to treat the corporation as a tax resident, the total foreign tax burden for the year of change and every subsequent year increases, as shown in Table 6.1.

Attention also needs to be paid to cases of dual residence (for example, a corporation organized in the United States and managed and controlled in a country using that test for residence) and stateless structures (for example a corporation organized in a country using a management and control test but managed and controlled from the United States). Stateless structures have typically arisen inadvertently, but dual resident companies have been employed in the past to maximize the benefit of current tax deductions. For example, suppose a United States corporation organizes a subsidiary to borrow and acquire the stock of another corporation that was organized in and managed and controlled in the United Kingdom. Assume that the subsidiary is incorporated in the United States and is managed and controlled in the United Kingdom. Assuming no further restrictive tax law provisions, a consolidated return

TABLE 6.1

Resident of Original Foreign Country		United Kingdom Resident		
			Foreign Tax on Residence Change	No Foreign Tax on Residence Change
Regular Earnings	100	Regular Earnings	100	100
36% Tax on Regular Earnings	<36>	36% Tax on Sales Gain	<36>	—
	64	36% Tax on Regular Earnings	<36>	<36>
15% Withholding Tax	<9.6>		28	64
	54.4	36% ACT	<9.1>	<23>
		1/2 ACT Refund	5.1	11.5
			23	52.5
		5% Withholding Tax	<1.2>	<2.6>
			21.8	49.9

could be filed in the United States by the parent company and subsidiary (giving effective deduction in the United States of the interest paid by the subsidiary against the parent's income, which was not taxed in the U.K.), and group relief could be claimed in the United Kingdom for the subsidiary and for the U.K. company (giving effective deduction in the U.K. of the interest paid by the subsidiary against the income of the U.K. company, which was not taxable currently in the United States). The effect is two separate current interest deductions for one interest payment.

Despite the apparent appeal from the prior example, dual resident companies do not appear to have been greatly used by United States acquirers, and for good reason. There can be numerous problems, particularly longer term, in being subject to tax on a full resident basis in two different tax jurisdictions simultaneously. Not surprisingly, governments have now made efforts to prevent the practice illustrated, including recent United States tax legislation that denies use of a dual resident company's losses in a United States consolidated tax return where the loss is available to be used abroad against the income of a non-U.S. corporation. The problems some companies now face with dual resident subsidiaries illustrate the need for caution in choosing a structure that cannot be readily changed later and the benefits of which are within the independent control of third parties (the governments involved) that can be expected to react hostilely to the structure.

1.3 Entity Characterization

Critical to the United States tax consequences is whether any foreign entity involved will be treated as a corporation for United States tax purposes. In some cases, there may also be a question about whether particular arrangements give rise to what must be treated as a separate entity for United States tax purposes. If a given foreign entity is treated as a corporation, the United States deferral-credit rules will be applicable; if it is treated as a pass-through entity, the United States taxation will be the same or very similar to what would apply if the business unit were the branch of a United States domestic subsidiary.

The relevant determinations for United States tax purposes will be made under United States tax law concepts. In many cases, there will be no question whether there is a foreign entity that must be taken into account and how it should be characterized for U.S. tax purposes. But hybrid arrangements that do not correspond to arrangements in customary use in the United States may be open to question. An example is the United States treatment of German *stillegesellschaft* arrangements. Under these arrangements, the party (the *stillegesellschafter*) providing funds to a GmbH has the status under German law of a creditor equal to other unsecured creditors of the GmbH and is not listed in any public records as having an equity interest in the GmbH. The return on investment paid to the *stillegesellschafter* is deductible by the GmbH and taxable to the *stillegesellschafter* for German tax purposes. But the investor's return on investment is typically a percentage of the GmbH's pretax profits, and the investor may also share in any unrealized appreciation in value of the business if and when the GmbH is liquidated. The bankruptcy of the GmbH automatically terminates the arrangement.

In a series of private letter rulings, the IRS first took the position that the arrangement constituted a second class of stock in the GmbH that would result in deferral of any U.S. income inclusion until the return on investment was actually paid. But if the actual payment of the investment return was delayed, it could leave the United States *stillegesellschafter* with a potential foreign tax credit for the tax paid Germany without any foreign source income against which to use the credit before the carryover period expired. The IRS subsequently reversed itself, and issued a private letter ruling treating the arrangement as the creation of a separate entity (solely for U.S. tax purposes) that had to be characterized as a partnership. The revised IRS position results in immediate United States tax and foreign tax credits for U.S. tax purposes when the *stillegesellschafter* is a United States entity, even when the investment return is retained in the business and not paid out currently.

2.0 FORMS OF TRANSACTION

In addition to deciding whether a foreign or domestic entity will be used to carry on the business, consideration must also be given to the basic form of the transaction: whether it is to be tax free, taxable, or a hybrid of the two. The United States deferral-tax credit system, discussed below, will bring into play the United States tax system. Consistency of treatment between the two tax systems generally will be desirable, often more so than in the case of an in-bound transaction involving an acquirer from the same foreign country acquiring a United States target. Transactions that are fully taxable in the foreign jurisdiction but tax-free under the United States rules generally should be avoided. Otherwise, there would be a full tax paid abroad but no new tax basis in the assets of the business for United States tax purposes. As a result, the same appreciation in values may be taxed a second time in the United States system without benefit of any credit for foreign income taxes paid by the sellers on the original acquisition when the acquirer receives dividends or otherwise realizes on its investment. The reverse situation (a transaction taxable under United States rules but tax free under the foreign rules) might be beneficial if the United States acquirer can fully use the additional foreign tax credits that the foreign target will generate later because of no new tax basis for foreign tax purposes.

2.1 Tax-Free Exchanges

The ability to accomplish a fully tax-free acquisition or a hybrid transaction is much more restricted for out-bound transactions than for in-bound transactions for several reasons. First, the more generous statutory merger forms of reorganization in the United States tax code are not available where the target is a foreign corporation. The transaction will therefore have to meet the more restrictive rules for B reorganizations (solely stock for stock) or C reorganizations (in practice, solely stock and assumption of liabilities for assets).

Second, foreign tax law systems frequently are less generous than the United States tax-free reorganization provisions concerning the form of consideration that can be used, especially with respect to allowing triangular transactions using a parent corporation's stock. Foreign law also may be more restrictive in the amount of nonstock consideration permitted or in the degree of required continuity of business enterprise or shareholder interest.

Finally, even if the transaction would be tax free for income tax purposes, there may be substantial transfer taxes in the foreign country. For a combination of government policy reasons, foreign countries frequently have high transfer taxes (value added or sales taxes) and title recording charges, including transfer taxes on such intangibles as goodwill. These taxes may apply even if the transaction involves acquisition of the stock of the corporation holding the assets. In France, for example, there was a time when acquisition of all of the stock of a corporation within a certain time frame resulted in transfer taxes being assessed with respect to the assets of the target (including goodwill) at rates up to 17 percent.

2.2 Taxable Exchanges

Issues of concern in transactions that are fully taxable on a current basis in both tax systems generally are fewer than for transactions intended to be wholly or partially tax free, but they can still be numerous. The applicable rules for both the foreign tax system and the United States tax system still must be considered because of the interplay with earnings computations for foreign tax credit allowances when the results of the foreign operations, or gains on disposition of the foreign investment, are brought into the U.S. tax system. Among the questions that frequently require attention are the tax treatment of borrowings and the tax treatment to seller and acquirer of such items as amounts paid for covenants not to compete and contingent purchase price payments. The possibility of significant transfer taxes and title recording charges also should not be overlooked.

3.0 FINANCING

3.1 Debt

Debt financing, both how much to borrow and which entity should borrow, should be taken into account in the structuring of a transnational acquisition in two different respects. Each is deceptively like the considerations in the purely domestic context, but each has an important twist. One aspect is restrictions on the deductibility of interest expense on acquisition debt. The United States currently has restrictions on convertible subordinated acquisition indebtedness (Internal Revenue Code, Section 279), and other restrictions have been a frequent topic of discussion in recent years. The country where the target is located may have a different set of acquisition indebtedness rules that gives a different effective benefit, at least initially. Differences in such rules between the two countries present obvious opportunities and pitfalls for relative competitive advantage in effective acquisition costs, depending upon where the borrowing and related interest cost are lodged in the overall corporate structure.

The second aspect is the possible use of debt to minimize the total tax burden within the overall corporate structure even when acquisition debt limitations do not apply. This applies particularly to intercompany debt, but it also applies to third-party debt placement viewed in the broader economic perspective. Not unlike state tax planning strategies, debt can be used to effectively shift earnings to or from the United States if that results in a lower tax rate. When the United States parent supplies its own funds by way of loans, it can also avoid the additional foreign withholding tax that might otherwise be imposed on repatriation of earnings through payment of dividends. On the other hand, savings of foreign taxes is only an interim cash flow benefit if all the foreign taxes can be used as foreign tax credit against United States tax liability. Unlike the purely domestic context, where the interest expense is lodged can have the effect of increasing the interim (or even the overall) effective tax burden when the interest expense generates more deductions than the payer can use currently. This is particularly likely to be relevant for cross-border intercompany loans since the related payee generally will be taxed currently on the interim income in the other tax jurisdiction.

As with limitations on acquisition debt, the ability to reduce the total tax burden on the earnings of a business through use of leverage and interest deductions is likely to vary from one tax system to the next, reflecting different attitudes and approaches to the debt versus equity problem generally and the extent to which a country wishes to offer a tax incentive to capital infusions from foreign investors. Canada, for example, has had a rule for some time that limits the principal amount of debt on which deductible interest can be paid to non-Canadian affiliates. The limit is no more than three times the Canadian company's equity. At the other extreme, Ireland still gives the taxpayer the option of interest-free loans both into and out of Ireland, effectively opening the opportunity for repatriation of capital without any withholding taxes.

3.2 Alternative Financing Forms

Nor should uniformity of tax systems necessarily be expected in rules for alternative financing forms, such as leasing and licensing. With the growth in international capital markets, cross-border leasing has experienced a rapid increase in recent years, particularly for relatively expensive equipment such as computers, aircraft, and ships that have relatively fungible market character. Differences in loan versus lease characterization rules between countries have sometimes afforded the possibility of "double dip" or even "triple dip" leases. In such cases, the lessor and lessee (and the sublessee in a triple dip) are located in different countries, and each is treated as the owner with depreciation allowances for its country's tax system, which usually allows more rapid tax allowances than would be allowed for rental payments. Where a multiple dip lease is possible, it is also usually possible to have the reverse case of a "no dip" lease where neither lessor nor lessee is treated as the owner in its tax system. A no dip lease generally is not attractive from a tax point of view although the possibility of appeal in very specialized circumstances cannot be dismissed entirely.

Leasing rules, like depreciation allowance rules, are often closely tied to government policy on how much incentive to give for new capital expenditure. They can change frequently. The point is well illustrated by the United States shifts in recent years on so-called "safe harbor" financing leases. Opportunities and limitations for leasing, therefore, should be reviewed afresh with each acquisition that may involve or permit a step-up in basis of a particular asset.

Licensing is another area where there are different rules from one country to the next, particularly for intangibles. The United States, for example, has special rules for amortizing acquisition costs of trademarks and other intangibles in certain circumstances. Other possible differences between the foreign and United States systems also need to be reviewed, since any differences will come into play in the operation of the United States foreign tax credit provisions.

The amounts of payments allowable with respect to intercompany transactions in intangibles and items like management services can also differ between the foreign and United States system, even when there is no difference in basic concepts. The United States now has special rules for intercompany licenses of intangibles under which the IRS can require second looks at the appropriate arm's-length royalty charges that will not necessarily be accepted by the tax authorities in the foreign country involved. Similarly, in some foreign countries it may be possible to negotiate an agreed, relatively nominal, charge for matters like corporate overhead, credit support, or technical assistance compared to what will be accepted on the United States side.

4.0 U.S. DEFERRAL AND CREDIT RULES

The tax area in out-bound transactions that can be the most elusive is planning for deferral of income and related foreign tax credit usage. In broad concept, the deferral-credit rules are designed to achieve two objectives. One is generally to allow active business operations owned by United States taxpayers to compete with foreign businesses without the disadvantage of current United States taxation at a higher rate than the effective rate of foreign taxation. The other objective is to avoid (or at least mitigate) double taxation of the foreign income when it ultimately is taxed by the United States. This relief must be tempered, however, to avoid going beyond double tax relief and allowing taxpayers to use the foreign tax credit provisions to recover from the United States treasury foreign tax paid at higher rates.

Efforts to implement these deferral-credit objectives within appropriate limits have led to one of the most complex and technical sets of rules in the United States Internal Revenue Code. For the businessman planning a foreign acquisition, the difficulty in coping with the complexity is compounded by the extent to which the better choice will be dependent upon future developments and the potential difficulty in being able to make structural adjustments to deal with those developments. Often the planning exercise needs to focus more on defensive steps to avoid potential problem situations than on affirmative tax reduction strategies.

4.1 Basic Rules

The basic deferral-credit rules are deceptively simple. If a business is conducted through a United States corporation, there will be current United States inclusion of net income or loss. If a business is conducted through a foreign corporation, there will be United States taxation only when a taxable distribution is paid to the United States shareholder (or deemed paid under deferral termination rules) or the stock of the foreign corporation is sold. In determining the extent to which an actual or deemed distribution from a foreign subsidiary gives rise to taxable income, substantially the same rules apply as in the purely domestic context, except that there is no dividend-received deduction. An actual and deemed distribution is taxed as a dividend only to the extent of current or accumulated earnings and profits of the foreign subsidiary. As and when the stock of the foreign subsidiary is sold, any gain on the sale is treated as a dividend to the extent of undistributed earnings and profits accumulated while the United States parent owned its stock; the balance of the gain, if any, generally is treated as a capital gain. Earnings and profits are computed in substantially the same manner as in determining the amount of a distribution that is a dividend from a domestic corporation, except that different (and generally somewhat slower) rules for computing depreciation charges apply.

When foreign source income is taxed in the United States, the resulting federal income tax liability (but not any state or local income tax liability) can be reduced by credits for foreign income taxes. The election to claim foreign income taxes as a credit against tax rather than as a deduction in computing taxable income is an annual election and applies to all foreign income taxes paid or deemed paid in that year by the U.S. taxpayer. The maximum permissible credit generally is not restricted to only foreign tax paid on the specific item of foreign source income, but it is subject to a number of limitations intended to insure that the total credit does not exceed the United States tax on total net foreign source income. It is also subject to a number of limitations intended to insure that the United States taxpayer does not shift the source of income, particularly passive or financial-type income, to increase the amount of tax liability against which foreign tax credit may be claimed. Within the maximum credit allowed, the United States taxpayer is allowed a credit for foreign income taxes imposed directly on it and foreign withholding taxes imposed on payments directly to it. In addition, if a United States corporation owns a requisite minimum percentage of the voting stock of the foreign corporation, the United States shareholder also receives a credit for the amount of foreign income taxes paid by the foreign corporation (or in certain cases paid by a lower tier foreign corporation) with respect to the earnings out of which the dividend was paid. There is a limited carryback and carryover of any excess foreign tax credits to other years, subject to the same limitation in each of those other years.

Future performance of the business and developments in each country's tax laws will obviously affect deferral and tax credit planning. There are, however, some points where investigation in connection with the planning and structuring of the acquisition can be useful. One involves determining which of the various foreign taxes imposed on the business will qualify as a creditable foreign tax rather than one that can only be deducted. Another involves assessing what permanent and timing differences may arise between the foreign tax system rules and the United States rules.

4.2 Creditable Taxes

A country's general tax levy normally will qualify as an income tax if it is based on gross receipts minus deductions of the same general type the United States allows in computing net income. Problems can arise, however, when there are alternative bases of assessment or supplemental taxes imposed on a business sector. Also, a tax does not qualify to the extent that it is imposed on the basis of the maximum amount available as a tax credit in another country.

4.3 Timing Differences

In the past, timing differences sometimes produced dramatic effects (some would argue distortions) in the amount of foreign tax credits that could arise from a dividend. Prior to 1987, the United States rules treated each year's earnings and related foreign taxes as separate pools, with dividends paid from the most recent pool in reverse chronological order. To illustrate the resulting possible effects, consider a subsidiary in the United Kingdom in the period in the recent past when that country was allowing an immediate deduction for new capital investment in equipment. Suppose the subsidiary had earnings before depreciation of 100 monetary units for both United Kingdom and United States tax purposes. Suppose also an equipment investment of 100 which would be depreciated evenly over four years for United States tax purposes. Finally, suppose the corporate tax rate was 40 percent in both the United Kingdom and the United States and that no withholding tax is imposed on dividends. If a dividend of 25 were paid at the end of each of year 1 and year 2, the tax burden would have been $40 of United Kingdom tax (from year 2) and 12.8 of net additional United States tax (a liability of 20 from year 1 and an excess credit of 7.2 from year 2). By contrast, if the entire dividend of 50 were paid in year 2, the total United States tax would change to an excess foreign tax credit of 4 that could produce a United States tax refund in that amount. Assuming full use of available foreign tax credits, the total taxes decreases to 36 when the entire 50 is distributed in year 2 (40 of United Kingdom tax less 4 from use in the United States of the excess credit).

The United States has now shifted to a single aggregate pool of

TABLE 6.2

	United Kingdom Tax Calculation		United States Tax Calculation					
			Prior Law			Current Law		
			25 Dividend Each Year		50 Dividend	25 Dividend Each Year		50 Dividend
	Year 1	Year 2	Year 1	Year 2	in Year 2	Year 1	Year 2	in Year 2
Income	100	100	100	100				
Depreciation	<100>	-0-	<25>	<25>				
Net U.K. Tax Earnings		100						
U.K. Tax (40%)	-0-	40		40				
Net U.S. Tax Earnings	-0-	40	75	35				
Dividend			25	25	50	25	25	50
Credit Carried By Dividend			— $\frac{25}{75} \times 40 = $ -10-	$\frac{25}{35} \times 40 = 28.6$ —	$\frac{35}{35} \times 40 = 40$ 15 $75 \times 0 = $ -0-	$\frac{25}{75} \times 0 = $ -0-	$\frac{25}{85} \times 40 = 11.8$	$\frac{50}{110} \times 40 = 18.2$
U.S. Net Earnings			25	53.6	90	25	36.8	68.2
U.S. Tax (40%)			20	21.4	36	20	14.7	27.3
Foreign Tax Credit*			-0-	<28.6>	<40>	-0-	<11.8>	<18.2>
Net Tax Liability			20	<7.2>	<4>	20	2.9	9.1

*U.K. Tax × (Dividend − Net U.S. Tax Earnings).

earnings and tax credits for years after 1986. But timing can still make a difference. In the above example, the United States tax would have been 22.9 for equal distributions in year 1 and year 2 under the new rules, but only 9.1 if the entire distribution were in year 2, as shown in Table 6.2. The total tax burden would converge (to 40 U.K. and an additional 20 U.S.) only if the entire remaining earnings and profits are distributed in year 2. As a practical matter, however, the total earnings are not likely to be distributed or otherwise reflected in income or gains taxable in the United States prior to the time the business is sold. Moreover, once a dividend is paid (even in year 2) the total effective tax rate increases to above the effective tax rate being borne by the local competing businesses, even though the nominal statutory rates in the example are the same in both the United Kingdom and the United States. In effect, the distributions, whether in year 1 or year 2, result in the loss of the more favorable effective foreign tax rate arising from the foreign government's more favorable tax incentive. The converse also will be true if the United States grants a more favorable effective rate and the excess foreign tax paid can be used as a credit against the United States tax liability on other foreign source income.

4.4 Foreign Exchange

One other factor that can produce dramatic effects is the potential difference in income recognition between the two tax systems due to changes in foreign exchange rates. Suppose, for example, the United States parent funds foreign subsidiary with $100, which it exchanges for £100 (units of the local currency). It acquires a machine with the funds on the last day of its tax year. Suppose both the United States and the foreign tax laws allow the machine to be depreciated in full the next year and that as a result of inflation, the exchange rate is $1.00 = £2 at the end of the next year. The depreciation calculated using the dollar cost or the exchange rate in effect when the machine was purchased produces a $100 (or £200) deduction compared to the £100 deduction from computing income using local currency costs.

Under the foreign tax law, the subsidiary may be allowed an additional depreciation deduction to help correct for the inflation (an allowance frequently given by foreign countries with chronic high inflation). But that benefit effectively will be lost, or at least deferred, if there is an actual or deemed dividend from the subsidiary and the United States computes its earnings in £'s without granting a supplemental depreciation allowance comparable to the foreign tax system. Conversely, the effect will be eliminated if the United States computes earnings using historical dollar cost.

Some years ago, a client was presented with this problem in classic fashion. Between the time it had purchased its operations in Brazil (through a Brazilian subsidiary) and the time when it wished to receive dividends from the Brazilian subsidiary, inflation in Brazil resulted in the devaluation of the cruziero from an exchange rate of a few hundred to the dollar to several thousand to the dollar. Brazil allowed a depreciation adjustment for the inflation so that the effective Brazilian tax rate on the earnings, on a constant value basis, was slightly more than the United States statutory tax rate. But if the effect of the currency decline were not taken into account, the depreciation allowance was so diminished that the unadjusted earnings were large enough to reduce the effective Brazilian tax rate (and therefore the amount of foreign tax credits carried by the dividend) to nil. As a result, the client faced significant additional tax liability in the United States on the dividend income.

The situation is exactly reversed, of course, if the foreign currency has appreciated against the dollar. The client mentioned in the preceding paragraph also had significant operations conducted through foreign subsidiaries in Europe. The currencies in those countries had appreciated against the dollar. While the effective tax rates in those countries was comparable to the United States rate when the earnings were computed on a constant value basis, application of the approach that caused the problem for a Brazilian dividend raised the effective foreign tax credit that would be carried by a dividend from the European subsidiaries. The client found that it could solve its tax problem without taking more extreme steps by taking dividends from both countries and using the excess credits on the European dividends to satisfy the United States tax liability on the Brazilian dividends—a happy, albeit fortuitous, set of circumstances.

In 1986, the United States adopted for the first time a systematic set of rules for the treatment of foreign exchange gains and losses. Under those rules, the income of a foreign subsidiary for United States tax purposes is generally computed in foreign currency, but a taxpayer may elect to compute the income of all subsidiaries in hyperinflationary countries in dollars (basing depreciation on historical dollar cost). Such an election can be appealing, but the decision often is more complicated than the simple example presented. The choice to use dollars will result in cancellation of indebtedness income or other taxable exchange gain from the benefit of repaying any local currency borrowings with the low valued local currency on the later payment date. As a result, the timing of earnings recognition and corresponding deduction in the United States tax system calculations still will not necessarily coincide. As a practical matter, the problems in the foreign currency area are likely to be so complex that prior planning will have to focus on evaluating exposures more than crafting perfect solutions.

The tax risks involved in foreign currency exposures are more than just a repetition of the basic economic risk. While an offsetting hedge position in the parent can neutralize the economic risk, the tax effects will not necessarily be as neutralized on a current basis if each part of the hedge is in a different tax jurisdiction. The current gain on the one part will not necessarily be offset by a current deduction in that tax system for the corresponding loss on the part in the other tax system. And even if the hedge needed to convert the risk to another currency is placed in the home tax system of the other currency (for example, the foreign subsidiary purchases a dollar futures contract), one part will still be in the currency of the tax system while the other is not; so only one side of the hedge will be taken into account in that system.

5.0 EMPLOYEE COMPENSATION AND BENEFIT PLAN REQUIREMENTS

Most transactions involve transfers of key personnel from the United States to the foreign country or vice versa. Such transfers are frequently made with an agreement to protect the employee from any increase in tax burden. Even where no such agreement exists, there will be a mutuality of interest in reducing the overall tax burden on the employee.

After the transfer, the tax residence of the employee may shift to the new location, particularly if the employee will remain there for a number of months and there is no applicable tax treaty. The United States taxes its citizens on their worldwide income, wherever they reside. Non-U.S. citizens generally are taxed on a worldwide basis only in the country where their tax residence is located (although cases of dual tax residence can arise, particularly where there is no applicable income tax treaty). As a consequence, a United States citizen whose tax residence shifts to a foreign country can become subject to taxation on worldwide income in two tax jurisdictions simultaneously. Even if tax residence does not change, transferred personnel are likely to become subject to tax on compensation in the country to which they are transferred.

5.1 Tailoring the Time Away

Relief provisions to help affected employees cope with the burdens and complexities vary too much from country to country to be surveyed. But consideration should be given to whether the period abroad can be adjusted to qualify for any overseas employment relief (such as the provisions of Section 911 of the United States tax code) and whether such provisions would provide a benefit in comparison to other available steps (such as claiming foreign tax credits) to avoid double taxation of the employee.

5.2 Tailoring, Timing, and the Nature of Compensation

Consideration should also be given to delaying or accelerating items of compensation or fringe benefits. Most individuals prepare their tax returns using the cash method of accounting, and it seldom is realistic for them to contemplate using an accrual method for any extended period of time. The United States taxes its citizens and tax residents on all income they must report under their method of accounting during the period they are United States citizens or tax residents, even if the income was earned for prior services or will be earned for subsequent services. Foreign countries frequently follow a similar concept with respect to periods of tax residence. The United States also generally taxes at its regular net income rates any income earned from services performed in the United States for a United States employer that would be reported by the employee in a period in which he is a nonresident alien. The income is taxable regardless of whether the employee was a United States citizen or resident when the services were performed. Foreign jurisdictions can be expected to have similar source taxation concepts. Some, however, may tax the employee on a gross withholding, rather than a net income basis, on amounts properly reported in a period when he is not a tax resident even if the services were performed while he was a tax resident.

Differences may also exist in the amount of income that may be assessed for fringe benefits, including car allowances and life insurance. Special attention should also be given to how to deal with moving expenses, both for the transfer to the new position and for the transfer back to the original employment location.

Coverage under funded benefit plans can pose special problems. Such plans generally involve special tax benefits that are available only if extensive, very specific requirements are met. The requirements are virtually never the same in the two tax systems. The problem is both deductibility for the employer for the amount of the contribution and taxation of the contribution to the employee currently on a constructive receipt theory. For the United States employee sent abroad, the U.S. tax law permits the employer to maintain a United States plan covering only U.S. citizens and residents. Within slightly relaxed limits, a U.S. citizen or resident may also be covered under a plan of a foreign employer. The degree of relaxation permitted, however, may not always allow the problem to be avoided.

6.0 CHECKLIST

A. Initial structural decisions.
   1. Foreign versus U.S. business entity.
      a. Factors affecting choice.
         i. Foreign law may have nontax restrictions on using U.S. entities.
         ii. Form of transaction likely to affect available options. Buyer

will probably have to accept existing entity if transaction is to be an acquisition of stock (see B, below).

iii. Tax residence rules.

(A) Rules on residence in each country: U.S. determines corporate tax residence by place of incorporation while other countries frequently use another test (such as place of management and control).

(1) May be possibility of dual resident or stateless entity. Generally desirable to avoid both.

(a) Can have an adverse effect (including loss of treaty relief) on withholding taxes on interest, dividends and other payments.

(b) Restrictions on use of dual resident company tax losses and other benefits in U.S. consolidated tax returns.

(2) Change of residence can result in substantial tax liabilities.

(B) Distinctions between taxation on branch versus residence basis by the foreign country.

(1) Possible exclusion of passive income.

(2) Possible differences in expense deductions allowable.

(3) Possible differences on withholding rates on items of income paid or received from another country.

iv. U.S. deferral-credit rules (see C, below).

v. Employee compensation and benefit plan requirements (see D, below).

vi. Tax planning needs of other equity participants for less than wholly-owned businesses.

b. If choice is for foreign entity.

i. How will entity be classified for U.S. tax purposes?

ii. Choice of direct U.S. ownership or ownership through intervening foreign entity.

(A) Utility of multicountry holding companies or chains of ownership limited by potential loss of deferral of U.S. taxation when lightly taxed dividends and passive income are paid by foreign subsidiary in one country to foreign subsidiary in another country.

(B) U.S. will not recognize foreign tax consolidations.

2. Financing of the acquisition and on-going business entity.

a. Debt, especially intercompany debt.

i. Tax planning factors to consider.

(A) Potential benefits from reducing foreign taxes.

(1) Is foreign marginal tax rate above U.S. marginal tax rate?

(2) Does U.S. parent face excess foreign tax credits?
  (a) Foreign tax law deduction for interest coupled with reduced withholding rate when treaty applies typically permits earnings stripping at reduced foreign tax burden.
  (b) Debt typically avoids foreign withholding tax on recovery of original principal.
  (c) Intercompany loan from U.S. affiliate may favorably affect allocation of U.S. interest expense among domestic and foreign source income.

(B) On intercompany loans to foreign subsidiary, will the subsidiary have and use additional current foreign tax law deduction equal to interest currently includible in U.S. income? If not, result can be net increase in total current taxes.

(C) Generally, possible to convert debt into equity without tax but not to substitute debt for equity, so initial capitalization with debt tends to give more flexibility.

(D) Special tax considerations on intercompany debt.
  (1) Interest paid to foreign sister companies generally taxed currently by U.S.
  (2) Arm's-length interest rules will apply. Is the interest charge within any safe harbor for intercompany interest under each country's tax laws, and if not, can the rate be sustained against attack in both jurisdictions?
  (3) Will interest expense on any borrowings by U.S. entities be offset against the interest deducted by the foreign subsidiary for U.S. foreign tax credit calculations?

(E) Other points of U.S. versus foreign tax law treatment to check.
  (1) Amount of allowable debt restrictions on total debt and related company debt, both generally and on borrowings to finance acquisitions.
  (2) Minimum and maximum restrictions (both tax and nontax) on interest rates.
  (3) Currency: foreign versus U.S. tax law treatment of exchange gains and losses.
  (4) Timing: foreign versus U.S. tax law treatment of
    (a) Installment and contingent payment purchases: when interest will be deductible and when amounts will be added to basis for depreciation allowances.
    (b) Interest deductions for debt issued at a discount or premium.

b. Equity.
  i. Issuance of parent company stock.
    (A) Will transaction be tax-free exchange for either U.S. or foreign tax purposes (see B.1 on this page).
    (B) U.S. taxation of foreign recipient on dividends and on subsequent sale of stock.
      (1) U.S. withholding on dividends (generally reduced to no more than 15% by any applicable treaty).
      (2) Sale of stock by nonresident alien, even on U.S. stock exchange, generally not taxed by U.S.
  ii. Possible avoidance of United States securities law restrictions but possible local securities law regulations.
c. Hybrid securities.
  i. Foreign tax law treatment of
    (A) Convertible debt.
    (B) Issuance and expiration of warrants to acquire stock in United States acquirer.
  ii. U.S. treatment of local country hybrids without direct U.S. correspondence (e.g., German *stillegesellschaft* arrangements).
d. Other funding sources.
  i. Lease and licensing financing.
    (A) May be useful in avoiding interest expense and other debt/equity limitations.
    (B) Likely to require sale of any assets involved for both foreign and U.S. tax law purposes.
      (1) May not be an additional concern where basic transaction is an asset purchase, but foreign transfer taxes can be substantial and should be checked in addition to foreign income taxes if done in connection with stock sale.
      (2) If stock acquisition, consider deemed asset purchase rules under I.R.C. §338 and consider potential foreign transfer tax costs.
    (C) Lessor-licensor likely to become subject to tax by foreign country either on net income basis or withholding basis.
      (1) Burden of tax on withholding basis frequently prohibitive unless reduced or eliminated by treaty.
      (2) Real estate lessor frequently taxed on a net basis or permitted that election if treaty applicable.
    (D) Special rules likely to be applicable to intercompany sale and license back of intangibles such as patents, trademarks, trade names, copyrights, etc.
  ii. Possibility of financing through indirect working capital support (e.g., extension of credit to subsidiary on inventory

purchases from affiliates of same payment terms offered third parties).
3. Expected on-going intercompany dealings.
   a. Funding transactions (see A.2.a, above).
   b. Home office management services and other intercompany services.
      i. Interplay of U.S. arm's-length and safe harbor rules with foreign tax law rules.
         (A) Consider whether a reasonable and systematic policy can be established for allocating corporate overhead charges.
         (B) Take steps to identify and segregate for retrieval any costs on which management charge is to be based.
      ii. Consider whether services will raise risk of service-provider being taxed in other country and steps (such as transferring employees or making them dual employees) to avoid.
   c. Purchases of Goods.
      i. Unless there are comparable uncontrolled sales to unrelated third parties as reference point, likely to be a point of potential dispute with tax authorities in at least one of the countries.
      ii. If a problem, consider feasibility of a marketing agency arrangement.
      iii. If transaction involves sale by U.S. affiliate, consider having sale terms with title passing on delivery abroad to maximize amount of foreign source income.
B. Form of Transaction.
1. Tax free versus taxable.
   a. Generally undesirable for transaction to be structured as tax free under U.S. laws and taxable under other country's laws.
   b. Restrictions on U.S. rules applicable to domestic transactions.
      i. More generous statutory merger forms of tax free reorganizations not available.
      ii. Check whether U.S. rules applicable to exchanges involving foreign corporation preclude tax free characterization (see I.R.C. §367). Generally should not be a problem where at least majority of target is owned by nonresident aliens or foreign-owned foreign corporation.
   c. Foreign tax laws generally not as generous as U.S. system in allowing tax-free corporate restructurings and ownership changes.
      i. Income tax issues.
         (A) Frequently less developed or less generous rules for use of parent company stock and types and amounts of other consideration that can be used.
         (B) Possible differences in continuity of business and continuity of shareholder interest required.

ii. Check foreign transfer taxes even if transaction is a stock purchase. Rates typically are substantial if they apply.
  (A) Will sale of stock be treated as sale of assets? If so
    (1) Transfer tax could also apply to goodwill involved as well as tangible assets and other intangible assets.
    (2) May be possible to avoid by purchasing stock in two traunches.
  (B) Stamp duties or other title recording charges may be imposed on registration or consummation of stock ownership change.
2. Taxable exchanges.
  a. Use of debt versus cash (see A.2.a, above).
  b. Foreign and U.S. law implications of allocation of purchase price.
    i. Treatment of intangibles, including in particular goodwill and covenants not to compete.
    ii. Permissible inventory practices.
  c. Check foreign law limitations on foreign tax benefit carryforwards (e.g., provisions like U.S. limitations on net operating loss carryforwards).
3. Hybrid transactions.
  a. Possibilities of combining taxable redemption and tax-free purchase to avoid more restrictive foreign income tax law provisions and maintain parity between U.S. and foreign tax law calculations.
  b. Typically foreign tax laws have no equivalent to I.R.C. §338 deemed elections and treat distribution of assets (other than to a local parent owning a very high portion or 100% of the stock of the distributing company) as a taxable sale by the distributing company.
  c. Some foreign countries have equivalent of mandatory I.R.C. §338 for at least transfer tax purposes if all the stock is acquired within a certain time frame.
C. U.S. deferral and credit rules.
  1. Check for differences between U.S. tax law calculation of taxable income (income inclusion measure for a U.S. subsidiary) and earnings and profits (income inclusion measure for foreign subsidiary).
  2. If foreign subsidiary used, will net income be taxed under deferral limitation rules before actual cash dividends are paid to the U.S.?
    a. Generally no deferral for Subpart F income where recipient does not bear effective foreign tax rate equal to 90% of maximum U.S. corporate tax rate.
      i. Will the foreign subsidiary earn investment income, provide services to, or purchase or sell goods to related parties in other countries?
      ii. Will foreign subsidiary invest in stock or debt obligations

of related U.S. corporations or residents, property to be used in U.S. or accounts receivable from related U.S. persons?

   b. Will foreign subsidiary be at least majority owned directly or indirectly by a few individuals or families?

   c. Deferral can also terminate in connection with arm's-length pricing adjustments.

3. Check differences between U.S. tax law computations of taxable income under foreign income tax law and taxable income (if U.S. subsidiary used) or earnings and profits (if a foreign subsidiary is used).

   a. Absolute differences may arise from

      i. Different characterization of form of acquisition.

         (A) Tax-free or partially tax-free transaction under only one of the tax systems (typically U.S.).

         (B) Hybrid transaction (particularly where I.R.C. §338 election made for U.S. tax purposes).

      ii. Treatment of intangibles (e.g. foreign systems that permit goodwill or covenants not to compete to be written off as a balance sheet equity adjustment instead of deduction on income statement).

      iii. Adjustments to asset basis for foreign government subsidies or tax credits.

      iv. Interest allowances.

         (A) Restrictions on acquisition debt or related party borrowings.

         (B) Imputed interest on interest-free or low-interest loans.

         (C) Treatment of accrued but unpaid interest.

   b. Timing differences.

      i. Depreciation and amortization allowances.

      ii. Inventory calculations.

      iii. Treatment of installment and contingent payment sales.

   c. Foreign exchange gain or loss exposures.

      i. Prognosis for inflation and changes in foreign currency exchange rates.

      ii. Election to compute earnings in dollars for subsidiaries operating in hyperinflationary currencies.

4. Check credits carried with amounts included in U.S. taxable income.

   a. Which foreign taxes constitute income taxes?

      i. Corporate taxes measured by net income and withholding taxes deducted from payments and distributions qualify.

      ii. Taxes not seeking to reach net income and taxes imposed for specific government services do not qualify and must be deducted as an expense or capitalized.

      iii. Tax does not qualify to extent it is not compulsory (e.g.,

constitutes a penalty imposed for noncompliance) or is imposed only to the extent a tax credit is available in another country for the assessment.
  b. Additional restrictions for income taxes imposed on foreign subsidiary.
    i. Foreign subsidiary cannot be lower than third foreign tier of corporate chain.
    ii. At least 10% direct ownership of voting stock of the foreign entity by immediate shareholder and at least a 5% flow-through voting stock interest by U.S. shareholder of the chain.
D. Employee compensation and benefit plan requirements.
  1. Cash compensation.
    a. Consider whether any U.S. citizens or residents transferred to the new operation will benefit from the foreign earned income exclusion under I.R.C. §911.
    b. Consider timing of payment of salary, bonuses and other fringe benefits for employees transferred to or from U.S.
      i. Effect of early or delayed payment of salary and bonuses on which country taxes and whether on a net income or withholding tax basis.
      ii. Treatment of fringe benefits, including housing, automobile allowances and life insurance.
      iii. Treatment of moving expenses.
  2. Check rules for funded benefit plan coverage as regards timing and allowance of deductions for contributions and taxation of contributions for transferred employees.

Chapter 7

Financing
Foreign
Acquisitions

Waldo M. Abbot
Managing Director

Daniel P. Tredwell
Vice-President

James B. Windle
Associate

Banking and Corporate Finance
Chemical Bank

The financing of an acquisition will be determined by the structure of the transaction, in particular, the form of consideration offered. The basic forms of consideration are cash, debt which provides deferred cash payments, and equity. The choice among these forms of consideration should be made to maximize the bids' chance of success, and to conform to the financing limitations of the acquirer. Thus, the acquiring firm's short- and long-term liquidity will be constraints on the financing structure. The goal is to finance the transaction in the least expensive way while maintaining an acceptable degree of financial flexibility for the company.

This chapter will present a sampling of the techniques that can be used to finance an acquisition. It cannot provide an exhaustive analysis of all the possibilities or of all the financing pros and cons. But *the chapter as a whole* will provide a checklist of what needs to be considered.

There is one key point to be remembered. From a financing perspective, the techniques and options for funding a foreign acquisition are essentially similar to funding a domestic acquisition.

1.0 CASH CONSIDERATIONS

Cash offers tend to be very attractive to shareholders of the target. Cash can be raised by a number of means, both long term and short term. The smaller the acquisition relative to the acquirer the greater the amount of the acquisition which can be financed through the acquirer's existing short-term liquidity facilities. Some acquisitions such as Merck's acquisition of Banyu Pharmaceutical Co., Ltd., in Japan or Pepsi's acquisition of Seven-Up International's Canadian assets have been financed through existing short-term facilities and cash balances. The use of cash balances or short-term debt facilities to finance acquisitions have the advantage, with a normal yield curve, of providing the cheapest financing possible.

1.1 Short-Term Sources of Cash

Cash and marketable securities.   The use of the acquirer's existing cash balances and marketable securities provide extremely cheap and convenient financing for an acquisition, but they will rarely provide enough funds for any but small acquisitions.

U.S. commercial paper.   Under U.S. law, commercial paper is not generally available as a means of takeover financing. However, if the commercial paper is privately placed, or issued with a bank letter of credit, the restrictions against using the commercial paper proceeds for acquisition funding fall away. Where feasible, commercial paper offers a low cost and highly flexible source of financing.

Eurocommercial paper and foreign commercial paper. These financing sources, including NIFs, RUFs, MOFs, and the like, offer very cheap funds without some of the registration or legal requirements of domestic commercial paper. The market for Eurocommercial paper is more name sensitive than is the demand for securities in U.S. domestic markets. Thus, this may not be an option for all companies or there may be limited appetite for paper with a company's name. However, the access to bank funds in an NIF or similar facility may give more certainty to the availability of funds.

Foreign commercial paper markets can provide acquisition financing for financially strong companies in that market. To finance its acquisition of Firestone, Bridgestone Corp. of Japan used one billion dollars from existing cash balances and obtained the balance from the sale of commercial paper in Japan.

Revolving credits.   Revolving credit facilities can be used to fund the working capital portion of an acquisition, or even the entire acquisition for a highly liquid, well financed company. An RC offers much flexibility because the borrower may repay and reborrow on an unscheduled basis, but is more expensive than some other short-term options. A syndicated RC, if available, may be slightly cheaper. The maturity varies between one and ten years, five to seven most common. Syndicated revolving credits are sold by assignment and novation because the regulatory authorities hold that there is a risk that the buyer may be unable to meet the funding obligation. Banks prefer to syndicate by selling participations; thus they tend to prefer syndicated term loans to syndicated RCs.

Cash and marketable securities of the target.   The target's liquid assets can be used to fund an acquisition, but their use will frequently be restricted. Depending upon the country, their use may be restricted until a certain percentage of equity is obtained; for a certain period of time after the merger, the movement of cash out of the country may be restricted. This affects not only the use of the target's cash for funding the acquisition, but also its use as a source of repayment for other sources of funds.

Bridge loans.   Short-term subordinated loans made by banks or investment banks and which are to be repaid from the proceeds of divestitures and/or subsequent permanent financing are becoming a much more important source of acquisition financing. These bridge loans frequently allow a deal to be completed by providing needed interim financing, but they are generally expensive, both in fees and rates. While not as flexible as revolving credits in repayment schedules, bridge loans usually will not have as many covenants as more traditional loans or debt issues.

1.2 Long-Term Sources of Cash

Senior term loans.   Senior bank financings typically comprise 60 to 70 percent of an acquisition's initial capital structure. Banks will generally provide loans of seven-year maturity, although the maturity can be one to fifteen years. Senior debt is a cheap source of funds compared to subordinated debt, but it will impose more restrictions through loan covenants. The amount of senior debt will be limited by asset and other coverage ratios. The foreign acquisition of a firm with a balance sheet richly laden with saleable and accessible assets can obviously support more senior debt than, say, a service firm with very few "hard" assets.

Syndicated loan facilities, in which the bank making the loan sells off all or part of it to other banks, allow for large loans to be completed very quickly and at competitive pricing. Syndicated loans tend to be more available than public issues because of the more stable investor base for syndicated loans. Term loans can be done in either the domestic or Euromarkets, and even if done domestically, the syndicate will generally include foreign banks. If the loan is made in the Euromarket, by a foreign bank, it may be done in a foreign currency. Term loans are almost always floating rate instruments, but they can be swapped into fixed rate obligations. Term loans are syndicated by the sale of participations which is preferred by the bank to assignments or novations, because the buyer of the loan has no recourse to the bank which sold it.

Public debt.   These are debt securities, registered with the SEC domestically, which can be traded after underwriting or publicly underwritten and traded Eurobonds, which need not be registered. Maturity will generally be 5, 7 or 10 years, although 15, 20, and 30 year bonds are also issued. Covenants in the indenture may not be as strict as bank debt. The priority given the bonds, along with the credit rating and maturity will determine the market interest rate of the bonds.

Unlike bank loans, debt bonds will generally not require prepayment from excess cash flow, and in fact, they may not even be callable. Bonds are generally fixed rate obligations, although floating rate bonds can be issued.

The successful selling of Eurobonds will generally require that the company's debt be rated or that the company's name be fairly well known in the Eurobond market. In issuing Eurobonds, care must be taken not to saturate the market because the market is name sensitive, unlike the demand for domestic corporates, which tend to be interchangeable with bonds of similar rating. Eurobonds can be issued in a number of currencies. However, the dollar market is the largest, and other markets have exhibited a lack of large demand for bonds, thus limiting opportunities. The demand for bonds of different currencies varies dramatically over time. Furthermore, currency swaps to hedge these exposures may not always be available.

Junk bonds.   Junk bonds are bonds with below investment grade rating or bonds for companies without credit ratings. The acceptance of these securities has opened the bond market to many companies which could not previously access it. Junk bonds are generally subordinated debt, and they carry few restrictive covenants. They are expensive, however, and their buyers will frequently require a slice of equity as well. The junk bond market is almost purely a U.S market, although there have been some "junk" deals in the Euromarkets. Most of the Euro-Junk issues have been swapped to give investors a floating rate yield.

Private placements. Private placements are debt securities which are not registered or traded but placed with sophisticated investors in privately negotiated transactions on a best-effort basis. Thus, the issuer will get the proceeds only when the final investor buys the bond, unlike in a syndicated loan or a "bought" deal in bond underwriting when the underwriter pays the issuer and then resells to the final investor. Because only a few, sophisticated investors are involved in private placements, they are very flexible and may incorporate unusual features or fund unusual and complicated transactions.

Debt/debt swaps. This source of funding is restricted generally to acquisitions in third world countries with large debt burdens. They are similar to debt/equity swaps except that the sovereign debt is exchanged not for equity but for the debt portion of an acquisition. These transactions are very complex and time consuming, but they may offer substantial advantages in the acquisition of assets in certain parts of the world because they allow a company to access local currency very cheaply.

Convertible debt. Convertible debt can either be convertible bonds or bonds with detachable warrants to buy equity, which generally can be traded separately. The most subordinated debt in a highly leveraged deal will frequently require some amount of equity participation as a reward for assuming the risk of this debt. Investors at this intermediate level are generally looking to net returns of around 25 percent annually. Thus, the amount of equity allocated to the bonds must raise the return on the securities to the 25 percent level from the coupon rate. Convertible debt can be used to raise low coupon debt, but because of the equity portion, its real cost to the acquirer can be very high.

Contingent payment or profit participation. In order to raise the return on securities to the level required by middle level investors, bonds are sometimes issued which have a redemption value that varies with the company's value or performance, or which have a minimum coupon which is supplemented by additional payments if the company's cash flow exceeds a certain level. Through this mechanism, these investors can get a higher rate of return while the acquirer of the foreign target can maintain a higher level of control over the investment.

2.0 DEBT CONSIDERATION

In debt consideration sometimes referred to as "seller paper" the seller of the acquired firm agrees to accept a debt security issued by the buyer which will provide the seller with a stream of deferred cash payments. Any of the debt securities discussed above that can be issued to investors by a company could also be issued to the seller as debt consideration. Debt consideration placed directly with the seller makes it unnecessary for the buyer to access the capital markets. This may reduce the buyer's cost and places fewer restrictions on the buyer as well.

3.0 ASSET SWAPS

Another option which can avoid accessing the capital markets is an asset swap. Asset swaps typically only work when no large cash payments are necessary to equalize the value of assets swapped. If a cash payment must be made along with the asset swap, the payment may be financed in any of the ways already discussed. An asset swap presupposes that the acquiring company has assets which it desires to divest, and that the owner of the assets to be acquired is willing to accept in return the assets to be divested by the acquirer. Because of this double coincidence of wants, assets swaps are fairly unusual. Doing asset swaps internationally requires careful examination of ownership restrictions and the special tax regulations which might apply.

Several transactions have been completed or proposed using asset swaps or divestiture through joint ventures. One of the most complex transactions in recent years was ITT's divestiture of its foreign telecommunications assets to a joint venture which it formed with CGE of France. The transaction was completed in two stages. First, CGE purchased the assets from ITT; then the assets were merged with CGE's assets and ITT was given a minority stake in the venture. This resulted in both a cash payment to ITT and a joint venture between ITT and CGE. CGE paid ITT $1 billion in cash and assumed $800 million of debt associated with the acquired properties. ITT then retained a 37 percent interest in Alcatel, the joint venture.

A more straightforward example of an asset swap was the General Electric, Thomson deal. In this transaction GE swapped its $3.2 billion revenue consumer electronics business with Thomson for Thomson's $770 million revenue medical equipment business and $800 million in cash. Thus, each company obtained the foreign assets it wanted and financed the acquisition by disposing of unwanted assets.

A further example of an asset swap was Atlantic Richfield's ultimately unsuccessful bid for Britoil. In this takeover contest, ARCO bought a toe hold of 7.7 percent of Britoil. After the shares were purchased, ARCO and Britoil would swap certain assets, and the value of these assets would be equalized by Britoil issuing new shares to ARCO, raising ARCO's holdings to 49.9 percent. This avoided the necessity of a tender offer while allowing ARCO to gain effective control. The offer was eventually withdrawn after a higher offer from British Petroleum.

4.0 EQUITY FINANCING

As with debt, equity may be used directly as a form of consideration such as a stock for stock swap, or it may be used to finance part of a cash acquisition. In a typical leveraged buyout structure, equity will comprise from 5 to 20 percent of the deal, and senior debt will typically comprise 50 to 60 percent of the typical financing, assuming there is adequate asset coverage and cash flow coverage. Equity is the most expensive form of financing for a company, but in a highly leveraged transaction it has the virtue of not requiring a fixed cash payment in the case of common equity. Preferred equity is more like debt in that it has fixed payments associated with it, although these payments are junior to the debt securities, and a missed payment is not considered an event of default.

Preferred stock. Preferred stock can be used in some leveraged acquisitions as a way to obtain more financing when debt capacity is almost used up and the company does not want to issue more common equity. The preferred issues are frequently convertible into common equity and have some kind of deferred cash payment such as a grace period or payment in kind feature. If they are not convertible, the preferred shares will frequently be redeemed quickly with the proceeds of a debt issue. By using preferred stock in this manner, the requirements of Regulation U in the U.S. can be met.

Another alternative is a Dutch auction rate preferred stock. This is reauctioned periodically to adjust the rate to market required yields similar to commercial paper. Because payments are dividends, these instruments can be attractive to corporate buyers enjoying the tax exemption on dividend payments.

Common stock. Common stock issues can be used to finance either a cash offer or to effect a stock for stock swap. There are a number of considerations in using equity financing. The considerations for common shares are also applicable to a warrant issue whether the warrants are created with a bond or separately. Stock for stock swaps, which may, on an after-tax basis, be very attractive to the shareholders of a foreign company, are subject to the same considerations. The issuer must also decide whether to place the stock domestically, in foreign markets, or both. Restrictions may be imposed by the foreign government, the central bank or the stock exchange.

4.1 Foreign Stock Ownership Restrictions

Many governments have restrictions on asset ownership by foreigners, and some governments have policies discouraging their citizens from owning foreign assets. Any such restrictions must be considered before issuing equity.

Before issuing your equity as part of an acquisition funding, it is important to know who the new shareholders will be and how their ownership will affect your firm. For example, the advantage of having European shareholders is that their ownership has historically tended to be more stable. This advantage is maximized with individual shareholders and lessened with institutional shareholders. Thus, if the acquiree's shareholders are predominately individuals, a stock for stock deal may provide a stable base of loyal shareholders for the acquirer. Some additional considerations about issuing your equity for foreign acquisitions are given below.

Discount.   A foreign corporation's stock may be unknown and not as desirable as the old company stock to shareholders, who may therefore place a discount on your shares, particularly if it is not actively traded in their country. This discount could indirectly affect the trading of your stock in the U.S.

Dividend restrictions.   In some foreign countries there may be restrictions on the currency in which dividends can be paid. This may cause an unwanted foreign currency exposure.

Class of shares.   To maintain control, one can issue shares with different voting privileges. The willingness of new shareholders, particularly foreigners, to hold stock with different voting rights must be considered.

4.2 Dilution

Dilution is always a concern in equity issues. Several forms of dilution must be considered.

Ownership dilution.   A new issue of shares, whether through an underwriting or a stock for stock deal will dilute the existing shareholders' ownership. The extent of this dilution and whether shareholders will accept it must be considered.

Earnings dilution.   How much earnings per share will be diluted and how much this dilution can be expected to reduce the share price must be determined.

Dividend dilution.   How will the dividend yield be reduced by the share issuance? How will this reduce share price? How much additional cash flow will be necessary to maintain the dividend at previous levels?

Book value dilution.   Measure the amount of net or tangible net asset value per share, before and after the acquisition.

4.3 Listing

Will the new share be listed on foreign exchanges or will the company maintain its present listing? If shares are to be listed and traded on a foreign exchange a number of considerations are relevant.

Market appetite.   Like the Eurobond market the Euroequity market is name sensitive. A large issue, whether the new shares are created to raise funds or in a stock for stock deal, may exceed demand for the shares.

Flowback.   The advantage of an international equity issue is that a new stable shareholder base may be tapped. If the shares are placed with short-term holders and there is not much other demand for the share in the foreign market, then as they are sold, they will flowback to the original domestic market where there are buyers. This defeats the purpose of the international underwriting. The risk of flowback can be reduced through good syndication practices (American and European investment banks tend to use different syndications methods), careful targeting of buyers in the syndication process, and effective investor relations. In particular, good "road shows" for institutional investors can dramatically increase the demand for a company's shares.

FX exposure.   If the shares are traded in a foreign market, they may be listed and traded in the foreign currency, or they may be put in a depository account and traded as International Depository Receipts which will be denominated in dollars. International Depository Receipts are similar to American Depository Receipts (ADRs). They are not actually shares but certificates issued representing actually shares held by a trustee bank. IDRs offer American companies the ability to have foreign shareholders but not to have its stock traded in a foreign currency. ADRs are traded in dollars but give foreign companies the advantage of reducing U.S. disclosure requirements since actual shares are not issued to the public.

Disclosure requirements.   A foreign listing may expose the company to foreign disclosure requirements which may be more extensive than or substantially different from domestic requirements. This may require expensive compliance measures.

Liquidity.   A new listing may increase the stocks' liquidity dramatically.

Asset restrictions.   A foreign listing may bring with it restriction on the ownership or transfer of certain assets. The most common are currency restrictions.

5.0 HOW DEBT FINANCIERS ANALYZE FOREIGN ACQUISITIONS

The first point to recognize about debt financing is that a bank or any other provider of financing will look at a foreign acquisition in exactly the same manner it would look at any domestic acquisition. Foreign exchange, foreign laws, and foreign cultures add layers of complexity to the exercise, but the essentials of credit, investment, and financial analysis will not change just because the deal is not domestic.

The rest of this section discusses the key points a banker or other debt investor will evaluate in analyzing transactions.

5.1 Business Fundamentals of the Target and Acquiring Companies

Particularly with foreign acquisitions, banks will require financings with recourse to the parent. Thus, in making its lending decision, the bank may look primarily to the financial strength of the acquiring U.S. corporation, regardless of the qualities of the prospective acquisition.

They will ask questions like what are the prospects for current business? Is the business maturing and declining? Or is it growing rapidly and requiring major cash infusions? Are profit margins falling or rising? Is the technology about to become obsolete? What other debt is the current business supporting?

The debt providers will also have to make a judgement about the foreign business being bought.

They will ask many of the questions management has already considered concerning the acquisition. For instance, is the target growing or declining? Are profit margins rising or falling? Is the business too heavily reliant on one or two products? Does the company have the capability to manage the foreign target? Is the firm's technology up-to-date? Will major new capital expenditures be required? Is it too reliant on the purchases of a small number of customers? Is it too reliant on a small number of suppliers? What are its major factors of production? How much are the costs of these factors likely to rise? Are distribution changes in the business changing? Are new firms preparing to enter the target's industry? Are firms exiting the industry? What is the target firm's market share? Does it dominate the industry as a price leader, or is it in an industry dominated by other large firms? Is the target subject to commodity pricing, or can it achieve premium pricing?

A good banker will analyze each of these questions, and if the answers are favorable, the bank may back the venture.

5.2 Quality of Management

Probably the most important consideration for any lender in any deal, foreign or domestic, is the quality and character of the prospective managers of an enterprise. Good business fundamentals and earnings projections are necessary, but are not sufficient for winning credit approval. If a bank or other lender does not trust and does not believe in management, it will not agree to provide acquisition financing. The managers of an acquisition must have a good record, they must have a credible operating plan, and they must be able to prove to the bank that their talents will not be spread too thin by the additional responsibilities of a new, foreign business.

5.3 Structure of Acquisition Financing

Under traditional credit policies, a bank or other financier will want to lend its funds to the level of the organization as close to the assets being acquired as possible. Banks generally do not like to lend to holding companies, for instance, because other lenders can lend directly to the entity owning a company's assets (not just its stock) and can achieve a superior security interest.

That traditional policy, however, may often be turned on its head in foreign acquisition lending. If a U.S. company is acquiring a firm whose primary assets are located in a Third World nation, the U.S. bank will very likely prefer to lend to the U.S. parent, not to the subsidiary that will own the assets.

5.4 Level of Leverage

There it is no secret that the higher the percentage of the equity capital that is committed to an acquisition, the more comfort debt providers take in the deal. That said, however, there is still no number that can serve as a standard for equity participation levels. Each transaction has to be viewed separately. In general terms though, the acquisition of a profitable, stable, foreign company can clearly support more debt than the takeover of a new firm in a cyclical industry. If a financially strong parent will guarantee the acquisition debt, leverage can reach 100 percent. If, on the other hand, the parent is weakly capitalized, and/or there will be no recourse to the parent, senior lenders will be reluctant to commit to more than 50 to 60 percent of the financing. Subordinated lenders, who are traditionally counted on to fill up the capital structure in today's domestic acquisition environment, have not yet become significant providers of debt for foreign deals.

5.5 Length of Repayment Terms

Senior bank lenders usually like to see projections that indicate that an acquisition loan can be paid off through the business' cash flows in seven years or less. Banks will often consider loans with longer lives, up to about ten years, but they get nervous when an acquisition cannot show an ability to pay down its debt within seven years. Senior lenders will almost always require that no other debt on the balance sheet will be amortized before the senior debt is paid off.

As stated earlier, various types of bonds can be sold for maturities of up to 30 years.

5.6 Using Foreign Assets as Collateral

In a higher leveraged transaction, most providers of senior debt will want to have some secured interest in the acquirers' assets, and those of the foreign acquisition before providing financing.

It is reasonably easy to assess the value of a domestic asset. The banker can just look at the prices recently paid for similar assets, check for any other financial encumbrances on the asset, and apply that net valuation to the property.

But when assets are located in foreign lands, outside the jurisdiction of U.S. law and the U.S. courts, the process becomes much more complicated. Foreign liens against assets are not always as well documented and recorded as those in the U.S. and are not as accessible. The banker is less sure of what other claims on an asset may have priority. This makes it much more difficult to insure the perfection of a lien, especially given varying perfection periods in different countries.

Even when the security claim on an asset is perfected, it may be impossible to attach assets located in a foreign land if that country's government decides to be uncooperative. It is not uncommon in foreign trade for a new claimant to simply seize and sell an asset, regardless of the prior claims on it, to satisfy a debt.

The bottom line is that to a U.S. bank, foreign assets represent a much higher degree of risk than domestic assets, and consequently, the U.S. bank will often *heavily* discount the security value of overseas assets. In fact, in many cases, the U.S. bank will assign a value of zero to foreign assets and look only at its recourse to the U.S. parent as security for debt.

5.7 Projected Synergies

One may visualize many millions of dollars in cost savings and/or increased sales and profits through the combination of the current firm's operations and those of the foreign acquisition target. A banker, however, will look very skeptically at the ability to actually realize these synergies.

For example, the foreign target may have excellent marketing and distribution skills, but that will not necessarily make it successful at selling the domestic firm's products in overseas markets.

It may seem reasonable to use existing management to eliminate a significant portion of the foreign target's overhead costs. In most cases, however, the management of far-flung enterprises will increase, rather than decrease, general and administrative spending, especially in cross-border situations.

Over the long run, the international merger may indeed create several synergies that improve the parent firm's performance. But bankers and other financial analysts have seen quite a few synergistic dreams fade into red ink. It will be tough to make them believers. Point out the savings and improvements expected, but realize that a banker will place more emphasis on historical performance, and will base assumptions on only a portion of the improvements projected.

5.8 Cash Flows on Conservative Projections

In any acquisition situation, the prospective lender will look very carefully at the cash flow projections from the foreign target.

Generally, bankers will not accept projections that show flat historical sales and earnings growth figures followed by magically improving results as soon as the takeover is completed. The bank simply will not believe the overly optimistic forecasts.

Debt providers are much more receptive to projections that are based on a thorough and tough analysis of the foreign target's operations and to credible explanations for any marginal improvements in anticipated earnings. Projections should be conservative estimates, not dreams.

It is also important in a foreign acquisition to show the banker projections of a realistic downside scenario. Show how bad the operating environment has to become before the parent and target will not be able to service the debt, and realistically estimate how probable that worst case is. The banker knows that when things go badly, the bank's stake in the acquisition quickly rises. Consequently, the banker needs to be comfortable with the downside analysis.

5.9   Other Lender Concerns

Virtually all the issues mentioned in other chapters of this handbook can impact the cash flow of the foreign acquisition and are, thus, very important elements of any lending decision. We will not duplicate here the work of our colleagues in this book, but be aware that prospective debt financiers will look very carefully at issues like:

Political and country risks that could severely damage the value of security interests,

Varying international tax treatments that could dampen cashflows,

Foreign accounting differences that could be creating illusory operating results,

Restrictions on the operations of foreign assets that could derail good business strategies,

Restrictions on purchases or sales that could place limitations on economic purchases from or sales to foreign countries, and

Restrictions on the use of foreign subsidiaries' cash, both in the country and in repatriation.

5.10   Impact of Lending Syndications

It has been common practice for decades for banks to spread the risk of larger credits by sharing portions of the loan to peer banks and selling participations to smaller banks. But in recent years, as the large money center banks have struggled to improve their return on assets, this syndication practice has become institutionalized to the point where the money center banks will rarely make a loan that they are not highly confident they can sell off quickly.

The potential impact to an acquisition financing results from a simple track of logic: If a loan is going to be sold down quickly, it follows that it must be a fairly homogenous corporate credit with fairly standard documentation that the participating banks can readily understand and analyze. To the extent that the acquisition of a foreign asset or company is highly complicated or unique, the financing for that acquisition becomes more difficult to syndicate.

Consequently, if the deal differs from the mainstream, and looks like it would amount to what bankers call a "story credit," the U.S. bank market may not be the best place to seek financing.

6.0 CONTROLLING FOREIGN EXCHANGE EXPOSURE

6.1 Defining Foreign Exchange (FX) Exposure

The first step to managing the risk to the foreign acquisition from FX movements is to understand the composition of that risk.

When making a cross border acquisition, FX exposure comes at two levels: the risk that the value of the target may change in the time interval between contract and settlement due to currency fluctuations, and the risk that the earnings stream from, and future value of, the acquisition will be impacted.

As a general rule, a banker and most other potential providers of debt financing will take the view that the parent is not in the business of betting on foreign exchange movements, and consequently, they will want it to hedge its FX risk wherever possible. But given that statement, while it is clear that the parent should hedge its exposure to the purchase price risk it is not so obvious that it should automatically hedge the ongoing transaction and/or translation (under FASB 52) elements of its FX exposure.

For instance, if the foreign assets being acquired consist primarily of a natural resource that is priced on the world market in U.S. dollars, cash inflows will be in dollars, and the only FX exposure is to the currency fluctuations of other factors of production. Similarly, if the firm being acquired manufactures goods and ships them back into the U.S., cash inflows will again be in dollars, and the local currency matters only on the expense side of the equation.

It is also possible that the foreign acquisition could serve as a hedging vehicle itself. If the parent corporation or one of its subsidiaries already has an exposure to a currency through foreign purchases or sales, an acquisition with sales or purchases in the same currency may serve as an excellent hedge for the ongoing operation, and the new acquisition should not be separately hedged.

FX exposure will also be impacted by plans for running the acquisition. No matter how the business is run, its financial statements will be affected under FASB 52 translation adjustments. But cash flow and transaction exposure could be minimal if the acquisition's earnings are reinvested into the business. If there is no plan to repatriate the target's earnings, the FX exposure to the business, in terms of cash flows, could be minimal.

In summary, to control the FX risk, the parent must understand its nature and its correlation with the parent's other businesses. If an exposure truly exists, it may be wise to hedge it, and the bank might require this. But in many cases, a full analysis may lead to less exposure than expected in the acquisition. The rest of the section sets forth some issues to be considered.

6.2 Hedging the Acquisition Price

In merger and acquisition transactions, the interval between the date the purchase offer is accepted and the date the target is acquired can run from a matter of only a few days to a period of more than a year. It is easy to see that in such an uncertain time span, currency fluctuations could significantly raise or lower the dollar cost of the acquisition without necessarily changing the value of the targets' earnings stream. Leaving aside this economic risk, there is also the potential of losing the acquisition financing. Take the example of a ten percent decline in the dollar relative to your target's currency. The bank that is willing to lend $500 million against an asset it thinks is worth $600MM, may not be willing to loan $550 million against an asset it still thinks is worth just $600 million, even though the dollar cost of the acquisition has jumped to $660.

Perhaps the two simplest and most effective methods of protecting against a currency related escalation of the acquisition cost deal with the risk in the contract. The acquisition price can be fixed in the contract in dollar terms. Alternatively, the contract can include some exchange rate adjustment clause. Both these techniques can provide an almost perfect hedge, and in the event the deal should fall through, the potential cash losses that may have occurred because some other FX hedging transaction are not at risk.

If for some reason this type of price hedge cannot be arranged within the contract, the acquirer might lock in the acquisition cost by buying forward today the foreign currency it will need to complete the acquisition. Most major banks sell foreign exchange at a forward rate for delivery at a specified future date.

A slightly more complicated hedge would involve borrowing the dollars needed for the acquisition on the contract date and immediately exchanging these dollars on the spot market for the target currency. Then foreign currency is held until settlement date.

The downside risk of borrowing immediately or buying forward is that these techniques cause a currency exposure if the deal falls apart. If there is uncertainty regarding the deal, some of the option hedging techniques discussed below may be preferable. But they, too, can involve costs and currency exposures. In most cases, if it is at all possible, the best protect against completion and currency risks is by putting the price hedge inside the contract.

6.3 Hedging the Acquisition's Future Cash Flows

Once the acquisition is completed and the FX exposure is defined, the acquirer must decide whether and how to protect itself against risking cash flow. The debt financier will strongly recommend, and in some cases will require, some technique to protect the cash flows of the acquisition from a currency devaluation.

There are dozens of strategies available for hedging the particular currency exposure the acquisition will cause, and there are a dozen variations (usually called "Bells and Whistles") that can be added to each technique. Each will present different advantages, disadvantages, and costs. The choice will depend on expectations about currency movements, the level of certainty regarding the earnings and cash flow the acquisition will generate, whether these expected cash flows will be required to cover any scheduled debt repayments, and the time factor of your investment.

We will not attempt in this chapter to present every feasible hedging strategy possibility, but we will outline a few of the basic hedging techniques and attempt to explain some of the costs and benefits of each.

Sell the foreign currency forward.   If the cash flows the acquisition will throw off are fairly certain, or if, for instance, a major asset sale is planned to pay down borrowings, it may be appropriate to lock in the dollar value of those proceeds by entering into a forward contract to sell the foreign currency expected to be received on a future date, for a fixed amount of dollars.

In the major currencies like yen, sterling, Deutschmark, and Swiss franc, it is quite easy to arrange forward contracts for up to four or five years. Such long-term foreign exchange agreements usually specify a series of exchanges spread proportionately over maturity of the contract and are usually arranged with a bank, which typically then tries to find another firm with a countervailing currency exposure to act as its other counterparty.

A final point should be noted here. It may be difficult to exactly match the timing and size of the cash flows with the long-term forward contract, resulting in at least a short-term exposure.

Borrow domestically and swap currencies.   If the acquiring firm can gain an advantage by borrowing in the U.S. capital markets to finance the foreign acquisition, it can reduce the FX exposure through the arrangement of a currency swap.

In the straight currency swap, companies agree to sell their respective currencies to each other with a concurrent agreement to buy back the currencies at a fixed exchange rate on a fixed date or series of dates in the future. The amount swapped is set in one currency and a spot exchange rate is used to establish the amount in the foreign currency. Typically, an annual fee also is negotiated between the parties to take account of possible interest rate differentials between the two currencies.

The currency swap technique is in many ways similar to arranging long-term currency forwards, with the advantage that the swaps can often be arranged on more flexible terms and can extend to maturities of five to ten years.

Borrow in the local currency.   One of the cleanest ways to finance a foreign acquisition is to base borrowings in the currency of the target. If the target is located in a country with well-developed capital markets, bonds can be issued in that country in the local currency. Alternatively, the funds needed for the acquisition might be borrowed at a bank in the target's country.

Basing acquisition debt in the local currency can accomplish two goals. First, since the local debt financiers will be much more familiar with the business being acquired than will be U.S. banks, they will be more likely to provide financing solely on the strength of the target business and will be less likely to require recourse to the U.S. parent for repayment.

Second, if acquisition borrowings are in French francs, and the cash flows of the target will be in francs, the ability to repay the debt will be insulated from movements in the foreign exchange markets.

This technique, however, will not totally eliminate FX exposure. The debt exposure will be hedged, but any repatriated earnings will be exposed to the risk of currency devaluations.

Hedging with foreign currency options.   If the acquisition will be producing a major cash flow in the near term (for instance, from a large dividend, or from the spinoff or divestiture of a substantial asset), but that cash flow is highly uncertain, it may make sense to hedge the currency exposure from this transaction by purchasing a put option on the currency.

The put option provides the purchaser with the opportunity to sell a currency at a specific strike price on or before a specific date, usually no more than a year into the future. As long as the transaction occurs before the put expires, the currency exposure is covered since the minimum exchange rate is known.

Buying the currency put option gives the acquirer two additional advantages. While the put locks it into a minimum rate of exchange, if the spot rate should move in its favor, it simply does not exercise the put and sells its foreign exchange at the more favorable spot rate. Secondly, if the transaction expected to produce the cash flow does not materialize, that acquirer is not locked into a large forward contract or swap agreement that creates its own currency exposure. The maximum sunk cost is the put premium which will depend primarily on the strike price and time to maturity chosen.

While the option is an ideal tool for hedging a contingent exposure, if an expected cash flow is fairly certain, and if hedging is the correct decision, the forward contract will always provide better results than an option contract. But if some risk is acceptable, and if the debt agreements allow it, buying the put protects some downside risk and lets the acquirer keep the benefits of favorable movements.

Hedging with option combinations.   By creating a somewhat more complicated position than the straight put, the acquirer can partially hedge the foreign cash flows of the acquisition at a greatly reduced cost.

For instance, the range forward is a combination of buying a put at one out-of-the-money strike price and writing a call option at a different out-of-the-money strike price. The range forward is constructed so that the premium cost from buying an option is completely offset by the premium income from writing an option. Almost by definition, this means that there is more room on the downside than on the upside. Using this technique, the acquirer is able to set a range of exchange rates within which it is willing to accept the currency risk. And the acquirer will have little or no net premium cost with a range forward.

Another method of creating an option position without the premium cost is the participation forward. A participation forward is a combination of buying a put option at an out-of-the-money strike price and writing a smaller (in contract size) call option at the same strike price. The participation rate is one minus the ratio of the size of the option written to the size of the option purchased. Thus, the further the put option bought is out-of-the-money, the higher is the participation ratio, because the call option written is even more in the money.

The participation forward is constructed so that the premium cost of buying an option is completely offset from the premium income from writing an option. The premium income from an in-the-money option is much greater than from an out-of-the-money option. Consequently, for the premium income to offset the premium cost, the in-the-money option will be smaller than the out-of-the-money option.

The participation forward essentially creates, at no premium cost, a situation whereby the acquirer will be able to benefit partially from any exchange rate moves in its favor while being completely protected from a drop in the currency's value below the strike price.

Problems with using the futures contracts to hedge. In theory, expected cash flows from the foreign acquisition can be hedged by selling futures contracts, but in practice the use of futures for hedging purposes is fraught with problems. For example, futures are traded only in major currencies and only in fixed contract sizes on fixed dates. Most of the cash flows coming out of the acquisition will be for odd amounts and on odd dates well into the future, leaving the acquirer unmatched and almost certainly exposed to currency risk in the long term. Additionally, the futures contract requires the up front cost of an initial margin to cover adverse changes in contract value, and if the currency moves too far, can require the deposit of additional margin funds, long before the corresponding cash flow will be received.

The proxy hedge.   The majority of the hedging techniques discussed in this chapter can be arranged in the major currencies: Deutschmark, sterling, yen, Swiss Franc, French Franc, and the U.S., Canadian, and Australian dollars. To protect against currency risk for an acquisition in Italy or New Zealand or some other nonmajor currency country, the proxy hedge can be used.

The exchange rates of most of the minor currencies track the movement of a major currency in its region. Movements in the lire, for instance, are highly correlated with the ECU and the New Zealand dollar tracks the Australian dollar. Thus, to cover an exposure for an acquisition in a minor foreign currency, a hedge in the major currency that is highly correlated can be established.

The proxy hedge still leaves the acquirer with some basis risk, but the potential losses due to this exposure are likely to be far less than the costs of setting up cross-rate hedges between the major and minor currencies.

The record on hedging.   In 1987, Chemical Bank's Foreign Exchange Trading Desk conducted a survey of its major trading customers to determine how they dealt with their foreign currency exposure; 369 firms returned the questionnaires.

61% hedged transactions exposure selectively,

13% did not hedge transactions exposure,

25% automatically hedged all transactions exposure,

only 18% hedged translation exposure, and of these 78% hedged translation exposure selectively, and

11% took positions for profit, but less than 10% acknowledged speculating.

Chapter **8**

People, Issues, and the American Target Company

Peter J. Clark
Managing Director
Maplestar Consulting Group

G. Christopher Wood
Managing Associate
Coopers and Lybrand

This chapter will address the plans made and actions taken to resolve the key "people issues" associated with the acquisition of an American corporation by a non-U.S. firm. By "people issues," we mean issues of organizational restructuring and process development; human resources and personnel policy; and corporate culture evolution[1] particularly as applied to major corporate change such as a shift in ownership and strategic direction resulting from an acquisition.

This chapter is not intended as a summary of prevailing concepts, approaches, and issues in the field. Rather, our emphasis is on the role of

---

[1]Our working definition for corporate culture as used in this chapter is the combination of shared beliefs, behavior and values that shape the corporation's self-identity.

senior company management in using people issues in their acquisition strategy. Management often relegates organizational and cultural issues to the status of postmerger afterthoughts. Yet people issues may also play critical roles before the bid is announced and during the interim period between bid announcement and at the time of the signing of the deal.

Our examination of inbound-organizational people issues in this chapter is divided into three sections, each corresponding to a distinct stage in the acquisition process.

In the *preplanning* period, the potential foreign acquirer is not known. There may be no indication of outside acquisition interest. The quality and depth of people issues examination during this period may influence the role of such issues in the subsequent stages of the acquisition process.

In the *transitional* period, people issues may either be used offensively, that is, to discourage undesired acquisition interest, or defensively to help protect employees in the event of a completed deal.

In the *postmerger* period, people issues are one set of concerns that must be addressed as part of the total integration plan. Retention of key individuals and development of a successful acquirer-acquiree work environment are key considerations in this stage.

A checklist is provided at the end of this chapter outlining key needs at each of these stages.

1.0 PREPLANNING PERIOD

Devising a workable organizational and cultural strategy within the context of future acquisition strategy.

In the preplanning stage, the identity of the potential suitor is not known. As a matter of fact, the U.S. company may not even consider itself to be a serious acquisition target at this stage. Why, then, should management spend any time in developing a knowledge base which might never be used? Two reasons:

U.S. merger activity since 1984 underscores that no public company can ever be fully insulated from corporate raiders. One must prepare for the unthinkable, because it may become the thinkable.

Knowledge gained from the preplanning analysis may improve corporate profitability and effectiveness. Higher profits mean higher stock prices, which are the most practical deterrents to undesired acquisition interest.

1.1 A Senior Executive for Corporate Organizational and Cultural Development

For people issues to be a factor in the preacquisition period, topics of organization structure and process, overall human resources policy, and corporate culture development must be elevated from the level of corporate politics. Ideally, a single senior executive will be assigned responsibility for corporate organizational development. To carry out that responsibility, he or she must be provided with the authority and resources to conduct an objective and comprehensive organizational-cultural investigation.

People issues are the most democratized topics in U.S. business today. Corporate structure, reporting relationships, compensation, and bonuses impact the pocketbook of every employee. It is not surprising, therefore, that virtually every employee views himself or herself as an expert.

But like the adage of the elephant being a mouse that was designed by a committee, more voices do not necessarily mean a better result. To prevent diffusion of effort and attention, corporate organizational-cultural development should be assigned to a single enabling executive within the firm. The role must not be a figurehead responsiblity, an invitation to chair ineffectual "focus" meetings. Rather, the officer must be responsible for developing workable programs and later, demonstrating that these programs yield specific results. "Quick fix" solutions such as the broadscale imposition of simplistic centralization or decentralization designs in an inadequate substitute for thorough investigation.

Who should be this corporate "people" officer? Traditional organizational theory may argue for the vice president of human resources or the executive vice president for administration. Corporate culture theorists will push for the leadership by the chief executive officer, arguing that the CEO is best positioned to empower values and beliefs in a new direction.

Our choice for the assignment is one of two individuals: either a chairman emeritus who has a close working knowledge of the company and its heritage or a CEO-designate with a similarly broad perspective. Neither choice is without risk, but the greater risk is to do nothing. Until responsibility for organizational and cultural development becomes focused, a workable development program may be impossible to achieve.

1.2 Assessment of Organizational and Cultural Strengths and Weaknesses, and Capacity for Change

The designee must next implement a program of corporate introspection that uncovers key people issues, strengths, and weaknesses.

A complete investigation is both objective and comprehensive; some corporate-cultural analyses conducted today fall short on both counts. If the culture analysis is contorted to be consistent with a management preconception, it constitutes little more than a rubber stamp for management's current or proposed structure.

The alternative is an analytical approach aimed at identifying the organizational structures, processes, and cultural and human resource elements critical to the corporation's ongoing success. Objectivity necessitates that most criteria are defined outside of the firm; the organizational assessment framework shown in Figure 8.1 suggests one approach.

The matrix shows organizational units along a vertical axis, with cost, market, and process factors along the horizontal axis.

The process column deals with the relationship between the corporation's formal organization structure and its informal mechanisms for getting things done. Are the two the same? If not, what is the difference?

Cost per employee is measured in comparison to competitors or a peer group. Without such a benchmark, the bureaucracy will multiply according to span of control rules of thumb rather than competitive needs.

The market column defines the organization's relationship to its customers. This is one way of asking how close is the subject organization to revenue creation?

The substitute column calls for a comparison of the business unit's overall budget to the cost of the next best alternative. If that department or unit were eliminated, what would be the net cost of replacement, including transition costs and the expense of finding a qualified substitute?

Thorough and rigorous investigation will raise objections and concern within the firm, since the analyses could lead to budget or staffing cuts in the business unit or department under examination. External assistance may be requested to develop this diagnosis.

The continuing value of a systematic analytical approach is the information developed as a result of exploring key issues. A thorough investigation should yield answers to the following questions.

Assessment Factor Function or Organizational Unit	Process Consistency with Informal Decision/Information Processes		Cost Costs per Employee, Relative to Competitor or Peer Group		Market Relationship to Customer: • Direct Contact • Coordination • Support			Substitute Elimination Risk: Budget versus Next Best Alternative	
	Yes	No	$ Company	$ Compare	DC	COR	S	$ B	$ NB
Administrative Departments									
Sectors/Regions									
Divisions/Separate Business Units									
Company Subsidiary									

Figure 8.1

What is the company's self-image, and how does that image contrast with perceptions of suppliers, key competitors, and customers?

What are the critical functions and activities *directly* related to the company's enterprise? Who are the key individuals or drivers performing those functions?

What has been the company's success in promoting and retaining key drivers in the past? Have past departures helped competitors? Has the company's turnover rate for key drivers been higher than the competition's?

How do these key drivers perform their functions? Do they manage through the formal organization structure, or do they devise and follow their own informal processes? Do the two coincide?

Which support functions, activities and procedures do the key drivers themselves view as most important to achieving success in their assignments?

What motivates, and demonstrates the key drivers? Are salary, bonus, and benefits the most important issues? Or are other factors such as speed of promotion or challenging work more important?

How does the company's total package of compensation benefits compare with competitors? Do more benefits mean a lower turnover rate?

1.3 Becoming Aware of Possible Postmerger Pressure Points

Excepting manufacturing capacity, proprietary manufacturing processes, and patents, people issues are the most critical elements in the acquisition value formula.

The non-U.S. acquirer will often cite strategy in rationalizing its acquisition. In many instances, strategy may actually be the byproduct of a successful people policy applied to the foreign acquisition. When a Japanese holding company purchased the U.S. subsidiary of a British tire manufacturer, the acquirer's highly personal distribution network was the reason underlying its U.S. market presence. When a Korean electronics manufacturer bought a Southwest U.S. distributor, the stated acquisition goal was to gain access to a "world gateway." The actual objective, however, was to benefit from a market image established by past key drivers from the target company.

In other cases, the acquirer's strategy may have undefined people implications which bring about loss of jobs for U.S. employees. A Japanese manufacturer and distributor of beauty aids acquired a U.S. company with a complementary product line after publicly announcing that much of their expansion would occur in the United States. As discussions progressed, the U.S. negotiators used this knowledge as a ploy to raise the minimum acquisition price. This tactic succeeded as the Japanese's desire to complete the transaction and save face overcame their price sensitivity.

However, the second phase of the acquisition strategy was implemented after the deal closed: New owners attempted to implement a plan which had proven highly successful in Japan—to convert the U.S. company's distributors into franchisees. However, because the foreign acquirers underestimated the complexity of U.S. franchise law, they achieved only limited success. In the end, two U.S. principals and many of their staffs were terminated.

In addition, hard-to-define acquisition concepts such as "fit" and "presence" sometimes translate into people issues and policies. A Scandinavian company's pursuit of a fine paper manufacturer in the U.S., on closer examination, was motivated by the company's need for U.S. market stamp of credibility for selling other products.

Trademark presence notwithstanding, the "magic" behind a highly recognized retail name often traces back to an original product team of managers and workers who created a quality image through sweat and dedication. A foreign acquirer may fail to recognize this aspect of brand name power and may temporarily continue the momentum of the marketplace. Later, however, surprises may occur and sales growth declines as does the real "value-added" of the acquired company.

The prospective U.S. acquiree places itself in an advantageous position by understanding the relationship between people issues and acquisition value, and by acting upon this understanding, as can be seen in the following examples.

A leading U.S. advertising conglomerate, interested in remaining independent, revises the terms of its employment contracts with its top salesmen so that five company superstars are released in the event of a hostile takeover.

A North American chemicals company, interested in attracting acquirers, eliminates two layers of management and slashes the number of company decision centers prior to entering into serious discussions. This makes the company easier to manage and, thus, more attractive to potential acquirers.

A Southern California middle-market bank highlights its traditional strength in Pacific Basin lending its capital and organizational restructuring. A European financial institution with existing Pacific loans pays an above-market premium for the bank to acquire the California institution's established infrastructure.

The intent of U.S. company management is not necessarily to use people issues to thwart an acquisition. As illustrated in the instances above, the goal may instead be to facilitate successful completion of the deal. For this to occur, however, the comprehensive diagnosis described earlier in the chapter must first be developed, findings evaluated, and action steps taken.

2.0   TRANSITIONAL PERIOD

People issues and announcement of the bid for a U.S. target company

The bid is announced. Analyses from the company's organizational diagnosis are mobilized to either assist or block the deal. Cultural and organizational patterns of the prospective acquirer are studied to support negotiations and to prepare for postmerger integration of the two firms.

2.1   Using Issues in Foreign Acquisitions

Corporate executive management must provide specific guidance to the people-issue executive concerning bid strategy: *who* is the acquirer group that is being encouraged, *who* is being discouraged, and what takeover defense tactics are being applied? Even before that however, preparatory steps can be taken, as illustrated in Checklist 1.3. Some additional ways for converting people issues into acquisition deterrents include the following.

Labor contract fragmentation.   U.S. Company management replaces master labor agreements with individual accords with each union. To a foreign acquirer unfamiliar with the nuances of negotiating with American labor unions, the added complexity poses an additional obstacle.

Technology and tradename licensing.   The U.S. company licenses its tradenames and products to third parties; so part of the attractiveness of name exclusivity and reputation in the marketplace is lost for a potential acquirer.

Benefits escalators.   "Golden parachutes" or top executive compensation programs triggered upon a successful unfriendly takeover bid have been used extensively by U.S. management in the past. In 1987, a U.S. money center bank extended the concept to middle management levels, to deflate an unwelcome acquirer's future cost reduction opportunities. Conceivably, these "tin parachutes" and their "golden parachute" counterparts run a possible risk of shareholder class action suits or IRS disallowance as excessive compensations.

Local support.   The culture of the company is often intimately entwined with the local community where the firm is headquartered. Philips Petroleum called upon its community image in Bartlesville, Oklahoma, to help in its defense against a raider.

Several methods for encouraging foreign acquisition interest are listed in Checklist 1.3. Other actions are aimed at encouraging outside interest.

Creation of an acquisition review committee.   Creation of such a committee signals that management is willing to talk about the sale of the company. The chairman of this committee should either be the chief executive or an outside director with the authorization to conduct preliminary discussions with highly qualified principals.

Union and key employee initiative.   In recent years, airline pilot unions have performed an increasingly active role in U.S. air carrier acquisitions, either independently or in coordination with other shareholder groups. Key employees, such as senior research scientists in technology firms, may be well positioned to initiate exploratory discussions in their professional communications with experts in other firms.

Strategic alliance environment.   Some U.S. companies are loners. Others actively pursue business alliances as an integral part of their growth strategy. The two partners become accustomed to each other's cultures and styles, smoothing future acquisition discussions if such discussions are warranted.

2.2   Identification of Acquirer's Organizational and Cultural Characteristics

The acquirer's past record may already suggest a distinctive operating style. Such information may be useful to acquiree management for two reasons.

Negotiation points: The acquirer's strategic objectives and operating style in its home nation may provide useful insight for the U.S. firm's negotiating team. For example, a U.S. company in the financial printing field changed its acquirer information package to highlight electronic prospectus preparation after potential Asian acquirers described their vision of a future era of worldwide electronic printing centers supported by satellite communications networks.

Postmerger integration: An understanding of acquirer organizational structure personnel policies and corporate culture is also essential preparation in advance of the postmerger phase. A U.S. acquiree with a six-deep organizational chart can anticipate deep cuts if it is acquired by a European company with half the number of layers.

Acquirer organizational and cultural characteristics may be divided into two categories: nationalistic and company-specific.

Nationalistic acquisition cultures are difficult to identify and even tougher to quantify. At Maplestar Consulting Group, we examined U.S. acquisition statistics of several nation-groups over a five year period. We searched for discernible patterns, examining acquiree standard industrial classification (SIC) code information, price-earnings multiples, ownership level data (100 percent, majority, or minority), and the acquisition of premium percentage over preannouncement stock prices.

While this analysis supported some initial hypotheses (for example, German acquirers have emphasized engineering-based acquisitions and companies in basic industries with worldwide distribution networks), few other consistent patterns emerged. No nation-groups were spend-thrifts; the Japanese were equally likely to pay the same substantial acquisition premium over prevailing market value as the French. All nation groups preferred 100 percent ownership over minority interest. In sensitive industries, the Japanese had started with minority positions, suggesting an understanding of American sensitivities and a desire to learn more about the acquiree before investing more money.[2]

On the other hand, some analysts are indicating that cash-rich Japanese companies are beginning to become knowledgeable about managing U.S. companies and more familiar with the mechanics of acquiring companies in the United States.[3] One area of general agreement, however, is that the Japanese fully intend to have global businesses in which they manufacture and sell in all markets to increase the market share of their product lines.

Our analysis showed that visible shifts in national economic policies provide a more predictable means for anticipating future acquisition patterns by acquirers from a particular country. Privatization, or denationalization of formerly government-owned enterprises, preceded the move by United Kingdom companies to acquire complementary businesses in the

[2]Examples: Nippon Life Insurance Company's minority stake in Shearson Lehman Hutton; the minority stake of Japanese banks and insurance companies in BankAmerica Corporation; and Yasuda Mutual Life Insurance Company's minority investment in Paine-Webber Group, Inc.

[3]Burnstein, Daniel, "Where Japan's Money is Going Next," Global Finance (October 1987), pp. 37–43.

(American) "colonies." British Telecom acquired Dialcom, a U.S. electronic information and database development company, while British Petroleum acquired Sohio. The new Japanese government has announced a budget calling for increased expenditures for essential national defense. Could this precede a bolder move into aircraft and avionics industries?

Company-specific organization designs and corporate cultures are easier to identify. One European client initially appears to have a four-tier organization structure, but decisions are not made in accordance with this structure. Upon closer examination, it becomes apparent that the company's information and decision process is essentially circular, with the entrepreneur-founder intervening in all decisions. At another client active in U.S. acquisitions and ventures, twelve recent corporate acquisitions are spread among five nations.

For a target U.S. company of the first company described above, the interventionist operations of the chairman means that a subsidiary can expect little real operating autonomy. An acquiree of the twelve business unit company would face loose operating controls, consistent with the entrepreneurial style of the parent.

2.3 Review of Adequacy of U.S. Executive and Key Employee Provisions

The transitional period between bid announcement and deal completion is the appropriate time to review adequacy and coverage of current executive employment contracts, severance arrangements, union contracts and employee benefits programs. Dr. Dee A. Soder, president of The Endymion Company, a New York-based executive assessment firm, states

> The predeal period is an ideal time to challenge actuarial assumptions, investigate funding requirements, and determine whether over-or-under funding exists in the corporate pension and other benefits. If plans are overfunded, the excess cash could be used to management's advantage to help discourage inappropriate inquiries. Or, excess funds could be used to reduce the acquirer's net cost. On the other hand, underfunding of liabilities could reduce the attractiveness of a target company.

2.4 Refinement of Key Employee List

The employees who are critical to the U.S. company's future success are not necessarily current department or business unit heads. Management's objective evaluation of critical processes and organizations (Checklist 1.2, 1.3) could indicate, for example, that a third or fourth level manager is the key to continuing a successful relationship with an important customer.

Because of the sensitivity of such assessments, the Key Employee List should be reviewed only with the CEO and board of directors. External assistance in conducting or reviewing the management assessments may be necessary to ensure (1) that consistent criteria were used in the assessments and (2) that the criteria selected directly relate to the future performance of the U.S. acquiree.

3.0 POSTMERGER PERIOD

Working with new owners to realize the potential of the U.S. acquisition

The role of the U.S. company's senior management changes abruptly as soon as the deal is signed. The people-issues executive may be the company executive, either on a temporary or permanent basis.

Acquirer company management wants to realize the full value of the U.S. comany for the new owners. If this desire is effectively communicated, it should become a key postmerger goal of acquiree senior management as well. A coordinated postmerger integration effort often means a joint team effort with representation from both companies.

A key to successful postmerger integration focuses attention on a carefully developed list of opportunities. Both too much change and the wrong type of change must be actively avoided. Ideally, the American acquiree group will use their advance knowledge of key drivers, formal organization structures, and informal processes within the company to smooth the integration process.

A structured PMI blueprint guides management from the time of deal signing until most of the important integration work is completed, usually four to six months afterwards. But some action steps must be taken immediately. For example, key employees and customer relationships must be stabilized; if management delays more than thirty days after deal completion, there could be permanent damage. A priority list of actions should be developed to guide postmerger assignments, based on the dollar impact of the issue, timing, and competitive urgency.

3.1 Action to Neutralize Immediate Acquisition Aftershocks

An abrupt change in ownership is a potentially catastrophic change, particularly as perceived by long-time employees. Under the previous ownership, the individual's roles and responsibilities were set, and his or her standing in an organization was well known. Acquisition of the U.S. company by a foreign firm brings the expected fears of streamlining, reorganization, and new policies. Fears may be accentuated because no one knows the foreign acquirer, how they think and operate, or what they value. A senior executive in a U.S. electronics firm acquired by a Taiwan trading company, for example, has no reference point for what the new owners will emphasize, and what they will discard. Uncertainty breeds fear, and the employee may act abruptly to lower that uncertainty, sometimes by joining a competitor.

If a key driver decides to leave, damage is two-fold: First, the departure will make it more difficult to achieve projected company performance; second, the departure can multiply, resulting in an "exodus of employees" prompted by whispers of "If *she* leaves, there must be something to fear."

The window of opportunity for retaining key drivers following an acquisition is notoriously short; less than a week in some instances. For planning purposes, management is advised to assume that the employee and possibly his whole staff are vulnerable to loss unless secured within two weeks of the deal completion. The best preparation for the possible management exodus is to develop a comprehensive assessment of top and middle management several weeks before the close of the transaction.

Whatever is done to retain key drivers and their staff must be consistent. Key drivers quickly learn the identity of others in the top performance group, and the comparison of notes and offers is inevitable. If management, say, offers two key drivers extended year contracts, others in the group will soon pressure for comparable terms.

By itself, retention of key drivers may not ease the tremors shaking the corporation. This is the time for the acquirer to use the U.S. acquiree's internal information grapevine to spread the word that solid performers have little to fear. Supplementing this, a personal series of appearances by the acquirer company CEO may achieve in one afternoon what one hundred memoranda could not.

The acquirer CEO should use initial visits to selectively meet with key suppliers and customers, particularly those actively contested by the rivals. A visit to a key account within the first month of a change in ownership is a highly visible gesture which competitors cannot match, at least not at that time. If the customer or supplier relationships are allowed to slip, twice the effort and expense will be necessary to regain lost ground in the future.

3.2   Planned Action for the Postmerger Period

Postmerger integration should resemble the action of a skilled piano tuner carefully adjusting and calibrating selective parts of the instrument according to a planned sequence, with particular care not to disturb other functioning parts. Frequently, however, the postmerger plan is a plan in name only. Too often, our experience is that acquiring management concentrates on shifting around organizational boxes instead of planning in advance which parts of the acquired firm should be changed, and how, and which parts should be left alone.

For such planning to be effective, a structured analytical approach to setting priorities before acting is essential. A temporary integration team with an assigned leader is critical. Without this discipline, postmerger momentum may collapse, with managers taking action on all issues but succeeding on none.

Figure 8.2 graphically represents a process for assigning priorities to alternative postmerger concerns. Even the most resilient U.S. acquiree can only withstand a limited amount of significant change in a short period of time. Therefore, use of some priority-setting mechanism by the integration team is necessary. These considerations are emphasized below.

> *The dollar size of the PMI opportunity* is the first consideration. Without such priority-setting, the CEO may be spending critical, early portions of the postmerger program time on minor matters rather than on critical concerns such as retention of new customers and key employees.
>
> *Timing of dollar opportunities* also should influence the selection of what action is taken first, second, and never. Staff cuts, for example, are difficult to make after the first few months following the close. Many changes are easier to achieve in the early months of the PMI program because the employees' hunger for resolving their uncertainty facilitates fast regulation of postmerger challenges. For example, the system's integration task team at one Maplestar client firm was called upon to consolidate four separate data centers into one within a few months of the close; what was considered impossible became achievable as employees wanted to be part of the new company's future.
>
> *Opportunity cost (cost foregone)* is more difficult to calculate in precise terms, but it may be the more important consideration over the longer term. A single customer up $100 million annual sales can be replaced with several smaller sales, but the new accounts may never support the same gross margins as the old one. Alternatively, management may put off purchase of a $20 million dollar computer system to appear frugal following the acquisition, but they spend twice that amount because of inflation and hidden costs.

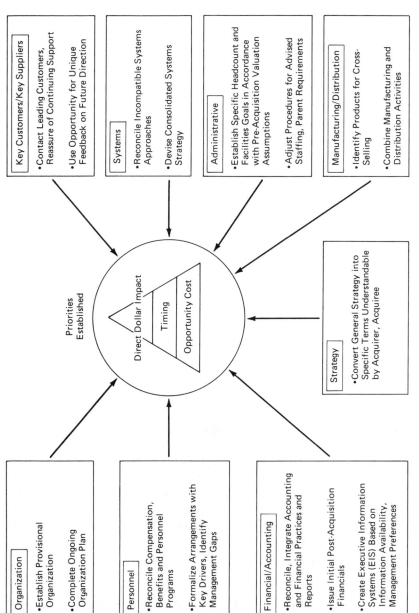

Figure 8.2

281

3.3 Developing the Joint Corporate Culture

Development of combined acquirer-acquiree culture should be delayed until critical postmerger integration work is well underway. Corporate culture is changed through indirect actions which shape the direction of shared experiences and beliefs. Until the two management teams actually work side-by-side, however, actions aimed at developing a combined culture are likely to be premature.[4]

Canadian Campeau Corporation acquired Allied Stores Corporation in December, 1986. The venerable American chain had difficulty adapting to the acquirer's executive operating style.[5] Since that time, Campeau also acquired Federated Department Stores, which includes New York's well-known Bloomingdale's. In January, 1990, Campeau's U.S. retail stores went into Chapter 11.

After a year of so of working together, the acquirer and acquiree cultures may be combined in one of four ways.

1. The predominant form of combination is actually *superimposed* with the acquirer imposing its values and beliefs on the acquiree. An aggressive cost-cutting mentality is one of the more visible values imposed by Computer Associates on Applied Data Research.

2. An alternative is to *mix* different cultures of the acquirer and acquiree, emphasized the strengths of each. Sometimes the combination works, sometimes not: Renault's investment in AMC Corporation was supposed to combine French design excellence with Mid-America manufacturing grit. On reflection, "Franco-American Motors" just did not work where it counts: in the showrooms.

3. A *replacement* culture may be necessary if the acquired U.S. company is culture-vacant. If senior American founders have left the acquired company, the foreign acquirer may choose a passive management approach. Midland Bank PLC's acquisition of Crocker Bank was an instance in which a replacement business culture was required but did not happen. Midland eventually sold its interest in Crocker to competitor Wells Fargo Bank, which followed the more abrupt superimposition approach.

4. A *fusion* of cultures results when the non-U.S. and U.S. Firms share core values and critical business objectives. For example, when Kas-

---

[4]The Samuel Armacost regime at BankAmerica Corporation provided one example of corporate culture analysis gone awry. While senior management concentrated on shared belief values, loan losses and adjustments continually mounted.

[5]Barmosh, Isadore, "Life with Campeau: Allied's Year of Constant Change," *The New York Times;* February 14, 1988; p. 11.

hiyama acquired J. Press, the transaction was the final event in a fifteen-year courtship which started with a licensing agreement. Cementing the relationship was the mutual discovery that both firms shared the same *value* (the desire to provide quality conservative clothing to the elite and their emulators) and *objective* (to improve profitability and expand into carefully selected markets).

The chief executive is the ultimate corporate culture bearer, whose actions and image shape internal beliefs within the new organization. If the foreign parent assigns one of its officers to the CEO position, a split may emerge between "old" American employees and their "new" managers from the parent corporation.

If the acquirer's culture is stacked upon the acquiree's, there is no successful integration of ideas, approaches, or abilities. A North American technology products company was acquired by a European firm in 1984. The acquiree's planner observed, "We go through a two-stage process to get things done around here. First, you get the old guard (former American management) all pulling the same way. Later on we need to get the parent company people on board, and that's when we fail."

At one North American acquiree, management tried to streamline the U.S. product line to be more responsive to customers' perceptions and requirements. The result was a recommendation to top management to discontinue a top-of-the-line machine with elegant technology, but which duplicated much of what was already in the market. Furthermore, customers had strongly perceived that the company was good at the low-tech end of the market but not at the high-tech end.

Acquirer and acquiree management were driven by different visions. The acquirers dreamed of becoming a world-wide force in telecommunications technology. Not surprisingly, the acquirer's vision prevailed. The recommendation for technology discontinuation was shelved and its advocates were discredited. The chief executive, who only visited the acquiree once each quarter, complained that no one had attempted to learn his view of what the acquiree should become.

The solution? The parent organization can attempt to force its own beliefs and approach on the acquiree through management staff replacement. However, a top management revolving door only slows the process of team-building essential to effective management. Threaten acquiree managers with capitulation or firing, and they avoid making any decisions at all, and the most competent ones leave.

One alternative approach calls for use of an office of the chief executive structure as a temporary bridge between the old corporation and the new. In a three-person office of the CEO structure, one appointee is usually from the parent, one is from original acquiree management, and the third is a new individual who is familiar with both organizations, but owes allegiance to neither.

Correctly implemented, the office of the CEO structure can help resolve major policy and strategic direction differences before they reach the rest of organization. Ideally, discussions and debates remain confined to the three-man group, with a mutual agreement to support the majority position. A fourth, nonvoting member of the group, sometimes the strategic planner, acts as agenda developer for issues requiring extensive advance analysis.

Carefully implemented, the postmerger office of the CEO approach provides the three members with daily experience in understanding each other's different cultures. That structure must be temporary, however. The three-person committee structure should give way to a traditional CEO-COO structure at the end of the postmerger period, but with each officer benefiting from an improved appreciation of the corporate culture that must emerge in the future for the company to be successful.

Within middle management levels and below, a similar structure can address perception and communication issues which, while not of a strategic or policy nature, can nonetheless undermine or sabotage otherwise well-conceived postmerger integration programs. For example, U.S. managers tend to form perceptions of foreign nationals which can block the establishment of effective business and working relationships. Some of the more common, and damaging, misperceptions are

- The (foreign nationals) do not promote U.S. managers above a certain level.
- The U.S. operations are run with a dictatorial and arrogant hand from afar by the foreign national parent.
- The motives and objectives of the "Swiss gnomes of Zurich" are mysterious and incomprehensible.
- The French think they are superior to us intellectually; so it is not worth the effort to propose new ideas to them.
- The Japanese do not trust anyone who does not speak their language, who is not Japanese, or who has been out of Japan for too long a period of time.

Such stereotyping can lead to misunderstandings, lack of full cooperation, or outright conflict. Integration teams at the middle management level composed of representatives from both nationalities can ameliorate these situations by providing a formal structure to resolve such problems *before* they affect business performance.

In summary, our experience has taught us that potentially crippling people issues which emerge during international mergers and acquisitions can best be resolved by appointing a single senior executive to serve as the focal point for corporate and organizational change during the pre-planning and transitional phases of the process. During the postmerger phase, organizational mechanisms should be created to ensure that the business objectives of the acquisition are not thwarted by corporate culture or related communication issues.

4.0 CHECKLIST

A. *Preplanning Period* (before the bid or tender)
   1. Designate a single senior executive to be responsible for corporate organizational and cultural development. Entrust this individual with sufficient resources to get the job done.
   2. Develop a comprehensive assessment of organizational and cultural strengths and weaknesses, emphasizing capacity for productive change. Periodically refine this knowledge base.
   3. Convert knowledge gained from the assessment into a working understanding of potential postmerger integration pressure points, that is, values structures or processes that can either facilitate or obstruct smooth integration of acquirer and acquiree.
B. *Transitional Period* (interim period before resolution of acquirer's interest)
   1. Articulate the role of "people issues" in discouraging or encouraging foreign acquisition interest, as executive management specifies.
   2. To the degree possible, identify general (national) and specific (company) organizational and corporate culture aspects which may assist U.S. company management in responding to outside inquiries.
   3. Review the adequacy and assignability of executive and employee labor arrangements, including (but not restricted to) fortification of "golden parachute" arrangements, and review of severance terms, key manager contracts and/or postemployment consulting arrangements.
   As part of this review, examine the current status of corporate benefits and pensions, both from the perspective of future personnel policy possible in negotiations.
   4. Assemble a list of key personnel in each of the U.S. company's departments and units critical to future success. Develop strategies for retaining key individuals after the acquisition is completed.
C. *Postmerger Period* (completed transaction)
   1. Quickly act to offset the immediate aftershocks of the transaction as felt by key employees, customers, and suppliers.

2. Develop a priority plan for post merger integration (PMI) action that takes into account the organization's capacity for change, required postacquisition cost savings or revenue increases, and the competing issues demanding immediate top management attention.
3. After the PMI program is well underway, shape the new culture required for the combined corporation, and take action to make that change occur.

Chapter 9

Personnel Policies, Human Resources, and Personnel Administration Offshore

Robert M. Battaglin
Manager, Human Resources—Business Divisions

Keith D. Engstrom
Retired as Director,
Salaried Compensation
Corning Inc.

1.0 PERSONNEL POLICIES AND PRACTICES

In any location—in the U.S. or offshore—it is important to recognize that planning and thinking in the human resources area must derive from business expectations and the operating situation you expect to face. Personnel policies and practices, the level and mix of people needed to successfully run the operation, development activities required to meet unique skill and management needs, as well as choices of salary administration programs, all are impacted. What must be recognized in many offshore ventures is the inability to adjust for change. That is, the ability to change personnel policies and practices or change people or change methods of operation can be severely limited in many non-U.S. locations. With that in mind, the initial consideration in the human resources area is to clearly understand the basic business expectations and operating plans, thus enabling personnel policies and procedures to be set in place correctly.

This entire chapter is a checklist for your use.

1.1 Overview Considerations

A. Can expectations for the venture be stated clearly?
   1. Why is it being done? What will be accomplished in a general sense?
      a. Export outlet for U.S. goods and services
      b. Low cost source of production
      c. Foothold in a key country or region for future opportunities
      d. Immediate profit or long-term payoff
   2. What will the business be? What are its basic operating strategies, goals, and objectives?
   3. How should the venture look five or ten years from now? The nature and complexity of personnel and human resource programs are definitely impacted by considerations such as these. A specific purpose venture with a limited mission will need significantly different personnel policies and practices than a venture with a diverse, ambitious mission regardless of size.
B. How much change is expected or required to meet business plans?
   1. Is it a start-up of a new operation or is an existing, ongoing business already in place?
   2. Are there immediate and urgent issues to resolve or is the operating situation stable?
   3. Is rapid growth and change expected or is the business to evolve more slowly over time?
   4. Is growth to be through new products, new directions, and new operations, or is it growth of an existing product or service base?
C. Are there unique needs for management and functional talent?
   1. What are partners and/or the local entity expected to bring to the venture in the way of management or functional talent?
   2. Are the key functional areas of the operation covered appropriately by either the local entity or partner or parent?
   3. Are the partner and local resources being used to the best advantage?
   4. Are there special technical needs?

The system in the U.S. allows much more immediate problem-solving potential than do other economic systems. Offshore there are two different ways to be caught relative to initiating change.

What is allowed or not allowed can vary widely, but developing countries are often much more restrictive than the U.S. The ability to fire people, for example, or the ability to change salary policies without government approval, especially for hourly workers, can be severely limited. Your entry decisions may stay with you much longer than expected.

What is doable, in a problem solving sense, can also be severely limited. There will usually not be a rich labor market to dip into to solve a problem and certainly not the easy access to it even if it is there. In the U.S. a large infrastructure is available (legal, business, engineering, and the like) and this is typically not available in developing countries. A wrong estimate of skills needed or a wrong estimate of the level and complexity of the workforce and organization is not necessarily correctable in the short term.

Corning entered Singapore a number of years ago with a small export sales organization and later expanded into a distribution company. It was assumed we could add more sophisticated marketing to better penetrate the marketplace. In fact, while sales talent was abundant in Singapore, marketing talent, especially talent that could related back to U.S.-based product divisions, was not at all easy to find. Our program had to be changed and directed primarily from the U.S., with resulting loss of on-site "touch" until we could develop more local talent.

In Japan, the difficulty in attracting talent is well known. Planning for growth and change takes on a new dimension when it might take two or three years to build a functional skill base rather than the instant mid-career hiring assumed in the U.S.

1.2 Operating Considerations

A. Evaluate how the venture will or must fit into the local culture and business environment.
   1. What is the level of operating flexibility expected or allowed?
      a. In China for example, direct interaction with workers even in a training or start-up situation may be limited. All communication must go through formal channels and workers' counsels. How this might affect the transfer of technical knowledge and impact the learning curve for the venture is obviously a serious question.
   2. What language can and will be used? Is it different at different levels in the organization, and how will that be handled?
   3. What are the local business practices and how do they differ from domestic practices?
      a. This can lead to interesting management and training problems if basic U.S. approaches are tried and they do not work. In Southeast Asia, there is, on the surface, a very western style of business. In fact, the "rules of the dance" are quite different, especially in dealing with local companies. For example, the ex-

pectation of performance and output from sales people might not apply.

b. One might find it difficult in Hong Kong, for example, to get a local salesperson to walk away from business to meet some broader strategic need; the order is *all* that counts. Or, in Japan, it is often difficult to get sales people to "pressure" a customer to adjust a requirement to help a manufacturing problem. The customer's requirements override other considerations.

c. Personnel evaluation techniques, motivation of people, the salary system, and the like often need to be adjusted to meet local needs. The U.S. system may appear to work, but long-term it may not.

B. How must or will the venture be operated relative to the partners or parent?

1. Are the people loyal to the venture or to the parent or to one of the partners? In Japan, for example, it may be difficult to separate people from the Japanese parent, regardless of other legalities.

2. Are policies and procedures derived from the parent or set in place by the venture itself?

3. Is it to be a standalone entity overseen by a board of directors or to be directly managed by the parent or one of the partners?

4. Who is to have basic operational control?

5. What influence is allowed from either partner in a joint venture and in which of the various aspects of the business?

6. How are parent-venture or partner conflicts to be resolved?

The point to be made is that the U.S. parent or partner must not assume it can impact operations, affect change, or install personnel policies and practices. The loyalty of the people, and situation and status of the local partner, and accepted local practices can all impact the degree of freedom the U.S. partner has and affect the ability to meet expectations in personnel matters.

1.3 Other General Considerations

A. How is the venture to be positioned in an overall "quality" sense relative to personnel policies and practices? That is, will attempts be made to duplicate the U.S. position or to meet local standards? For example, if the acquirer ranks in the top quartile in the U.S., is the plan to do so in Singapore as well?

B. How will the company be positioned in relation to other multinationals or local companies? This is somewhat dependent on the management issues in B, above. If the U.S. parent is operating the company, multinational standards tend to apply; if the local partner is in charge or if it is a standalone entity, it might fit into the local company group. This can lead to very different results in the human resource area.

C. What style or philosophy of management will be used? Will it work in the local culture?

D. Are the support systems and infrastructure available to carry out the desired personnel policies and practices? Are the computer systems consultants, training facilities, schools, and so on available?

E. Are the operating and personnel plans based on the local reality? Approvals, cultural delays, and bureaucracy can significantly delay or slow change. Consider the need to deal with all legal and governmental issues before actually embarking on the venture, before the normal start-up point.

In general, Americanize the venture (if that is the objective) with caution, over time rather than immediately. The more developed the country, the closer an operation can be to expected personnel policies and practices; but they can be expensive and may not be required or may not work at that. In Singapore, for example, the government mandates a savings program which essentially precludes the need for pension and savings plans and many other social services. In other countries, the social welfare system has totally different parameters than we are used to.

1.4 Government Issues

A. What are the employment security rights and privileges in the country?
  1. What are the strong local practices and/or legally mandated issues?
  2. What are the layoff requirements?
  3. Are there specific termination and severance requirements?
  4. Note that the implications can be different in each country, but relative to U.S. practices they will usually be more restrictive.
     a. There are legal restrictions in Western Europe where professional people work under contract. Termination is possible but at severe cost. If the process is not managed well, the system can literally prevent action for a considerable period.
     b. In Japan, termination is allowed and severance costs are not that high, but the social implications for the remaining workforce is very serious. A multinational trying to build a viable company will let someone go at great risk. I worked with one company that added a number of specially skilled people to introduce a new product line. The business failed, and they initially assumed they could let the people go; everyone of course would understand that those skills were no longer needed. Not

so; after some discussion, the people were carried until they could be absorbed in other businesses, and considerable effort was expended in retraining. This consideration is obviously important if operation plans and strategy call for major restructuring or dramatic change in the skill mix of the employees.

    c. In many countries, workers may not be laid off except with severe penalty. Once a personnel level is committed to, say a second shift, it may have a permanency not expected. A U.S. planning system may not work as effectively in an offshore venture.

B. What are the staffing requirements or restrictions at the location?

    1. Are there limits to the use of expatriates? For example, in India and China, nonlocal management is typically not allowed. Even in places like Mexico and Brazil, the use of expatriates is often discouraged.

C. What restrictions and/or requirements are there about compensating employees? Consider all aspects of pay.

    1. Pay for time worked: base pay levels and bonuses.

    2. Pay for time not worked: vacation and holidays, sick leave and personal days, military or government service, and special religious observations and restrictions.

    3. Benefits pay: pensions and savings plans, medical and life insurance programs, and workers' compensation programs.

    4. Pay increases or reductions.

    5. Note that in many cultures pay action has only a one-way aspect to it. It is very difficult to cut or change pay schedules in place. Caution is in order before adding or improving a benefit. Bonuses in Asia, for example, are fixed by practice and essentially lose the variable pay implication unless there is a severe business situation. In Brazil, once a bonus is paid, it becomes legally required; it soon loses its "pay for performance" implication.

D. What are the specific labor relations requirements in the country?

    1. What are the implications of labor law?

    2. What are the local practices relative to hourly workers? For example, shift work in many cultures is not accepted or understood; finding people for a midnight to seven shift may be a very different situation than in the U.S.

    3. What is the general militancy of the workforce and the culture? Are unions severe or are they relatively benign or nonexistent?

E. Can the government and/or local entity deliver on the various infrastructure needs necessary for successful operation?

    1. Is there a labor pool with the required skill and ability? Are they available and reliable in the right numbers?

    2. Can the safety and security requirements of the facility be ensured?

3. Are there transportation and other employee services available in the country and at the site?
4. Is there adequate power, water, sanitation, and the like?

1.5 Environmental and Cultural Issues

A. What management style and operating practices will be used or required?
   1. Do not assume that U.S. style management, whether it be consensus, confrontational, or team, is necessarily the style of management used abroad. We remember vividly one case where we took over operation of a factory and immediately put responsibility onto key department heads expecting them to rise to the challenge and be delighted with their new-found authority. In fact, this was not at all the cultural practice. People were confused and behaved in ways that thoroughly confused our management. Only after some serious start-up and learning problems did we discover that they were waiting for us to tell them what to do.
B. Are an acceptable work ethic, experience base, and ability to learn embedded in the available workforce or is much basic training and development required?
C. Are there ethnic, race, or sex issues relative to workforce interactions that will limit flexibility?
   1. Women are not acceptable in management or supervisory positions in many cultures. Often highly skilled, intelligent women are in a company but not in positions of authority. The U.S. company that casually tries to change that could have problems.
   2. Certain nationalities may not be allowed to supervise or work in close proximity with other nationalities.
D. What is the general outlook in the country and, specifically, of the workforce relative to business, capitalism, the U.S., the West in general, ownership, and the like?
E. Consider language implications for operations.
   1. How hard is the language to learn?
   2. Are there single or multiple languages in the workplace?
   3. What degree of English capability will exist and at what levels in the organization?

1.6 Evaluation of Existing Operating Situation or Expected Situation

A. What are the implications of any existing local facilities or sites to be used?
   1. What is the availability of workforce at the site?

2. Are there transportation issues and problems?
3. Are services and facilities available to meet the basic health and safety requirements necessary?

    We recall discussing such issues with a human resource person from a major international construction company. Our problems paled next to his. For one project they had to create the total infrastructure, including building access roads, before even starting the project.

    Then there was the case of the U.S. plant manager who found that water and power were intermittent at best at the operating site. The availability during the construction phase had been a very special effort. In developed countries, obviously, the issues are not as severe. But to presume U.S. conditions prevail relative to fulfilling basic personnel needs is risky to say the least.

B. What key relationships do the existing management and/or partners bring to the venture? That is, what relationships already exist with suppliers and dealers and agents or customers, industry organizations, key competitors, and so on?

C. What are the capabilities of the partner as an individual or as part of your management team? Does it fit with the vision and business strategy anticipated for this venture?
   1. What is the business, technical, and functional expertise of top management?
   2. What is their credibility, honesty, and stature in the community?
   3. Is their operating style compatible with the operating style envisioned for the venture?

1.7 Training

A. What type and intensity of training will be needed to operate the facility?
B. Are there government mandates on safety and personnel policies and practices? What amount of training is necessary for the workers?
C. How will the literacy of the workforce affect training needs and concepts? Can your standard procedures and manuals be used, or must new ones be developed for the country?
D. Has sufficient time been allotted to accomplish training through a complex process which could require developing basic training needs then translating these to the management supervisory force and then retranslating them to the actual worker?
E. What will be taught?
   1. Basic operating skills?
   2. Functional skills?
   3. Management philosophy and vision?

In Brazil, Corning built a complex television bulb factory in a rural area where the only mechanically inclined people to be found were those in the bicycle repair business. There were no other trades available so all had to be developed and trained.

During the construction of turnkey operations in Rumania, Hungary, and China, finding enough people with engineering or trade skills was difficult. Again, extra development and training time was a critical element in the project.

2.0 HUMAN RESOURCE PLANS

The previous section was intended as an overview, raising issues to be addressed at an early stage of the venture project. They would probably be addressed by the key manager involved or the project team evaluating prospects, not necessarily by a human resource professional. This section addresses issues at a later point, when someone with more specific personnel responsibility begins to look at human resource issues in detail. Note that there might be redundancy in some of the questions, but the need now is to go into more detail relative to human resource planning.

As a starting point a total review of the information gathered and evaluated in the overview section would be in order, with a specific focus on the personnel implications of the expectations, strategy, and operating plans for the venture.

2.1 Requirements for People: Organizational Structure

A. What is the basic manning plan for the venture? Consider both immediate needs as well as what is needed at key future check points for the business.
  1. In broad terms, how many people will be needed in total and in general personnel groupings (management and professional people, clerical people, factory workers, people with special skills, and so on)?
  2. What are the functional requirements (the basic mix of skills required), again for various categories of people?
  3. Are there any areas where special personnel policies and practices might be needed to attract and keep the kind of people required in key positions?
B. What will be the structure of the organization?
  1. What is needed to get started with essentially the existing company in an acquisition or the initial start-up organization for a new venture?

2. Is the organization expected to change significantly over time? If so, how will it look at various check points?
3. How will the organization look when it meets longer term expectations?
4. It is important at this point to anticipate personnel needs and consider what it will take to address them. As explained earlier, the ability to adjust and problem solve may be much less than anticipated.

C. What capabilities and skills are required for key positions?
1. Evaluate and spell out the expertise, skills, and experience needed for key functional areas.
2. What level and scope of management and administrative ability is required?
3. Are there specific technical areas that need special attention?

D. What are the key positions that need to be filled or upgraded in order for the venture to successfully meet the operational requirements?

2.2 Resources Available

A. Spell out clearly how the venture is to be staffed.
1. Are some people coming along with the acquisition?
2. Are people to be supplied by the partner?
3. Will the venture be hiring new local nationals and to what extent?
4. How many expatriates will there be? Where will they fit into the management structure and how long might they be expected to stay?

B. Analyze and evaluate the existing workforce and especially the management team. What is the supply of people and skills?
1. What are their capabilities and skills in relation to the projected needs?
2. Do the attitudes and ability of the key people fit the vision, culture, and operating plans?
3. Is there basic demographic data available, such as age, sex, service, education, experience, and the like, on the total workforce?
4. Is there a sense of the flexibility in the organization? Can it accept and work with change? If not, can this be developed?

C. Is there information available on people to make it possible to forecast likely personnel changes? That is, who is likely to or should retire, be terminated, quit, change jobs, or stay and fit in productively?

D. Evaluate the local talent pool. Consider the educational and training facilities available. Will there be a need to upgrade as well as bring in new people?

E. Is there an agreed to consensus on the techniques to be used in the evaluation of people? This is especially important in taking over an existing organization or working with a partner who has a strong presence in the venture.

2.3 Human Resource Plan

A. Compare the need for people—staffing levels, specific skills, functional and management talent—against the available talent in the existing company or parent or partner organization. What is the gap?
 1. Spell out the need for hiring to fill the key needs, immediately and over time.
 2. Spell out the need for expatriate talent or specific talent from the partner.
 3. Are there needs to rearrange roles or significantly change existing jobs?
 4. What is the timing and pace of such changes and people needs?
B. Set a specific manning plan and timetable.
 1. For a new venture, this is usually an evolutionary process.
    a. There will typically be one or two key people with responsibility to initiate the venture and manage financial, legal, and government affairs, usually an expatriate or key partner.
    b. The next group is the operating functional people such as manufacturing, sales, and marketing personnel.
    c. Finally, other managers and operating people are added as the business expands.
 2. For existing organizations, this would primarily be a plan to adjust and change the organization and key people over time to meet strategic and operational needs.
 3. As noted earlier, carefully consider the local hiring and employment practices and evaluate the risks, legal commitments, and liabilities they might entail.
 4. Inevitably mistakes and failures will occur so contingency plans are critical for key positions. Is there adequate backup in either company to fill critical management and functional needs if it becomes necessary? Again, note that the ability to adjust by going to the marketplace for people can often be limited.

3.0 PERSONNEL ADMINISTRATION

3.1 Compensation

A. What is to be the basic level, quality and philosophy of the program?
 1. How does the operation compare to the parent or partner, other multinationals, or local companies in the locale, industry, or market?

2. Will U.S. practice, local practice, or a hybrid be followed?
3. Are programs in place in a local entity, or do they need to be developed? How much change is needed?
4. It is important to remember that the ability to adjust and change later can often be restricted; designing programs to meet initial as well as ongoing and future needs is essential.

B. Acquire the basic data to evaluate local practices and levels of compensation to help determine the program.
   1. In many cases, formal data specific to the local situation may be difficult to obtain, although excellent regional surveys do exist. Make use of all of the informal channels available, such as other multinationals, partners, accounting firms, and consultants.
   2. In using the data, be especially sensitive to its reliability and accuracy, and note well the assumptions and conditions underlying the numbers. For example, in most Asian countries multiplying monthly pay by 12 *does not* yield gross yearly pay; the practice is to pay 1 to 5 extra months as a fixed "bonus" at specific times of the year. Other factors, such as housing allowances, car allowances, and transportation, can be factored in in various ways.

C. Establish a basic outlook on pay for time worked.
   1. Identify the pay groupings. There may not be the clearly visible equivalent of U.S. pay groups such as exempt/non-exempt/hourly, but there undoubtedly will be categories to consider both formal and informal.
   2. Have a clear idea of base pay levels from survey data.
      a. What will it take to hire people as well as to keep them?
      b. Do multinationals pay a premium to attract people or are they seen as preferred employers?
   3. What types of adjustments to pay are generally used? Which are flexible and which are preset and/or mandated?
      a. In many countries, merit programs are not key elements in the pay system as they are in the U.S.
      b. Cost of living adjustments, set or strongly influenced by the government, often are the norm.
      c. Promotions.
      d. Seniority or time in the job.
   4. What bonus program and/or performance incentives are planned? As mentioned earlier, be careful in this area. Bonuses can become fixed either formally or informally once they are put in place.

D. Develop a clear picture of the practices relative to pay for time not worked.
   1. Vacations and holiday practices can vary widely, but there also can be a wide range of other personal, family, or cultural events that require special pay considerations. Some are legally mandated and

others are local practice. All must be understood and considered in the compensation program.

2. Consider various other pay enhancements such as transportation allowances, cafeteria or food allowances, and the like.

E. Have a sound understanding of the health, medical and social welfare policies and practices required or expected.

1. These can vary widely in cost and implications, from Europe, where the benefits programs are more comprehensive than in the U.S., to countries in Asia, where mandatory programs hardly exist.

2. Should local standards be met or exceeded? This is always an important complex question.

3. Consider all aspects of the health and welfare area.

   a. Medical and other insurance programs.

   b. Pensions and/or savings plans.

   c. Workers' compensation and other government programs.

   d. Severance and layoff requirements.

F. Carefully evaluate the financial liabilities imposed on the company relative to all aspects of compensation, whether legally mandated or due to local practice and expectations.

Chapter 10

Pricing
and
Negotiations

Arthur H. Rosenbloom
Chairman of the Board
MMG Patricof & Co., Inc.

1.0 PRICING

Many merger and acquisition specialists cherish the thought that their
particular specialty, be it legal, tax, accounting, or something else, holds
the key to the success or failure of the negotiation. We are not immune
from such bias when we assert that the pricing or valuation element is,
in our judgment, the most critical element in the deal. By valuation, we
mean the process by which, through the use of objective yardsticks and
informed judgment, the seller's fair market value can be determined. Fair
market value, however, may or may not equate to purchase price in a
given merger or acquisition context. The fair market value concept takes
into account only those elements which would be considered by theoretically arms-length parties, both reasonably well informed and equally in-

terested in and capable of doing the deal. In the real world, different buyers will pay higher or lower than fair market value prices as a function of variables like additional business synergy or the need to shore up a sinking business. Sellers may demand a premium price, for example, when management is reluctant to convey control or sell for a reduced price when selling stockholders (even with good successor management) are old, sick, or just tired.

Nevertheless, pricing indices set objective price ranges for discussion. Desire to close, bargaining power, and bargaining strength move a price within and sometimes above or below the range of fair market value. The discussion which follows will describe pricing and negotiation in negotiated transactions. Analyses of offensive and defensive measures in hostile transactions are beyond the scope of this chapter.

Let us assume that a non-U.S. buyer seeks to acquire Jones Widget Manufacturing Co. Inc. (JonesCo), an automotive parts manufacturer. What criteria will enter into the pricing process?

CRITERIA FOR PRICING

1. The percentage ownership to be acquired and attendant voting rights of each class of stock to be acquired.

2. Voting and other rights of the shares involved and any past transactions in the company's securities that may be probative of value.

3. JonesCo's history and management, the nature of its business strengths and weaknesses, and factors affecting those businesses.

4. JonesCo's financial condition, historical, at the valuation date, and as projected, and an analysis of the company's assets, liabilities, invested capital, and net worth.

5. Historical operating results, particularly earnings generated and factors affecting these.

6. JonesCo's outlook at the valuation date; the outlook for the overall economy of the United States; the structure of and outlook for automotive parts industry in which the company is engaged.

7. Bases of investor appraisals of publicly traded stocks of companies that could be employed for comparative purposes in this case, together with comparisons between the financial performance of JonesCo. and the comparatives, discounted cash flow, asset analyses, payback and other elements. The closest competitors may not be public and so data may not be available. A comparative company may not be a competitor, but is close enough in business type to be used for comparison.

8. Recently completed merger and acquisition transactions in industries usable for comparative purposes.

9. The marketability of the subject securities.
10. Premium for control elements.
11. The strategic importance of JonesCo to the buyer in question.

The list above sets forth a list of criteria typically considered as part of an informed pricing analysis. While all such elements need to be considered, different fact patterns will make some elements more important in one case and less so in another. In a pricing analysis for a producer of phosphate rock a number of years ago, value turned largely on an element in Item 6, in that case prices of imported Moroccan phosphate. A pricing analysis arising out of the need to sell an apparel business upon the death of its founder and CEO made the management portion of Item 3 a critical element. A recent chemical industry transaction considered by us involved two classes of stock, one with superior voting power, thus making Item 1 of key importance. A 55 price-earning ratio recently paid for a French cognac company by a Canadian liquor company illustrated the strategic importance of the seller to a particular buyer (see Item 10). However, all of the items in Example 1 need to be considered even if some play little or no part in the ultimate pricing process.

After setting forth the pricing criteria but before the pricing analysis takes place, it is important for the buyer to do a thorough due diligence investigation of the seller. If the seller is taking the buyer's shares or notes, he will be foolish not to do the same with the buyer. We will cover the rudiments of this in the discussion later about the selling brochure. It is sufficient for present purposes to note that among other elements, the process should include a consideration of (1) details surrounding the seller company's founding, (2) the principal milestones during its corporate history, (3) a description of the process by which new products or services are created, (4) if the potential seller is a manufacturing company, details respecting raw material procurement, production, plant and equipment, (5) the seller company's labor situation, (6) details related to the seller company's sales and marketing efforts, (7) the company's current and projected competitive position, (8) information respecting the company's senior management, (9) a thorough consideration of the seller company's historic and projected financial statements, and (10) the company's future plans.

The importance of the due diligence process cannot be overstressed. No sooner had Bridgestone Corp. of Japan acquired Firestone Tire & Rubber Co. for $2.6 billion in 1988, than General Motors who reportedly accounted for 25 percent of Firestone's OEM business announced it was dropping Firestone as a supplier. Due diligence is critical in all deals; it is imperative in international transactions where it is usually the case that the buyer is exposed to greater informational gaps.

Special attention must be given to those areas in which it is relatively easy to overstate earnings purchase in order to maximize the price for the seller with potentially disastrous consequences to the buyer in future years (lower than appropriate R&D or capital improvement expenditures or overvalued inventory).

Similarly, one should scrutinize with particular care elements purportedly resulting from conservative accounting treatment whose purpose is to minimize taxable income. Areas in which such practices are likely to be present include (1) understated inventories, whose income statement consequence is an increase in cost of goods sold and a corresponding decrease in taxable income, (2) travel and entertainment expenses and charitable gifts at levels exceeding those reasonably required for business purposes, (3) redundant personnel (often family members) on the company's books, and (4) unreported sales, particularly in countries in which value added taxes or other sales taxes are high. Many prospective sellers will attempt to reconstruct current or historic earnings and assets by adding back the difference between the earnings reductions resulting from the practices described above and normal expenses in the areas. An earnings multiple attached to that difference can frequently result in a dramatic increase in sale price. Thus, the parties should recognize that reasonable persons may differ on the extent to which earnings in these or other categories are properly reconstructable. In addition, we believe that the quality of reconstructed earnings or assets is usually less persuasive concerning the seller's future earning power than historically generated earnings and assets. Given this presumption, it may be appropriate to attach lower earnings or cash-flow multiples and lower market-book value ratios to reconstructed earnings and assets in relation to their historical counterparts.

Correlatively, projections of the "hockey stick" variety (curving dramatically upward from historical levels) need to be viewed with a healthy dose of skepticism. A rigorous testing of the assumptions upon which such projections are made is strongly advised.

Clearly, the ability of projected cash flows to support the interest charges and amortization of purchase price debt should be given close scrutiny.

Thus, due diligence turns the pricing analysis from an exercise in number crunching to a tool from which, based on the facts revealed to the due diligence process, a realistic price range can be determined. Please note that the pricing exercise is a necessary tool for each side; it is most assuredly not the exclusive preserve of the buyer.

Comparative company analysis. This form of analysis compares the financial performance of a prospective seller to that of other companies, usable for comparative purposes usually. Factors considered include growth in revenues and profits, profit margins, return on assets, return on equity, working capital and leverage ratios, and inventory and asset turnover ratios. It is often useful to consider industry specific kinds of ratios such as revenues per passenger mile and passenger load factor for the airline industry or sales per square foot in the retail industry.

The kind of comparative company analysis just described determines the value of a freely traded minority interest in the seller. A control premium is added to this result. An alternative form of comparative company analysis is to consider the price-earnings ratios and market-book values paid in recent acquisitions of companies in the same industry as that of the seller. While this kind of data is very useful when available, it may be difficult to find recent transactions of companies sufficiently close in business to that of the seller. Older transactions reflecting investor appraisal ratios at times removed from the valuation date may reflect stock market realities not relevant to pricing at a later date. In addition, comparative transaction pricing is made more difficult in transactions used for comparative purposes which have noncash components (the need to value bonds or preferred stock which may be worth other than face or par).

Single company analysis.   This technique attempts to measure the seller by itself in terms of discounted cash flow and asset valuation.

Affordability.   The ability to pay what may be a fair price is a real world constraint on price, for even if the prospective seller measures up under both comparative and single-company analyses, the transaction may not be cash affordable by the buyer, or may be excessively dilutive or have some other incurable impediment to "doability."

Let us now look more closely at comparative analysis and single company analysis.

1.1 Comparative Analysis

The basis of this analysis is to compare the financial performance of prospective seller against that of a group of companies offering a comparable product or service in order to infer a value for the company being priced as a result of how well or poorly its financial performance compares to that of the array chosen for such purposes. That is sometimes more easily said than done. For one thing, the best comparisons may be from closely held companies where little or no public data is available or from subsidiaries or divisions of publicly held companies primarily engaged in other business areas. Even when companies report on a separate product line basis, the price-earnings ratio is a function of the total company.

These problems notwithstanding, it is usually possible to develop a defensible array of companies usable for comparative purposes. Assuming a non-U.S. buyer and a U.S. seller, probably the best way to start the search is by determining the seller's SIC Code (the United States Commerce Department Standard Industrial Classification Code) and, through Standard & Poor's Corporation Records, the Directory of Companies Filing Annual Reports with the SEC, or Standard & Poor's Compustat data base, determine the potential universe of publicly held comparative companies having the same or a similar SIC Code. After determining the potential universe, it is necessary to start weeding out companies on what, given the facts of a particular seller's operations or finances, are logical grounds. Such grounds include differences between the seller and the potential comparative in product line, profitability (if the seller has been generally profitable, exclusion of consistently unprofitable potential comparatives may be warranted), facts affecting market price such as merger rumors, and the like. After selection of the comparatives, accounting adjustments may be required to put the comparative companies on the same footing as the subject company. Adjustments in, for example, inventory reserves and depreciation methods will result in greater comparability.

We can consider how a defensible array of comparatives can be picked in our JonesCo, a hypothetical situation. The comparatives should share with each other and with Jones a series of common characteristics. If the comparative company selection process has been correctly performed, there should, other than the array chosen, be no other publicly held companies who meet all of the criteria. Thus, the only attack would be upon the rationality of the manner in which the array has been developed.

COMPARATIVE ARRAY

The automotive parts manufacturers to be used for comparative purposes were selected on the basis of the following criteria.

1. Each was a U.S. corporation operating principally as a manufacturer of automotive or truck parts for both the OEM and replacement parts markets found in SIC Code 3714, with at least two-thirds of total revenues generated by such sources.

2. Companies who met the first criterion, but were distinguished from JonesCo because their primary products were body parts, bumpers, wheels, or other nonconsumable parts were not included, nor were those who produced parts primarily for stationary or other non-over-

the-road engines. Likewise, those companies that were primarily producers of speed or custom parts were not included, as they represent different markets than those served by JonesCo.

3. The company could not primarily be a wholesale or distribution company, nor a nonproducing importer of foreign car parts.
4. The company could not primarily be a wholesale or distribution company, nor a non-producing importer of foreign car parts.
5. Each company had most recent total revenues of less than $1 billion and was profitable four of the last five fiscal years.
6. No company was the subject of an ancillary transaction, such as a merger, tender offer, or going-private offer.
   Companies meeting these criteria, and the principal trading market of the common stocks of each, are as follows:

Atlantic Auto Parts	NYSE
Edison Spark Plug Company	NYSE
E-Z Air Filter Company	NYSE
Hercules Gasket Mfg. Co.	AMEX
Miracle Muffler Company	NYSE
Winning Motor Products, Inc.	AMEX

The above makes clear that in order to be within the comparative company array, each comparative company, like JonesCo, had to be (1) principally an OEM producer of automotive or truck parts, (2) one that specialized in consumable parts for nonstationary over the road engines, (3) a manufacturer and not a distributor or importer, (4) one having shares that were publicly traded in quantity, (5) within specific revenue and profit constraints, and (6) one whose freely traded value was not affected by an ancillary transaction. The effect of such a transaction would be to raise the company's stock market price over the levels of a freely traded minority interest because of the addition of speculative elements in contemplation of a "premium for control," "going private" premium, or otherwise.

For U.S. companies seeking to acquire abroad, the process is much the same. One should attempt to identify a universe of companies usable for comparative purposes in the seller company's country of origin, although the supply of companies usable for such purposes outside the U.S. may be more limited due to less developed public markets and less stringent disclosure requirements. Caveat: It is frequently the case that investor appraisal ratios for companies in a given industry in the public markets of one country may be quite different from those in another country at the same date.

At the time of the acquisition of Belgium's Continental Pharma

Company by Monsanto, in which we participated some time back, there was a 10 to 20 percent disparity between U.S. pharmaceutical price-earnings multiples on the one hand and price-earnings ratios for such companies in Europe or elsewhere. Given this fact, it is desirable wherever possible to develop comparatives in the same country as that of the subject company.

Once the comparatives have been selected, the process of comparison begins. The measuring period is typically either five years or an average business cycle (whichever is longer) for each principal industry in which the seller company operates. This is an exercise as important for the seller as it is for the buyer to prepare for subsequent price discussions.

The following compares JonesCo's growth trend in revenues, operating income, and net income versus that of the comparatives. Using year 1 as the 100 percent or base year, it demonstrates that in all three categories JonesCo compares poorly to the median of the comparatives.

TABLE 10.1   Revenue Comparison

Year	1	2	3	4	5
Revenues					
Atlantic Auto Parts	100	115	120	140	182
Edison Spark Plug Co.	100	102	98	96	102
E-Z Air Filter Co.	100	138	163	187	229
Hercules Gasket Mfg. Co.	100	109	111	118	131
Miracle Muffler Co.	100	118	142	165	194
Winning Motor Products	100	125	142	164	188
Median	100	117	131	152	185
Jones Widget Mfg. Co.	100	120	127	143	168

Source: Company financial reports. Computations by MMG Patricof & Co.

TABLE 10.2   Operating Income Comparison

Year	1	2	3	4	5
Operating Income					
Atlantic Auto Parts	100	130	120	192	329
Edison Spark Plug Co.	100	85	98	75	81
E-Z Air Filter Co.	100	182	263	291	394
Hercules Gasket Mfg. Co.	100	138	157	201	268
Miracle Muffler Co.	100	158	190	242	290
Winning Motor Products	100	344	420	577	635
Median	100	148	174	222	310
Jones Widget Mfg. Co.	100	114	148	173	158

Source: Company financial reports. Computations by MMG Patricof & Co.

TABLE 10.3 Net Income Comparison

Year	1	2	3	4	5
Net Income					
Atlantic Auto Parts	100	164	143	242	398
Edison Spark Plug Co.	100	85	72	72	76
E-Z Air Filter Co.	100	145	303	350	500
Hercules Gasket Mfg. Co.	100	119	121	149	193
Miracle Muffler Co.	100	135	194	247	351
Winning Motor Products	100	342	457	640	693
Median	100	140	168	245	375
Jones Widget Mfg. Co.	100	125	164	192	132

Source: Company financial reports. Computations by MMG Patricof & Co.

Measuring growth trends in operating income and net income allow one to determine, in the former instance, how well the seller's base business, uncomplicated by other elements, compares with the comparatives; and, in the latter instance, the impact of interest income and expense, taxes, and other items on its financial performance. Note that there is no reason to slavishly compare the subject company against a median. Although a median irons out statistical highs and lows better than an average, if one or more comparatives are strikingly more similar to the subject company than the others, recognition of that fact should be given in the analytical process and ultimately be reflected in the choice of investor appraisal ratios.

The three preceding tables compare JonesCo's profit margins to those of the comparatives in terms of the relationship of gross income, operating income, and net income, respectively, to sales. While JonesCo has turned in superior gross margins and operating margins (Tables 10.4 and 10.5), its after tax profit margin in year 5, while still exceeding the me-

TABLE 10.4 Gross Margin Comparison

Year	1	2	3	4	5
Gross Margin					
Atlantic Auto Parts	18.3%	17.5%	18.1%	17.9%	17.4%
Edison Spark Plug Co.	35.3	32.6	33.5	33.0	32.1
E-Z Air Filter Co.	33.0	31.6	33.1	32.7	32.5
Hercules Gasket Mfg. Co.	38.5	38.1	40.7	41.5	42.1
Miracle Muffler Co.	29.5	31.1	32.9	33.1	32.3
Winning Motor Products	38.4	43.9	44.7	47.4	47.3
Median	34.2%	32.1%	33.3%	33.1%	32.4%
Jones Widget Mfg. Co.	40.6%	46.4%	46.8%	48.4%	46.8%

Source: Company financial reports. Computations by MMG Patricof & Co.

TABLE 10.5 Operating Profit Comparison

Year	1	2	3	4	5
Operating Profit					
Atlantic Auto Parts	4.0%	4.5%	4.0%	5.5%	7.2%
Edison Spark Plug Co.	9.1	7.5	9.0	7.1	7.2
E-Z Air Filter Co.	6.4	8.5	10.4	10.0	11.1
Hercules Gasket Mfg. Co.	4.5	5.7	6.4	7.7	9.2
Miracle Muffler Co.	8.5	11.5	11.6	12.7	12.9
Winning Motor Products	5.3	14.6	15.6	18.7	17.9
Median	5.9%	8.0%	9.7%	8.9%	10.2%
Jones Widget Mfg. Co.	13.5%	12.8%	15.7%	16.3%	12.7%

Source: Company financial reports. Computations by MMG Patricof & Co.

TABLE 10.6 Profit After Taxes Comparison

Year	1	2	3	4	5
Profit After Taxes					
Atlantic Auto Parts	1.8%	2.5%	2.1%	3.1%	3.9%
Edison Spark Plug Co.	4.9	4.0	3.6	3.7	3.6
E-Z Air Filter Co.	2.9	3.1	5.4	5.4	6.4
Hercules Gasket Mfg. Co.	3.0	3.3	3.3	3.8	4.5
Miracle Muffler Co.	4.6	5.2	6.2	6.8	8.3
Winning Motor Products	2.6	7.2	8.4	10.2	9.7
Median	3.0%	3.7%	4.5%	4.6%	5.5%
Jones Widget Mfg. Co.	7.4%	7.7%	9.6%	10.0%	5.9%

Source: Company financial reports. Computations by MMG Patricof & Co.

dian, are less attractive than its gross or operating margin. This suggests some care in analyzing elements such as JonesCo's Other Income and Expense category and the company's historic tax rates. In the real world company from which JonesCo was drawn, the answer was to be found in high social costs (a day care center) adversely affecting pretax income and a higher than normal tax rate (few investment tax credits) both of which ultimately and adversely impacted net income.

A consideration of return on average total assets or net income divided by average total assets (Table 10.7) shows an attractive performance for JonesCo, evidence of its relatively unleveraged state. Its return on average common equity (Table 10.8) is likewise attractive. These ratios test the extent to which a company's asset and equity bases are effective engines for the development of profits.

JonesCo's working capital ratio (current assets divided by current liabilities) is also attractive as is its quick asset ratio (cash, marketable securities and accounts receivable divided by current liabilities).

TABLE 10.7   Return on Average Total Assets Comparison

Year	1	2	3	4
Return on Average Total Assets				
Atlantic Auto Parts	4.2%	3.6%	5.7%	8.9%
Edison Spark Plug Co.	5.2	4.6	4.8	5.1
E-Z Air Filter Co.	4.4	7.3	7.8	10.1
Hercules Gasket Mfg. Co.	6.1	6.0	6.9	17.5
Miracle Muffler Co.	6.4	7.9	9.1	24.3
Winning Motor Products	9.6	10.9	12.9	26.1
Median	6.6%	6.7%	7.4%	13.8%
Jones Widget Mfg. Co.	12.4%	14.9%	16.5%	16.8%

Source: Company financial reports. Computations by MMG Patricof & Co.

TABLE 10.8   Return on Average Total Equity Comparison

Year	1	2	3	4
Return on Average Total Equity				
Atlantic Auto Parts	7.9%	6.7%	10.6%	15.7%
Edison Spark Plug Co.	8.3	7.5	7.8	8.2
E-Z Air Filter Co.	7.4	12.9	13.8	17.8
Hercules Gasket Mfg. Co.	9.2	9.6	13.2	35.9
Miracle Muffler Co.	9.6	11.5	13.1	34.9
Winning Motor Products	16.7	17.0	20.1	40.9
Median	8.8%	9.5%	13.1%	26.3%
Jones Widget Mfg. Co.	36.3%	34.1%	32.5%	32.0%

Source: Company financial reports. Computations by MMG Patricof & Co.

Table 10.11 displays JonesCo's ratio of total debt-equity with the comparatives. This ratio is only one of many ways of testing leverage or debt bearing capacity. Other ratios by which to measure leverage include common stock equity to total invested capital (the sum of all the long-term debt and equity accounts), long term debt to common or total equity, and the like. Which leverage ratio to choose depends on the capital structure of each particular seller, patterns of analysis common to a particular industry or a specific country, among other factors. Table 10.11 demonstrates that JonesCo was far more leveraged than the median of the comparatives in years 1 through 3; its leverage in years 4 and 5 demonstrates that JonesCo's leverage was reduced to levels close to the median, thus, making it more leverageable as a leveraged buyout vehicle and hence more attractive. (In the real world, the company from which this case was drawn was slowly working down the nonrecurring debt from an industrial revenue bond.)

TABLE 10.9 Working Capital Ratio Comparison

Year	1	2	3	4	5
Working Capital Ratio					
Atlantic Auto Parts	3.5	4.1	3.5	3.0	2.8
Edison Spark Plug Co.	2.6	2.3	2.2	2.4	2.4
E-Z Air Filter Co.	4.0	2.8	2.5	2.7	2.4
Hercules Gasket Mfg. Co.	3.3	2.8	3.4	3.0	3.2
Miracle Muffler Co.	2.4	2.7	2.7	2.7	2.9
Winning Motor Products	2.7	2.7	4.1	3.8	3.5
Median	3.0	2.8	3.1	2.9	2.9
Jones Widget Mfg. Co.	4.6	4.9	6.0	6.3	4.1

Source: Company financial reports. Computations by MMG Patricof & Co.

TABLE 10.10 Quick Asset Ratio Comparison

Year	1	2	3	4	5
Quick Asset Ratio					
Atlantic Auto Parts	2.0	2.2	1.8	1.7	1.5
Edison Spark Plug Co.	1.0	0.8	0.9	1.1	1.0
E-Z Air Filter Co.	1.1	0.9	0.8	1.1	0.9
Hercules Gasket Mfg. Co.	1.2	1.0	1.4	1.3	1.5
Miracle Muffler Co.	1.0	1.0	1.0	1.1	1.0
Winning Motor Products	1.2	1.1	2.0	1.7	1.4
Median	1.2	1.0	1.2	1.2	1.2
Jones Widget Mfg. Co.	2.7	2.6	3.6	3.6	2.3

Source: Company financial reports. Computations by MMG Patricof & Co.

TABLE 10.11 Debt-Equity Ratio Comparison

Year	1	2	3	4	5
Debt Equity Ratio					
Atlantic Auto Parts	1.0	0.8	0.9	0.8	0.8
Edison Spark Plug Co.	0.6	0.6	0.6	0.6	0.6
E-Z Air Filter Co.	0.6	0.7	0.8	0.7	0.8
Hercules Gasket Mfg. Co.	0.5	0.6	0.6	0.8	1.1
Miracle Muffler Co.	0.6	0.5	0.5	0.5	0.4
Winning Motor Products	1.1	1.0	0.6	0.5	0.6
Median	0.6	0.7	0.6	0.8	0.7
Jones Widget Mfg. Co.	2.4	1.5	1.1	0.9	0.9

Source: Company financial reports. Computations by MMG Patricof & Co.

Tables 10.12 and 10.13 demonstrate JonesCo's turnover ratios (revenues divided by assets and revenues divided by inventory). These ratios demonstrate how effective a company has been in converting its assets and inventories into revenues. The data illustrate that JonesCo has, in both instances, exceeded the median of the comparatives.

Note that all of the ratios we have described must be understood as attractive or unattractive relative to the same ratio for other companies usable for comparative purposes. There is never an absolutely correct ratio at any given time. Industry norms, the accounting and regulatory environment of a specific country, and stock market conditions at a particular valuation date are the relevant factors.

The preceding tables represent a limited array of ratios usable in comparative company analysis. Other general ratios including dividend yield (per share dividends to common stock price), dividend payout ratio

TABLE 10.12 Asset Turnover Ratio Comparison

Year	1	2	3	4	5
Asset Turnover Ratio					
Atlantic Auto Parts	1.4	1.7	1.7	1.8	2.2
Edison Spark Plug Co.	1.3	1.3	1.3	1.3	1.4
E-Z Air Filter Co.	1.3	1.2	1.3	1.4	1.5
Hercules Gasket Mfg. Co.	1.8	1.8	1.9	1.9	2.0
Miracle Muffler Co.	1.3	1.4	1.3	1.4	1.5
Winning Motor Products	1.3	1.4	1.4	1.4	1.4
Median	1.3	1.4	1.4	1.4	1.5
Jones Widget Mfg. Co.	1.6	2.1	1.9	1.8	1.9

Source: Company financial reports. Computations by MMG Patricof & Co.

TABLE 10.13 Inventory Turnover Ratio Comparison

Year	1	2	3	4	5
Inventory Turnover Ratio					
Atlantic Auto Parts	6.0	7.7	7.9	9.0	9.6
Edison Spark Plug Co.	3.1	3.2	3.5	3.8	3.8
E-Z Air Filter Co.	2.9	2.8	3.1	4.0	3.9
Hercules Gasket Mfg. Co.	4.0	3.9	4.1	4.1	4.8
Miracle Muffler Co.	4.1	4.9	4.4	4.8	4.3
Winning Motor Products	3.2	3.0	3.5	3.1	2.7
Median	3.6	3.6	3.8	4.1	4.1
Jones Widget Mfg. Co.	6.7	6.2	6.9	6.2	6.3

Source: Company financial reports. Computations by MMG Patricof & Co.

(percentage of net income to dividends) might be used. Industry specific kind of ratios described earlier are often extremely helpful.

1.2 Earnings and Cash-Flow-Based Approaches to Value

From the analysis of JonesCo's performance versus that of the comparatives, we can develop a comparative company *earnings* approach to value.

Table 10.14 considers price-earnings multiples for the comparatives based on average five year, three year, latest year, latest twelve months, and latest current fiscal year projected earnings. The multiple for each such period results from dividing the company's current price (typically an average price over a week to a month prior to the valuation date to avoid the possible atypicalities from single day prices) by the earnings per share for the period in question. Practitioners vary on whether to use primary or fully diluted earnings per share and how to calculate earnings per share when, in a given year, earnings have been impacted by an atypi-

TABLE 10.14 Jones Widget Mfg. Co. Versus Comparative Companies Investor Appraisal Ratios

Company	Price-Earnings Multiples					Ratio of Market Price to Tangible Book Value
	Latest 5 Years	Latest 3 Years	Latest Year	Latest 12 Months	Year Projected	
Atlantic Auto Parts	15.6	12.5	8.3	7.9	7.6	114%
Edison Spark Plug Company	10.8	11.9	11.8	11.8	10.5	89
E-Z Air Filter Co.	21.6	16.3	12.6	12.0	13.0	213
Hercules Gasket Mfg. Co.	10.4	8.2	5.5	6.3	5.9	98
Miracle Muffler Co.	12.2	10.6	8.0	8.0	7.8	139
Winning Motor Products	10.6	8.2	7.1	8.2	8.5	146
Median	11.5	11.3	8.2	8.1	7.0	127

Source: Company annual and interim reports. Projected earnings from Standard & Poor's Earnings Forecaster. Stock prices from Barron's Magazine. Computations by MMG Patricof & Co.

cal event which nonetheless falls short of being an extraordinary item for accounting purposes.

In this instance as in many others in the pricing process, the decision should be based on an examination of the facts of a particular case (the extent to which dilution is reasonably foreseeable or the earnings enhancing or depressing event are isolated ones).

Which of the five earnings periods should be used? The answer is a resounding "it depends." Where the seller is involved in a cyclical industry (ranching, oil and gas, and the like) a pricing analysis that fails to consider price-earnings multiples based on longer periods (average *five* or *three* year earnings) may well be incomplete. In industries characteristically priced on recent results (like microelectronics and biotechnology) or where a company has recently changed the nature of its business, *latest year, latest twelve months* or *projected* results are generally more pertinent. Whether to consider latest year or latest twelve months results involves a balancing of the equities between the greater certainty of audited versus unaudited numbers and picking a date closest to the valuation date. The *ability* to price based on *projected* earnings depends upon the availability of earnings forecasts by the company or brokerage firm research reports and the extent to which projections made by or for the company have been on target in the past.

Quite often, when pricing a company where both cyclical and current elements are relevant, more than one earnings period is used. Moreover, pricing a company with operations in a number of industries may result in one pricing period for one company subsidiary and another for other subsidiaries. In pricing Hyatt Corporation a number of years ago, we used longer pricing periods for its hotel and then existing medical business and, due to the then existing stock market, a shorter period for its casino operations.

The illustrations displayed in Table 10.14 are based on multiples of net income. In some industries (publishing, for example) companies are sometimes priced on multiples of pretax operating income. This proved to be the case, for example, in the acquisition by VNU (a Dutch publisher) of Hayden Publishing, a U.S. publisher of technical magazines. (In some high tech industries where constant earnings patterns have not developed, companies are priced by reference to *revenues*.)

In industries characterized by high levels of depreciation, amortization, and other noncash charges like real-estate, equipment leasing, and the like, a variant on the price-earnings multiple approach, called a price-cash flow multiple, may be considered, in which price is divided not by earnings per share but by total cash flow per share from operations.

In our analysis of Trans Union Corporation some years back, we priced that company's railcar leasing operations (a high cash flow business) on a price-cash flow multiple basis while pricing other elements of the business (its finance subsidiary) on a price-earnings multiple basis.

A second way to value earnings is through the analysis of the seller's future earnings or cash flows. A conventional tool for doing this, particularly in the case of the leveraged buyout scenarios, is the use of payback analysis.

Table 10.15 considers the period over which a 100-percent common stock equity investment of $100,000 will be fully paid back. Projected pretax profits are reduced by 40 percent (the presumed sum of then applicable federal, state, and local taxes) to yield an after tax profit. Depreciation (a kind of shorthand for the sum of depreciation, amortization, and other noncash charges) is added back to yield a cash flow number. This number, added to subsequent years' cash flows produces a cumulative cash flow. Table 10.15 demonstrates that, under the facts presented, the investment will be returned in three years. Comparing the payback periods of a series of alternative investment opportunities and judging the payback period of each offers one means for investing in one company versus others. As in the case of any projections, in order to make this analysis a practical tool for decision making, one must be thoughtful in the as-

TABLE 10.15 Payback Period On $100,000 Investment Made in Year

Year	1	2	3
Pre Tax Profit	$25,000	$41,667	$50,000
Income Taxes			
(40% Total Rate)	$10,000	$16,667	$20,000
After Tax Profit	$15,000	$25,000	$30,000
Depreciation[1]	$10,000	$10,000	$10,000
Cash Flow	$25,000	$35,000	$40,000
Cumulative Cash Flow	$25,000	$60,000	$100,000

1. Straight Line

Reconstituted for Leveraged Buyout

Year	1	2	3	4
Investment	$100,000	—	—	—
Pre Tax Profit	$25,000	$41,667	$50,000	$80,000
Interest at 10%				
Unpaid Balance	$10,000	$6,667	$3,333	—
Adjusted Pre Tax Profit	$15,000	$35,000	$46,667	$80,000
Taxes	$6,000	$14,000	$18,667	$32,000
After Tax Profit	$9,000	$21,000	$28,000	$48,000
Depreciation	$10,000	$10,000	$10,000	$10,000
Cash Flow	$19,000	$31,000	$38,000	$58,000
Amortization of 3 year loan	$33,333	$33,333	$33,000	—
Adjusted Cash Flow	$(14,333)	$(2,333)	$ 5,000	$58,000
Cumulative Cash Flow	$(14,333)	$(16,666)	$(11,666)	$46,334

sumptions going into the process. Thus, careful scrutiny needs to be given to the likely levels of pretax earnings and the effect on such earnings of investments in property, plant, equipment, people, R&D, and the like, over the period studied required to realize them. Current and foreseeable changes in tax rates and depreciation practices must also be considered in order to produce "real world" results.

Table 10.15b considers the same $100,000 investment described in Table 10.15a but reconstitutes it. Whereas 10.15a assumes a 100 percent common equity investment, 10.15b assumes a 100 percent debt investment (the ultimate expression of the leveraged buyout art form) in which the $100,000 is borrowed with interest at 10 percent over a three year amortization period. Because of the debt service and amortization requirements, the payback period becomes five rather than three years. Clearly, the same cautionary advice respecting the appropriateness of the assumptions described for Table 10.15a applies here too. A typical merger and acquisition scenario will see a financing structure somewhere between the extremes shown in Table 10.15a and 10.15b.

Another form of single company analysis is the *discounted cash flow* (dcf) method. Dcf proceeds on the assumption that dollars, pounds, francs, marks, liras, yen, and so on received today are more valuable than those to be received in the future because today's currency in hand can be invested to yield a return. The higher the return, the lower the present value. If the current market return is five percent, the value to be received in a year is $.95 cents but if the current market return is eight percent, that value is only $.92 cents. In countries where no useful universe of comparatives exists, dcf may become the primary or the only pricing methodology. There are four components to dcf in mergers and acquisitions: One is the *net free cash flows* projected for the seller (net profits plus depreciation, amortization, and other noncash charges less cash required for reinvestment, retirement of debt or otherwise, and dividends).

A second dcf component is the period over which the cash flows are to be measured. That period is typically five to ten years. Discounting over shorter periods tends to produce more reliable cash-flow projections but higher sensitivity to the terminal value calculation, since the earlier the time for measuring terminal value, the higher the present value decimal. The converse is true when discounting over longer periods. We suggest that the dcf exercise consider the results based on both shorter and longer term discounting.

A third element in the dcf process is the discount rate. The discount rate is generally chosen after considering *cost of capital* and premiums over risk free rates elements. Cost of capital is a combination of the cost of debt and equity capital weighted in proportion to their presence on a company's balance sheet. Average borrowing costs at the valuation date is generally a good proxy for debt cost of capital considerations. A public

company's price-earnings ratio and a private company's return on equity
are typical means by which to determine equity cost of capital. Thus, if
XYZ Corporation has an average cost of debt capital of 10 percent and a
cost of common equity of 12 percent and debt and common equity components represents 50 percent each of XYZ's capitalization, the discount
rate would be 11 percent.

A second methodology for determining the discount rate attempts
to calculate the investment opportunities available to shareholders by adjusting for risk. This form of analysis has three components, the first of
which is the so-called riskless rate (typically the rate for long-term U.S.
Treasury instruments). Added to the riskless rate is a second feature, an
amount equal to the subject company's *beta*. A beta is the stock market
deviation of the subject company's stock from an appropriate index of
other stocks. In the case of a closely held company, the beta must be
inferred. The third component is the *risk premium*, the risk that the subject company will face to generate the projected cash flows in relation to
the stablest of comparable kinds of stocks. The sum of the riskless rate
plus the beta plus the risk premium produces the discount rate.

At whose discount rate should the seller's net free cash flows be
discounted: its own discount rate or that of the buyer? This question is a
particularly vexing one in international transactions where costs of capital, betas and risk premiums may vary dramatically from country to
country at the same valuation date. Discounting at the *seller's* cost of
capital provides the most realistic means by which to measure the risk of
its projected cash flows not materializing. Discounting at the *buyer's* cost
of capital best measures the buyers opportunity cost. The benefit from
choosing the first alternative is the opportunity cost of not having chosen
the second. Since persuasive arguments are available for discounting at
both seller and buyer costs of capital, it pays to run models using both
such approaches. By doing so, one will be best armed for the price discussions to come.

The fourth element in dcf analysis is that of terminal value. Terminal value expresses the theoretically perpetual value capable of being generated by the seller's cash flow. One can arrive at terminal value by a
variety of means: (1) a perpetual dividend stream, (2) a price-earnings ratio that assumes the seller will be sold at the end of the discounting period
for a price which may be a fixed industry common price/cash flow ratio
(most often used when industry price-cash flow have been fairly constant
over the years), (3) a price-cash flow ratio (over whatever period measured)
equal to that paid by the buyer at the closing, (4) a figure equal to the
sum of the seller's cash flows generated during the measuring period
(which has the merit of not requiring the use of a second independent
variable), (5) at the projected net asset value at the end of the period (a
methodology generally providing the most conservative result without

the use of an independent variable), (6) At a price-cash flow multiple representing the reciprocal of the discount rate (an approach most useful when the risk factors at the end of the discounting period are presumed to be the same as those present at the beginning of the period).

Table 10.16 assumes a seller with $24 million in most recent year net profits seeking a purchase price of $240 million. From our comparative company pricing analysis, we can determine whether the resulting price-earnings ratio of ten times the latest year profits is reasonable (assuming the appropriateness of a price-earnings ratio based on latest year's net profits). Table 10.16 attempts to answer the same question from the perspective of dcf analysis.

Table 10.16 discounts ten years' worth of projected net free cash flows at 18 percent (as a result of one of the two most common methods for picking discount rates previously described) to yield a discounted cash flow of $179,939,435. Terminal value was determined here by using the reciprocal of the discount rate as a price-cash flow multiplier applied to year 10 net free cash flow to yield a terminal value figure of $56,104,899. Adding the sum of ten years of discounted cash flows and terminal values results in a value of $236,044,334, thus suggesting that a $240,000,000 price is a bit tight. Real world considerations, however, make clear that because of the many variables in the process, pricing exercises like this cannot be expected to produce results with micrometer like precision.

TABLE 10.16   Discounted Cash Flow Analysis
of Jones Widget Mfg. Co.

Year	Cash Flow ($)	18% Present Value	Discounted Cash Flow ($)
1	34,680,000	.84746	29,394,768
2	35,547,000	.71818	25,529,144
3	36,457,350	.60863	22,189,037
4	40,303,218	.51579	20,787,997
5	41,306,886	.4371	18,055,653
6	42,360,724	.37043	15,061,683
7	46,357,247	.31392	14,551,467
8	47,519,114	.26604	12,641,985
9	48,739,070	.22546	10,988,710
10	52,910,033	.19106	10,108,991
			179,939,435
		Terminal Value	56,104,899
		Total	236,044,334

Terminal Value or 52,910,033 × 5.55 (Reciprocal of 18% = 293, 650, 683 × , 19106 = Terminal Value of 56,104,899)

Source: Company projections.

Thus, that where, as here, measurement is within three percent of the targeted sum, a "buy" decision by the buyer and persuasive case by the seller to the same effect might be supportable.

1.3   Asset-Based Approaches to Value

Thus far, we have discussed only the valuation of earnings or cash flows. What about *asset* valuation? There are, at least, two basic methods of asset valuation: (1) a return on equity-market-tangible book value approach and (2) an asset by asset approach. We shall take them up one by one.

The comparative company methodology offers a useful means by which to measure the way the investor community values assets by measuring the relationship between a company's return on average common equity and its market price to tangible book value. It is usually the case that the higher the return on equity, the higher the market price to tangible book value. This is true because, as we have mentioned, investors will bid up or bid down a stock in relation to its equity base as a function of how well or poorly that equity base serves as an engine by which to generate earnings.

Consider the illustration of this methodology in Table 10.17.

Note in Table 10.17 that companies like Edison and Atlantic with a low return on equity (ROE) sell at low market-tangible book value ratios, whereas high ROE companies like Hercules and Winning sell at higher market-tangible book value ratios. This relationship is almost never a perfect one. Note that E-Z with a 17.8 percent ROE, one exceeded by three of the comparatives, has the highest market-book ratio. Still, the relationship generally holds true. If such is the case with an array of compara-

TABLE 10.17   Jones Widget Mfg. Co.
Versus Comparative Companies

	Return on Average Common Equity	Ratio of Market Price to Tangible Book Value
Edison Spark Plug Co.	8.2%	89%
Atlantic Auto Parts	15.7	98
E-Z Air Filter Company	17.8	213
Miracle Muffler Company	34.9	125
Hercules Gasket Mfg. Co.	35.9	139
Winning Motor Products, Inc.	40.9	146
Jones Widget Mfg. Co.	36.0	—

Source: Company financial statements. Stock prices from Barron's Magazine. Computations by MMG Patricof & Co.

tives in a manner demonstrable through a linear regression analysis (plotting ROE on one axis and market-tangible book value on the other to determine whether the plot results in a reasonably straight line relationship among the companies plotted), the technique may be useful. Here, we can *infer* a market-tangible book value relationship for JonesCo, given its 36.0 percent ROE of about 140 percent (a bit greater than Hercules' market-tangible book but clearly lower than that of Winning). A variant on the same approach is to compare the relationship of return on average total assets to the ratio of market price to tangible book value.

A second method for determining asset value derives from single company methodology. It is an asset by asset approach, under which each asset and liability is written up or down from the historical cost manner in which it appears on the balance sheet, to its fair market value. Assume a hypothetical balance sheet as follows.

Cash.   This is the first balance sheet item on U.S. balance sheets. Note that cash may not always be equal to its stated balance sheet value. For example, $10,000,000 in free and unencumbered cash is clearly worth more than $10,000,000, some portion of which was the subject of a compensating balance at the company's bank or part of a "carve out" pursuant to a restriction in a private placement agreement.

Marketable securities.   The next U.S. balance sheet item requires some scrutiny. Not only must share or bond prices current to the valuation date for the securities held by the seller be checked, but care should be taken to see that what purport to be marketable securities are in fact freely tradeable under applicable law and not subject to contractual restrictions or restrictions by operation of law. Finally, trading volume for each security should be compared to the size of the holding of that security on the balance sheet to determine whether, given the size of the holding compared to then current trading levels, that security could be sold at once without depressing its market price. Sometimes (albeit rarely) a common share holding on a seller's balance sheet may be worth a premium if it represents a control block.

Accounts receivable.   This also requires careful scrutiny. Their quality, and hence their value, depend on the answers to several questions.

Are They Really Receivables?   That is, has more than order taking occurred? Have the goods actually been shipped? What is the purchaser's obligation? Is it, perhaps, only a conditional sale with a right of refusal by the customer. What are the practices of the trade in this regard?

How Collectible Are They?   Old receivables are less valuable than current ones since they are less likely to be collected. The process of attributing value to receivables based on dates on which payment is due is called aging. An aging schedule should be prepared.

How Fast Are They Collectible?   A simple measuring rod to determine the speed of collection is to divide the ratio of receivables to sales into 365 days. The resulting answer must be judiciously applied. Assume the following example.

$10 million in annual revenues

$2 million in annual accounts receivable

$10 million divided by $2 million results in a revenues-receivables ratio of 5:1, 365 days in a year divided by 5 equals 73 days on average from billing to collection.

Whether this 5:1 ratio is a good or bad one depends to a large degree on how it compares to the company's historic experience, and the experiences of other companies in the same industry and country at the same time. Consideration should therefore be given to how the seller compares to the comparatives used in the pricing analysis or to general industry norms (data contained in the Robert Morris Annual State Survey which, organized by SIC codes, contains this and many other ratios).

The business under review may be subject to seasonal variations; therefore, balance sheets for different periods in the year should be examined.

Inventory.   Inventory consists of raw materials, work in process, and finished goods. The value of the inventory includes the cost of labor and manufacturing expense necessary to transform the inventory into the finished product. Buyers shall look for and sellers be prepared to answer a series of inventory related questions including the following.

Is This Really Inventory?   Similar to the need to verify the quality of receivables, the buyer must examine the inventory to make sure that it contains only materials and goods pertaining to the sellers' business. Inventories of other people's goods held for sale on consignment or which includes goods of the seller sold on consignment are obviously not the same as inventories that are the subject of unconditional sales.

What is the Accounting Procedure?   Material variations can result from differences in inventory accounting. Both the buyer and the seller must reconcile the method used by the seller with the buyer's method of inventory accounting and make adjustments up or down as required.

How Fast is the Inventory Turning?   Here it is necessary to go back to one of the basic ratios, revenue divided by inventory, to determine how fast the goods move out. As in the case of receivables, use of comparative company methodology and industry wide statistics provide useful measuring rods by which to gauge seller company financial performance. Poor inventory turns are a warning to the buyer of the possibility of significant amounts of obsolete inventory. Sellers having low inventory turns will need to explain why such is the case.

To What Extent is There an "Inventory Cushion"?   To what extent have inventories been stated ultra conservatively with tax avoidance in mind? (Understatement of inventories causes an increase in cost of goods sold and hence a diminution in taxable income.) As previously indicated, sellers frequently seek to be paid on the basis of reconstructed income which adds back the amount of the cushion. Buyers are usually less than fully accommodating on this score. An "earnout" consisting of additional post closing purchase price contingent upon future years financial performance and described later in this chapter, during which the seller reduces or eliminates the cushion, may be the only viable way of addressing the problem. Even then, the solution is less than perfect. Thoughtful sellers should, several years before making their companies available for sale, consider the reduction of inventory cushions, since reconstructed earnings are generally capitalized at lower multiples than historical ones and there are many variables that may hinder or make impossible the full realization of contingent earnouts.

Thus far, we have devoted our attention exclusively to the valuation of current assets. What of *fixed assets* like property plant, and equipment?

The most commonly used approach to valuing these is to determine the cost required to buy the seller's facility new, less physical deterioration and functional obsolescence of each major asset. While each appraisal of physical assets stands alone, there are certain measuring rods that should be used.

Depreciation.   The buyer should examine the seller's plant and equipment and get a feel for real values by independent appraisal, especially if the industry being examined is unfamiliar to the buyer. Comparing these results to the way in which such items are booked may reveal a very different picture (often more favorable) of the seller company than that apparent from a reading of the financial alone.

Use to the Buyer.   In all asset valuations, it is important to consider opportunity cost elements. If, for an equivalent price, the same facility can be built in one year, what is the value of the one-year lead time?

The value thus derived may vary considerably from the value recorded on the seller's books, from fair market value, liquidation value, or replacement value—other criteria by which to determine asset value.

A commonly used formula in the valuation of assets is

$$E = WC + (PP + I)$$

In which   E = Enterprise value
              WC = Working Capital (current assets minus current liabilities)
              PP = Property plant and equipment
              I = Intangibles (patents, trademarks, etc.)

Note that in many service businesses (like advertising and public relations) or businesses with uniquely proprietary features covered by nominally booked patents, copyrights or trademarks (computer software or biotechnology), or by mandatorily booked development expenses, intangible asset values may represent substantially all of the company's fair market value. Thus, intangible assets such as favorable leases (leases at less than market rate), trained work forces, customer lists, brand names, and business goodwill, which may not appear on the balance sheet at all, require close scrutiny. Separate analysis of these intangibles is a must.

Not only the asset side, but the liability side, of the balance sheet must be measured. Usually, however, this involves rather less difficulty since the accounts payable, notes payable (if any), and income tax payable are described in the company's books and records. The same is true with respect to long-term obligations of the company, on which the fixed payment schedules make analysis fairly simple. Be certain, however, where footnotes are scanty to fully understand the terms of such debt.

In analyzing the liability side of the balance sheet, *caution must be taken* in at least three areas.

1. See that current earnings and cash flows are not puffed by the delaying of payments of accounts payable beyond the accounting period under scrutiny. Vigorous short term collection of receivables while delaying the payment of accounts payable can create a picture of current profits or cash flow that is largely illusory.

2. Look carefully at the terms and conditions of loan agreements and particularly at items such as floating rate interest provisions and repayment schedules. Consider the affirmative and negative covenants in bank loan agreements, trust indentures, and elsewhere which can, given an unwaived breach, turn long-term debt into debt due immediately by reason of acceleration clauses in such agreements.

3. Study off-balance-sheet liabilities. These include actual or impending product liability, tax disputes, and the costs associated with

compliance with governmental regulation over issues such as environmental pollution, workplace safety, and employee pension and termination rights.

1.4 Deriving Conclusions on Price

We have thus far considered the values derived under comparative company analysis from two points of view: a price-earnings or price-cash flow multiple approach and an asset based relationship between return on equity and market price to tangible book value. We have also considered an asset-by-asset approach. Usually, a weighting of the conclusions derived under the earnings approach and the asset approach is made with the result under the earnings approach weighted more heavily since investors tend to value companies more nearly on the basis of their earnings than their assets. Assume a company with $1.0 million in net profits and a tangible book value of $4.0 million. Assume further, an earnings approach which led one to conclude that the proper price-earnings was six times and that based either on the ROE-market tangible book or asset by asset approach that fair market value of assets was 120 percent of tangible book. A typical weighting system might be to weight the earnings approach at twice the asset approach. Thus, the calculations would proceed as follows.

Earnings Approach
     $1.0 million × 6 = $6 million × 2 = $12.0 million

Asset Approach
     $4 million × 1.2 = $4.8 million   4.8 million
                                        $16.8 million

     $16.8 million ÷ 3 = $5.6 million

This $5.6 million figure represents a freely traded minority interest value without giving effect to a premium for control. It represents a value comparable to that of the publicly traded common stocks of the companies against which it was compared.

However, sale of control of a profitable company carries with it a bundle of rights which are not enjoyed by minority shareholders. A control block carries with it the right to determine day-to-day corporate policy, to increase, decrease, or withhold dividends. If the block is sufficiently large in size, it carries the right to sell, merge or liquidate the company. In the case of the closely held company, some of this premium otherwise applicable may be eroded by a discount which gives recognition to the lack of marketability of the company's closely held stock. While many practitioners believe that a premium for control is inherent in the terminal value calculation in discounted cash flow analysis, comparative company analysis demands that it be separately determined. One objective yardstick by which to determine the amount of the premium for control is to consider the range of premiums paid for control in transactions involving companies usable for comparative purposes with the seller. In the U.S., data bases organized by SIC code such as those provided by Standard & Poor's and publications such as *Mergers & Acquisitions Magazine, Mergers and Corporate Policy,* and *The Acquisition/Divestiture Weekly Report* may be used. If these are unavailable, a general range may be established by looking at a number of sale of control situations by merger or tender offer close to the valuation date. Table 10.18 illustrates typical ranges measured on the basis of premium over unaffected market price and relationship of price to tangible book value in a particular industry group. Note that in all instances, price is determined by a premium over a market price presumably unaffected by news of the transaction. Thus, it is conventional to consider a price from which the premium is derived that dates back 30 days from the date of the announcement of the proposed transaction. To avoid questions of valuation of noncash consideration in the form of securities or other noncash considerations, it may be best to confine the premium analysis to all cash offers.

While these statistical measurements offer some general insight on ranges of premiums (the median premium over market price has been in the 40 to 50 percent range for a number of years), the ultimate premium will depend on the facts of a given case. Here, a number of elements need to be considered. These include (1) the seller's historic and current results, (2) its future prospects, on a stand-alone basis and within the framework of the buyer company giving effect to such synergies as may exist, and (3) the strategic importance of the seller to the buyer,[1] (4) the willingness (rational or otherwise) of buyer or seller management to complete the transaction, (5) the presence or absence of other bidders, (6) in public transactions, the influence of arbitrageurs, and (7) in international transactions, the opportunity to buy at investor appraisal ratios lower than those payable in one's home country or when currency exchange relationships effectively lower the price for overseas buyers. (A cheap dollar attracts buyers with marks, pounds, francs, or yen.)

1.5 Preferred Stock and Debt Security Valuations

Sometimes preferred shares or debt securities are issued as part of the purchase price consideration. In such instances, a variant of common share valuation methodology is required. Unlike common shares, both

---

[1]One of the reasons generally assumed to account for why non-U.S. buyers generally pay higher premiums for U.S. sellers than do U.S. buyers (see Merrill Lynch Mergerstat Review) is the strategic importance for some such buyers of obtaining a toehold in the U.S.

TABLE 10.18 Successful Cash Offers for Common Stock Control[1] January 1–December 31, 19XX[2]

Company	Where Traded	Date of Initial Offer	Market Price of Stock 30 Days Prior to Announcement		Indicated Premium	Latest Available Tangible Book Value	Price to Tangible Book Value
			Price Per Share	Price Per Share[3]			
Arkansas-Smith Inc.	PSE	5/27/XX	24.00	15.75	52.4	18.60	129.0
Bullett Templates	ASE	4/8/XX	6.25	5.00	25.0	4.92	127.0
Caroll Industries Inc.	OTC	2/16/XX	6.50	5.75	13.0	6.14	105.9
Deca Amp Corporation	ASE	4/30/XX	6.30	4.00	57.5	6.16	102.3
Elliott Supreme Inc.	OTC	4/14/XX	7.80	6.00	30.0	13.57	57.5
Famous Industries, Inc.	ASE	2/24/XX	12.00	7.50	60.0	9.45	127.0
Georgette & Sons Inc.	OTC	2/1/XX	5.00	3.25	53.8	8.38	59.7
Median					52.4		105.9

1. In cash tender offers or in merger proposals.

2. Period within which transaction was completed.

3. Closing price of stocks.

Sources: The Wall Street Journal; Standard & Poor's Corporation Records; Daily Stock Price Index; Stock Guide and Stock Reports; SEC Forms; 10-K, 10-Q; Interim and annual reports to stockholders; Proxy statements; Offer to purchase documents. Computations by MMG Patricof & Co.

preferred shares and debt securities derive their value principally from their internal characteristics (dividend or interest rate, seniority versus other classes of the subject company's securities, liquidation preference, coverage ratios, and the like). Thus, the form of comparative company methodology employed here compares the subject securities to securities having like characteristics irrespective of the industry of the issuer.

Assume that if XYZ Corp. was offering a $10 par value 8 percent cumulative nonvoting preferred shares to acquire ABC Ltd., XYZ's preferred stock might be valued as follows: (1) Determine XYZ's ability to cover preferred dividends (pretax income divided by total annual dividends required to be paid on the preferred stock), (2) compare XYZ's preferred dividend coverage with the dividend coverage of an array of preferred shares with similar internal characteristics (see Table 10.19), (3) determine the current yield of the comparative company preferred stock, and (4) divide XYZ's proposed dividend by the current yield or yields of companies having similar preferred dividend coverage to arrive at a percent of par value.

Thus, if XYZ's coverage were around 3.18 times (the median of the comparatives in Table 10.19), its current yield might appropriately be 9.6 percent the median current yield.

$$.08 \div .096 = 83.3\% \text{ of par}$$

Thus, XYZ's preferred would be worth 83.3 percent of $10.00, or $8.33, assuming a freely traded preferred stock. Lacking a freely traded market, a discount of 10 to 15 percent would be typical. This discount is smaller than the typical common stock discount because of the fixed dividend and greater seniority of the preferred stock.

A debt security analysis is very similar to a preferred stock analysis except that interest rather than dividend coverage is sought and comparative bonds rather than comparatives preferred are used.

1.6 The Contingent Earnout

The contingent earnout is a device by which to bridge the seller's characteristic optimism about the future of its business and the buyer's customary unwillingness to pay for earnings materially higher than those historically recorded by the seller company. In this circumstance, assume a seller whose company has the following characteristics.

Sales	£ 10,000,000
Net Profits	£ 500,000
Net Worth	£ 3,000,000

Further assume that the seller wants £6,000,000 for the business (12 × earnings) and the buyer is willing to pay only £5,000,000 (10 × earnings).

TABLE 10.19 Publicly-Traded Preferred Stocks

Company	Description	Exch.	S&P Rating	Cumul	Voting	Annual Div.	Coverage Year 1	Coverage Year 2	Current Price	Average Coverage	Current Yield
Arthur Industries Inc.	$4.50 Pref.	NYSE	AA	Y	N	$4.50	2.88	3.47	$47.00	3.18	9.6%
Beechwood Corp.	$3.50 Pref.	NYSE	AA	Y	N	3.50	2.88	3.47	36.75	3.18	9.5%
Casual Time Inc.	$3.75 Cum Pref.	NYSE	AA+	Y	N	3.75	3.00	5.00	39.50	4.00	9.5%
Dinsmore Development Corp.	$5.00 Cum Pref.	NYSE	AA+	Y	N	5.00	3.00	5.00	52.25	4.00	9.6%
Edwards & Co.	$3.75 Pref.	NYSE	AA−	Y	N	3.75	6.10	10.05	35.00	8.08	10.7%
Furrey Bros. Inc.	4.25% Pref. A	NYSE	AA−	Y	Y	4.25	3.07	3.20	42.50	3.14	10.0%
Gowanus Rubbish Corp.	$5.45 Cum. Pref.	NYSE	AA−	Y	N	5.45	2.77	2.06	54.63	2.42	10.0%
Median										3.18	9.6%

Source: Company financial statements, and Standard & Poor's Stock Guide. Computations by MMG Patricof & Co.

"But," says the seller, "My company's financial statements do not truly reflect its value. For years I've been depressing earnings to save on taxes. I've been undervaluing my inventory [the inventory cushion described earlier] so that may inventory is understated by £1,000,000. My salary, instead of being £100,000 [which might be considered normal for a company this size] is £200,000. I charge my car and the mortgage on my house to the business and several of my relatives are on the payroll to perform jobs that could be filled for much smaller salaries. If I had a financial incentive to uncover my earnings, I could show considerably more. Maybe even 50 percent more."

In response, a buyer might propose a transaction with £4,500,000 payable at closing and the opportunity to earn more (typically over a three to five year period), if future earnings warrant it.

What then follows is an earnout proposition. While there are limitless variations on the earnout approach, Tables 10.20 and 10.21 describe two of the more common ones.

Table 10.20 shows an average earnout. As indicated, the seller receives £4,500,000 at closing. To this is added the contingent feature here an amount equal to 10 times the net after-tax profits in the five years following the acquisition minus base year earnings. If the seller realizes the projected earnings levels, it receives an additional £1,500,000 earnout payment at the end of year 5. While it is true that the sum of the £4,500,000 payment at closing plus the £1,500,000 earnout payable in

TABLE 10.20   Contingent Earnout/Average Earnout

Deal Structure

At Closing: £4,500,000
Earnout: 10 × average net after tax earnings in the five years following the acquisition less base year net after tax earnings paid at the end of year 5.

Net After Tax Earnings Assumptions

Base Year	Year 1	Year 2	Year 3	Year 4	Year 5
£500,000	£550,000	£600,000	£650,000	£700,000	£750,000

Results

Total Net After Tax Earnings: £3,250,000
Average Net After Tax Earnings: £ 650,000
£650,000 − £500,000 (Base Year) = £150,000
£150,000 × 10 (P-E multiplier)   = £1,500,000

£4,500,000	at Closing
1,500,000	Contingent
£6,000,000	Total

TABLE 10.21   Contingent Earnout/Percentage of Profit Earnout

Deal Structure

At Closing: £4,500,000
Earnout: 50% of net after tax earnings (either annually or at the end of
           a specific period)
Net After Tax Earnings Assumptions

Base Year	Year 1	Year 2	Year 3	Year 4	Year 5
£500,000	£550,000	£600,000	£650,000	£700,000	£750,000

Results

1. Base year not considered
2. Total Net After Tax Earnings: £3,250,000
3. .50 × £3,250,000 = £1,625,000

   £4,500,000
   1,625,000 (payable at end of Year 5)
   £6,125,000

   OR

4. Payment as follows:

Year 1	Year 2	Year 3	Year 4	Year 5
£275,000	£300,000	£325,000	£350,000	£375,000

year 5 is, on a present value basis, clearly less than the £6,000,000 sought by the seller, it is likewise greater (on any reasonable present value basis) than the £5,000,000 the buyer was prepared to pay without an earnout.

Table 10.21 illustrates a percentage of profit earnout in which the seller receives a percentage of the profits earned over a period of years, either annually or at the end of the period. On a present value basis, the annual earnout clearly favors the seller. Waiting until the end of the earnout period before paying the earnout clearly favors the buyer, which has the benefit of the use of the earnout funds over the period in question and, in addition, a means to lessen the seller's incentive to generate earnings early in the earnout period at the possible expense of future earnings.

There are limitless varieties of earnouts. In an overseas magazine transaction completed for a client of ours some time back, the earnout was limited to the results generated by one particular magazine. In one of our leveraged buyouts of a motor carrier, the earnout was related to increases in revenues subject to the maintenance of operating margins at agreed upon levels. In our sale of an equipment leasing company, the earnout was based upon a sharing between buyer and seller of profits after the buyer obtained a designated return on the capital representing that portion of the price paid at the closing. We have seen earnouts that require the seller, as a condition to receiving earnout payments for a particular year, to have achieved earnings in that year higher than in any previous year.

Some fact patterns are less conducive to earnouts than others. (1) Where the businesses of the parties are to be closely integrated following the transaction (as, for example, in the case of a consolidation of factories or a merger of sales forces), it may be difficult or impossible to determine which of the parties will have been responsible for future results. (2) Earnouts seldom work unless key members of seller company management are prepared to continue to operate the business for the length of the earnout period. (3) Earnouts are uncommon where the seller is publicly owned, presumably due to the perception that only those shareholders responsible for producing incremental future earnings should receive earnout payments. This perception notwithstanding, General Motors' acquisition of Hughes Aircraft and of Electronic Data Systems illustrate instances of contingent earnout payments being made to public shareholders.

A seller may find an earnout acceptable if the following conditions are met.

Is it reasonably attainable?   A seller should consider the answer to questions such as the following. (1) How much hidden earnings can I uncover? (2) What is the future of my business? (3) Will I have a genuine chance at earning the contingent portion of the purchase price? (In that connection, seller may be well advised to negotiate in the purchase contract a kind of "nonmolestation" clause granting seller company management control over day-to-day operations, placing limits on buyer's ability to upstream cash from seller, negotiating an agreement, granting seller management certain expenditure authority and a say on the sums to be reinvested for R&D capital improvements, and the like. (4) Will affiliation with buyer make it harder or easier to earn the earnout?

Is it sizeable enough?   The seller should determine whether there is enough of an earnout to induce it to forego some of the money that might be paid at closing by agreeing to take the earnout. In short, how high a contingent price-earnings ratio or what percentage of profits is the seller receiving?

Note that under U.S. tax laws, with no escrow, tax free exchange rules provide a limit on the number of shares issuable for earnout purposes. To ensure tax free treatment, the number of earnout shares issuable may not exceed the number of shares issuable at closing, although there is some flexibility on this if the disparity between the two is not great and there is a genuine hurdle to attain in order to make the earnout.

From the buyer's point of view, the earnout offers the buyer the advantage of paying only for earnings actually achieved. Conversely, contingent shares issued for earnouts must be reported by the buyer as part of fully diluted earnings under U.S. accounting principles. Moreover, under U.S. accounting rules, the issuance of shares for contingent earnouts makes pooling of interest accounting impossible.

2.0 NEGOTIATION

Next we consider the merger process as just that, a play in five acts, the scenario of which can generally be described as (1) the finding stage, (2) the qualification stage, (3) the preliminary investigation stage, (4) the serious negotiation stage, and (5) the contract and closing stages. Some of the stages may take place concurrently (like contract and closing), and there are blurry lines about when the qualification stage becomes the preliminary negotiation stage and when the preliminary negotiation stage changes to the serious negotiation stage. How long each stage takes also depends on the specific transaction (whether there were prior negotiations, if the companies are in similar or different businesses, if the transaction is an international one, and the like), but in general, the outline suggested here generally holds true. We shall consider each stage.

2.1 The Finding Stage

This is the point at which *someone* (a broker, attorney, accountant, commercial, investment or merchant banker, company employee, supplier, customer, or someone else) approaches either of the two parties and makes it aware of the possible interest of the other side in initiating a transaction.

2.2 The Qualification Stage

Each party now decides whether it wishes to go forward. If the introducer's role was performed effectively, the buyer should have some idea of the seller's company, including its basic business, sources of supply, production and selling processes, and some information on seller management. For the buyer's part, it is usually best to have a set of acquisition criteria against which to measure the seller. This includes data such as product line sought, size of the seller, required investment returns, whether seller management will be expected to continue, and so on. Much wasted time and effort can be avoided if the buyer has clearly defined acquisition criteria, for most acquisition prospects are fatally flawed in one or more of the areas stated above. For the seller, the initial considerations include (1) how good an investment the buyer's shares or debt are (if the transaction involves other than all cash), (2) a consideration of how financially strong the buyer is, particularly if direct funding from the buyer or parent company guarantees are important reasons for selling, (3) whether the seller's organization is culturally similar to that of the buyer (for example, if seller-company seeks management autonomy, is it likely to be realized with the buyer with whom the transaction is being negotiated), (4) whether an affiliation with the buyer will provide the seller company with benefits otherwise unavailable to it (sales, marketing, R&D, production or financial synergy), and (5) how badly the seller wants to sell.

The international transaction adds an extra layer of complexity to the qualification stage for both parties. Each must consider the likely impact of language and cultural barriers and differences respecting issues like tax compliance and "sensitive" payments (a legally cognizable commission in one country may constitute a bribe in another) and the impact of local statutory or case law on the conduct of business. Here the litany includes the impact of local antitrust laws, "social" laws affecting compensation, benefits and termination of personnel, export control laws, and currency control laws. To this potentially threatening array of laws must be added a consideration of potentially positive legal developments, including the easing of trade barriers among members of the European Economic Community in 1992, the United Nations Convention on Contracts for the International Sale of Goods, adopted in 1988, and other statutory changes that simplify international transactions. Other important considerations are the effect of different labor conditions, economic circumstances, exchange rates, and competitive environments in other countries and issues relating to government policy such as percentage of ownership, if any, allowed to foreign businesses or individuals, and attitudes toward public ownership.

If the would-be seller is genuinely serious about sale, it ought to be genuinely prepared. This involves having a decent idea on what the business is likely to be worth to a given buyer and a written brochure which tells the company's story fairly and fully. This brochure generally contains the following elements.

1. A history of the company and the principal milestones in its business life.
2. If the company is a manufacturer, details about its raw material sources and procurement, the issues of criticality of certain materials and their availability, supplier dependency, a description of the flow of production, and the equipment used in the process including capital expenditure budgets.
3. Data on the company's R&D and product development or the way that new services are conceived.

4. A synopsis of the company's sales and marketing efforts: who sells the company's products (house salespeople, representatives, company principals), to whom sales are made (wholesalers, retailers, consumer, governments and customer dependency), terms of sales, marketing, advertising, and other promotional efforts.

5. A description of the company's principal officers including name, title, age, educational background, state of health, job function, length of services, and (if not overly sensitive) compensation.

6. Employee data including the number of nonexecutive personnel, union status, wage scales, fringe benefits, and the basic terms of any existing collective bargaining agreements.

7. Information about governmental regulatory compliance and areas of contingent liability (taxes, product liability, and the like).

8. Full financial statements for the longer of five years or an average business cycle and projections, if available, accompanied by the assumptions on which the projections are made.

9. Details on capital structure and equity ownership.

10. A discussion of the company's plans for the future. Will it be in the same business or a different one? What changes in procurement, production, sales, marketing, and capital expansion are needed to realize the goals of the plan?

No company's story is one of unadulterated success. It is often best to disclose a company's weaknesses in the brochure. If, for example, the seller is dependent on a single supplier, it should tell why such is the case, what the seller is doing about it, or why no action is needed. The prospective buyer is likely to find out anyway. Sellers should spare themselves the buyer's perception that seller has been hiding unfavorable facts by disclosing them initially, in a manner which can put them in perspective.

2.3 The Preliminary Investigation Stage

If the negotiations continue, there will often be a face-to-face meeting of principals at the seller's office or on neutral ground such as a broker's office or at a private club. If the companies are well known to each other or in the community, it may be best to hold the meeting in a private rather than a public setting. (We have frequently held quite confidential meetings at airport hotels.) Premature merger talk can get employees, customers, and suppliers very upset and make the transaction more difficult to close. At the first meeting, the parties will get to know one another, define their businesses, and have a brief discussion of price. Some preliminary understanding of the price range may be necessary if the buyer is to have access to the seller's records. The buyer, of course, will make any statement on its part dealing with price, subject to a thorough due diligence investigation of the seller's operational and financial affairs.

2.4 The Serious Negotiation Stage

As the parties begin to collect data on the other party's business and begin their pricing analyses, the hard bargaining begins. The following are some suggestions on how to get the most out of your negotiation.

Understand the Personalities on the Other Side of the Table.   If you are the buyer, judge whether the seller is risk averse or a maximizer of upside potential. Offer a fixed price to the former and a contingent deal to the latter. If you are the seller, attempt to satisfy the corporate culture of the buyer. If the buyer demands detailed company descriptions and projections, do your best, within reason, to supply them. Protect proprietary data with a confidentiality agreement signed by the buyer.

Understand the Constituents of Fit.   The experience of the years is that the transactions that succeed the best are the ones where the fit is best. The company fit analysis, which is part of the due diligence process, is also a subject for discussion at the bargaining table. Each side should stress what it can bring to the postmerger process in terms of financial fit, business synergy, and management fit.

Financial fit involves whether, ideally, the greater financial resources of one party can feed the faster growth potential of the other in a way which gives each superior investment returns to those which would occur were no transaction to take place.

Business synergy involves exploring R&D, production sales, marketing, or economies of scale, with the recognition that incremental costs or less dramatic synergies than were anticipated are frequently the case.

Management synergies involve considerations such as whether either part has managers to be retained for whom there are limited growth opportunities within the company and the extent to which investment returns of either party could be enhanced by the infusion of new management. These and related matters need to be explored at the bargaining table.

Some Suggestions for Prospective Buyers.   Do not approach sellers with a condescending attitude which says that you are bigger and, hence, probably smarter than they are. Project yourself as ready, willing, and able to complete a fair and reasonable transaction.

Avoid a long due diligence checklist until the parties get to know each other. Remember that deals are like courtships.

Have a backup person on your team to field questions by the seller in your absence.

Do not haggle over small differences in the purchase price. You will either lose the deal or create postmerger ill will.

Don't waste time. If it really is not a worthwhile proceeding, get out quickly. Prescreen carefully to avoid this time wasting process. Recognize that international transactions often take longer to complete than domestic ones because of time differences and differences in legal, tax, and accounting principles.

Develop with the seller a clear plan for postmerger integration, including reporting relationships, plans for integrating the businesses, and details regarding financial accountability of the seller to you.

Remember that no deal is perfect and that you will have to work hard to optimize results in the postmerger period.

Some Suggestions for Prospective Sellers. Don't assume that the buyer will behave badly on price and terms. Assume that the buyer wants the deal and will complete it on reasonable terms if you are fully prepared on price, terms, and fit.

Do a good due diligence on the buyer. If it is a public company, get its annual reports, summaries of meetings with security analysts, and research reports of brokerage firms.

Get good legal, tax, and accounting advice early enough in the deal so that you do not make a concession on price and terms that you will later regret. A concession once made is generally retrievable only at a cost. This advice takes on critical importance in international transactions where one may be dealing with a series of very different legal, tax, and accounting concepts than one is accustomed to.

Don't bargain for every last bit of the purchase price and don't use price as an excuse for withdrawing from the transaction when, in reality, you never really wanted to sell at all. Make that decision *before* you get into the negotiation.

Cooperate with the buyer to smooth out the people, financial, and operating problems that will inevitably attend the postmerger process.

Professional Advisors. Good professional advisors can make the transaction considerably easier to complete. Use your *lawyer* not only as a negotiator and draftsman for the purchase contract and employment agreement (but only on the legal not the business terms of these), but also for checking the legal and regulatory status of the other side. Use your *intermediary* to help you price and negotiate the deal. Your *accountant* can offer valuable advice on the tax and accounting implications of the deal and assist in the business review. Other experts like real estate appraisers, actuaries, and consulting engineers may be needed in specific instances.

Negotiating Style. Adopt a negotiating style calculated to minimize conflict while still getting all or most of what you want. To what purports to be a *nonnegotiable demand*, shift the dialogue to items that are easier to resolve. A difficult demand, when there are 30 items to bargain for, can become considerably easier if it is the only one left on the table. If you have to say no to something the other side wants, state why it is unacceptable and try to offer an alternative that you can live with. If you want something (like a formula for fixing renewal rates on a long-term lease) have one to present (increases in accordance with an index) and an alternative (three appraisers) if your first idea is rejected. *Trade off* a provision that will not cost you much, like additional registration rights on common stock issued, against something you may want very badly, like strong indemnification language.

Agreements in Principle.   Not everybody likes agreements in principle. We think they have some usefulness because, even though they are not legally binding, they reflect a general understanding that most parties will honor and help avoid convenient loss of recollection by either side on key points. However, agreements in principle probably do not make sense unless the basic structure of the deal, including price and terms, have been worked out or if the deal is near completion, at which point one might just as well go to the contract stage. In situations involving an agreement in principle in a sizeable deal with a publicly held buyer or seller, generally applicable disclosure rules will probably necessitate a public announcement. If the parties regard that disclosure as premature, it would be best not to have an agreement in principle.

Management Contracts.   Part of the serious negotiations will usually involve a consideration of mangement employment contracts for key executives. Where the people who are going to run the company to be sold are not the recipients of the purchase price (as in a divestment), these contracts can be of critical importance. They generally include length of term, base and bonus compensation, scope of responsibilities, and a restrictive covenant. Restrictive covenants in the U.S. are enforceable only if they are reasonable in nature, balancing the buyer's reasonable need for exclusivity and the executive's right to make a living in the field in which he or she has acquired expertise.

The final stages of the serious due diligence phase generally involve a great deal of time and paper work. Detailed inspections of physical facilities and analyses of the historic, current, and projected operations and of the financial picture of each party take place. Side by side are lawyers working on things like assignments of proprietary rights from seller to buyer and regulatory clearance. In the U.S., many transactions will require Hart Scott Rodino antitrust clearance. Transactions involving U.S. sellers may require Treasury Department approval under the Exon Florio statute. Mergers involving U.S. sellers in defense, media, or other industries may require certain kinds of regulatory scrutiny. In the on-again off-again confusion typically found at this stage, there are always problems which, if not adequately addressed, threaten to abort the transaction. Typical of these are the date on which the transaction will be completed (that is, whether the buyer or seller gets the benefit of recent earnings). The selling stockholder who wants either an extremely generous employment contract or a very small one to maximize his or her earnout is another. Opposition to the transaction from employees or from the outside (the selling company's local community, suppliers or customers) may have to be anticipated and dealt with.

2.5   Contract and Closing

Since a discussion of representations and warranties, covenants, conditions to closing, escrows, and other elements of the acquisition agreement is beyond the scope of this chapter, it is sufficient to point out that these are the very stuff of which transactions are made or not made, they form the basis upon which claims for breach of the agreement are asserted, and need to be negotiated with care. Full recognition must be given to the unique drafting problems in international transactions like conflict of law issues, remedies for breach of agreements that vary from country to country, and cultural differences in which contracts drafted by U.S. lawyers generally tend to be longer and more complex than those drafted by their non-U.S. counterparts.

While contract signing and closing may be simultaneous, generally they are not. At the closing, the seller surrenders its stock certificates, the buyer issues its own stock or cash or whatever constitutes the consideration, opinions of counsel and/or those of the accountants appear, necessary approvals from national or regional regulatory bodies are produced, loan agreements are signed, checks for fees are drawn, and the transaction is concluded.

The merger and acquisition process frequently is a long, complex, and demanding one, but rather exciting as well. Length, complexity, demands, and excitement tend to be multiplied in international transactions. However, with thoughtful planning, hard work, and some luck, the process can, for both sides, be a rewarding one.

3.0   PRICING CHECKLIST

I. Precede the pricing analysis with the most rigorous due diligence investigation available under the circumstances surrounding the specific transaction.

II. Where required, have the historical and projected financial statements of either or both the buyer company and the target company restated up or down. Typical areas of inquiry include
   A. Inventories.
   B. Travel, entertainment, and charitable contribution expenses.
   C. Personnel.
   D. Property, plant, and equipment.
   E. Impact of the transaction on projected earnings and cash flows.
III. Elements in a defensible comparative company analysis.
   A. Pick the array of comparative companies properly.
      1. Be sure each comparative shares with the others and the subject company a series of operating and financial characteristics.
      2. Know there is a sufficiently viable public market and financial data available to make these companies appropriate for comparative company purposes.
      3. Be certain that no companies that might have been used are missing and have a reason for all those that are excluded.
      4. If the seller is in a market outside the U.S. (or less often, in the U.S. itself) where no good comparative companies appear, come as close as possible picking the best possible array of comparatives.
   B. Compare the subject company with the comparatives on all of the important ratios.
      1. Generally applicable ratios (growth in revenues and profits, profit margins, return on equity, return on assets, debt-equity, working capital, and quick ratios).
      2. Industry specific ratios and data (sales per square foot, revenues per passenger mile, etc.).
   C. Pick an appropriate price-earnings or price-cash flow multiple.
      1. Choose P-Es that reflect a period appropriate to the business under scrutiny (P-Es based on average 3 or 5 year earnings for businesses in cyclical industries, and latest year or latest 12 month or projected earnings for new businesses or companies that have recently and materially changed the nature of their businesses).
      2. The P-E or price-cash flow multiple should be reasonably related to the subject company's financial performance against that of the comparatives.
   D. Explore the comparative company methodology to develop an assets approach to value.
      1. Determine if there is a relationship between return on average common equity or average assets and market price-tangible

book value among the comparatives, either on the basis of the most recent fiscal year or an average over several of the most recent years.

    2. Determine if a linear regression analysis will support this conclusion.

E. Weigh the results under the earnings and assets tests properly in light of all the facts in arriving at freely traded minority interest value.

F. Pick an appropriate premium for control.

    1. Try to find relatively recent transfers of control for companies in the same general line of business. Were these applied?

    2. Consult general data on premiums for control (Mergerstat, Houlihan, etc.).

    3. In applying the premium, give due recognition to the historic and current results and projected prospects for the target company.

      a. On a stand-alone basis.

      b. Within the corporate framework of the buyer.

      c. Within the corporate framework of a competitive bidder.

IV. Elements in a defensible single company analysis.

A. Payback analysis.

    1. The assumptions giving rise to the projections should be realistic in terms of the target company's projected growth or lack of growth.

    2. Include incremental costs or benefits.

      a. Factor in debt service from the transaction.

      b. Include additions to property, plant, equipment, sales force, R&D, etc. required of the seller.

      c. Give consideration to the disposal of nonessential assets to generate cash.

    3. Identify and calculate potentially beneficial aspects of the transaction.

      a. Cost reduction through elimination of redundant property, equipment, or personnel.

      b. The positive effects of business synergy in R&D, procurement, sales marketing, production, insurance, etc.

    4. Consider at least three scenarios (conservative, optimistic and average).

    5. Consider scenarios of the target company both on a stand-alone basis and within the framework of the buyer company.

    6. Consider characteristics unique to international transactions (including the effect of time and distance on the proposed business relationship between buyer and seller).

      a. Currency fluctuations.

      b. Exchange controls.

      c. Export controls.

      d. Applicability of local laws to the business relationship.

      e. High "social costs" respecting job terminations in certain countries.

      f. Reconciliation of non-U.S. accounting concepts to "generally accepted accounting principles."

      g. Tax effects of repatriation of earnings from affiliates outside the parent company's country.

B. Discounted cash flow analysis.

  1. In determining the net free cash flows, discount rate and terminal value elements, consider the items described in IV.A, above, respecting payback analysis.

  2. In selecting the number of years over which the net free cash flows are to be discounted, consider

      a. The relative certainty or variability of the projected net free cash flows.

      b. The sensitivity of the ultimate conclusion to the terminal value element.

  3. In selecting the discount rate, consider

      a. Both the buyer's and the seller's cost of debt and equity capital.

      b. What increment over a risk free rate is appropriate for the specific seller.

      c. The buyer's or target's alternative opportunity costs.

  4. In selecting the approach to terminal value, consider

      a. Whether the perceived risk elements are the same at the end of the discounting period as at the beginning.

      b. Whether relevant industry price-earnings or price-cash flow multiples have been relatively constant in the past.

      c. The advisability of a capitalized dividend approach.

  5. Use the discounted cash flow methodology to present an internal rate of return calculation.

C. Asset and liability analysis.

  1. Current assets.

      a. Does the cash account represent free cash available to the buyer (less that needed for the target company's working capital needs) or is it encumbered or restricted by compensating balance requirements or other elements?

      b. Are marketable securities or what purport to be marketable securities immediately convertible to cash or are the holding of such securities so large in relation to the public market for them or trading in them so thin that they need to be discounted for a partial lack of marketability?

2. Have marketable securities booked at the lower of cost or market been marked to the current market (allowing in international transactions for the effect of currency translations)?

D. Accounts receivable.

1. Are what purport to be receivables really receivables?

2. How collectible are they? Has an aging schedule been prepared?

3. How fast are they collectible? Has a "days sales" schedule been prepared?

E. Inventory.

1. Is what purports to be inventory really inventory?

2. What is the accounting procedure and how are disparities between U.S. generally accepted accounting principles and non-U.S. accounting principles to be reconciled?

3. How fast is the inventory turning? Has an inventory turn schedule been prepared?

4. To what extent have inventories been understated with tax avoidance in mind? What effect does a restatement of these have on asset value and earnings? What civil or criminal liabilities under relevant local law exist?

F. Fixed Assets.

1. Value each principal physical asset, giving recognition to the costs to acquire that asset new less physical deterioration and functional obsolescence?

2. Consider fixed asset value in light of the value of such assets
   a. On a fully depreciated basis.
   b. On a replacement value basis.
   c. On a going concern value basis.
   d. In an orderly liquidation.
   e. In a forced liquidation.

3. Consider fixed asset values as a part of buyer's opportunity cost. (The value of assets in place versus having to build or buy them.)

4. Consider variables affecting asset value associated with the acquisition of overseas assets, including their insurability against loss, expropriation, etc.

5. Assign all intangible assets a fair market value.
   a. Patents, trademarks, copyrights, brand names, capitalized computer software, future publishing rights, back lists, etc.
   b. Covenants not to compete.
   c. Favorable leases.

   d. Trained work force and competence and sophistication of management.
   e. Customer lists.
   f. Business goodwill.
6. Current liabilities.
   a. Mark each current liability to market.
   b. Give particular care to the exposure of future earnings to the slow payment of accounts payable.
7. Long term liabilities.
   a. Mark each long-term liability to market.
   b. Check affirmative and negative covenants in loan agreements to see if the target company is in or near a default status.
8. Determine how price will be affected by off-balance-sheet liabilities, actual or threatened, for items such as
   a. Tax liability.
   b. Product liability.
   c. Pension and retirement plans.
   d. Workplace liability.
   e. Equal opportunity in employment liability.
   f. Law unique to the place in which the buyer or the target company operate.

V. For transactions that might call for a contingent earnout.
   A. Are there reasons to believe that historical earnings do not necessarily reflect future financial performance?
      1. "Hidden" historic earnings.
      2. Something in the future suggesting greater or lesser earnings than those historically achieved.
   B. Have a variety of earnout scenarios been considered?
      1. Cash versus common stock earnouts.
      2. Average earnout (with or without hurdles).
      3. Percentage of profit earnout.
      4. Highest previous year earnout.
      5. Earnouts based on revenues versus those based on earnings.
   C. Whether to accept an earnout-target company's point of view.
      1. Is it reasonably attainable?
         a. How many dollars of "hidden" earnings can be uncovered?
         b. How attractive does the future of the business appear to be?
         c. Is the deal structure one that gives the seller company a reasonable ability to earn the earnout?
            i. Does the acquisition agreement or management contract allow seller company management to control day-

to-day affairs (including R&D and capital expenditures)?

    ii. Are there limits on the buyer company's ability to upstream cash from the target company?

    iii. Will the target company not be burdened with professional or home office expenses higher than those traditionally borne by it?

  2. Will seller company's affiliation with buyer make it harder or easier to attain the earnout?

  3. Is there enough of an earnout to make it more attractive than a noncontingent deal? (How high a contingent P-E or what percentage of profits can be bargained for?)

  4. Will the proposed earnout run afoul of U.S. tax law or tax free reorganizations?

D. Whether to offer an earnout-buyer company's point of view.

  1. Is the advantage of paying for results only when they are achieved offset by difficulty in attempting to integrate the businesses?

  2. Will an earnout reduce incentive among buyer company personnel in like organizations who have no such incentive?

  3. To what extent is pooling of interest accounting treatment important for the buyer? If it is important, an earnout will probably be forgone.

VI. Is the transaction one which might call for an installment sale?

  A. Is more than one payment to be made?

  B. Can it be coupled with an earnout?

4.0 NEGOTIATION CHECKLIST

I. The finding stage

  A. As buyer

    1. Make known your acquisition goals to those able to identify target companies.

      a. Employees.

      b. Investment or merchant bankers.

      c. Commercial bankers.

      d. Attorneys.

      e. Accountants.

      f. Suppliers.

      g. Customers.

    2. Determine your internal staff sufficient to find, screen, price, structure, and negotiate merger and acquisition transactions

and to identify the various sources of financing that may be required to fund the transaction.

3. Clearly describe the characteristics you deem important in seller companies.
   a. Industry or industries in which you seek to acquire.
   b. Target company size and price range.
   c. Required investment returns to buyer.
   d. Required market position of target.
   e. Species of payment preferred (shares or cash).
   f. Whether initial earnings or book value dilution is acceptable should other characteristics of the target company be attractive.
   g. Whether senior management in place is a requirement.
   h. If particular kinds of fixed assets are sought, a description of these.
   i. Characteristics unique to overseas acquisitions including
      i. Product or markets sought to be attacked.
      ii. Whether certain characteristics of overseas acquisitions will be difficult to assimilate into the buyer's corporate culture (social costs, sensitive payments, etc.).

B. As seller or divestor
   1. Ascertain if your internal personnel are sufficient to do the job or whether you will require help from others.
   2. Do the following.
      a. Price the company for sale.
      b. Describe the business. Take the time to
         i. Describe the founding of the business, when, where, by whom.
         ii. Detail the history and principal milestones in the life of the business.
         iii. Tell how new products or services are conceived and developed.
         iv. Supply data respecting raw material procurement (historic availability, number of suppliers, supplier dependency, price fluctuations, and the ability to pass these along to customers).
         v. Develop data respecting shipment of raw materials to the target company facility (by what means, who bears risk of loss in transit).
         vi. Supply information respecting flow of production that transforms raw materials to finished goods (plant and equipment required, plant and equipment age, when these need to be replaced).
         vii. Offer details on plant including ownership or lease

              terms and adequacy of plant and equipment for current and future needs.

     viii. Enumerate data on production and office personnel including how many, adequacy of local labor pool, terms of existing union agreements or other agreements with labor, current and planned and number of work shifts.

       ix. Include sales and marketing data including compensation (by whom, to whom, customer dependence issues, and details on marketing and advertising).

        x. Set forth information on competition and market share.

      xi. Describe senior management (age, education, title, work history prior to joining the target company, history and current duties at the company, state of health and compensation and benefits).

     xii. Enumerate share ownership including number of shareholders and how much each owns.

    xiii. Set forth legal and regulatory issues facing the target (product or work place liability, pension or tax claims, etc.).

     xiv. Include historical financial statements for five years together with projections and the assumptions on which they are based.

     xv. Candidly explain the weak points as well as the strong points of the business.

     xvi. Generally describe plans for the business (same or new products or services, what the future goals are and what it will take to get them accomplished).

    xvii. State why the business is for sale or divestment is being considered.

   xviii. Explore why the company might be an especially attractive fit for an overseas acquirer.

       (A) Ability of the target company to provide new markets for the buyer or vice versa.

       (B) Other business synergies.

II. The qualification and preliminary negotiation stage

  A. As buyer

    1. Be able to analyze some preliminary information on the target company.

    2. Make a preliminary assessment about whether the target company meets your acquisition requirements.

    3. Make some preliminary judgments about completing an overseas transaction.

        a. Language and cultural barriers (including issues like tax compliance, sensitive payments, etc.).

        b. Legal implications.

            i. Local antitrust laws.

            ii. "Social" laws.

            iii. Export control laws.

            iv. Currency control laws.

            v. Laws affecting foreign ownership.

        c. Differences in the market versus conditions in your own market in terms of

            i. Labor conditions.

            ii. General economic conditions.

            iii. Competition and market share considerations.

        d. Issues relating to government policy.

            i. Percentage of ownership allowed.

            ii. Favoring or not favoring public ownership.

            iii. Favoring or not favoring foreign suppliers.

        e. Issues relating to political stability.

  B. As seller

    1. Develop all the information you can on the prospective buyer.

    2. Make a preliminary judgment on whether you really want to sell assuming a reasonable price and reasonable terms. Consider the following.

    a. Personal liquidity.

    b. Management succession.

    c. Access to

        i. Funds with which to grow the business.

        ii. The ability to effect synergies in R&D, production, marketing, or otherwise.

    d. Elements unique to an overseas acquisition.

        i. International expansion opportunities.

        ii. Likelihood of greater autonomy.

  C. Both buyers and sellers should enter into preliminary negotiations

    1. With a willingness to hear what the other side has to say.

    2. Without a great number of checklists.

  D. Hold the first meeting at a neutral place.

    1. Investment bankers office.

    2. Airport hotel.

    3. Other site where confidentiality of discussion can be maintained.

III. The serious negotiation stage

  A. In framing your position on price and terms, take into account the personalities of the other side.

1. "Downside risk hedgers" versus "upside potential maximizers."
2. The "corporate culture" of the other side.
   a. Entrepreneurial versus structured.
   b. Centralized versus decentralized.
   c. Foreign versus domestic.
B. In planning for the serious negotiation, fully consider the complexities of an international merger and acquisition transaction.
   1. Given what may be significant time differences and distances between countries, allow sufficient time for due diligence activities and negotiations.
   2. Be prepared to investigate and try to design around specific problems in the international merger and acquisition.
      a. Cultural issues like the need for consensus building in certain countries.
      b. The issues described in II.A.3, above.
C. In the serious negotiation, fully explore the constituents of fit (and especially the international implications of these) including:
   1. Financial fit.
   2. Business synergy fit.
   3. Management synergy fit.
D. Both sides should begin to discuss how the postmerger period will be handled in terms of
   1. The kind of advisory information about the deal to be given to executives and workers.
      a. By whom.
      b. In what form.
      c. At what point.
   2. Effecting business synergy by removing redundancies in
      a. People.
      b. Property, plant, and equipment.
   3. Reporting relationships.
      a. Who from target to whom from buyer.
      b. Nature of written reports.
         i. Frequency.
         ii. Their form.
         iii. Nature of operational and financial information required.
   4. Desirability of establishing or not establishing a key executive or executives from the buyer company of the target company.
      a. On an interim basis.
      b. On a permanent basis.

E. DOs and DON'Ts for buyers.
   1. Avoid buyer hubris. Being the buyer does not make you the superior company in the transaction. Present yourself as ready, willing, and able to complete a transaction that is fair and reasonable to both sides.
   2. Avoid long due diligence checklists until the parties get to know each other. Remember that mergers and acquisitions are like courtships.
   3. Be sufficiently well staffed to conduct a good due diligence investigation from an operational and financial point of view but have a clearly defined team leader and a second in command to that person.
   4. Do not negotiate for the last bit of purchase price lest the transaction fail to close over trivial amounts of money or close with a sense of ill will from the other side.
   5. Consider the postmerger integration process (see III.D, above).
   6. Balance the attractive versus the unattractive elements of the transaction recognizing that no deal is perfect.
F. DOs and DON'Ts for target companies.
   1. Assume that the buyer will pay a reasonable price for your business, but only if you are thoroughly prepared to defend your asking price and have appropriately described your company.
   2. Perform the best possible due diligence on the buyer. If it is publicly held, obtain
      a. Its annual and interim reports.
      b. Summaries of its meetings with securities analysts.
      c. Research reports of brokerage firms.
      d. Whether or not publicly held.
         i. Ask to meet executives in companies previously acquired by the buyer.
         ii. Make your own evaluation of the transaction from a business point of view.
   3. Get good legal, tax, accounting, and investment banking advice early enough in the transaction so that you do not make concessions whose full implications you have failed to consider.
   4. Do not try to exact the last drop of purchase price or use price as an excuse when you did not really want to sell in the first place.
   5. Cooperate with the buyer in addressing the people, financial, and operational problems necessarily associated with the postmerger process.

G. Intelligent use of professional advisors. In planning the international merger or acquisition, consider how you will staff the transaction with
   1. Attorneys to
      a. Negotiate legal and tax points and draft agreements.
      b. Determine the legal and regulatory issues requiring work.
      c. Issue legal opinions on the legal capacity of the parties to complete the agreement.
   2. Accountants to
      a. Perform the audit work with related opinions.
      b. Offer assistance on tax issues.
      c. Perform a businessman's review of the financial aspects of the target company's business.
   3. Investment or merchant bankers, finders and brokers for
      a. Assistance in pricing and negotiation.
      b. In the case of target companies or divestors, preparing the selling memorandum to be sent to a group of prospective buyers.
   4. Other professionals sometimes used.
      a. Real estate and property appraisers.
      b. Consulting engineers.
      c. Actuaries.
      d. Marketing consultants.
H. Whether as buyer or target, develop a negotiating style calculated to minimize conflict while getting all or much of what you want.
   1. If there is disagreement over nonnegotiable demands, shift the dialogue to matters easier to resolve and go back to the difficult ones after the easier ones have been settled.
   2. State why a proposal advanced by the other side is unacceptable to you and, if possible, try to help solve the other side's problem in a way that will be acceptable to you.
   3. Trade off provisions that do not cost you much against provisions you want very badly.
I. Agreements in principle. Consider their use and limitations as follows.
   1. Uses.
      a. To reflect a general understanding between the parties.
      b. To avoid convenient loss of recollection on key business points later in the transaction.
   2. Limitations.
      a. They are not legally binding.
      b. They are not usable too early in the transaction, if the basic

structure has not been worked out, nor too late in the transaction, when one might as well go to contract.

    c. They cannot be used with a publicly owned party if the nature of the transaction requires an unwanted public disclosure.

J. Management contracts for key executives of the seller. Whether as buyer or as a key executive of the target company, consider with counsel

    1. The desirability of entering into such agreements.

    2. The terms of such agreements including differences in compensation for U.S. and non-U.S. citizens in the U.S. or abroad.

       a. Scope of authority.

       b. Base and incentive compensation.

       c. Fringe benefits.

       d. A reasonable restrictive covenant.

K. Typical issues in the late due diligence stage. Whether as buyer or target, be prepared for

    1. Detailed inspections of physical facilities.

    2. Negotiation on financial areas giving rise to questions including all of the areas described in the pricing checklist.

    3. Assignment of proprietary rights.

    4. Issues dealing with regulatory clearance.

       a. The U.S. Securities and Exchange Commission and comparable bodies outside the U.S.

       b. Other regulatory clearance designed to protect certain national interests (Federal Trade Commission, Interstate Commerce Commission, Federal Reserve Board, Department of Defense, Exon Florio, Hart, Scott, Rodino clearance, and their overseas counterparts).

       c. Shareholder approval if required.

       d. Clearances required to obtain funding (documents involved in rights offerings and other public filings on securities used as purchase consideration in the transaction).

    5. Issues involving target company shareholders.

       a. "Sellers remorse."

       b. Contractual issues.

          i. Purchase agreement.

          ii. Selling shareholders.

    6. Opposition to the transaction.

       a. From regulatory authorities.

       b. From other would-be buyers.

       c. From local communities.

       d. From workers or their unions.

IV. Contract and closing stage. Consider the typical acquisition agreement as a series of promises and limitations by buyer and target, bound within specific time frames.
   A. Forms of contractual promises and limitation.
      1. Warranties and representations. A statement that certain facts are true or correct.
      2. Covenants. Promises to act or to refrain from acting.
      3. Conditions to closing.
      4. Escrows.
   B. Time frames in which promises and limitations are effective.
      1. As of the date of the target company's most recent audited or unaudited financial statements.
      2. In the period between contract and closing.
      3. At the closing.
      4. After the closing.
   C. Closing. Consider the typical characteristics of the closing.
      1. May be, but is usually not, simultaneous with the contract.
      2. Typical happenings at the closing.
         a. Purchase agreements and other agreements conveying title to the target company are signed.
         b. Opinions of counsel and the accountants are delivered.
         c. Documents providing the financing are executed.
         d. Regulatory approvals are received.
         e. Intermediaries fees are paid.

References

1.0 STRATEGIC CHOICES

ANGEAR, THOMAS A. *How to Buy a Company*. Cambridge, U. K.: Director Books, 1989.

BIBLER, RICHARD S. *The Arthur Young Management Guide to Mergers and Acquisitions*. New York: Wiley, 1989.

BUSINESS INTERNATIONAL RESEARCH. *Acquisition Strategy in Europe*. Geneva: Business International S. A., 1987.

———. *Making Acquisitions Work: Lessons from Successes and Mistakes*. Geneva: Business International S. A., 1988.

COOKE, TERENCE E. *International Mergers and Acquisitions*. New York: Arthur Young International, 1989.

CRAWFORD, EDWARD K. *A Management Guide to Leveraged Buyouts*. New York: Wiley, 1987.

GILBERT, NATHANIEL, and LIVINGSTON, ABBY. "One Plus One Equals Three." *Venture* 11 (Jan. 1989): 45–47.

HUTCHINSON, G. SCOTT, ed. *The Business of Acquisitions and Mergers.* New York: President's Publishing House, 1968.

MCCANN, JOSEPH E. *Joining Forces: Creating and Managing Successful Mergers and Acquisitions.* Englewood Cliffs: Prentice Hall, 1988.

The Morgan Grenfell Handbook of International Mergers and Acquisitions. Oxford: University Printing House, 1988.

MORRISS, JOSEPH M. *Acquisitions, Divestitures and Corporate Joint Ventures.* New York: Wiley, 1984.

PRATT, SHANNON P. *Valuing a Business.* Homewood, IL: Dow Jones-Irwin, 1981.

RAPPAPORT, ALFRED. *Creating Shareholder Value.* New York: Free Press, 1986.

SCHARF, CHARLES A. *Acquisitions, Mergers, Sales, Buyouts, and Takeovers.* Englewood Cliffs: Prentice Hall, 1985.

SMITH, WILLIAM K. *Handbook of Strategic Growth through Mergers and Acquisitions.* Englewood Cliffs: Prentice Hall, 1985.

WARREN, JOSEPH H. *Mergers and Acquisitions.* Homewood, IL: Dow Jones-Irwin, 1988.

2.0 & 3.0 LAW

Books

ABA SECTION OF INTERNATIONAL LAW AND PRACTICE. *National Institute on International Mergers and Acquisitions: A Practical Guide to the Legal and Financial Issues.* New York: American Bar Assoc., 1987.

FFRENCH, H. LEIGH. *International Law of Take-Overs and Mergers: Asia and Oceania.* Westport, CT: Greenwood (Quorum), 1986.

——. *International Law of Take-Overs and Mergers: The EEC, Northern Europe, and Scandinavia.* Westport, CT: Greenwood (Quorum), 1986.

——. *International Law of Take-Overs and Mergers: Southern Europe, Africa, and Near East.* Westport, CT: Greenwood (Quorum), 1987.

FORRY, JOHN I. *Foreign Investment in the United States.* 2nd ed. Washington: BNA, 1982.

FOX, BYRON E., and FOX, ELEANOR M. *Corporate Acquisitions and Mergers.* New York: Bender, 1968.

KLEINMANN, WERNER, and BECHTOLD, RAINER. *Kommentar zur Fusionskontrolle.* Kartellrecht-Heidelberg: Recht u. Wirtschaft, 1989.

PRENTICE HALL INFORMATION SERVICES. *Corporate Acquisitions, Mergers, and Divestitures.* Englewood Cliffs: Prentice Hall, 1983.

RAYBOULD, D. M. *Comparative Law of Monopolies.* London: Graham & Trotman, 1988.

Periodicals

Mergers and Acquisitions. Philadelphia: MLR Enterprises, 1965—.

Articles

GOELZER, DANIEL L.; MILLS, ROBERT; GRESHAM, KATHERINE; and SULLIVAN, ANNE H. "The Pole of the U. S. Securities and Exchange Commission in Transnational Acquisitions." *International Lawyer* 22 (1988): 615–41.

"JOCKEYING FOR POSITION." *International Mergers and Acquisitions* (March-April 1989).

MACLACHLAN, SIMON, and MACKESY, WILLIAM. "Acquisitions of Companies in Europe: Practicability, Disclosure, and Regulation: An Overview." *International Lawyer* 23 (1989): 373–400.

MORROW, JOHN E. "Legal Issues in Acquiring Western European Companies." *Journal of Buyouts and Acquisitions* (March-April 1986).

TAQI, S. J. "Europe's Dealmaking Surge." *International Mergers and Acquisitions* (May-June 1989).

4.0 ACCOUNTING

OREINI, LARRY L.; MCALLISTER, JOHN P.; and PARIKH, RAJEEV. *World Accounting.* Matthew Bender & Company Incorporated, 1986.

PEAT MARWICK MAIN & CO. *Public Sale of Securities in the United States: A Guide for Foreign Enterprises.* 1987

———. *Accounting for Income Taxes: A Summary of FASB Statement 96,* 1988.

———. *Businessman's Review Practice Guide.* 1981.

———. *Action Plan for Reviewing Internal Accounting Controls.* 1978.

———. *Worldwide Financial Reporting and Audit Requirements: A Peat Marwick Inventory.* 1986.

5.0 & 6.0 TAX

ANGELINI, JAMES P.; HICKOX, CHET; and MATONEY, JOSEPH P. "Covenants Not to Compete and Goodwill." *Tax Adviser* 19 (1988): 576.

ARNOLD, BRIAN J. *The Taxation of Controlled Foreign Corporations.* Toronto: Canada Tax Foundation, 1986.

BITTKER, B., and EUSTICE, J. "Federal Income Taxation of Corporations and Shareholders." Para. 14.36 in "Reorganizations of Foreign Corporations (Sect. 367). 5th ed. New York: Warren, Gorham and Lamont, 1987.

BLOOM, GILBERT D. "Buying and Selling Corporations after Tax Reform." *Journal of Corporate Taxation* 14 (1987): 167–72.

CANELLOS, PETER. "The Over-Leveraged Acquisition." *Tax Lawyer* 39 (1985): 91.

———. "Buying or Selling a Business: Representing the Buyer." *New York Univ. Annual Institute on Federal Taxation* 44 (1986): 24–1.

COHEN, ALAN, and MILLMAN, STEWART. "Buying or Selling a Business: Representing the Seller." *New York Univ. Annual Institute on Federal Taxation.* 44 (1986): 25-1.

COLBY, L. "Tax Considerations in Financing Leveraged Acquisitions." *New York Univ. Annual Institute on Federal Taxation* 45 (1987): 1-1.

FREISCHLAG, PAUL H., JR. "Practical Tax Planning for Mergers and Acquisitions." *Tax Executive* 38 (1986): 157.

International Tax and Business Services. New York: Deloitte, Haskins, and Sells, 1982.

MALONEY, DAVID M., and BRANDT, MICHAEL G. "Taxable and Nontaxable Acquisition Techniques: A Case of Basics Not Being Basic." *Journal of Corporate Taxation* 14 (1987): 203-26.

TILLINGHAST, DAVID R. "Problem for Foreign Acquirer of Corporation in the U.S." *New York Law Journal* 184 (1980): 1.

7.0 FINANCING

ASQUITH, PAUL, R. BRUNER, F. MULLINS. *Merger Returns and the Form of Financing,* photocopy. Boston: Harvard Business School, October, 1986.

DIAMOND, STEPHEN C. *Leveraged Buyouts.* Homewood, IL.: Dow Jones-Irwin, 1985.

MARSH, P. "The Choice Between Equity and Debt: An Empirical Study." *Journal of Finance* 37 (1982): 121-44.

RAPPAPORT, ALFRED. "Financial Analysis for Mergers and Acquisitions." *Mergers and Acquisitions* 10 (Winter 1976): 87-88.

SMITH, C., JR. "Investment Banking and Capital Acquisition Process." *Journal of Financial Economics* 15 (1986): 3-29.

WANSLEY, J., W. LANE, and H. YANG. "Abnormal Returns to Acquiring Firms by Type of Acquisition and Method of Payment." *Financial Management* 12 (1983): 16-22.

8.0 PERSONNEL ISSUES AND POSTMERGER INTEGRATION

ADELSON, ANDREA. "Talking Deals: More Japanese Investing in U.S." *New York Times,* 18 Feb. 1988, p. D2.

ALTER, STEWART. "JWT Group Sold." *Advertising Age,* 29 June 1987.

BURKE, RONALD J. "Managing the Human Side of Mergers and Acquisitions." *Business Quarterly* (Winter 1987).

CALLAHAN, JOHN P. "Chemistry: How Mismatched Managements Can Kill a Deal." *Mergers and Acquisitions* (March-April 1986): 47-51.

CHIRA, SUSAN. "Japan's Next Goal: U.S. Companies." *New York Times,* 22 April 1989, pp. D1 and D5.

"Country Differences in Accounting for Takeover Costs." *GAO Report* (Dec. 1987).

FERRACONE, ROBIN. "Blending Compensation Plans of Combining Firms." *Mergers and Acquisitions* (Sept.-Oct. 1987): 57–62.

JOHNSON, ROBERT. "More U.S. Companies Are Selling Operations to Foreign Concerns." *Wall Street Journal* 24 Feb. 1988.

NATHANS, LEAH. "Anatomy of a Japanese Takeover." Business Month (June 1987): 46–48.

NOBLE, KENNETH B. "A Clash of Styles: Japanese Companies in U.S. under Fire for Cultural Bias." *New York Times,* 25 Jan. 1988.

PAINE, FRANK T., and POWER, DANIEL J. "Merger Strategy and Examination of Drucker's Five Rules for Successful Acquisitions." *Strategic Management Journal* 5 (April-June 1984): 99–110.

PANOS, JOHN E. "Postmerger Integration: Taking the Humane Approach to Postacquisition Layoffs." *Mergers and Acquisitions* 23 (March-April 1989): 44–47.

PRITHETT, PRICE. *After the Merger: Managing the Shockwaves.* Homewood, IL: Dow Jones-Irwin, 1985.

SCHWEIGER, DAVID M.; IVANCEVICH, JOHN M.; and POWER, FRANK R. Executive Actions for Managing Human Resources Before and After Acquisition." *Academy of Management Executive* 1 (1987): 127–38.

TOLCHIN, MARTIN, and TOLCHIN, SUSAN. *Buying into America: How Foreign Money Is Changing the Face of Our Nation.* New York: Times Books, 1988.

9.0 VALUATION

Books

DESMOND, GLENN M., and KELLEY, RICHARD E. *Business Valuation Handbook.* Marina del Rey, CA: Valuation Press, 1981.

DIAMOND, STEPHEN C., ed. *Leveraged Buyouts.* Homewood, IL: Dow Jones-Irwin, 1985.

EARL, PETER, and FISHER, FREDERICK G., III. *International Mergers and Acquisitions.* London: Euromoney Pubs., 1986.

Evaluating the Financial Performance of Overseas Operations. New York: Financial Executives Research Foundation, 1979.

Information Guides for Doing Business Abroad. New York: Price Waterhouse & Co. Center for Transnational Taxation. This series is updated periodically. Books are country and topic specific.

JUREK, WALTER. *How to Determine the Value of a Business.* Stow, Ohio: Quality Services, Inc., 1977.

LIPPER, ARTHUR, III. *Venture's Guide to Investing in Private Companies.* Homewood, IL: Dow Jones-Irwin, 1984.

PRATT, SHANNON P. *Valuing a Business: The Analysis and Appraisal of Closely-Held Companies.* Homewood, IL: Dow Jones-Irwin, Second Edition, 1989.

Property Asessment Valuation. Chicago: International Association of Assessing Officers, 1977.

RICKS, DAVID A. *International Dimensions of Corporate Finance.* Englewood Cliffs: Prentice Hall, 1987.

SILTON, LAWRENCE C. *How to Buy or Sell the Closely Held Corporation.* Englewood Cliffs: Prentice Hall, 1987.

Articles

GROSS, PAUL H. "Establishing Fair Market Value of Intangible Assets." *Journal of Business Valuation* 4 (July 1977): 5–17.

"International Mergers and Acquisitions." Special Section. *Mergers and Acquisitions* (July-Aug. 1987): 56–87.

LaFLEUR, GERALD W. "The Financial Investigation of Acquisition Candidates: How It Affects the Purchase Price." 7–21 in *Acquisitions 1978,* ed. Lewis B. Merrifield, III. New York: Practicing Law Institute, 1978.

POPOELL, S. D. "Mediating the Value of Small Businesses and Professional Firms." *Community Property Journal* (Winter 1983): 17–27.

PRATT, SHANNON P. "Developing the Valuation Model: Comparisons, Approaches and Sources." Proceedings of the 7th Biennial Conference of the Canadian Association of Business Valuators, 1984. *Journal of Business Valuation* (1985).

—— and HUGO, CRAIG S. "Pricing a Company by the Discounted Future Earnings Method." *Mergers and Acquisitions* 7 (Spring 1972): 18–32.

RAPPAPORT, ALFRED. "Financial Analysis for Mergers and Acquisitions." *Mergers and Acquisitions* 10 (Winter 1976): 87–88.

ROSENBLOOM, ARTHUR H. "Planning Divestment of Foreign Affiliates." *Journal of Buyouts and Acquisitions* (Feb. 1984).

——. "International Firms Find U.S. Publishing a Fertile Ground for Acquisitions." *Folio* (Dec. 1984).

——. "Opportunities and Pitfalls in Selling Your Company to a Non-U.S. Buyer." *Food Production & Management* (Jan. 1985).

——. "International Acquisitions Add Layer of Complexity." *Computer & Software News,* 3 Mar. 1986.

——. "A Seller's Guide to International Acquisition." *The President* (Sept. 1986).

——. "Update on International M&A Activity." *Merger Management Report* (Nov. 1987).

SOLBERG, THOMAS A. "Buy-Sell Agreements Can 'Freeze' Asset Values and in Some Cases Make Them Disappear." *Taxes* 59 (July 1981): 437–42.

10.0 NEGOTIATIONS

BARTOS, OTOMAR J. *Process and Outcome of Negotiations.* New York: Columbia University Press, 1974.

COFFIN, ROYCE A. *The Negotiator; A Manual for Winners.* New York: AMACOM, 1973.

FISHER, ROGER and URY, WILLIAM. *Getting to Yes: Negotiating Agreement without Giving In.* New York: Penguin Books, 1983.

JANDT, FRED EDMUND. *Win-Win Negotiating: Turning Conflict in Agreement.* New York: Wiley, 1985.

KOCHAN, THOMAS A., and VERMA, ANIL. *Negotiations in Organizations: Blending Industrial Relations and Organizational Behavior Approaches.* Cambridge: Sloan School of Management, M.I.T., 1983.

NEALE, MARGARET ANN. *Improving Negotiation: A Decision Making Perspective.* PhD Thesis, University of Texas at Austin: Social Science Research Council, Dec. 1982.

WALL, JAMES A. *Negotiation, Theory and Practice.* Glenview, IL: Scott, Foresman, 1985.

Index